International Series on Consumer Science

Series Editor

Jing Jian Xiao, University of Rhode Island, USA

For further volumes:
http://www.springer.com/series/8358

Evgenia Krasteva-Blagoeva
Editor

Approaching Consumer Culture

Global Flows and Local Contexts

Springer

Editor
Evgenia Krasteva-Blagoeva
New Bulgarian University
Sofia, Bulgaria

ISSN 2191-5660 ISSN 2191-5679 (electronic)
International Series on Consumer Science
ISBN 978-3-030-00225-1 ISBN 978-3-030-00226-8 (eBook)
https://doi.org/10.1007/978-3-030-00226-8

Library of Congress Control Number: 2018957319

This Springer imprint is published by the registered company Springer Nature Switzerland AG
The registered company address is: Gewerbestrasse 11, 6330 Cham, Switzerland

Preface

This edited volume comprises a collection of papers presented at the international conference "New Consumer Practices: Anthropological Perspectives" held at New Bulgarian University, Sofia, in April 2015. The main aim of the conference was to track current cultural transformations in the context of "global" consumer culture. Globalization is perceived here not simply as a process of cultural homogenization but as a flow and exchange of goods, people, information, knowledge, and images. In fact we see it as a process of communication conducted on a global level. Following Featherstone's ideas of studying contemporary consumer culture using framework that seriously displaces the "West" from center stage, the research interests of the contributors of this volume are focused on different ways of the production of locality through consumption. In other words, what we are concerned with are glocalization processes occurring in cultures perceived as "non-Western" or "not enough Western." The production of local consumer cultural contexts, or cultural *scapes*, to follow Appadurai, is empirically recorded and analyzed in detail through the methods of fieldwork and participant observation. Most of the chapters focus on consumer transformations that arose in southeastern European countries after the fall of communism. They offer theoretical approaches and empirical data about consumer culture in the region over the last 30 years, to allow the comparison of different ways of experiencing these processes and coping strategies "from below" in different postsocialist countries. Other chapters take up the issue of consumer culture in East Asia like China and Japan in particular.

Professor Featherstone was the conference's keynote speaker. His chapter, "Consumer Culture and Its Futures: Dreams and Consequences," brilliantly theorizes the emergence of the global cultural situation, from the rise of consumer culture in Western European courts to current global ecological changes caused by consumer culture and its 24/7 consumption patterns, so deeply transformative of human sensitivities and sociability. His chapter provides a global framework for the problems discussed in other chapters and thus may serve as a general introduction to this book.

The global-local axis is present in all the chapters, yet the scope of problems addressed by the authors is quite diverse. Socialism as a context for consumption development is the central topic of several chapters. Some local differences in eastern bloc and in the Balkans in particular are outlined and verified empirically. Yugoslavia, for example, can be seen as an "exception" and an instance of the so-called market socialism resulting in various consumer practices that were close to Western consumption yet at the same time were anchored in the dominant paradigm of socialist values and norms (Ildiko Edrei). This sharply contrasts with the Bulgarian experience of constant deficits, which led to illegal commerce, overvaluation of Western and other hard to access goods, different customization, and even subversive customization practices, which had an impact on the construction of individual and group identities (Krasteva-Blagoeva, Kristian Bankov).

Postsocialist transformations and their consequences for consumption practices and consumer culture in southeastern Europe are investigated in detail. Yuson Jung examines difficulties of establishing consumer activism in Bulgaria, due to the widespread distrust of civil society and its ability to ensure real protection of consumers against false products and deceptive practices. Studying everyday shopping in a Serbian town, Marina Simić concludes that buying Western goods and imitating Western consumer practices in a specific way reaffirms the non-Western status of the buyers as "cultural others." Tsvete Lazova theorizes the commoditization of archeology as a discipline through marketing of the archeological site of Perperikon, Bulgaria, via the specific "production of antiquity" and the construction of an archeological narrative designed to territorialize national space.

Two chapters are dedicated to food and food practices in postsocialism. Monica Stroe studies the revival of homemade preserves in Romania, a shortage-driven practice from socialist times that was given new meaning as a "creative domestic activity of self-provisioning." Domestication processes of pizza (as a culturally close product) and of sushi (as utterly different as viewed from a "traditional" perspective) are interpreted by Iskra Velinova as examples of the production of local meanings of urban culinary culture in the context of globalization.

The "Asian" part of the book consists of three chapters: two on Japan and one on China. Tomoko Tamari studies Mitsukoshi Department Store as an emblematic site for the formation of Japanese modernity. She sees the so-called modern girls as symbolic figures of the new Japanese consumer culture, dating from the early twentieth century. Japanese middle strata consumption patterns are analyzed by Maya Keliyan as a way of tracing the transformation of postmodern Japanese society from "middle class" to "middle mass" and finally to "divided middle mass." Min Zhou traces the historical roots and cultural premises of conspicuous consumption in China and contrasts it with Western conspicuous consumption practices.

This book combines illuminating theoretical discussions of global consumer culture "from above" with intriguing empirical analyses "from below" of the consumption patterns of people belonging to several different "non-Western" cultural milieus. This volume no doubt is fated to be consumed in a variety of ways as it navigates its way through international academic circles. At its core it will remain a significant result of a collective effort to advance the horizons of our understanding of consumer culture in a globalized world.

Sofia, Bulgaria Evgenia Krasteva-Blagoeva

Contents

About the Authors

Mike Featherstone is a professor of sociology at Goldsmiths, University of London. He is founding editor of the journal *Theory, Culture & Society* and the *Theory, Culture & Society Book Series*. He is editor-in-chief of the journal *Body & Society*. He is the author of *Consumer Culture and Postmodernism* (1991, 2nd edition 2007) and *Undoing Culture: Globalization, Postmodernism and Identity* (1995), and coauthor *of Surviving Middle Age* (1982). He is editor of over a dozen books and author of numerous journal articles and book chapters on social and cultural theory, consumer and global culture, aging and the body. His books and articles have been translated into 16 languages. He has spent time as a visiting professor in Barcelona, Geneva, Kyoto, Recife, São Paulo, Singapore, Tokyo, and Vancouver. He is founder and coordinator of the *Theory, Culture & Society* New Encyclopaedia Project, a research network of scholars at universities in Europe, Asia, Latin America, and Africa, which has held 20 colloquia and is producing a series of cluster volumes (the first on Problematizing Global Knowledge was published in 2006 and is currently being translated into a number of languages).

Evgenia Krasteva-Blagoeva is an associate professor in the Department of Anthropology, New Bulgarian University, Sofia. Her research interests are in consumer culture, ethnography of socialism and postsocialism, urban anthropology, communities and identities in the Balkans, names and name giving. She is a member of the Executive Committee of InASEA (International Association of Southeast European Anthropology) (2007–2014, 2016–2018) and elected president of InASEA (2014–2016). She was twice guest lecturer in the Institute of Ethnology, University "Ludvig Maximilian," Munich (2006, 2008), and in Konitsa Summer School of Balkan Anthropology (2006, 2008). She is a leading scholar in several research projects such as "Fast Food and Slow Food Culture in the Beginning of 21st century" and "New Consumer Practices: Anthropological Perspectives." She is the author of *The Personal Name in Bulgarian Tradition* (1999, in Bulgarian) and editor in chief of *Total Sale. Consumer Culture in Bulgaria* (2014, in Bulgarian). She has also authored more than 30 articles in refereed journals and edited volumes in English and German.

Ildiko Erdei is an ethnologist and anthropologist. She is an associate professor at the Department of Ethnology and Anthropology, School of Philosophy, Belgrade University. Her research interests range from politics of time and space in contemporary political rituals, relations between media and rituals as symbolic systems, and creators of "meaningful universes" to problems related to childhood and growing up during socialism, while her recent research interest includes cultural and symbolic dimensions of postsocialist transformation in Serbia and former Yugoslavia. She published articles and chapters in edited volumes on consumption and consumer culture in socialism and postsocialism and two monographs, *Anthropology of Consumption* (Biblioteka XX vek, 2008, in Serbian) and recently *Waiting for Ikea: Consumer Culture in Postsocialism and Before* (Belgrade, School of Philosophy, SGC, 2012, in Serbian).

Kristian Bankov is a professor of semiotics at New Bulgarian University and Department Chair of the Southeast European Center for Semiotic Studies. His interest in semiotics dates back to the early 1990s when as a student in Bologna he attended the courses of Prof. Ugo Volli and Prof. Umberto Eco. Bankov graduated in 1995 and has since taught semiotics at NBU. In 2000 he defended a doctoral thesis at Helsinki University under the guidance of Prof. Eero Tarasti. In March 2006 he was awarded the academic title "associate professor in semiotics" and in 2011 he became full professor of semiotics. Currently Professor Bankov is the Secretary General of the International Association for Semiotic Studies. His scientific interests were initially in the field of continental philosophy of language, philosophy of Bergson, and existential semiotics. He then focused his research on sociosemiotics and issues of identity. Since 2005 he has been exploring consumer culture, while recently his interest has been directed to the new media and digital culture. Kristian Bankov is the author of four books and numerous articles in Bulgarian, English, and Italian. Together with Paul Cobley he started the "Semiotics and its Master" series, and the first volume was published in 2017.

Marina Simić is an associate professor of cultural theory and cultural studies at the University of Belgrade, Faculty of Political Sciences. She obtained her PhD in social anthropology at the University of Manchester. She writes about postsocialist transformation in Europe and everyday life, consumption, and popular culture. She is also a published poet and libretto writer. Her book, *Cosmopolitan Longing: Ethnography of Serbian Postsocialism*, has been awarded by Ethnographic Institute of Serbian Academy of Arts and Sciences as the best anthropological book in Serbian language in 2014 and 2015.

Yuson Jung is an associate professor in the Department of Anthropology, Wayne State University. She is a sociocultural anthropologist and food scholar whose research explores issues of consumption, food, globalization, and postsocialism. Her publication includes her monograph, *Balkan Blues: Consumer Politics after State Socialism* (Indiana University Press, 2019) and a co-edited (with Jakob Klein and Melissa Caldwell) volume, *Ethical Eating in the Postsocialist and Socialist*

World (University of California Press, 2014) as well as numerous peer-reviewed articles and book chapters. She is completing her long-term ethnographic study on the cultural politics of the Bulgarian wine industry and has also been engaged in a collaborative research project (with Andrew Newman, WSU) about food politics and urban governance in Detroit.

Monica Stroe is an assistant professor of social anthropology at the National University of Political Studies and Public Administration, Bucharest (SNSPA), where she teaches anthropology of food, sociology of consumption, heritage politics, and ethnographic writing. She studied Nationalism Studies at Central European University in Budapest and Anthropology at SNSPA, Bucharest, with fellowships or short study grants at Goldsmiths College, University of Perugia, and Universite Libre Bruxelles. Her research interests and publications focus on food heritage, food and social class, consumption and morality, identity politics, and cultural landscapes.

Iskra Velinova is an independent scholar based in Sofia, Bulgaria. She has a PhD in philosophy from Sofia University. She has taught courses on Culture and Consumer Society and Youth Subcultures at New Bulgarian University. She has been conducting ethnographic research in Bulgaria for over 18 years. She has been observing cultural transformations and changing of consumption practices in the postsocialist society. She is the author of the following book chapters and articles: *Postmodernity and Political Identity. Observing Youth in the Anticommunist Revolutions of the 1990-s* (1999, in Bulgarian);*On Needs and Consumption During Socialism* (2004, in Bulgarian); *Global Food in Bulgaria, Between Domestic and Foreign* (2014, in Bulgarian).

Tsvete Lazova is an associate professor in history and theory of culture at the New Bulgarian University. She received her MA in classical studies and PhD in history from "St. Kliment Ohridski" University, Sofia. Her research interests include history and theory of anthropology and archeology; cultural studies; the politics of archeology and its commoditization in the formation of national identity; construction of media narratives on archeology of antiquity embedding them in the collective imagination; reflexivity in research practice; professional and ethical responsibilities in archeological practice of antiquity. She is the author of the book *Antiquity, Archaeology and National Imagination: Anthropological Perspectives* (2016, in Bulgarian), in addition to a number of articles.

Tomoko Tamari is a lecturer in the Institute for Creative and Cultural Entrepreneurship and a member of the Centre for Urban and Community Research, Goldsmiths, University of London. She is the managing editor of *Body & Society* (SAGE). Her long-standing research interests focus on consumer culture in Japan and Japanese new women, which will be discussed in her forthcoming book entitled, *Women and Consumer Culture: The Department Store, Modernity and Everyday Life in Early Twentieth Century Japan* (Routledge). She has recently published "Metabolism: Utopian Urbanism and the Japanese Modern Architecture Movement," *Theory Culture & Society*, 2016, vol. 31(7–8); and "Body Image and Prosthetic Aesthetics," *Body & Society*, 2017, vol. 23(1). She is currently working in the following areas: body image and disability; human perception and the moving image; probiotics and immunity; Olympic culture and cities.

Min Zhou is a professor and associate dean of the Institute of Literary Studies, Shanghai International Studies University. She is deputy editor-in-chief of *The Journal of British and American Literary Studies*. She worked as a Fulbright research scholar at the Department of English and Comparative Literature at Columbia University (2014–2015). She is the author of *What is Postmodernist Literature* and *The Transcription of Identities: A Study of V. S. Naipaul's Postcolonial Writings*, and translator of *J. Hillis Miller: Selected Works*. Her research area includes contemporary American and British literature, postcolonial studies, cultural theory, and media studies.

Maya Keliyan is a professor at Institute for the Study of Societies and Knowledge, Bulgarian Academy of Sciences. Her research interests are in the field of social stratification, middle classes, local communities, studies of consumption patterns, and lifestyle and social structures in comparative perspectives: Japan, Bulgaria, China, and Taiwan. She published numerous articles and five monographs, among which *Japan and Bulgaria: Modernization, Middle Strata and Rural Communities* (1999, in Bulgarian), *Japan and Bulgaria: Stratified Consumption Patterns* (2008, in Bulgarian), and *Local Community Lifestyle: Contemporary Japan* (2010, in Bulgarian). She is teaching courses on contemporary Japanese society, family, social stratification system, middle classes, consumption, and lifestyle at Sofia University "St. Kliment Ohridski."

Consumer Culture and Its Futures: Dreams and Consequences

Mike Featherstone

Introduction

The rise of consumer culture has frequently been presented as evidence of the success of capitalist modernity. Industrialisation and technological developments have produced massive transformations of human living space with over half of humanity now living in cities. This urban and industrial revolution has been accompanied over the last 30 years, by what some herald as a further revolutionary change: the impact of a new set of communications technologies with digital micro-computing mobile devices.[1] We can now instantly interact with distant others in an increasingly integrated global culture. Consumer culture is centrally inscribed into both the urban landscape and the new modes of digital communication such as the Internet. Contemporary societies, then, have become increasingly dominated by consumption, which has now become the driving force for the global economy. Yet the very success and extensiveness of consumer culture have more recently made visible problems, risks and doubts about its viability, along with a series of major dilemmas about how to deal with its consequences.

From one perspective this should be no surprise, as production is often seen as intimately linked to consumption. The capacity to produce more necessarily generates more consumption, with improvements in the standards of living and increased capacity to purchase new goods and experiences. At the same time we should be careful not to make the assumption that people are necessarily predisposed to produce or consume more. Max Weber was the one who took exception to this

[1] Some would see the communications revolution as a second industrial revolution, or even a third industrial revolution with the second being the phase from 1870 to 1914 dependent on the increasing use of technology. For advocacy of the Internet as stimulating a new bottom-up industrial revolution in manufacturing (3D printers, etc.) see Anderson 2012.

M. Featherstone (✉)
Goldsmiths, University of London, London, UK
e-mail: m.featherstone@gold.ac.uk

E. Krasteva-Blagoeva (ed.), *Approaching Consumer Culture*, International Series on Consumer Science, https://doi.org/10.1007/978-3-030-00226-8_1

form of naturalisation of the entrepreneurial impulse. In his Protestant Ethic thesis he sought to investigate the origins of the propensity for people to want to produce more, and to engage in constant work discipline and rational accounting. For Weber traditional societies showed a more direct and immediate relationship between production and consumption; the annual production (especially foodstuffs) was more or less directly consumed with little inclination to continue to work beyond the satisfaction of immediate needs (Weber 1981). The question of why people continued to work and accumulate when they did not need to was his central *problemstellung*, and his answer to the question sought to pin down the origins of the unique capitalist spirit which he held had world-changing consequences. Yet we could equally apply this mode of problematisation to consumption as to production. Indeed, one of the striking dispositions Weber found in the Protestant sects that was transferred to the early American capitalists was that one should value work highly and not consume indulgently. The focus was on the sober disciplined life dominated by work, with luxuries and worldly pleasures denigrated and frugality praised as the means to salvation. This demanded the methodical life of the monk, but not confined to the monastery, but out in the world, in the marketplace and everyday life.[2]

The followers of the Protestant sects were not directly interested in consumption as it took people away from work and the ordered life, the pursuit of pleasure and luxury needing to be carefully governed.[3] Rather, consumption needed to be modest, curtailed and well circumscribed; otherwise it threatened both other-worldly salvation and inner-worldly business success. Weber's own life and academic interests echoed these sentiments and he showed little interest in the governance of consumption, or the problems it opened up for modern societies. Yet one of Weber's contemporaries, Werner Sombart, took a very different view. Sombart argued that it was not the development of the production side, the capitalist spirit, but rather the stimulus to demand from the consumption side, which was crucial in bringing about the leap into modern capitalism (Sombart 1967). Crucial here was the demand for luxuries from court societies. Courts brought together nobles, courtiers, clergy, and beautiful women in sumptuous setting such as the 'gilded cage' of Louis XIV's Versailles, for ceremonial displays and pageantry (Elias 1983). Court life involved elaborate prestige contests, in which nobles engaged in ruinous consumption in the chance that they would gain the favour of the king. Courtiers and nobles were obliged to wear fine clothes, jewellery and adornment which stimulated the fashion system, they ate gourmet food with new dishes prepared by skilful chefs, they listened to music performances, they watched plays and pageants which stimulated the arts and high culture, and they socialised and performed in specially constructed palatial architecture replete with sumptuous interior design, décor and objects of art. As centres of consumption courts stimulated employment and the courtesans,

[2] As Weber remarked 'Christian asceticism ... strode into the marketplace of life, slammed the door of the monastery behind it, and undertook to penetrate just that daily routine of life with its methodicalness, to fashion it into a life in the world, but neither of nor for this world' (Weber 2001: 154).

[3] For a critique of the Weberian position see Campbell 1987.

tradesmen, artisans, fashion designers, cooks, architects and financiers involved not only furnished goods and services, but also observed their use by royalty and aristocrats. This stimulated demand in neighbouring capital cities such as Paris and London amongst the middle classes. Cities became centres of innovation in luxury consumption, manufacture and culture (Featherstone 2007: ch. 11, 2014b; Goody 2006: 144). Courts led to the development of the spice trade, but also silks, fabrics and dyes (indigo being more valuable than gold at one point), which increased the trade between Europe and Asia and led to the opening of the Americas. This stimulated consumption in the middle classes and wider urban life (McCracken 1988).

Whatever the outcome of historical debates about the role of consumption in the origins of capitalism, it is indisputable that today consumption plays a central role in the global economy. In the case of the United States' economy, around 70% of US gross domestic product (GDP) now comes from consumer spending; indeed personal consumption levels have fluctuated between 60 and 70% in the post-war period (Ivanova 2011: 342).[4] The reaction to the recession following the 2007 financial crisis was to flood the market with cheap credit in an attempt to reinvigorate consumer demand. This contrasts with the strategy of public works and infrastructure investment programmes that followed the Great Depression of the 1930s. One consequence has been the rapid increase in not just sovereign debt, but private debt in the United States and other parts of the world (Graeber 2011; Lazzarato 2012). The rise in consumption levels in China, India and other parts of Asia along with the development of the BRICS, and their up and coming rivals the CIVETS (Colombia, Indonesia, Vietnam, Egypt, Turkey and South Africa), as well as the more recent term, the MINT economies (Mexico, Indonesia, Nigeria and Turkey),[5] is also notable. Consumption then is firmly established as central to the world economy; in effect it is the driving force for the expanding manufacturing sector in the BRIC, CIVET and MINT countries to produce the consumer goods to be consumed in North America, Europe and Japan, but also increasingly by their own consumers who aspire to the same consumer lifestyles. In the West, Japan and other affluent parts of the world,[6] the strength of the service sector of the economy is a further indication of the importance of consumption.

Since the 1980s there has been a notable expansion of neoliberalism as the major form of governmentality, first in the United States and the United Kingdom and gradually extending to other parts of the world. While neoliberalism has a complex history and is not a unified doctrine, its main characteristics draw on liberalism, with the assumption of the benefits arising from the extension of the market and

[4] In May 2017 it stood at 69.45%—see US Personal Consumption Expenditure in *Y charts* http://ycharts.com/indicators/personal_consumption_gdp. Accessed 7.7.2017.

[5] See 'The Mint Countries: Next economic giants?' *BBC Magazine*, 6 Jan 2014, http://www.bbc.co.uk/news/magazine-25548060. Accessed 5.4.2015.

[6] It is increasingly difficult to continue to use terminology such as 'the West', the Global North and Global South. The rich and super-rich are now in all countries, not just the West, leading to a focus on inequalities within, not necessarily between, countries. The additional problems are the mobility of the rich and super-rich and difficulty in establishing their residence patterns.

competition to all corners of the world.[7] Neoliberalism is not anti-state per se, but favours the use of the state to deregulate state industries, monopolies and the state sector in general. This also entails the reduction of welfare support and the promotion of the self-reliant individual: in effect, people who must finance their own investments—in education and accumulation of social and cultural capital—in order to succeed in life. In effect people need to compete to accumulate property and must become entrepreneurial beings.

This is something Foucault highlights in his biopolitics, in the lectures he gave towards the end of his life at a time when neoliberalism was becoming more evident as a project in the form of Thatcherism and Reaganomic in the 1980s (Foucault 2008). On the one side this involved financial deregulation, bolstered by the integration of the global markets in the wake of the introduction of 24-h trading in 1986, which created a new financial infrastructure and form of global governance based on the sovereignty of the markets (Latham 2000). This not only increased the flows of money, shares, financial instruments and investment, but also led to the expansion of offshore financial services and tax havens which greatly benefitted corporations, the rich and the super-rich and also increased social inequalities (Featherstone 2013a, 2014b; Urry 2014a, b). People were also encouraged to actively invest in their own human capital (Becker 1993), a form of individualism that was also seen as beneficial in terms of increasing the collective societal wealth (see discussion in Featherstone 2013a).

One important manifestation here is the blurring of the lines between work and leisure, production and consumption. To gain the rewards that life offers and succeed, people needed to be enterprising and creative in their work (Foucault 2008: 226; McNay 2009). But this attitude needs to be carried over into their nonwork activities. Again, Foucault is instructive here in his suggestion, following Gary Becker that we should think of consumption as enterprise activity too (Foucault 2008: 226). In effect the consumer should also be seen as a producer, whose activity is geared towards the production of his/her own satisfaction. The consumer needs to be creative and enterprising if they are to maximise their own satisfactions and pleasure. They need to be lifestyle innovators and invest in themselves. Hence the active enterprising attitude is important in this apparently 'secondary' level, in terms of generating the right dispositions and orientation to life to make neoliberalism work. To maximise one's potential one needs to invest in one's nonwork activities: to borrow, buy, sell, accumulate and re-evaluate, in terms of house, consumer goods, vacations, etc., and weigh up the levels of short- and long-term satisfactions that can be derived. Yet the investment in sustaining this neoliberal consumer culture dream can be risky; it can be a gamble that goes wrong with negative consequences for both individuals and the system.

The 2007 financial crisis and subsequent recession have seen a massive rise in debt—the sovereign debt of government borrowing (also known via the euphemism

---

[7] For discussions of neoliberalism see Davies 2014a, b; Gane 2014, 2015. There has also been a good deal of discussion about the extent to which Foucault sympathized with or opposed neoliberalism—Gane 2015; Davies 2014b.

'quantitative easing' in the United Kingdom) and also individual household debt. Referring to the dramatic decline of household 'net worth' in the United States, one commentator remarks that 'the collapse of credit for the working classes signifies the end of debt-driven consumer capitalism' (Ivanova 2011: 346). The situation is little better in many other countries. Is consumer culture, then, facing endgame with 'shopped-out' 'debt-burdened' consumers unable to renew their credit rating and move forward? Is this not just the end of the American dream, but the more widespread consumer dreams of the rest of us around the world? It is possible to respond that for some sectors consumption continues to be healthy—the luxury sector and super-rich consumption are doing well. But there is a growing groundswell of criticism of the consequences and fairness of the system, raising many questions about the future of neoliberal economies and the consumer way of life. The growing inequalities evident in the United States, the United Kingdom and other countries raise questions about the sustainability of democracy, equality and social improvement, seen by many as positive by-products of modernity.

In this chapter we seek to address a range of questions about the dreams and consequences of consumer culture. Firstly, if consumer culture is central to neoliberalism and maintenance of the global economy, how far can this be seen as a deeper-seated process related to long-standing dreams of abundance and unrestricted consumption? How far were these consumer dreams significant in helping to overcome previous restrictions on consumption (sumptuary laws) and religious prohibitions against luxury, greed and avarice? The birth of economics and the rise of liberalism and utilitarianism in the eighteenth and early nineteenth centuries provided one set of answers which drew on major shifts in the attitude towards the pleasure and consumption and legitimated the desire for material self-improvement of ordinary people (Smith 1776; Berry 1994). How do these dreams relate to the American dream, which became a dominant force in the twentieth century? As consumer culture globalises are these dreams still viable? With the rise of new wealth in the form of the rich, super-rich and celebrities, does the desire for more excessive luxury lifestyles gain further legitimation?

Over two centuries beyond what has been referred to as the birth of the consumer society in eighteenth-century England (McKendrick et al. 1982), and what are the consequences of 200 years of an extensive and sustained consumer culture? Some would argue that with increasing climate change and impending planetary disaster, the ecological consequences of a consumer society are evident. There has been an expanding production of machinery and infrastructure for the manufacture of goods, along with the volume of goods themselves, which has also meant a largely uncosted and unknown set of risks, along with the accumulation of excessive waste. We are by now familiar with scenarios that suggest that if everyone in the world consumed like the United States we would need three earth-size planets to resource our consumption. If the unintended consequences of the consumer society now threaten planetary existence of living being, then, what is the potential for thinking beyond a consumer culture anchored in neoliberalism? Could there be a move from material to immaterial consumption, with limited consumption of new goods coupled with a focus on experience and sustaining interpersonal rhythms of life?

In addition there are important questions about the social consequences of consumer culture: How do we evaluate the way it works as a form of social organisation? Does consumer culture merely provide an extension of work, in the sense that the rhythms of nonwork life involve increasing public and self-surveillance through digital devices that under the guise of increasing sociability are effectively locking people into compulsive patterns of behaviour? Is the price of increasing consumption decreasing free time and does material affluence mean the loss of time affluence? Are there ways of being together, sharing and joint enterprise (open source, employee benefit trusts) that could reverse the excessive individualism, egoism of the enterprise and consumer cultures? Does continued regular and excessive consumption lead to the constant search for new goods, resulting in diminishing satisfaction? If more people possess more desirable luxury goods, does the prestige value satisfaction diminish too? Would diminishing satisfaction support a scaling down of the impulse to buy? Does consumer culture really lead to the good life and an increase in people's sense of happiness?

Dreams of Consumption

'We live in dreams like fish in water' (Halton 1992).

It is possible to identify two dreams of consumption that have been influential in stimulating consumer culture desires. The first is the peasant dream of effortless abundance manifest in luxury food, satiation and fulfilment. The second entails luxury, but closely linked to the dream of splendour, of magnificent luxurious surroundings, architecture and interiors of the palaces of rulers and nobility. This entails the sumptuous clothes, furnishings and full range of sensory sensations provided to stimulate the sophisticated tastes of refined and powerful people.

Cockaigne and Peasant Dreams of Abundance

The well-known overture by Elgar 'Cockaigne' composed in 1900–1901, subtitled 'In London Town', was intended to provide a musical portrait of London Life. At the time the term 'Cockaigne' was used to humorously point to the idleness, gluttony and drunkenness of the turn-of-the-century London and it is generally assumed that this is the origin of the term 'Cockney'. But Cockaigne has a long history and refers to the vision of a 'land of all delight', the land of luxury and idleness.

References to Cockaigne are prominent in numerous European societies, especially in medieval folklore and peasant culture. It refers to a dreamlike mythical land of plenty replete with rivers of wine, houses built of cakes and barley sugar, and streets paved with pastries. According to Herman Pleij in '*Dreaming of Cockaigne: Medieval Fantasies of the Perfect Life*':

> Roasted pigs wander about with knives in their backs to making carving easy, where grilled geese fly directly into one's mouth, where cooked fish jump out of the water and land at one's feet. The weather is always mild, the wine flows freely, sex is readily available, and all people enjoy eternal youth.
>
> (Pleij 2003)

The etymology of the term is thought to derive from a word meaning cake. But it also suggested more than special food, luxury and ease, for it also played of the logic of a land of contraries, where not only food was plentiful (skies that rain cheese), but also social restrictions were reversed (sexual liberties freely taken, authority figures humiliated by their juniors, etc.).[8] There are clear resonances between Cockaigne and carnival in the ways in which the annual medieval Christian carnival offered an inversion of conventional everyday life: with expensive and luxurious things made cheap and abundant, with normal sexual restrictions waved (Featherstone 2007: ch. 5; Bakhtin 1968).

Court Society Dreams of Splendour and Luxury

The realities of medieval peasants living with austerity, shortages and underemployment with sumptuary laws in place to restrict consumption can be contrasted to the court society of the monarchs, princes and nobility. Yet there was one important sense in which court life was very much the opposite of the dreams of excessive consumption found in the depictions of Cockaigne, or its carnival version. Court consumption was highly ordered and ritualised through careful ceremonials in which good manners, correct etiquette and social rules dominated and consumption could not be seen as only directed at the satisfaction of bodily appetites, pleasures and desires (Elias 1983). Nobles and courtiers were highly visible in the carefully orchestrated ceremonial displays, which necessitated a high level of self-control, careful presentation and performance skills, confidence and wit.

The splendour of palaces such as Versailles built by Louis XIV, lavish interiors with the finest materials, large windows, hall of mirrors and carefully controlled ornamental gardens were designed as a setting for displays of monarchical power and wealth. This pattern was found across Europe in the sixteenth and seventeenth centuries. The English Stuart kings (James I and Charles I) staged magnificent processions or pageants called masques, sometimes involving thousands of people in Roman or Greek costumes to depict heroic episodes from the ancient world in their full splendour (Peck 2005). The provision of such elaborately staged spectacles involving actors, animals, music and fireworks, in pageants and masques, was prohibitively expensive. But such was the power of kings that it was impossible to avoid the royal request and lords and courtiers were obliged to engage in the provision of competitive display and entertainments to the point of ruin.

---

[8] See Encyclopaedia Britannica entries for Cockaigne. See also the satirical Kildare 'The Land of Cockaygne' (circa 1330) critical of the local Cistercian abbey.

According to Sombart Louis XIV embarked on a phase of ruinous expenditure to impress his mistresses, building numerous chateaux, including Versailles (Sombart 1967). Mistresses and coquettes gained great prestige and power and set trends in fashion and style through wearing fine silks and latest fashions. Cuisine involved attention to the creation of new dishes and tastes by specially appointed cooks, who attained power and influence under the patronage system. Yet there were also backstage areas, in private quarters, or visits to the city to explore the greater informalities of the *demi-monde*.[9] The life of the noble and courtiers, then, involved careful ordered consumption with swings to excess, but it also involved the choosing and sampling new goods in the latest styles—be it furniture or clothes designed in the finest silk fabrics and carefully finished and coloured in the latest dyes. Men and women wore elaborate make-up, coiffeur and wigs. The fashion system first developed in court society through the overland Silk Road and eventually the regular sea routes to Asia. This search for luxuries and new tastes, such as rare spices and exotic fruit and vegetables for elaborate banquets, along with fine fabrics and dyes (silk, indigo)[10] being highly valued, helped usher in the race for colonies and greater competition between European powers.[11]

Court life stimulated its own sets of dreams and desires in the rest of the population, via the servants who prepared and catered along with the merchants and tradesmen who furnished the goods, settings and architecture. Courts and nobles needed financiers, bankers, merchants and the market, even if the noble and courtier despised the pedantry, caution and lack of style of the middle classes. But the middle classes and inhabitants of the expanding cities were by no means passive observers of the court. The competition for trade after the opening up of the Americas made new fortunes for the middle classes and led to a greater circulation of global trade after the flood of Spanish silver from the Potosí mines in Bolivia from the mid-sixteenth century onwards made its way to China across the Pacific (Pomeranz 2000, 2009). Wealth accumulated in the middle classes and they developed a taste for luxury goods. The expansion of the luxury trade between Europe and Asia not only linked cities together, but it also stimulated broader occupational specialism

[9] Elias suggests that one of the powerful dreams in court societies was to escape the formality and elaborate consumption rituals for the simple virtues of peasant life—a theme taken up in romantic novels and plays about shepherds and shepherdesses (Elias 1983).

[10] The valuable blue dye, indigo, tended to be more valuable than gold (Taussig 2008), pointing to the importance placed on fashion and appearance in early modern times. See also Braudel (1981) on the emergence of the fashion system.

[11] If European haute cuisine originated in the French court of Louis XIV, it had occurred earlier in China in the Ming dynasty (1368–1644). Ming was an era of governmental reform, social improvement and trade with the rest of the world in which China almost industrialized. Court life boosted by the building of the Beijing Forbidden City involved display, splendour and finery. It is said that one of the Ming Emperors never ate the same dish twice in his life. Certainly the opening up of trade under Admiral He facilitated the scouring of the empire and Southeast Asia for exotic fruit and vegetables and invention of new dishes such as bird's-nest soup (allegedly originally from swifts' nests from Borneo).

and expansion of middle-class cultural and knowledge occupations: lawyers, bankers and accountants, along with teachers, scholars and doctors.

Cities, then, became centres of innovation in luxury and learning, consumption and culture (Featherstone 2007: ch. 11; Goody 2006: 144). The court society opened up the visions of splendour and elaborate ritual for the middle classes. They observed the fine dress, fashionable clothes and demeanour of the nobles and courtiers, and the way they ate haute cuisine involving the latest spices and ingredients at elaborate banquets. Courts were centres of fashion and cultural innovation, but they were also centres of pleasure and enjoyment, where beautiful women engaged in love and romance. This dream of refined stylish sociability in attractive sumptuous surroundings, together with refined, witty people who displayed good manners, elegance and fashionable demeanour, provided a powerful stimulus to their dreams and ambitions of consumption.

The Birth of a Consumer Culture

It is now generally accepted that in eighteenth-century England there was not just an industrial revolution, but a consumer revolution too, with the provision of a whole range of new exotic goods stimulated by the colonial trade and manufacturing (McKendrick et al. 1982). The development of factories and eventually mass production made a wide range of cheap everyday households and staple goods (pots, pans, iron bedsteads, tinned food, cotton clothes) readily available in the nineteenth century. The department stores which developed in France, England and the United States from the mid-nineteenth century onwards provided not only new cheaper manufactured goods, but also luxuries for the masses, the 'democratisation of luxury', with new mass fashions which imitated more exclusive and luxurious goods. A key aspect of the department store was the way in which customers could walk around goods which were carefully displayed and lit, often in themed displays produced by an expanding set of commercial artists and designers which brought elements of fantasy and exotic imagery into window and store interior displays. It is in this sense we can refer to the stores as encouraging aestheticisation processes (Miller 1981; Tamari 2006; Williams 1982; Featherstone 2007).[12]

Goods were presentation and framed in carefully constructed settings designed to encourage the transfer of associations from the painted or increasingly photograph images, mannequins and mythological backgrounds and props. The application of the term 'dream palaces' is significant, to indicate not only the plushness and

[12] The ability to make the themed image seem real, or to actualize the imaginary, is something which was developed in world fairs and international exhibitions in the second half of the nineteenth century with national pavilions designed to replicate key elements of particular cultures. This became more developed in twentieth-century theme parks such as Disney World, in which fictional entities such as the Swiss Robinson family house could be replicated or simulated, so that the public could step inside and explore full-scale hyperreal versions (Simmel 1991; Baudrillard 1983; Bryman 1995).

sumptuousness of the settings of the interior and architecture of department stores, but also the way the stores played with imagery from cultural traditions, myths and folk tales to add an extra dimension to the goods. In some cases stores brought in performers and themed a series of spaces in the store to look like stage sets, which added to the illusion and dreamlike effect.[13] If department stores can be thought of as central sites of consumer culture that both nurtured and materialised dreams, another equally important site for the production of dream images was the cinema. The Hollywood cinema that developed in the 1920s has been referred to as a 'dream factory', through its capacity to draw on and actualise material taken from a wide range of past cultural traditions, myths and epics, or to graphically depict tales and epics taken from ancient civilisations, the Bible and well-known historical figures. Increasingly from the late 1920s onwards people watched the movies in plush, luxurious settings, and cinemas became 'picture palaces' (Hansen 1991).[14]

The American Dream

The cinema reinforced the power of images and it is hard to underestimate the way that images stimulated desires and helped to give form and depth to dreams. Stuart and Elizabeth Ewen mention the effect of mundane images on stimulating dreams and desires (Ewen and Ewen 1982). They recount how a young Czech immigrant girl was powerfully influenced by the image design on an American bale of cotton. Such images, on a can of fruit, packet of cigarettes and bag of flour, can be powerful in fostering the dream of a better life, the dream of abundance and opportunity in a land of plenty.[15] Images opened up the space of possibility: the dream, the desire. The Hollywood movies, like consumer culture advertising, marketing and display, played with transcultural and quasi-universal themes such as love, youth, romance, adventure, exotica, luxury, 'wonder' and 'the new'. These were often linked to a series of themes that include just reward, ambition, persistence, transformation and success.

---

[13] See Mica Nava's description of the London store Selfridges' use of the Ballet Russes' performance of Scheherazade just before World War I, to produce in-store themed spectacles which also encouraged women customers to enthusiastically purchase turbans and harem trousers and play out the dream (Nava 2002).

[14] For a discussion of the 'Hollywood ideal' with its images of youth, fitness and beauty along with the growth of fan magazines based on the wide interest in the backstage and off-duty lives of the stars, their grooming, fitness and beauty tips, see Featherstone (1982).

[15] This was especially the case in the Long Depression of 1873–96, and not just the United States proved attractive: migrants from Ukraine, Poland and other parts of Eastern Europe were attracted to Brazil via handbills distributed in many parts of Eastern Europe to the extent that the phenomenon became known as 'Brazil fever'. For discussions of the United States as a land of plenty and abundance and how this impacted on advertising see Leach (1993) and Lears (1994, 1998). It also occurred *within* the United States: in the 1930s Great Depression with the banks' foreclosure of farms, Oklahoma farmers were lured to California, by handbills depicting succulent peaches and the good life in the land of plenty (see John Steinbeck's novel *The Grapes of Wrath*).

The latter themes in particular were central to what became known as 'The American Dream': the United States presented as the land of opportunity in which everyone could rise up to their appropriate station and potential in life and enjoy the fruits of success: the car, and the suburban family home crammed full of the latest consumer goods. The American Dream proved to be enormously powerful globally, especially so when harnessed to the Hollywood Cinema. It helped open the horizons of dreams, desires, ambitions and scope of what it would like to live in exotic places, amidst stylish, knowledgeable beautiful people in comfortable surroundings. Especially in eras such as the 1920s, the American Dream offered what Scott Fitzgerald noted as 'the extraordinary gift of hope'.[16] This can be linked to the broader theme of transformation—the hope of self-improvement and betterment. The self-help, 'pulling yourself up by your own bootlaces' idiom, is particularly strong in the United States. We have the Pygmalion myth, first popularised by George Bernard Shaw as a play, then taken up as a stage show in the 1950s, and adapted into a 1960s Hollywood movie, *My Fair Lady*, starring Audrey Hepburn and Rex Harrison, remade and revamped in the 1990s as '*Pretty Woman*' with Richard Gere and Julia Roberts.[17] There is widespread media interest in transformation, in the highs and lows, of stars and celebrities, their permanent adolescence, constant renewal of partners and relationships, opulent lifestyles and consumer goods, along with their constant battle to transform their bodies against the ravages worked by the ageing process. The fall and rise of stars as they battled against drink, drugs, career failure, divorce, abused childhoods, etc. also provided an endless supply of material for novels, feature stories, movies, television documentaries, chat shows and of course more recently the Internet, including social media sites (see Turner 2004; Featherstone 1982, 2010a, b, c).[18]

It is also interesting to note the way in which the success stories of those who become enormously wealthy are central to not only the American Dream, but also the various globalised versions. With the extension of neoliberalism since the 1980s, those who are wealthy, especially those who have become so through their own enterprise, tend to be presented as efficient contributors to the economy and social life. The contemporary wave of new rich, the expanding strata of successful millionaires, multimillionaires and billionaires, who are increasing in China, India, Russia and other parts of the world as well as in the United States and Europe, can be contrasted with the imagery of the traditional aristocracy and 'idle rich'. They are

[16] This is how Scott Fitzgerald describes Gatsby, the central character in *The Great Gatsby* (p. 6), and most of the people in the novel are full of hope. Yet Gatsby sacrificed himself to fulfil the dream and get into the upper class, but ultimately fails. See the synopsis of *The Great Gatsby*, www.ovtg.de/3_arbeit/englisch/gatsby/dream.html, Accessed 6.2.2015.

[17] The opposite case to the achievement success stories would be movies like *Dawn of the Dead* (1978, director George Romero) set in a mundane suburban shopping centre taken over by zombies, with the consumers endlessly circulating, unable to escape. Repetition, closure and consumer nightmare.

[18] American dreams were also very important in European youth culture, especially the Sixties Generation (see discussion in Frith 1983). See also Rosen on movies and the American Dream (Rosen 1972).

immensely confident in their own qualities: that they are self-made persons who have risen to the top through their own talent, hard work and creative enterprise. They are given increasing prominence with their business successes and failures, relationships and scandals, leisure activities and adventures that are regularly featured and glamorised in the media. In short their wealth and enterprise make them celebrities and featured in the expanding celebrity culture (Turner 2004). Their lifestyle and excessive luxury consumption, their new 'toys' (classic cars, super-yachts and customised private jets), sumptuous homes full of art treasures, antiques and designer goods are generally presented with admiration in media features, narratives, advertising and popular culture imagery. In many ways they are presented as the heroes of consumption, and the success stories of consumer culture, and they are not slow in proclaiming their own social contribution and justifying their excessive rewards and luxurious consumer lifestyles (see Peretti 2015; Freeland 2012; Featherstone 2013a, 2014b).

Consumer Rhythms and the Timing of Consumption

Within consumer culture, then, the consumption of images and looser associations such as dreams are important. Advertisers are eager to attach experiences to particular goods, so that the consumption of the immaterial aspect, or the cultural experience that they want to become associated with particular goods, becomes dominant. It has been argued that over time there has also been a more general shift from the consumption of goods to the consumption of experiences to the extent that we have references to 'the experiential society' (Schulze 1992) and 'experiential economy' (Pine and Gilmore 2011). This fits in well with the dreams of consumer culture, the emphasis on the freedom to travel and enjoy a mobile lifestyle and to sample cultures and new experiences, catered for by the expansion of the tourist and leisure sectors. At the same time the basic organisation of the rhythms of consumer culture points not just to escape from routine through tourist vacation breaks, but also to the intensification of regular consumption patterns by increasing the amount of time available to consume, not only in extending the hours of stores and malls, but also through Internet shopping, which offers the potential for around the clock consumption. Two observations can be made here in relation to time and the rhythms of everyday life. The first relates to the discouragement of people wasting time. The second relates to the extension of biopolitical regimes by which populations are regulated through consumption.

The ways in which workers were subject to capitalist discipline not just in the factory, but outside the workplace too, were noted in a book by Paul Lafargue, *The Right to be Lazy* (Lafargue: orig.1883). Lafargue argued that the working class had to overcome their passion for work, which he saw as leading to the exhaustion of their vital energies and creativity (Lafargue 2011). Lafargue's concerns about the spread of work discipline chime with the evidence provided by EP Thompson in an important essay 'Time, Work Discipline and Industrial Capitalism', which points to the difficulties in establishing the work discipline and punctuality necessary for the factory system in eighteenth-century England (Thompson 1967).[19] Eventually clock time became internalised with the workers engaging in self-surveillance and displaying a high degree of time consciousness. While EP Thompson sketched out the implications for the sphere of work, Michel Foucault addressed more fully in developing his theory of biopolitics.[20] Foucault identified two distinctive technologies of power: one technique is disciplinary; it centres on the body, produces individualising effects, and manipulates the body to make it useful and docile. The second technology is centred not upon the body but upon social life and brings endeavours to control and predict the series of random events that can occur in a living mass (Foucault 2008: 249).[21] We will return to the discussion of how to gain productive statistical knowledge of population sets shortly, as this has become central to consumer culture data analysis and marketing and in particular Internet consumption. For the moment the important point is how these general changes in work and social life laid the basis for the development of a particular rhythms of everyday life and how our consumption practices became readily fitted into the larger disciplinary, surveillance, and biopolitical social matrix, albeit still seeking to incorporate consumer culture dreams of abundance, excess, and yearning for a better life.

---

[19] Prior to the factory system, families working at home in the pre-industrial putting out system and receiving yarn to weave on a weekly basis were paid for completed work only, so that work, leisure, and everyday life were not strongly differentiated. This casual attitude carried over into the early factory system with high absenteeism (many workers observed 'Saint Monday' and 'Saint Tuesday'—i.e. they were not motivated or too drunk to turn up to work after the weekend). It proved difficult to convert a rural workforce who had enjoyed long periods of nonwork, chatting, or daydreaming. Clocks came in very gradually, initially only showing the hour hand, and started to proliferate with the industrial system. By the nineteenth century many workingmen had internalized the time rhythms to the extent that they possessed pocket watches. The introduction of the factory system meant people living close to the workplace responded to the sound of the factory hooter, which encouraged new habits. The old tradition did not decline uniformly, and in some areas it continued and flourished. The various bohemian (artists and fellow travelers who had irregular work patterns and often worked at night and slept by day) and counter culture movements (1960s' hippies) also attacked conventional work and time discipline, seeking alternative work rhythms and time structures (see Seigel 1986; Pels and Crebas 1988; Abrams and McCulloch 1975).

[20] In *Discipline and Punish* Foucault noted the systematic application of disciplinary techniques in a range of sites: the prison, the hospital, the school, and the barracks, which were based on a new architecture of visibility, along with the differentiation and documentation of bodies (Foucault 1979). In effect the undifferentiated mass of the people became increasingly confined, regulated, and controlled through the disciplinary and normalizing techniques of state power. In addition to this set of disciplinary technologies to order and control the body, Foucault identified a second 'regulative technology of life', in which people were analysed on the population level.

[21] Modern governance took the population as its primary object, and through statistical knowledge was able to analyse and conceptualise the constituent parts: birth rates, death rates, forecasting, and estimates. This newly analysed collective body of the population became productive through the development of the science of economics in the eighteenth century, with the subsequent successful arguments of liberalism, Adam Smith, laissez-faire, and utilitarianism (see Featherstone 2013a, 2014a, b).

Consume Productively 24/7

Contemporary consumer culture encourages even more disciplined and intensive rhythms of consumption. In his book *24/7* Jonathan Crary addresses the shift towards a life with no respite, in which consumers are expected to live to the full every minute of the week (Crary 2013). The term 24/7 also conjures up machinic performance, a world in which it is impossible to hide, or expect time out, where the machine clocks abstract time, rather than the rhythms of day and night or the annual seasons, dictate. Crary mentions that North Americans now sleep on average six and a half hours a night, down from 8 h a generation ago and down from 10 h in the early twentieth century (Crary 2013: 11). The problem is that you can't consume when you sleep, and this brings with it the consumer culture corollary that sleep is wasted time, bereft of efficiency or enjoyment. The tendency in many of the affluent parts of the world is one of dissolving the boundaries between work and professional time, between work and consumption with the accent always on productive tasking. The hours city centre shops, stores, and malls are open are progressively extended. There is a constant cycle of new goods, new advertisements, and refurbished store designs to entice customers. This is something which Hannah Arendt detected in the 1950s when she remarked,

> 'if we were truly nothing but members of a consumer society we would no longer live in a world at all, we would simply be driven by a process in whose ever-recurring cycles things appear and disappear' (Arendt 1958: 134, cited in Crary 2013: 22).

We will turn to examine things and material commodities shortly, but first it is useful to examine more closely the rhythms of consumption.

Increasingly the pressure is to make our lives follow the financial benefits of maximum use of resources and become 24/7 consumers: extended shopping hours in the malls, and the 24-h city of entertainment with clubs, bars, cafes, and other leisure facilities open all night. The city permanently illuminated, serviced, and provisioned with transport and infrastructure: round-the-clock television, radio, and cable channels, accompanied by the Internet that never sleeps, forever updating itself, constantly accessible from the widening range of mobile devices such as smartphones, tablets, and laptops. This leads to the 24-h city with extensive Wi-Fi coverage overhead, but also cabled and wired below the streets and in buildings. The digital networks provide information for whatever desires or whim springs to mind: the nearest Japanese sushi restaurant, bar with Belgian beer, pancake café, designer perfume shop, fashion boutique, etc. Yet, this is the city not just furnishing information for us, but the city tracking us and gathering our information.

The digital networks and informational infrastructure along with the constant stream of innovative mobile machines are altering the rhythms, speeds, and formats of an increasingly accelerated and intensive consumer culture. They are also helping to reshape the nature of experience and perception, which is increasingly mediated through a screen culture. Currently we are familiar with people on public transport gazing at miniature screens (reading emails, newspapers, playing computer games, reading books, learning languages, window-shopping online stores). Some have headphones and are listening to music, books, sporting events, newscasts, or language programmes. Yet the handheld screen plus audio device is itself vulnerable and could well be displaced by newer display formats and technological innovations.[22] There is a massive R&D investment into technologies that speed up and reduce decision-making time and hence eliminate reflection and contemplation (Crary 2013: 40). Large transnational corporations such as Microsoft, Apple, Google, and Facebook are constantly seeking to innovate and produce new information technologies which offer consumers greater strategic empowerment, save time, capture and control experience, and enhance personal security and comfort too.

The new digital communicative technologies offer forms of empowerment and multi-tasking, always holding out something enticing in the endless stock of apps and entertainment content just a download away. The worry or hope is that there will always be something online that is more interesting, amusing, or impressive than the everyday life around you. As the gaze turns to the screen, many things in the immediate surroundings go unnoticed, and there is an atrophy of shared experience and attentiveness to others and traditional forms of sociality. This is captured by those people we see walking down the street who are highly animated and gesture dramatically while talking on a mobile phone headset, who are totally indifferent to passers-by. Everyday life until recently amounted to the bits left over, after work, consumerism, and dictates of the state administration—it was relatively free and eventless time. But as critics such as Lefebvre Debord and others suggest, the accent has been on the intensive colonisation of this time by the market and administration (Lefebvre 1971; Debord 1970).

These tendencies have also been noted by Deleuze with his concept of 'societies of control' (Deleuze 1992), which he saw as replacing and filling in the gaps between the institutions and sites Foucault described in terms of 'disciplinary societies': prisons, hospitals, barracks, schools, clinics, asylums, etc. But it has also been ratcheted up more with the move to financial capitalism since the 1980s and the institution of less visible forms of digital control. There is certainly greater camera surveillance and monitoring, plus swipe cards and coded and biometric access to restricted areas, along with monitoring of phone and Internet traffic. But what is interesting is the convergence and overlap between consumer culture and control society (see discussion in Crary 2013: 71ff). Of course, it may seem that time spent looking at Facebook, checking favourite sites, reading blogs, and downloading free music is enjoyable free leisure time. Yet, whatever we do is increasingly trackable and traceable—our movements by foot or car in the city, or our browsing and purchasing in the Internet (Crandall 2010). The browsing, the click and pointing, the tasking, and the searching point to an attentive economy, one of whose data indicators is to record the number of 'eyeballs' (looks or glances at a webpage). Facebook, Google and associated Internet corporations make money through high use of their platforms, so they

[22] One example being the see-through interface, as occurs with Google glasses. There is also the development of gesture-based computing where a nod of the head or blink of the eye serves as the command. Screens with voice commands and touchscreen devices could well be rendered obsolete.

want to achieve near-continuous involvement with content through computers and mobile devices as possible. The screens engage us and demand responses; they track us and harvest our data. Increasingly people check devices for emails before they go to bed and when they wake up, with some persons even waking several times in the night to check for messages. In the 24/7 screen culture sleep, the time or remission, the pause, and the waiting time become increasingly seen as unproductive and even wasteful. It becomes a luxury to seek release, to sleep, to forego, and to forgive.

Profiling, Tracking, and Data Harvesting

Consumption invariably leaves traces. Traditionally purchasing goods involved coins passed from hand to hand and was generally not receipted. Today it is more and more common to buy things with debit and credit cards, which are near-instantaneously linked electronically to bank accounts along with credit-worthiness checks.[23] Increasingly consumers are encouraged to use credit or debit cards for all purchases, including small items via 'touch and debit' for small items or metro and bus travel. Larger items, which include practically everything from department store durable goods, motorcars, package holidays, and air flights and health insurance, can be now purchased via the smartphones which can potentially replace credit and bank cards in the future, given their host of additional functions, which include Internet banking access of the details of multiple sets of purchases. The specialist information service agencies that are rapidly gaining global extent, such as Experian (originating in the United Kingdom, but now a leading transnational corporation), mediate between banks and consumers to make credit checks.

In doing this they amass a massive amount of data not only on credit worthiness, but also on purchasing habits and preferences of customers. Once this is coupled with other personal data, people's address, age, occupation, salary, and other deductions can be made about the person. This accumulated geodemographic data compounds the assumption that people with similar occupation and age characteristics

[23] According to CredCards.com United Kingdom, 75% of all spending in the UK retail sector was made using plastic cards at the end of November 2013 (UK Cards Association Annual Report 2014). Payment card spending amounted to £141.9bn during Q3 2014, representing an annual growth rate of 6.6%, http://uk.creditcards.com/credit-card-news/uk-britain-credit-debit-card-statistics-international.php. Accessed 21.2.2015. People in the United Kingdom owed £1.463tn in total personal debt at the end of November 2014. This is up from £1.43tn at the end of November 2013—an extra £591 per UK adult. The average total debt per household—including mortgages—was £55,384 in November 2014. Total lending to individuals increased by £3.3bn in November 2014, compared to the average monthly increase of £3bn over the previous 6 months. The 3-month annualised and 12-month growth rates were both 2.4%. At the end of 2013, credit card debt accounted for 4% of total personal borrowing; mortgages accounted for 89%. Total outstanding credit card debt averaged £57.4b a month. Unsecured consumer debt, which is mostly made up of credit card debt, almost tripled between 1993 and 2013, reaching nearly £160bn in November 2013. The United Kingdom is the biggest card payment market in the European Union, accounting for more than 30% of all EU card spending, and 73% of the EU credit card market.

often have similar consumer tastes, which include choice of housing—in effect as the old adage goes 'birds of a feather live together', meaning university professors and lecturers tend to be found in the same type of areas of cities and decorate their houses in similar ways, dress in similar clothes, and drive similar types of cars (cf. here the type of analysis Bourdieu used in *Distinction*—Bourdieu 1984).[24] Such databases and value of the information they provide will increase in significance if current trends continue. E-commerce is currently the fastest growing retail market in Europe with sales in the leading countries expected to grow by 18.4% to 185.39bn euros in 2015. The sales in the United States were expected to amount to $398.78bn for 2015.[25] While the UK online percentage share of the total consumer retail market was estimated to be 15.2% in 2015, it is suggested that this percentage will be sustained or increase to the expense of conventional stores.[26]

It is important to see this as not just a consumer culture business opportunity, but also an advantageous accumulation of data, with money to be made from the digital data traces, not just the actual goods sold. Indeed, in many ways the data side is highly lucrative, given that companies constantly seek more precise market information about their customers.[27] The financial and business deregulation accompanying the

---

[24] Richard Webber has been a central figure in the development of geodemographics (see Burrows and Gane 2006; Beer and Burrows 2013).

[25] According to the Centre for Retail Research, sales in the United Kingdom, Germany, France, Sweden, the Netherlands, Italy, Poland, and Spain were expected to grow from £132.05bn [€156.28bn] in 2014 to £156.67bn [€185.39bn] in 2015 (+18.4%), reaching £185.44bn (€219.44bn) in 2016. In 2015, overall online sales were expected to grow by 18.4% (same as 2014), but 13.8% in the United States on a much larger total. These figures relate only to *retail spending*, defined as sales of merchandise to the final consumer. In the United States, online sales were expected to rise from $306.85bn [£189.26] in 2014 to $349.20bn [£215.39bn] in 2015 and $398.78bn [£245.96bn] a year later. This independent study for 2015–2016 has been funded by Retail Me Not, Inc., the world's largest digital coupon marketplace with 655mn customer visits to its sites in 2014. The Retail Me Not, Inc. portfolio of coupon and deal websites includes RetailMeNot.com, VoucherCodes.co.uk, Deals.com, Bons-de-Reduction.com, Deals2Buy.com, and Poulpeo.com. Within the EU market the United Kingdom is expected to grow to £52.25bn sales in 2015, an increase of 16%, followed by Germany with £44.61bn, a growth of 23%. Poland's growth in 2015 was estimated to be £4.33bn, an increase of 21%, http://www.retailresearch.org/onlineretailing.php. Accessed 19.2.2015.

[26] Some conventional stores are fighting back and trying to utilise digital technologies within the stores and also encourage customers to interface with online material and their own website pages on Facebook and other sites for an enhanced consumer experience. Within the stores digital devices in the form of screen/mirrors in changing cubicles enable women to see not only the dress they are wearing, but also their previous saved collection of items on the stores' website, with an additional Facebook link to enable them to post the composite digital images to solicit the views of friends and family (Coleman 2013). This response to the expansion of Internet shopping is an attempt to create a new hybrid enhanced shopping experience and younger customers in particular seem enthusiastic.

[27] In our earlier discussion we emphasised that Foucault's (Foucault 2008; see discussion in Featherstone 2013b) focus was not just on panopticism (disciplinary control of bodies), but also on biopolitics, governing the population aggregate, with the state utilising demographic data to increase its populations' productivity (increasing the birth rate through better maternal and infant care, etc.). Importantly, the statistical information was not just about people, but also about goods

move to neoliberalism has worked well in tandem with the digital communications revolution. This has dramatically increased the capacity to gather information on the part of Internet corporations, especially the growing number of Web analytics firms, who trawl data in real time to constantly update information on Internet website usage via computer algorithms.[28] Through the use of software algorithms, commonalities between data patterns can be identified to enable real-time access and matching (Cheney-Lippold 2011; Beer 2009). Users' profiles can be continually updated with each piece of information on new preferences or changing tastes and the set of recommended purchases altered accordingly. This is the typical pattern we experience on Amazon Books: 'if you liked this book you could like this other one', and 'people who bought this book, also bought …'. This type of profiling and targeting is increasingly becoming standardised across sites and Internet providers. If one browses for cosmetics, or a holiday in Paris on one site, mysteriously a range of relevant margin advertisements spring up on other provider's sites.[29] In effect we are tracked, we are monitored, we are profiled, we are enticed, and we are trained to be productive by the corporations. It is in this sense that we can understand the massive corporate investment in the Internet which has taken place since the dot.com boom.[30]

This is a long way from the dreams of the World Wide Web in the 1990s with the efforts of its founder Tim Berners Lee and others to create a free Web where people could find easy access to data across different cultural and informational domains. The Internet today increasingly entails data harvesting, tracking, and

and movement of commodities (the shiploads of corn arriving at the ports, the number of cartloads being ferried to cities, etc.), which furnished highly useful data, which led to the birth of economics. Indeed, the two became connected when in the eighteenth-century Europe through the physiocrats in France (Quesnay et al.) and especially liberalism and then utilitarianism in England (Adam Smith, Mandeville, Bentham et al.), it was assumed that the most efficient form of governance involved laissez-faire, let the market work itself and encourage competition and minimal state interference.

[28] The sophistication of the data sets is impressive and puts into shade the traditional social research methods with sample surveys, and also the type of data accumulated by governments in their population census gathering exercises, that occur each decade. Now there is a new social life of methods outside the academy, with social science quantitative data techniques such as sampling and census surveys seen as far inferior in terms of energy expended, completeness of data sets, and a host of other factors (Ruppert et al. 2013). Many of these new databases are now vastly superior to those constructed by social science research in terms of their extent, scope, and real-time updating, and provide much more fine-grained information about the consumption, lifestyle, and cultural values of different groups (Burrows and Gane 2006; Beer and Burrows 2013).

[29] If, for example, I email a colleague in Sofia using Google gmail, I will notice out of the corner of my eye that a series of small advertisements for hotels and flights to Sofia have popped up. Apparently the Internet providers bid against each other in terms of fractions of a pence in real time to be able to place the appropriate advert in the margin of my Internet pages, based upon data analytics which reveal not only my profile and buying habits, but also set of tastes which enables them to make a decision (or rather one of their machines to make a decision) on the probability that I will at some point make a purchase.

[30] The fact that Facebook was valued at $104bn just before flotation and Mark Zuckerberg in his late 20s rapidly accumulated a personal fortune of some $35bn. Or the fact that Google paid $1.65bn for YouTube.

online purchasing. Some people might see the emergence of social media platforms such as Facebook as a countermove against this tendency. Yet the high flotation value of Facebook which was valued at $114bn in May 2014 is one sound indicator of the financial market's estimation of the value embodied in the product and the returns expected to be realised. With Facebook it is not just the capacity of algorithms to filter, sort, and extend the networks of people we can meet online, and hence the usable data for profiling. Rather, it is also the visibility of other people or particular sites, which seem attractive to browse through, to perhaps leave a like 'tick' or 'swoosh' next to a particular image which endorses them. The activity of people relating to other people, searching, looking, adding photographs, adding news, and updating their profiles, is what creates value. Inscribed into the algorithm logic of the Facebook News Feed is the idea that greater visibility functions as a reward for providing the type of news items favoured and relates to having a large number of friends commenting that they like a particular post. In effect there is a disciplining process that encourages users to be attentive, to monitor their own behaviour, and to train themselves to perform as required. From the Facebook perspective a useful individual is one who 'participates, communicates and interacts', with the big danger being the threat of invisibility (Bucher 2012: 1175).

High visibility can also bring a range of commercial rewards. Take the case of Zoella, who in 2015 had over 5 million following her YouTube channel with more than 2.3 million watching her vlog (video blog) episode 'Chopping Off My Hair' (February 2015). Zoella, now aged 24, started her blog 6 years ago as a teenager in her bedroom. She allegedly commands some £20,000 a month from advertisers and bought a £1 million five-bedroom mansion in Brighton (*Daily Mail*, 17 February 2015). Zoella provides beauty, fashion, and relationship advice. She is proving to be an ideal vehicle for brands that want to reach young consumers. Zoella has also learnt to diversify, having just written her first novel *Girl Online* (Zoe Sugg 2014).[31] YouTube is more dialogical than television, offering more direct connection with audience who can offer immediate feedback by commenting on videos and blogs, and it is in process of establishing its own superstars for a younger generation attuned to screen culture and mobile devices. Yet while there is potential stardom for some and the possibilities to post material on YouTube or Facebook for many, and the potential that others could see, comment, and potentially admire your efforts, the chances of becoming another Zoella are very limited. In many ways the logic of YouTube and Facebook fits well with that of the talent contest, which has undergone a revival over the last decade or so, through television shows such as 'America's Got Talent', 'X-Factor', and 'Come Dancing' along with the reality television programmes such as 'I'm a Celebrity Get Me Out of Here', where stars and ordinary people are seen to mix and engage in potentially dramatic and humorous ordeals, or

---

[31] See Wendy Marr 'Zoella, Tanya Burr and the UK's YouTube Superstars', *Telegraph,* 16 August 2014; Alice Audley 'Social Media Sensations: Top UK Beauty You Tubers', *Telegraph*, 3 April 2014. There are also articles on the Internet such as '12 Social Media Secrets from World's Top Superstars', Tia Dobi, *Social Media Examiner*, April 6 2010 full of tips to 'take your social media marketing to max'.

put up with mundane boredom in a confined environment designed to induce pressure and bitchiness. The talent and skill required to be a good performer, along with the ambition to become famous, a proto-celebrity, persona, and perhaps a star, very much reflect the competitive individualism central to neoliberalism. The assumption of talent, that those who win possess it and the corollary, that those who fail do not, is central to the philosophy of success of the rich and super-rich often presented as a justification for their incredible wealth (see Featherstone 2013a, 2014b).

Immaterial and Informational Lifestyle Construction

Consumer culture for some is associated with a crass materialism, with the unregulated desire for objects, things, and possessions, to hoard and amass for one's own purposes and exclusive pleasure. This connects to one meaning of the term consume: to exhaust and destroy like a fire (Featherstone 2007; Williams 1976). Clearly the person who greedily consumes expensive and prestigious food and drink, or constantly buys new clothes and goods, fits this stereotype. As Durkheim indicated in the late nineteenth century this behaviour carries the danger that the consumers themselves will be consumed, as the pursuit of the new, of the latest nameless sensations, carries with it the danger of psychological disorders, anomie, and social deregulation (Durkheim 2014). Yet this does not apply to all purchases as there are many goods that have different life spans and functions. The purchase of a house as a space to dwell and display possessions is a very different type of consumption from buying a meal, bottle of wine, or music download. The materiality of a house or apartment seemingly contrasts with the immateriality of Internet consumption. The latter doesn't involve consumption of an object, but use of a means, or medium for information. It encourages searching, researching, browsing, checking, and learning. It encourages sampling, planning, monitoring, rehearsing, and testing. The Internet is interactive and offers feedback.

This raises the question of the different durability, consumability, and life history of things, along with their shifting relationships to other objects and people (Appadurai 1986). There are major differences in the timing and duration of purchase and consumption time, between for example luxury and everyday consumer goods. The symbolic significance of special social occasions or ceremonies often requires high-value luxury goods to be used or consumed.[32] Means of transports,

[32] Some things are immediately consumed on purchase (an ice cream in the park on a hot summer's day demands immediate consumption), and other objects may be put away for years before being brought out to consumer (the bottle of Chateau Lafite 2005 Bordeaux wine may last 50 years before it is opened). Valuable paintings may be carefully displayed and protected by security systems to be gazed at with reverence along with the comforting expectation that they are constantly gaining in value. Other things have more mundane uses (see Miller 2008). The Internet encourages researching and comparison of things in terms of value and price. But other items may be defined as special luxury presents to oneself so that price is less relevant and the time spent learning how to use the good is not seen as wasted (e.g. the new Porsche sports car may need extra driving les-

such as automobiles, are not only complex things in terms of their intricate machinery and computer technologies, but to drive the car is not merely to put in motion an object; it is more than a vehicle. It is part of a complex material and information assemblage, which includes not only the management of the car's own performance and safety, but also the highway traffic management systems, refuelling stations, automated e-toll payment systems, etc. (Featherstone 2004). The shift from objects to quasi-objects suggests the difficulty of gauging the boundaries and extent of objects, and the difficulty of definition given their embeddedness in networks of externalities, relationships, and objects.[33]

This moves attention away from the materiality of the object to wider material, informational, and immaterial networks. Indeed, it is possible to see what has been happening to the motorcar as symptomatic of wider changes in the nature of the commodity within capitalism. Increasingly, it has been argued that we have seen a shift not just from use value to exchange value, as Marx and others emphasised in pointing to how the useful qualities things have become subordinated to their monetary value as commodities to be bought and sold. Rather, it is argued that there has been a further displacement from both use value and exchange value to sign value (Baudrillard 1983; see discussion in Featherstone 2007). This has also been characterised as a shift to post-Fordism, involving a much greater informational and cultural input into branded commodities (Lash and Urry 1993; Lash and Lury 2007). Jean Baudrillard, in particular, has drawn attention to the shift from things to signs and images within contemporary consumer culture (Baudrillard 1983). It is assumed that we no longer are confronted by goods with fixed meanings, because the rapid flow of signs and images through advertising and consumer culture manages to elide new meanings onto things. The surfeit of floating images and signs saturates the fabric of everyday life to produce an unstable field in which secure meanings are lost. In effect the proliferation of signs and images has effaced the distinction between reality and images, to the extent that we now 'live in an aesthetic hallucination of reality' (Baudrillard 1983: 248; Featherstone 2007).

While Baudrillard's language may be unduly hyperbolic, it does point us to a significant shift in the volume and intensity of images and signs. Baudrillard's prime concern is in documenting this sign overload and new simulational world; it is not his concern to ask how this world is made, but following Bourdieu we can point to the expansion of the cultural and information sectors and with it the rise in the numbers of cultural specialists and intermediaries (Bourdieu 1984). Many of these work in culture and creative industries which have flourished on the back of the increasing salience of cultural, artistic, fashion design, and consumer activities in contemporary societies, an expanding sector of the economy to deal with the informational aspect of goods and the wider cultural matrix within which goods are increasingly

---

sons to learn how to handle it). Some goods, then, may open up a prestigious learning process, which brings with it numerous social and psychological benefits (Boscagli 2014).

[33]The term quasi-object was initially developed by Michel Serres (Serres 1982, 1995; see also discussion in Brown 2002; Schiermer 2011). Latour also refers to the impact of quasi-objects on subjects and raises the question whether subjects are becoming quasi-subjects.

encountered. A further important aspect of the new cultural sector is the significance of emotional and affective labour (Hochschild 1983; Neilson and Rossiter 2005).[34] The attractions of working in the cultural sector, in fashion, design, television, film, music, theatre, and advertising occupations and the increasing numbers have led to an oversupply.[35]

If the expansion of the cultural sector is considered alongside the rise of YouTube Superstars and the mass of cultural production and interactivity entailed, we can see that Internet consumption is opening up new dimensions for consumer culture. The act of purchase no longer stands alone as a simple task: it is only one moment in a wider set of activities, involving searching, researching, updating, communicating, and blogging which can no longer be easily separated, or considered as ancillary or peripheral. To buy a product endorsed by Zoella is very different from a traditional star product endorsement in a 30-s television advertisement clip. It is also different from accustomed consumer culture 'research' which could involve checking newspapers, consumer magazines, women's magazines, or occasional 'window-shopping' trips to city centres. The type of knowledge building and the levels of interactivity between the followers and stars on the Internet can be seen to break new ground. But even to engage in Internet purchase from Shiseido, Estee Lauder, or other major cosmetic companies on the Internet now contains an experiential dimension. The major brands have invested in high-value designed complex sites with beautiful images, detailed information, and multiform advice in their endeavour to make the experience as complete as possible.

In addition, there has sprung up masses of beauty blogs with varying degrees of independence. They tend to have their own Facebook pages along with links to other sites, plus product reviews, posts, and comments; everything is liberally sprinkled with high-definition arty or professional-shoot-style colour photographs of models or would-be models. This suggests that consumers who enter into the Internet tend to be drawn into a good deal of systematic work, planning, and knowledge accumulation. They are encouraged to become enterprising, engage in

[34] Affective strategies are evident in department store, boutique, restaurant, and café interior design (with attention given to lighting, music, mood to create atmosphere, and ambience), but also evident in advertisements, especially television, cinema, and online (attention to imagery, colour, text layout, and choice of language, music, voice, and mood). Major transnational corporations in the cosmetic industry for example engage in careful attention to the affective dimensions of their products in terms of in-house department store makeup bars, the shape and materials of products, the uniforms of assistants, the advertising imagery, use of celebrity endorsement, and choice of leading film makers to produce advertisements (Oyama 2011). For a discussion of affect and body image in consumer culture see Featherstone (2010a, b, c).

[35] This in turn has diminished job security and remuneration leading to more part-time, flexible, and temporary work along with a range of hybrid employer/employee statuses on the part of a group of people who are 'neither wage earners, nor entrepreneurs nor employees', but share greater insecurity and 'precarity' (Gill and Pratt 2008; Lazzarato 2012: 53; McRobbie 2011). A 'winner takes all' total mobilisation and unsustainable level of self-belief, sacrifice, and entrepreneurialism are demanded of workers in this sector who increasingly have to put up with a quasi-proletarianisation and forms of flexible home working as the Internet becomes the increasing means of work connectivity.

endless self-improvement, and become conscious of the importance of their image, personal style, and need to be fashionable and innovative. There are also endless possibilities for self-monitoring and archiving of one's own photographs on social media websites like Facebook, or the development of blogs with similar-minded people, or in the endeavour to reach out to the widest audience possible and gain acknowledgement of one's talent in order to become famous and make money as in the case of Zoella et al.[36]

In addition there are those companies that seek to forge stronger links with their customers: not by traditional modes of brand identification, but by involving their followers, fans, and customers as co-producers in product design by opening sites which ask for suggestions on new products, or engage in blue-sky open thinking about the nature of their sector. Car manufacturer designers who encounter a particular problem in say engine design may now eschew secrecy and put the problem onto a website to invite followers to make suggestions. The latter could no doubt be flattered or thrilled to be involved and are aware of the career advantage of having something in their portfolio; but they are also effectively providing a free consultancy (cf. the practice of interns working for leading politicians and others).

Consumption Experiences, Prosumption, and Curating Lifestyles

It has often been observed that there has been a shift in consumer culture from the consumption of goods to the consumption of experiences. Activities such as watching a music concert, play, movie, football match, having a special dinner, visiting a museum or a foreign country, enjoying a weekend break, short course to learn a new sport or hobby, or 'once-in-a-lifetime vacation' all promise in varying degrees to be an experience. In some cases this could be classed as 'mere entertainment', but in others the premium is on the eventfulness of the experience, and the payment is made in the expectation of something vital and memorable. Consumer culture industries, with novels, adventure stories, travel guides, movies and documentaries, and more recently the Internet with its mixture of text and images, but also blog feedback, provide a major outlet. With the expansion of education in modernity, especially within the middle classes, there has been a premium placed upon experience, with the eventful and creative life often contrasted to the boredom and routines of everyday life (Featherstone 1992, 2007). The potency of this repertoire of experiential themes

[36] The increased capacity to record experiences and post material on the Internet has opened up new forms of blogs, social media sites, and archives (Featherstone 2006; Beer and Burrows 2013). High-street stores also are keen to use the new technologies such as 'digital mirrors' (a combination of a real mirror and digital screen in changing rooms to enable women to upload images of themselves on Facebook websites in order to get opinions of their friends and family about the suitability of potential purchases) (Coleman 2013). There is also a darker side via phone-camera filming, sharing, and eve Internet posting video clips of violent assaults or sexual offences (Schwarz 2012).

means that they are constantly reworked and repackaged within consumer culture marketing and become associated with a wider range of goods (Schulze 1992, 1997; Pine and Gilmore 2011). It has also been argued that brands have undergone a series of changes and should be thought of more as 'emerging potentials', a developing unstable field of associated characteristics than a fixed object (Lash and Lury 2007). As mentioned above, brands are also increasingly interactive in asking consumers to engage with the total experience of goods and offer a wide range of ancillary expertise, seductive imagery, and pleasurable browsing via their websites. Consumers are therefore increasingly asked to not just use goods blindly, or to purchase impulsively, but to study, research, and work at capturing the full range of capabilities and pleasures a product and its ancillary field of information and experience can supply over time, in short, to adopt a learning mode to life.

All this suggests that consumers can no longer be conceived as passive and manipulated behind their backs by advertising. Rather, the consumer is drawn into working the array of material that exists alongside goods: in effect the consumer is encouraged to be productive. As mentioned earlier, this was one of the points made by Foucault with reference to neoliberalism and consumption: people are encouraged to be enterprising and self-reliant, to increase their human capital through a range of investment strategies, but also to see consumption as an extension of these activities, by addressing consumer culture with a similar orientation: 'How can I maximise my satisfaction and pleasure?' As the boundaries between production and consumption blur, it is not surprising that people talk about productive consumption and the term 'prosumer' (Toffler 1980; Ritzer 2014) has been invented to capture this. The prosumer points to the way in which consumption ceases to be a largely passive activity of reception, but becomes one in which consumer businesses manage to externalise some of their costs: we return our trays, leftovers, and rubbish in McDonalds and Starbucks, we buy a flat-pack wardrobe from IKEA which we assemble at home, etc.

More recently Ritzer has discussed smart machines in terms of prosumption, with examples such as mobile phones passing location data to providers, or e-tolls allowing data on car journeys to be figured automatically by electronic devices and deducted from bank accounts (Ritzer 2014). Likewise wearable monitoring devices can automatically communicate blood pressure, pulse, glucose levels, and other data to hospitals and clinics. The potential of this area has been noted for some time and increasingly barcodes and RFIDs (radio frequency identification devices) mean objects can be tagged and coded and can send data back to home server databases, or exchange data with mobile phones with code readers (Hayles 2009).[37] Effectively an enchanted world opens up, a 'disneyfied world' in which things not only speak back to custom-

[37] Biometric devices, embedded chips in people and pets, are also one aspect of the Internet of Things. Along with wearable computing (smart clothes which can also adapt to environmental conditions or wearer's mood) it will produce a network that will enable greater monitoring and interactivity of things as they move around, but also greater sensory enhancement devices—cf. the new 4HD cameras which have twice the capacity of human vision in the dark. Google glasses, fulfilling some of the science fiction speculations of William Gibson's cyberspace, also point in this direction (Kuchler 2008; Anderson and Rainie 2014).

ers, but are also able to exchange information, perform set information repertoires, and hold limited conversations. This points to the upsurge of interest in smart houses, smart cars, home robots, and a host of smart devices. The material fabric of the urban world, shopping centres, theme parks, and resorts begins to talk back to consumers. Things carry embedded information, but increasingly can display it with an affective charge. There are two further points, relevant to briefly mention here: the first relates to customisation and mass consumption, and the second to lifestyle.

One of the key dynamics within consumer culture has been that of mass and luxury. The age of mass consumption opened up in the nineteenth century and twentieth century offered the availability of cheap mass-produced goods. At the same the department stores were quick to promote luxuries, and the availability of cheaper versions of luxuries gave rise to the notion of the democratisation of luxury (Williams 1982). While mass goods were often disposable or incorporated 'built-in obsolescence', luxuries were crafted and singular; with the emphasis upon enduring quality, they would continue to retain their value both economically and culturally.[38] The potential of new technologies such as 3-D printers offers an intermediate category, goods which can be machine produced, but which are singular and can be produced on demand at home. In addition to customisation, consumer culture seeks to persuade people that the research and careful accumulation of knowledge of consumer goods will result in greater satisfaction. The full set of goods and services which promise new or valid experiences should be chosen with care as they amount to a lifestyle. That is, they need to be deliberately pursued and given due consideration for their overall style and level of appropriate compatibility; within consumer culture advice and publicity lifestyle are generally presented as active transformative terms, and not a set of characteristics people gradually and unknowingly accumulate over time (Featherstone 2007).

Consumer culture therefore demands the careful purchase, assemblage, and care of sets of goods and services selected on the assumption that they will yield maximum satisfaction and care. Yet the goods also demand curating, they can become obsolete or outmoded (*démodé*), and they need to be periodically assessed and evaluated with some relegated to the attic or the rubbish bin. At the same time, the turnover of goods is essential to keep the neoliberal global economy functioning. To this end, despite the risk of debt, consumers must be persuaded to continue actively consuming, to become aware of the range of new options and possibilities available, and then make new purchases to maximise their satisfaction—a form of 'calculating hedonism' (Featherstone 2007: ch. 2). In some ways this activity is similar to that of a curator, but more of a lifestyle curator. Like the museum or gallery curator, each assemblage or show disturbs the previous classification. Assembling and presenting collections and curating lifestyles need careful work, along with continual research and evaluation.

[38] A Savile Row suit is a good example of a customised luxury good. It is not just a fine piece of tailoring, but also meant to instil confidence in its wearer and the tailors make every effort to educate their customers (who can pay £10–20,000 for the suit) into knowledge of every aspect of the quality product they are getting. Indeed, many customers, especially the nouveau riche, do report that the magic confidence does actually occur (personal comment from Javier Caletrio). This is also the case with high-end luxury fashion brands, which seek to present their clothes as art and enhance the charisma of the designers (Dion and Arnould 2011).

The Consequences of Consumption

What are the consequences of the opening up of new forms of consumption? It can be argued that the shift towards 24/7 Internet consumption is helping to change the rhythms of everyday life and producing new forms of social behaviour. There are numerous social consequences in terms of interacting with screens on a regular individual basis, and also the consequences of handling, selecting, and digesting the vast quantities of information now available. What effect do these new modes have on existing forms of sociality and sociability? Secondly, there is the question of how far the integration of Internet and other forms of immaterial consumption into the activities of purchasing, researching, and using goods is really immaterial. What are the energy consequences and levels of waste generated by the new digital technologies?

In terms of the first question, the Internet provides a massive increase in the scope and volume of information available; it opens up a vast archive of material. This can be conceived in terms of the problem that Georg Simmel referred to over a century ago in terms of the buildup of objective culture (knowledge of the past, and the range of cultural media and forms such as novels, books, newspapers, magazines, scientific and art objects, image and data banks, etc., beyond the capacity of assimilation into individual subjectivity (Simmel 1997a, b, c, Featherstone 2000, 2006; see also Bell 1973)). It is impossible to read or be aware of the parameters of the archive and database the Internet opens up, amounting to a veritable Borghesian Library of Babel. On the subjective level it is not just a question of how to navigate a sea of data, but also how to handle 'the over-optioned life', with too many choices, raising the problem of selectivity and value choice. In addition the fateful wager of our life paths, chosen or unchosen, opens up: the fact that our chosen path amounts to a bet on a particular course of life, which given the finitude of human life necessarily eliminates the remaining time available for sampling alternatives. One of the aporias of consumer culture is that however much one searches and researches in order to make an informed choice, this eats into the time to live out the choice or try alternatives when a particular becomes deemed unsatisfying or boring. The new screen culture and mobile devices open up the myriad of possibilities on a mundane daily basis.

There are further consequences of the Internet screen culture in the way that it trains us to be attentive. We are encouraged to regularly check mobile devices anytime and anywhere. Checking devices for new messages, or aimlessly flicking through various windows, and refusing to shut down can become a compulsion. Indeed, it has been remarked that like television, which has been linked to autism and depression, Internet viewing may produce similar disorders.[39] A related consequence is the impoverishment of the capacity to daydream or engage in absent-minded introspective reflection. The tempo of reverie, of idly succumbing to ran-

[39] As Crary comments 'Even the quasi-addictiveness associated with internet pornography and violent computer games seems to lead quickly to a flattening of response and the replacement of pleasure with the need for repetition' (Crary 2013: 87).

dom or loosely associative thought chains or images, does not sit easily with 24/7 screen culture. This in turn can lead to a deterioration of memory and failing in the capacity to imagine or dream of another time.[40] If we are seeking a forceful critique of the consequences of consumer culture and its dreams, then for Crary one of the worst consequences is the elimination of dreams and wishes, of daydreaming and musing, which leaves little space to creatively think beyond the performative repertoires, the repetitive cycles, of the Internet screen culture (Crary 2013).

A further consequence is diminishing of sociality. Computer screens tend to be individualised; they are designed for one person and their personal habits and preferences become incorporated into the device set-up and way of operating.[41] Communication increasingly works through seriality, the transmission of individual-tailored messages into the aggregate, conceived as an inchoate mass of isolated consumers with only a limited need for, or potential for, collective encounters or forms of sociality, with the dangers of increased loneliness and 'generalised autism' (Crary 2013: 120). It can be added that this seriality is increasingly tempered by profiling: the collection of individual data on subjects to enable marketing to match individual taste profiles (see discussion in earlier section above).

In terms of the second question, the consequences of the shift from material to immaterial consumption, it could seem that the new information technologies such as the Internet and the range of related mobile devices are shifting the balance towards immaterial things and the 'knowledge economy'. Yet this ignores the material infrastructure and maintenance activities, which sustain the electronic networks (Graham and Thrift 2007).[42] This means that there are substantial quantities of 'e-waste' that is often exported from the Global North to the South with the recycle process involving toxic hazards. A desktop computer or mobile device often appears to be an efficient and stylish device incorporating a high level of design

[40] Indeed, the Internet can be seen as an enhancement of a process which gathered pace from the 1840s onwards, which tightened the associative relationship between image production machines and consumer goods. The new image-making industries sought to replicate and replace the human capacity to retain retinal after-images—to retain after-images or bring visions into focus with one's eyes closed (Crary 2013: 106). The new image-making technologies went through a series of shifts, in terms of quality of images with the production of high-quality chromolithographs being a significant step (Ewen 1988: 37ff), as well as the development of collective spaces for spectators to view images, the series of form: panoramas, dioramas, etc. that preceded cinema (Crary 1990, 2001; Schivelbusch 1986; Friedberg 1994).

[41] See discussion in Cubitt on the ways computer screens or terminals could have been designed for more collective viewing (Cubitt 1998). Collective viewing of sports programmes or national or global events in collective situations, offices, student halls, bars, etc. tends to provide a totally different viewing experience and in some situations it is possible for a quasi-religious sense of the sacred to be generated (see discussion of Katz's work in Featherstone 2007: ch. 8). But in many everyday public and quasi-public situations, people tend to be absorbed with their mobile devices, and interpersonal sensitivities tend to be switched low.

[42] The Internet depends on a surprising amount of hardware such as cabling—the transoceanic cables, for example, are vital for not only the Internet, but also the financial markets (Toscano 2013). In addition there is the turnover of computer hardware, the constant need to purchase new upgrade models, with companies like Apple bringing out new models or upgrades on an annual basis.

input. Yet the amount of energy expended to manufacture such devices can be surprisingly large, with a few microchips able to have as much embodied energy as a car (De Decker 2009).[43] Consumer culture, therefore, generates a massive amount of waste from the so-called immaterial consumption. The rapid turnover of goods and the continuing throwaway mindset within contemporary consumer culture means that we are only beginning to consider the implications of the accumulation of discarded things and their by-products.[44] The drive for technological innovation decreases the half-life of products. Yet, the increasing embedding of microchips into an expanding number of objects and environments means that the complexity of waste and the subsequent difficulties of recycling will grow.[45]

In contradistinction to social theories of modernity, which apart from Marx hardly considered energy, or if they did saw it as effectively an infinite resource, we currently have entered a phase of global life in which we have to relinquish the modernist Faustian view of nature as an endless resource. In short in the face of an expanding global population, over-exploitation of natural resources, and climate change, we have to contemplate the transition to a post-carbon society that relies on renewable energy and recycled materials too. This suggests a profound social, economic, and political challenge for humankind with planetary consequences for all life forms (Clark and Yusoff 2017). Yet there are few current signs that this has been digested. Consumer culture as mentioned earlier is central to the global economy and held up by the vast majority of nation-state governments as the incentive and reward for economic growth, which is still part of the implicit social contract, which legitimates governance and furthers social integration.

Despite intermittent acknowledgement of the mounting scientific evidence about the need to heed climate change and curb carbon emissions, there are still many powerful nation-states who argue that they have exceptional circumstances. Others

[43] It is difficult to get reliable data about the energy used in the production phase to make a desktop PC or mobile phone. De Decker remarks the 'embodied energy of the memory chip alone already exceeds the energy consumption of a laptop during its life expectancy of 3 years' (De Decker 2009). There is also the energy and Wi-Fi needed to make the devices functional. If we add in constant upgrading performance costs, energy use costs, and safe ecological disposal costs, then we get the total carbon footprint of Internet devices (see Walsh 2013). In addition, cars nowadays contain increasing numbers of computer chips and it has been estimated that around 40% of the cost of a vehicle now comes from the electronic components (Hedge et al. 2011).

[44] In some sectors such as home design and furnishings it may be possible to encourage small-scale artisanal sustainable forms of production, but for the moment this looks to be something for a minor sector of the middle classes. See discussion of ethical consumption below.

[45] One solution would be more biodegradable materials and recycling. Currently in the United Kingdom we have to separate household rubbish, yet around a third of recycle waste is shipped abroad to China, Korea, Indonesia, and other places. An estimated 250,000 tonnes a year of used electronic and electrical products is sent to Ghana, Nigeria, India, Pakistan, and China, generally dismantled by unprotected workers, often children under the guise that these used goods are 'charitable donations' which allows them to elude safety laws (Moses 2013). China is the leading importer of waste, including plastic waste, and also is the leading country that allows plastic waste to reach the oceans. The infamous Great Pacific Garbage Patch, a floating mass of non-biodegradable plastic, is a small part of the estimated five trillion pieces of plastic floating in the world's oceans—anticipated to double over the next decade (Sample 2014).

too, are committed to delivering the long-cherished consumer culture dreams to their populations. A life full of the latest goods, fashions, and gadgets remains powerfully seductive. In addition, the heroes and role models of consumer culture, the stars, celebrities, and super-rich enjoy unlimited consumption of luxuries, along with a high-mobility lifestyle (private jet travel).[46] Few politicians today want to dismantle this system, one which they tend to benefit from. Yet the consequences of the consumer culture dream have been under attack since the 1960s' counter-culture, and the criticisms and the warning reports on the lack of sustainability of global resources (Club of Rome *Limits to Growth Report*) alongside the 1973 oil crisis. One of the voices at this time, Andre Gorz, presciently suggested:

'"Better" may now mean "less": creating as few needs as possible, satisfying them with the smallest possible expenditure of materials, energy, and work, and imposing the least burden on the environment' (Gorz 1980: 27; cited in Urry 2014a).

The inability to implement a low-expenditure and limited-consumption society, in the intervening 40 years of so, has been marked. Indeed, the problems of dealing with waste, carbon accumulations, and climate change have accumulated to a level that would have been impossible to imagine in the early 1970s (Cubitt 2015, Reno 2014).

It is now argued that the changes that face us, which are now becoming acknowledged, result from irresponsible human intervention, which is of sufficient magnitude to amount to a new geological epoch. The term Anthropocene, a period of human history which follows after the Holocene era, was developed by Paul Crutzen in 2002, to point to the way in which human activity had interfered with the geophysical forces of the planet, with the extraction of fossil fuels in the industrial revolution, the significant marker event. Crutzen now locates the start of the Anthropocene era to a key event: the Trinity detonation of July 16, 1945: the first nuclear explosion, which released invisible radioactive decay into the atmosphere. The new era is marked by the release of waste, in the form of nuclear fallout. It can, therefore, be argued that waste has become the most enduring and abundant trace of the human (Hird 2017). In one sense the beginning of the Anthropocene era and the buildup of waste are premised on human's capacity to burn fossil fuels, in effect to turn rocks back into gases, to generate energy, which is now producing significant climate change (Dalby 2017).

In short this is one of the consequences of consumer culture: the dreams end in waste, in the accumulation of planetary depletion and toxicity, which defines a certain narrowed-down limited future for humanity and the planet, which is far from the earlier optimism dreams of a modernity harnessed to an unlimited bountiful nature coupled with complete faith in the human capacity for mastery and the delivery of ingenious technological solutions. But now we face the possibility that our waste will be the end of us. At this juncture it could be useful to outline briefly a number of possible futures for consumer culture.

[46] This is a lifestyle based on not only efficient forms of wealth generation, but also tax avoidance through offshore tax havens—Birtchnell and Caletrío (2013); Featherstone (2013a, 2014b); Urry (2014b).

Consumer Culture Futures

1. *Continue Consuming, Scenario Planning, and Business as Usual*

   Firstly, it would seem to be very difficult to turn around, or alter the course of contemporary consumer capitalist societies. Some critics such as Ulrich Beck, Anthony Giddens, and Zygmunt Bauman have used metaphors such as a juggernaut out of control to attempt to depict a world recklessly accumulating global risks (Beck 1993, 1996, 2010; Beck and Levy 2013; Giddens 2011; Bauman 2000). This is also a phase in which the state has retreated from direct involvement in a number of areas of social life, in part to reduce budget expenditure and in part to open up domains for private business competition under the banner of efficiency.[47] Attempts to rely on the business community to deal with waste and climate change, or the carbon trading schemes, in which excessive carbon expenditure in the Global North is offset through financing ecological schemes in the Global South, have met with very limited success. Indeed, there are many voices arising now, which bemoan the lack of a single institution to cover and manage the various ecological issues, which preoccupy us (Latour 2017). Despite the evidence, the implementation of this type of institution, or a concerted international response, continues to be denied for a range of pragmatic reasons. Instead, we are offered limited short-term contingency planning.[48]

[47] The calls for reduction of the state role is not new—US President Calvin Coolidge remarked back in 1925 'the business of America is business'. The birth of neoliberalism from the 1930s onwards can be seen as partly motivated by the desire to counter the expansion of centralised planning by governments along with various forms of keynesianism, socialism, and totalitarianism, which were significant in the 1930s and immediate post-war era up to the 1970s (Gane 2014; Peck 2012; Mirowski and Plehwe 2012).

[48] In the late twentieth and twenty-first centuries, there has been an increasing rejection of long-term planning in the light of the complexities, turbulence, and unexpected events, on the increase around the planet. On one level this could be said to arise from the difficulty of managing a divided and fractious configuration of interests, as the number of significant participants in global politics, international finance, and business grows: the larger the number of players involved in a game, the greater the possibility of unstable alliances and shifts of opinion and power, which can potentially create more uncertainty. This is especially the case as the world moved from a bipolar system (the Cold War and 'the American Century') to a multipolar system, leading to a more unstable geopolitics more difficult to govern. The ecological shifts arising from the accumulation of waste and climate change we have already spoken of are generating more unpredictable and volatile weather, whose ramifications on state action are uncertain and difficult to predict, or plan for in the long term (Urry 2010). The response has been the growth of 'scenario planning'; the emphasis is upon flexibility and the capacity to strategically plan in an unstable environment, which better fits the business and financial mentality with limited objectives and strategic horizons. Scenario planning is based on games theory and involves the construction of numerous simulational models, which are designed to better further decision-making under conditions of uncertainty and unknowable contingencies (Cooper 2010). It has been influential in business, but also on the US Government and military thinking about responding in a post-equilibrium world with greater risk of natural disasters and food and water shortages, one in which environmental manipulation of resources along with geoengineering could become weapons of war.

2. *The Search for Alternatives: Reduced Consumption, Conservation, and Environmentalism*

In the wake of the collapse of state socialist regimes after 1989 in many parts of the world, socialism and communism as viable alternatives to capitalism became discredited. A particular Western triumphalist interpretation of global history that had culminated in 'the end of history' was proclaimed.[49] The logic of history had delivered the victory of the superior market philosophy of free trade and competition. For some this may not necessarily be linked to universal peace. A more Darwinist view of powerful nation-states locked in international competitive struggles for limited resources, in some cases through the use of force, still held sway for those of a more Weberian persuasion. A counterview to both these positions entails the creation of an active global public. It is difficult to envisage the generation of global public opinion, given the limited opportunities for people to interact and develop common agendas. But some would follow the logical of the Habermasian public sphere scaled up from the nation-state level (Featherstone 2001) and the development of a form of global opinion capable of forcing governments to acknowledge climate change and face up to the need for radical resource and energy depletion along with a more conservationist way of life. One of the main proponents of this view is Ulrich Beck who argues that a process of cosmopolitanisation from below is emerging globally (Beck 2002, 2010; Beck and Levy 2013; Featherstone 2002; Hume 2010; Mythen 2013).[50] Public opinion shifts will take place, with wealth redefined and new forms of freedom, power, creativity, and invention of new institutions, new ways of production, and ways of consumption sensitive to the globalisation of waste (Beck 2010: 262).[51] Beck has painted a big vision based on the assumption that we are moving into a second modernity, the risk society, which will generate new institutions and transformations to take us out of the old industrial modernisation framework, but the question is how might this work on the everyday level.

---

[49] Books like Francis Fukuyama's *The End of History and the Last Man* (1992), J.M. Roberts' *Triumph of the West* (1985), and earlier Landes' *Prometheus Unbounded* (1969) put forward a particular Western-centric view of world history, one which has been strongly contested by post-colonialism (Venn 2001, 2006; Featherstone and Venn 2006) and comparative history (Goody 1996, 2006, 2009; Featherstone 2006, 2009b; Pieterse 2006). There is now wider acknowledgement of the Chinese contribution to global history in many quarters accompanied by a rewriting of the archive, in the light of the expansion of Chinese global power along with the oft-voiced predictions that the twenty-first century could well be a Chinese century.

[50] Beck envisages a world public generated by the awareness that the nation-state system is undermined by the global risks such as climate change, which bind all nations, developed and underdeveloped, together. This releases a 'cosmopolitan moment', an opportunity for greater interconnectedness through media events such as environmental disasters with their globalised images of shared suffering.

[51] Beck in his major work *Risk Society* sees a move from concerns with wealth in first modernity to a concern with risk in second modernity (Beck 1993). But the dynamics of neoliberalism, the emergence of the super-rich, and the return to levels of inequalities prevalent around a century ago (Featherstone 2013a, 2014b; Piketty 2014) would throw some doubt on this claim.

There are others who if not following the word of Beck certainly write in the spirit of Beck, and see a shift to more restricted forms of consumption and self-limitation based on a simpler and more frugal post-consumerist lifestyle entailing new ethical modes of conduct and responsibility (Featherstone 2010c). Zygmunt Bauman, for example, asks the question in the title of one of his books: *Does Ethics have Chance in a World of Consumers?* (Bauman 2008). For Bauman the danger is that we pursue our selfish consumer lifestyles and dreams to the detriment of our capacity to empathise, to engage in sociability, dialogue, and care for others. In short the excesses of consumer culture need to be anchored in new forms of ethical conduct. Currently this could be seen as a predominantly idealistic dream generated in fractions of the middle classes. To date it has had minimal electoral impact, with only limited inroads in countries like Germany, Sweden, or New Zealand where the environmental and green political support is stronger. The problem of implementing new forms of ethical conduct, which involves commitment to care for the other, for other life forms, nature, and objects, entails major shifts in values. It is not easy to change values, or implement an ethic, even with a strong education programme. After the failed experiments at engineering or creating new values, over the last two centuries, few today would wish to follow Saint-Simon, one of the founders of sociology's optimism that one can build a new religion or ethics, like one can build a bridge. In addition to the powerful effects of consumer individualisation, it suggests that new technological developments such as the Internet and other mobile technologies are difficult to contain. They offer forms of empowerment and independence, which have widespread appeal, but increase the volume of information in circulation, including 'false news', making the faith in the 'power of the better argument' difficult to uphold.[52]

3. *Global governance and the emergence of a global state*

The possibility of global governance in which sovereignty is vested in some form of supra-nation-state entity which would have the power and resources to disciple business, organisations, and nation-states which did not cut back on carbon emissions and implement low-emission consumption lifestyles. In its ultimate form this would be a global state, most likely based on a federation. Governance would occur through the essentials of statehood identified by Max Weber and Norbert Elias: the monopoly of the means of violence and the monopoly of taxation.[53] Historically states have tended to emerge in a figuration

[52] George Steiner wrote about the difficulties of reversing or holding back technological development once the genie is out of the bottle (Steiner 1971). Cf. here Virilio's discussion of 'the museum of accidents' and other accounts about how we embrace new technologies without fully testing their dangers and consequences (Virilio 2006). The same can be said in not only forms of transportation, living space, and urban infrastructure, but also alleged modes of body care and health cure through drugs.

[53] The monopoly of taxation, which Norbert Elias drew attention to, refers to the need from early civilisational times to raise revenue through taxation (Elias 1987). He refers to how in Ancient Egypt drawings show peasants having to pay taxation to tax collectors accompanied by soldiers, with scribes recording the payment details on a scroll. In terms of taxation beyond the nation-state,

of competing nation-states with nationalism, the sense of common belonging as an 'imagined community', central to the state formation process. As many have pointed out, it would be hard to scale this up to the global level.[54]

4. *Beyond neoliberalism*

We have mentioned the ways in which neoliberalism is tightly linked to consumer culture with a large proportion of the GDP of the most advanced economies dependent on consumer spending. To reduce consumption would be exceedingly difficult, not least in terms of people's belief in their right to spend their money on whatever they want as one of their entitlements and rewards for work. Restricting consumption, say in terms of taxes on transportation or high-carbon goods, could be seen as increasing austerity and unfairly targeting those in the lower regions of society who have limited ability to cope. Restrictions on purchasing or any form of rationing could further threaten the legitimacy of the system, especially if the rich and super-rich were seen to continue consuming without limit. Today the rich sometimes justify their excessive wealth in terms of their superior ability and talent: the just rewards for the winners in a society that vaunts competition, enterprise, and creativity. As yet there is only limited critique of their lifestyles, although there is a good deal of scepticism that their excessive financial rewards are deserved.[55] In short the rich and super-rich seem to enjoy a high degree of immunity from laws, which apply to ordinary people. Avoiding taxation has become a specialist art for the super-rich, through the intricate web of offshore tax havens. The response of many governments around the world has often been not to condemn this, but to openly compete to welcome in the rich for their alleged economic advantages in their capacity to make deals and mergers and stimulate innovation and creative growth.[56] The super-rich's lack of allegiance, mobility,

there has been interest in 'Tobin tax' proposals—a small tax of 0.01% on financial taxations. The idea was taken up in the EU, and despite opposition is still being discussed with some experimental implementation in France and Italy.

[54] Unless we imagine an invasion from interplanetary or interstellar invaders—as in H G Wells' novel *War of the Worlds*. Such threatening events could potentially generate the in-group/out-group solidarities, to bind people together into a global culture (Featherstone 1990, 1995). Yet, whether the threat of planetary disaster through global warming and climate change, without humanoid enemies, is an equivalent event that could force nation-states to suspend their competitive national interest is a moot point. Many, Max Weber included, would have been negative about overcoming the Darwinist elimination contest between nation-states.

[55] Likewise in the fallout from the 2007 financial crisis, scarcely any bankers or financial specialists faced legal proceedings or prison. Currently in the run up to the UK National Election the Labour Party is talking about reversing the immunity of foreign domiciled rich people living in London from taxation on their foreign earnings.

[56] See Kirkup's 'New VIP visa service for wealthy foreigners', who tells us that home secretary Teresa May was about to announce that 'wealthy foreign business executives will get a new "VIP" visa service to speed their entry to the UK' (Kirkup 2013). Currently foreign domiciles and their families, provided that they have sufficient funds (i.e. are rich or very rich and can deposit a large sum such as £1 million), can live in London tax-free and also obtain extended visas.

> and familiarity with a variety of cultures, then, can make them 'the true cosmopolitans' (Bauman 2008), who are welcome in practically any country.

The rich and the super-rich are often presented as obsessed with time, especially saving time (cf. Linder 1970). In contrast to the unemployed urban poor who often have to waste time, queuing for benefit payments or charity handouts, the rich seldom have to wait. In effect they are locked into the 24/7 capitalist rhythm of life that does not provide time to pause, or indeed, time to look around and see if there are others who need helping or are suffering misfortune (Crary 2013: 125). It leads to a lifestyle in which the care of others is minimised or impossible. This tight schedule with every moment purposefully employed, the high-tech friendly spaces, and the latest communication and surveillance devices contrast with the portraits of 'time-affluent societies' which encourage sociability, reciprocity, care, and a certain amount of unregulated drift (see Baudrillard 1998: 151; Featherstone 2007). Indeed, it can be argued that the super-rich no longer live in society in any meaningful sense.[57] But today's elites do not need the equivalent of court society, to being confined to a tightly knit social world with its rivalries and suspicions, forever open to gossip and surveillance, engaged in a complex set of strategies to maintain their prestige and status, under the gaze of the powerful figure of the monarch or sovereign. Rather, they have the private jet fuelled and ready to take off to a wide range of destinations around the world. While there may be a certain amount of philanthropy, or 'philanthro-capitalism' (Bishop and Green 2008) engaged in through setting up private foundations, it is on their own terms and in tune with their own priorities and involves little sense of obligation to others' agendas.

5. *Generosity, Gifts, and General Economics*

   There seems to be little way to recycle their financial advantages for more general benefit: rather it stays within their own chosen priorities, be it their charitable foundation, ownership of arts or sporting bodies, or family dynasty's agenda. It is in this context that the quest for radically alternative notions of finance become popular. One alternative is Bataille's formulation of a general economy. At one point he pointedly remarks:

   'it is not necessity but its contrary, "luxury," that presents living matter and mankind with their fundamental problems' (Bataille 1988: 12; McGoey 2018).

   The display of luxury, the accumulation of wealth, and the exclusive use of property, along with the assumptions that somehow it is a just reward for talent and hard work, should not be seen as the legitimation of a fairer social order

---

[57] The term society, which is central to the emergence of sociology, not only refers to society in the abstract sense as we have come to know it (French society), but also indicated the emergence of a sphere with forms of sociability dating back to the eighteenth century. In England as Raymond Williams has shown the term society also refers to the upper-class sense of its own bounded community and world, as in 'polite society', or 'good society', with its round of mandatory sociability and annual 'season' (Williams 1976). The rich may choose to meet or socialise at annual or periodic events such as December in the Caribbean, January at the World Economic Forum in Davos, June in Cannes or Wimbledon, the Olympic Games, and other festivals.

based on equality of opportunity, but rather the persistence of wealth itself can create and sustain lasting social inequalities and a range of social problems.[58] Bataille refers to the latter economy (what we today understand as neoliberalism) as a restricted economy. Against this restricted economy with its utilitarian mindset and accumulation of economic value, property, and waste, a general economy is premised upon generosity, upon the expenditure of the accumulated surplus. Often this can take the form of festivals, where the surplus is collectively consumed and then a whole new cycle of accumulation initiated. This destruction of the unproductive value that has been stockpiled, Bataille (1991) held, was a way of getting rid of the 'accursed share' (la part maudite). In some societies, this can lead to destructive prestige contests as in potlatch, but it can also lead to positive aspects of gift giving.[59]

In modern societies the restricted economy can result in stockpiling and massive accumulations of surplus with the excess used in catastrophic outpourings of energy as in warfare. A more benign alternative would be to expend the surplus in festivals, or the arts. For Bataille the concentration and distribution of economic surplus were central to economic thought and it is interesting to see that after relatively isolated voices like Veblen, JM Keynes, C Wright Mills, and Galbraith in the past, there has been a return to issues of wealth distribution and inequality as we find around the work of Thomas Piketty (2014 I) and the growing interest in the contribution of the super-rich (Featherstone 2013a, 2014b). Bataille can also be located in this tradition with his interest in the Marshall Plan in the wake of the Second World War, which brought him very close to liberal thinkers such as Keynes (see Bataille 1991; McGoey 2018). For Bataille the Second World War concluded with the United States becoming the richest nation-state in the world, yet for it to prosper it needed to sacrifice its own riches to get rid of the potential negative consequences of the accumulated wealth. The Marshall Plan for Bataille was an ideal vehicle for this and could reverse some of the negative consequences of the 1944 Bretton Woods agreements which furthered the global restricted economy and in particular the self-interest and domination of the United States. In effect economic surpluses would be recycled in the form of gifts, to the benefit of all globally, and of course this would feedback for the benefit of the United States too through the increased volume of trade. In this context it is interesting to note that Naomi Klein in her new book argues we

[58] It is a point emphasised in many of the books on the super-rich that large income inequalities can be dispiriting for those in the middle and lower levels. The dramatic rise in the ratio of top to bottom salaries occurs not only in banks, but also in many businesses and other organisations since the 1980s. This itself was then used to justify the increase in the salaries of public-sector managers: a stark contrast to the situation in 1950s United States where the differentials were far less and apparently people experienced higher levels of satisfaction (see Featherstone 2013a, 2014b).

[59] Bataille suggested that in potlatch societies gift-giving could be used to increase one's status and power through the wasteful extravagant squandering of accumulated gifts and wealth. The gift for Bataille was an amazing device by which the gift-giver 'enriches himself with a contempt for riches' (Bataille 1991: 69; McGoey 2018).

need a response which is 'a Marshall Plan for the Earth' to deal with climate change (Klein 2015).

Bataille's thinking here chimes with recent discussions of a debt jubilee and the emergence of various Jubilee Debt coalitions (Graeber 2011), as well as the new social movements such as Occupy and the Indignados, which target the financial and banking system and advocate a very different form of economy. Currently financiers, bankers, and super-rich enjoy a privileged status and high level of immunity from prosecution (Lorey 2014; Papastergiadis and Esche 2014).[60] The argument is that the periodic dispensation with the massively accumulating levels of national sovereign debt and personal debts, that sustain our current neoliberal economy, could open up another space for a different type of economy with different priorities (Lazzarato 2012). The problem is that the shift towards greater inequalities and the predilection of the super-rich and rich to preserve and expand their wealth and ensure the continuity of the existing global consumer capitalist system only encourage further social discontent and waste of talent, as well as increase the chances of planetary climate change disaster.[61]

6. *The Pursuit of Happiness*

A life lived around the accumulation of wealth misses the ephemeral nature of wealth and its inevitable dissipation. Bataille reminds us that all wealth, like all matter, will inevitably decay. The avoidance of coming to terms with death and the concern to extend the lifespan through longevity technologies, including cryonics and nanotechnology, in the quest to overcome mortality and live forever, is currently fascinating the super-rich and is the source of major invest-

[60] Roberto Esposito unfolds the various meanings of immunity and focuses on the Latin term *munus*, the term which implies gift-giving and is at the heart of community as well as immunitas (Esposito 2011). It also opens up the whole question of the inside and outside in terms of species, and our varying capacities to live with and generate co-responsibilities with other non-human entities, including not only the glamorous animals, but also bacteria and viruses (see discussion in Featherstone 2010a, b, c).

[61] A problem with the Bataille approach in terms of climate change is that it involves a very different mindset, with the inversion of the conventional neoliberal and consumer culture logics and attitude towards saving and debt (Bataille 1988). It is also based on an energy expenditure model, which although assumed to be more socially efficient by sacrificing the accumulated surpluses in excessive festivals, potlatch, etc. involves its own form of destruction. This involves a very different indeterminate relationship to excess to that found in consumer culture-restricted economies with their utilitarianism. But to show how a general economics could work as a better option to cope with the specifics of climate change would be an exceedingly difficult option to actualise. Doubtless many would find the crises of impending climate change demand strategic action and clearly workable policies.

ment.[62] Death is seemingly pushed away and no longer hangs over life.[63] Images of gruesome deaths abound in the media and popular culture with the level of graphic realism increasingly heightened; but although they have a certain fascination, they are generally distanced from the everyday experience of most people in which we rarely encounter death, or see a dead body, or minister to the dying (Elias 1985; Featherstone and Hepworth 1991). Certainly there is little that would seem to make the rich give up their fortunes to the poor and focus on saving their own souls, as has been the case in some previous historical eras. Here we think of the fellow feeling, which can be generated by the sense of contingency and fate which propels some up and others down the social scale, which can lead to a sense of contingency and solidarity with others that manifests itself in care. This is a sentiment that in some cases was extended beyond the human to all living beings (St. Francis of Assisi, being a good example).

Some people may of course not be impressed by the call to give up their riches and lead a simple life of austerity and faith in God, even though this is a powerful message from the New Testament and lives of Christian saints and martyrs, with strong resonances in other traditions such as Buddhism and Islam. It does not sit easily with consumer culture. Yet there are also good social reasons for curbing wealth and increasing taxation on the rich. Higher levels of social inequality have been shown to actually impede economic growth.[64] The expanding levels of inequalities since the 1970s are taking us back to levels found in the late nineteenth and early twentieth centuries (the Gilded Age in the United States and Belle Époque in France), an earlier phase that has been referred to as 'incredible

[62] Silicon Valley hedge fund manager Joon Yun says that the probability of a 25-year-old dying before their 26th birthday is 0.1%; if it were possible to keep that risk constant throughout life instead of it rising due to age-related disease, the average person would—statistically speaking—live 1000 years. In 2014 Yun launched a $1 m prize challenging scientists to 'hack the code of life' and push human lifespan past its apparent maximum of about 120 years. Ultimately he believes that it is possible to 'solve ageing' and get people to live, healthily, more or less indefinitely. He says that our society faces growing numbers of loved ones lost to age-related disease and suffering extended periods of decrepitude, which is costly to economies. Yun's quest is part of the wave of enthusiasm to disrupt death, engulfing Silicon Valley. Billionaires and companies are bullish about what they can achieve (Corbyn 2015: for a discussion of ageing and longevity see Featherstone, 2017; Featherstone and Hepworth 1998).

[63] Google co-founder Sergey Brin has talked of 'curing death' one day. Head of Google's investments, Bill Maris, says that it will be possible to live to 500. 'Solving ageing' becomes another investment project, which also promises massive financial returns on investment for any success (Leonard 2015).

[64] According to a recent OECD report 'Inequality hurts economic growth, finds OECD research' (http://www.oecd.org/newsroom/inequality-hurts-economic-growth.htm 09/12/2014), countries where income inequality is decreasing grow faster than those with rising inequality with the key factor being investment in education. 'This compelling evidence proves that addressing high and growing inequality is critical to promote strong and sustained growth and needs to be at the centre of the policy debate', said OECD Secretary-General Angel Gurría. The paper finds new evidence that inequality affects growth by undermining education opportunities for children from poor socio-economic backgrounds, lowering social mobility, and hampering skill development (OECD 2014).

rise of the one percent' (Piketty 2014). In addition people's sense of well-being tends often to be higher when levels of inequality are lower.[65]

There is a basic assumption within neoliberal consumer economies that the more income, wealth, and purchasing power people achieve the more things they can buy and the happier they will be.[66] Nevertheless, there is a good deal of controversy over the sources of happiness and a good deal of counter-evidence (Freeland 2012) and more recently there has been the construction of various 'happiness indexes'[67] as well as the United Nations adopting a non-binding resolution in 2011 that happiness should be included in development indicators (Buncombe 2012). Happiness may well be ephemeral, but it is a persistent aura hanging over consumer culture leisure activities, practices, and use of goods. Yet the promise of valid experience, of encountering something eventful and absorbing, which generates strong affective sensations and feelings that stimulate recollection and memories, can also be intangible and difficult to actualise via the consumer culture modalities of life.[68]

Two final comments on this are in order. Firstly, there would seem to be a trend among the rich and those possessing lesser amounts of wealth to preferring the purchase of experience to goods or possessions: the once-in-a-lifetime type of vacation to Machu Picchu, or Bhutan is within their reach, and available on a regular basis. There are those gurus who argue strongly that the purpose of accumulating wealth should be to enjoy experiences, with work cut down to a

---

[65] The disparity in remuneration between average workers and CEOs stood at around 30 to 1 in 1970. It now is well above 300 to 1—in the case of McDonalds about 1200 to 1 (Harvey 2014).

[66] There are of course many attempts to show that money can lead to happiness with recent one being from the British Prime Minister's Downing Street's 'Nudge Unit'—the Behavioural Insights Team. They draw on research incorporated into a book by American psychologists *Happy Money*. The authors Elizabeth W Dunn and Michael Norton suggest that the secret to everlasting happiness is to eschew rampant consumerism by paying for experiences over possessions, helping others instead of yourself, and delaying gratification (Dunn and Norton 2014). In addition it is suggested that philanthropy, giving to charity, brings positive results in terms of self-age (Cooper 2012).

[67] One of the countries which tends to regularly come top is Bhutan, a small landlocked country in the Himalayas which until the last 10 years or so has had few travellers and only recently got television. The vast majority of the 700,000 population is Buddhist. The Bhutan Government advocated a 'gross national happiness' index as an alternative to stand alongside GDP. Incidentally in 2011, the United Nations adopted a non-binding resolution that happiness should be included in development indicators. Buncombe remarks, 'It's not just about happiness as it is understood in the West', he explained, saying that a more accurate translation of the king's original concept might be 'gross national contentment'. 'Bhutanese people are generally content. In the Buddhist tradition, wherever you are in this life is because of your previous life. Contentment leads to happiness' (Buncombe 2012).

[68] The arresting subtitle of Francois Jullien's book *Vital Nourishment* is 'Departing from Happiness' (Jullien 2007). The author wants to encourage us to take seriously the Chinese tradition, with its very different approach to happiness from the West. In China the focus was not on pursuing experiences which will allegedly bring happiness; rather the focus is on the cultivation of the ground, the accumulation of 'vital capital', which involves a systematic approach to body care (diet, food, exercise, longevity, etc.), effectively nourishing the life capacity potential, remaining open to change, which will create the conditions of sustainability within which happiness could appear.

minimum as is the case in the bestselling book *The 4-Hour Work Week: Escape the 9-5, Live Anywhere and Join the New Rich* by Timothy Ferris (2011). In one way this offers to go beyond the harried leisure class idea of status orientated, other-directed consumers amassing goods and prestige. It holds out the promise of a certain degree of 'time affluence'. On the other hand, it still involves various forms of consumer purchasing: air travel, equipment, hotel stays, restaurant meals, local transport, etc., all involving service labour and goods; there are carbon costs and planetary consequences of the desire to leave home and experience the world. Of course not all travel and vacations need to be luxurious and high-carbon jet travel. It is possible to walk, or move by local buses or trains: slower forms of travel provide a different rhythm of life and give more latitude for experiences.

Secondly, this takes us into the great outdoors. One of the many significant points in the genealogies of consumer culture was the Great Exhibition of 1851, which was moved from Hyde Park to Crystal Place, South London. It housed the latest technologies along with simulations and representative elements from all the world's cultures, starting a trend followed by the spate of subsequent exhibitions in the nineteenth century and later taken up in the second half of the twentieth century in Walt Disney World, Orlando's 'World Showcase of Cultures'. In his book *In the World Interior of Capital: Towards a Philosophical Theory of Globalization* Peter Sloterdijk argues that we now live in the interior, with the glass and steel great exhibition, being a first opening to this new era (Sloterdijk 2013). This is seen as highly detrimental to our sense of creativity and adventure and weakening the capacity to live as men. A further book, *You Must Change Your Life* (Sloterdijk 2014), takes these sentiments further with the stark message that we must constantly quest for new experiences and ring the changes at regular intervals. The quest for experience then is part of the urgent critique of consumer culture and seen as the way towards a meaningful valid life. Yet it is also something easily marketed, packaged, and rolled out surrounded by advice books, simulations, and constant flow of images of digital screen culture. It is not too easy to find a way beyond or out of consumer culture.

References

Abrams, Philip, and Andrew McCulloch. 1975. *Communes, Sociology and Society*. Cambridge: Cambridge University Press.

———. 2012. The Internet Has Created a New Industrial Revolution. *Guardian*, September 18.

Anderson, Janna, and Rainie Lee. 2014. The Internet of Things Will Thrive by 2025. *Pew Research Centre*, May 14.

Appadurai, Arjun. 1986. Introduction. In *The Social Life of Things: Commodities in Cultural Perspective*, ed. A. Appadurai. Cambridge: Cambridge University Press.

Arendt, Hannah. 1958. *The Human Condition*. Chicago: Chicago University Press.

Bakhtin, Mikhail. 1968. *Rabelais and His World*. Cambridge, MA: MIT Press.

Bataille, Georges. 1988. *The Accursed Share*. New York: Zone Books.

———. 1991. *The Accursed Share*. Vols. 2 and 3. The History of Eroticism; Sovereignty. New York: Zone Books.
Baudrillard, Jean. 1998. *The Consumer Society*. London: Sage.
———. 1983. *Simulations*. New York: Semiotext(e).
Bauman, Zygmunt. 2008. *Does Ethics Have a Chance in a World of Consumers?* Cambridge, MA: Harvard University Press.
———. 2000. *Liquid Modernity*. Cambridge: Polity Press.
Beck, Ulrich. 1993. *Risk Society*. London: Sage.
———. 1996. World Risk Society. *Theory, Culture & Society* 13 (4): 1–32.
———. 2002. The Cosmopolitan Society and Its Enemies. *Theory, Culture & Society* 19 (1–2): 17–44.
———. 2010. Climate for Change, or How to Create a Green Modernity? *Theory, Culture & Society* 27 (2–3): 254–266.
Beck, Ulrich, and Daniel Levy. 2013. Cosmopolitanized Nations: Re-imagining Collectivity in World Risk Society. *Theory, Culture & Society* 30 (2): 3–31.
Becker, Gary. 1993. *Human Capital*. Chicago: Chicago University Press.
Beer, David. 2009. Power Through the Algorithm? Participatory Web Cultures and the Technological Unconscious. *New Media & Society* 11 (6): 985–1002.
Beer, David, and Roger Burrows. 2013. Popular Culture, Digital Archives and the New Social Life of Data. Special Issue on the Social Life of Methods. *Theory, Culture & Society* 30 (4): 47–71.
Bell, Daniel. 1973. *The Coming of Post-Industrial Society: A Venture in Social Forecasting*. New York: Basic Books.
Berry, Christopher J. 1994. *The Idea of Luxury*. Cambridge: Cambridge University Press.
Bishop, Matthew, and Michael Green. 2008. *Philanthrocapitalism: How Giving Can Save the World*. London: A & C Black Publishers Ltd.
Birtchnell, T. and Caletrío, J. (eds.) (2013) Elite Mobilities. Oxford: Routledge.
Boscagli, Maurizia. 2014. *Stuff Theory: Everyday Objects, Radical Materialism*. London: Bloomsbury.
Bourdieu, Pierre. 1984. Distinction. London: Routledge
Braudel, Fernand. 1981. *Civilization and Capitalism, 15th–18th Century*. 3 vols. New York: Harper Collins.
Brown, Steven D. 2002. Michel Serres: Science, Translation and the Logic of the Parasite. *Theory, Culture & Society* 19 (3): 1–27.
Bryman, Alan. 1995. *Disney and His Worlds*. London: Routledge.
Bucher, Taina. 2012. Want to be on the Top? Algorithmic Power and the Threat of Invisibility on Facebook. *New Media & Society* 14: 1164–1180.
Buncombe, Andrew. 2012. Is Bhutan the Happiest Place in the World? *Independent*, January 14.
Burrows, Roger, and Nicholas Gane. 2006. Geodemographics, Software and Class. *Sociology* 40 (5): 793–812.
Campbell, Colin. 1987. *The Romantic Ethic and the spirit of Modern Consumerism*. Oxford: Blackwell.
Cheney-Lippold, John. 2011. A New Algorithmic Identity: Soft Biopolitics and the Modulation of Control. Special Issue on Code and Coding in Crisis. *Theory, Culture & Society* 28 (6): 164–181.
Clark, Nigel, and Kathryn Yusoff. 2017. Geosocial Formations and the Anthropocene. *Theory, Culture & Society* 34 (2–3): 3–23.
Coleman, Rebecca. 2013. Sociology and the Virtual: Interactive Mirrors, Representation Thinking and Intensive Power. *The Sociological Review* 61 (1): 1–20.
Cooper, Charlie. 2012. 2013's Big Idea? Money Can Buy Happiness. *Independent*, November 24.
Cooper, Melinda. 2010. Turbulent Worlds: Financial markets and Environmental Crisis. Special Issue on Changing Climates. *Theory, Culture & Society* 27 (2–3): 167–190.
Corbyn, Jeremy. 2015. Live Forever Scientists Say They'll Soon Extend Life 'Well Beyond 120'. *Observer*, January 11.

Crandall, Jordan. 2010. The Geospatialization of Calculative Operations: Tracking, Sensing and Megacities. *Theory, Culture & Society* 27 (6): 68–90.
Crary, Jonathan. 1990. *Techniques of the Observer: On Vision and Modernity in the Nineteenth Century*. Cambridge, MA: MIT Press.
———. 2001. *Suspensions of Perception: Attention, Spectacle and Modern Culture*. New York: October Books.
———. 2013. *24/7: Terminal Capitalism and the Ends of Sleep*. London: Verso Books.
Cubitt, Sean. 1998. *Digital Aesthetics*. London: Sage.
———. 2015. Integral Waste. Theory, Culture & Society 32 (4): 133–145.
Dalby, Simon. 2017. Anthropocene Formations: Environmental Security, Geopolitics and Disaster. Special Issue on Geo-Social Formations. *Theory, Culture & Society* 34 (2–3): 233–252.
Davies, William. 2014a. *The Limits of Neoliberalism*. London: Sage.
———. 2014b. A Response to Nicholas Gane's 'The Emergence of Neoliberalism'. *Theory, Culture & Society* 31 (7–8): 299–302.
Debord, Guy. 1970. *Society of the Spectacle*. Detroit: Red and Black.
De Decker, Kris. 2009. The Monster Footprint of Digital Technology. Edited by Vincent Grosjean; artwork by Grace Grothaus, *LOW-TECH MAGAZINE*, June 16.
Deleuze, Gilles. 1992. Postscript on the Societies of Control. *October* 59: 3–7.
Dion, Delphine, and Eric Arnould. 2011. Retail Luxury Strategy: Assembling Charisma through Art and Magic. *Journal of Retailing* 87 (4): 502–520.
Dunn, Elizabeth W and Norton, Michael 2014. Happy Money: The New Science of Smarter Spending. London: Oneworld Publications.
Durkheim, Emile. 2014. *The Division of Labour in Society*. New York: Free Press.
Elias, Norbert. 1983. *The Court Society*. Oxford: Basil Blackwell.
———. 1985. *The Loneliness of The Dying*. Oxford: Basil Blackwell.
———. 1987. The Retreat of Sociologists into the Present. *Theory, Culture & Society* 4 (2–3): 223–247.
Esposito, Roberto. 2011. *Immunitas: The Protection and Negation of Life*. Trans. Zakiya Hanafi. Cambridge: Polity Press.
Ewen, Stewart. 1988. *All Consuming Images: The Politics of Style in Contemporary Culture*. New York: Basic Books.
Ewen, Elizabeth, and Stewart Ewen. 1982. *Channels of Desire*. New York: McGraw Hill.
Featherstone, Mike. 1982. The Body in Consumer Culture. *Theory, Culture & Society* 1 (2): 18–33 reprinted in Featherstone, Mike, Mike Hepworth and Brian S. Turner (eds.) *The body*. London: Sage, 1991.
———. 1990. Global Culture: An Introduction. *Theory, Culture & Society* 7 (2–3): 1–14.
———. 1995. *Undoing Culture: Globalization, Postmodernism and Identity*. London: Sage.
———. 2001. Globalization Processes: Postnational Flows, Identity Formation and Cultural Space. In *Identity, Culture and Globalization*, ed. Eliezer Ben-Rafael and Yitzhak Sternberg, 483–527. Leiden: International Institute of Sociology and Brill Academic Press.
———. 2002. Cosmopolis: An Introduction. *Theory, Culture & Society* 19 (1–2): 1–16.
———. 2004. Automobilities: An Introduction. Special Issue on Automobilities. *Theory, Culture & Society* 21 (4–5): 1–24 Also reprinted as a *TCS Book Series* title, London: Sage, 2005.
———. 2006. Archive, In Special Issue on Problematizing Global Knowledge. Edited by M. Featherstone, C. Venn, R. Bishop and J. Phillips. Theory, Culture & Society 23(2–3): 591–596.
———. 2007. *Consumer Culture and Postmodernism*. 2nd ed. London: Sage.
———. 2009. Introduction to Jack Goody: Occidentalism and Comparative History. *Theory, Culture & Society* 26 (7–8): 1–15.
———. 2010a. Body, Image and Affect in Consumer Culture. *Body & Society* 17 (1): 193–221.
———. 2010b. Luxury: Consumer Culture and Sumptuary Dynamics. Special Issue on Le Luxe, *Les Cahiers Européens de l'Imaginaire,* No. 2, CNRS Editions, Mars: 166–72.

———. 2010c. Ethical Consumption: Some Prefatory Remarks. In *Ethical Consumption: A Critical Introduction*, ed. Tania Lewis and Emily Potter. London: Routledge.

———. 2013a. Super-Rich Lifestyles. In *Elite Mobilities*, ed. T. Birtchnell and J. Caletrío, 99–136. Oxford: Routledge.

———. 2013b. Preliminary Reflections on the Visible, the Invisible and Social Regulation: Panopticism, Biopolitics, Neoliberalism and Data Consumption. *The Journal of Critical Studies in Business & Society* 4 (1): 6–37.

———. 2014a. Mass Culture. In *Concise Encyclopedia of Comparative Sociology*, ed. Masamichi Sasaki, Ekkart Zimmermann, Jack Goldstone, and Stephen Sanderson, 252–261. Leiden: Brill Publishers.

———. 2014b. The Rich and the Super-Rich: Mobility, Consumption and Luxury Lifestyles. In *Consumer Culture, Modernity and Identity*, ed. Nita Mathur, 3–45. New Delhi: Sage.

———. 2017. Forming a Life and Learning to Live with the Dilemmas of the Ageing Process. In *Anthropologia na Iztok ot Raia [Anthropology East of Eden]*, ed. Magdalena Elchinova and Vassil Garnizov, 428–449. Sofia: New Bulgarian University Press (in Bulgarian).

Featherstone, Mike, and Mike Hepworth. 1991. The Mask of Ageing and the Postmodern Life Course. In *The Body*, ed. M. Featherstone, M. Hepworth, and B.S. Turner, 371–390. London: Sage.

———. 1998. Ageing, the Life Course and the Sociology of Embodiment. In *Modernity, Medicine and Health: Issues Confronting Medical Sociology Toward 2000*, ed. G. Scrambler and P. Higgs, 147–177. London: Routledge.

Featherstone, M. 1992. 'The Heroic Life and Everyday Life' Theory, Culture and Society 9(1) Reprinted in Featherstone, M. (1995) Undoing Culture: Globalization, Postmodernism and Identity. London: Sage.

Featherstone, M. 2000. 'The globalization of mobility: experience, sociability and speed in technological cultures,' in E.E. Busto Garcia and F. Lobo (eds) Lazer numa sociedade Globalizada/ Leisure in a Globalized Society. São Paulo: SESC & World Leisure & Recreational Association, 2000.

Featherstone, Mike, and Couze Venn. 2006. Problematizing Global Knowledge: An Introduction. In *Special Issue on Problematizing Global Knowledge*. Edited by M. Featherstone, C. Venn, R. Bishop and J. Phillips. *Theory, Culture & Society* 23(2–3): 1–20.

Ferris, Timothy. 2011. *The 4-Hour Work Week: Escape the 9-5, Live Anywhere and Join the New Rich*. New York: Vermillion, Random House.

Foucault, Michel. 1979. *Discipline and Punish: the Birth of the Prison*. Harmondsworth: Penguin.

———. 2008. *The Birth of Biopolitics: Lectures at the College de France 1978–79*. Houndsmills: Palgrave Macmillan.

Freeland, Chrystia. 2012. *The Plutocrats: The Rise of the New Global Super-Rich*. London: Penguin Books.

Friedberg, A. 1994. *Window Shopping: Cinema and the Postmodern*. Berkeley: California University Press.

Frith, Simon. 1983. *Sound Effects: Youth, Leisure and the Politics of Rock*. London: Constable.

Fukuyama, Francis. 1992. *The End of History and the Last Man*. New York: Free Press.

Gane, Nicholas. 2014. The Emergence of Neoliberalism: Thinking Through and Beyond Michel Foucault's Lectures on Biopolitics. *Theory, Culture & Society* 31 (*4*): *3–27* first published on November 26, 2013.

———. 2015. Review Article Trajectories of Liberalism and Neoliberalism. *Theory, Culture & Society* 32 (1): 133–144.

Giddens, Anthony. 2011. *The Politics of Climate Change*. Oxford: Polity Press.

Gill, Rosalind, and Andy Pratt. 2008. In the Social Factory? Immaterial Labour, Precariousness and Cultural Work. *Theory, Culture & Society* 25 (7–8): 1–30.

Goody, Jack. 1996. *The East in the West*. Cambridge: Cambridge University Press.

———. 2006. *The Theft of History*. Cambridge: Cambridge University Press.

———. 2009. *The Eurasian Miracle*. Cambridge: Cambridge University Press.

———. 2010. *The Immaterial*. Chicago: Chicago University Press.
Gorz André .1980. Ecology and Politics. Boston, MA: South End Press.
Graeber, David. 2011. *Debt: the First 500 Years*. London: Melville House.
Graham, Stephen, and Nigel Thrift. 2007. Out of Order: Understanding Repair and Maintenance. *Theory, Culture & Society* 24 (3): 1–25.
Halton, Eugene. 1992. The Reality of Dreaming. *Theory, Culture & Society* 9 (4): 119–139.
Hansen, Myriam. 1991. *Babel and Babylon: Spectatorship in American Silent Film*. Cambridge, MA: Harvard University Press.
Harvey, David. 2014. Afterthoughts on Piketty's Capital, David Harvey Website. http://davidharvey.org/2014/05/afterthoughts-pikettys-capital/. Accessed 5 March 2015.
Hayles, N. Katherine. 2009. RFID: Human Agency and Meaning in Information-Intensive Environments. Special Issue on Ubiquitous Media. *Theory, Culture & Society* 26 (2–3): 47–72.
Hegde, Rajeshwari, Geetishree Mishra, and K.S. Gurumurthy. 2011. An insight into the hardware and software complexity of ECUS in vehicles. In *Advances in Computing and Information Technology*, ed. David C. Wyld, M. Wozniak, I. Chaki, N. Meghanathan, and D. Nagamalai. Basel: Springer Nature.
Hepworth, Mike, and Mike Featherstone. 1982. *Surviving Middle Age*. Oxford: Blackwell.
Hume, Mike. 2010. Cosmopolitan Climates: Hybridity, Foresight and Meaning. *Theory, Culture and Society* 27 (2–3): 267–276.
Hird, Myra J. 2017. Waste, Environmental Politics and Dis/Engaged Publics. *Theory, Culture & Society* 34 (2–3): 187–209.
Hochschild, Arlie. 1983. *The Managed Heart*. Berkeley: California University Press.
Ivanova, Maria, N. 2011. Consumerism and the Crisis: Wither 'the American Dream'. *Critical Sociology* 37: 329–350.
Jullien, François. 2007. *Vital Nourishment: Departing from Happiness*. New York: Zone Books.
Kirkup, James. 2013. 'New VIP Visa Service for Wealthy Foreigners,' Who Tells Us that Home Secretary Teresa May Was About to Announce that 'Wealthy Foreign Business Executives Will Get A New "Vip" Visa Service to Speed their Entry to the UK.' *Daily Telegraph*, November 6.
Klein, Naomi. 2015. *This Changes Everything: Capitalism and Climate Change*. London: Penguin.
Kuchler, Susanne. 2008. Technological Materiality: Beyond the Dualist Paradigm. *Theory, Culture & Society* 25 (1): 101–120.
Lafargue, Paul. 2011/1883. *The Right to be Lazy*. London: AK Press.
Landes, David. 1969. *The Unbound Prometheus: Technological Change and Industrial Development in Western Europe from 1750 to the Present*. Cambridge: Cambridge University Press.
Lash, Scott, and Celia Lury. 2007. *Global Culture Industry*. Oxford: Polity.
Lash, Scott, and John Urry. 1993. *Economies of Signs and Space*. London: Sage.
Latham, Robert. 2000. Social Sovereignty. *Theory, Culture & Society* 17 (4): 1–18.
Latour, Bruno. 2017. Why Gaia is not a God of Totality. *Theory, Culture & Society* 34 (2–3): 61–81.
Lazzarato, Maurizio. 2012. *The Making of the Indebted Man: Essay on the Neoliberal Condition*. Cambridge, MA: MIT Press.
Leach, William. 1993. *Land of Desire: Merchants, Power and the Rise of a New American Culture*. New York: Vintage.
Lears, T.J. Jackson. 1994. *Fables of Abundance: A Cultural History of Advertising in America*. New York: Basic Books.
———. 1998. Reconsidering Abundance: A Plea for Ambiguity. In *Getting and Spending: European and American Consumer Societies in the Twentieth Century*, ed. S. Strasser, C. McGovern, and M. Judt. Cambridge: Cambridge University Press.
Lefebvre, Henri. 1971. *Everyday Life in the Modern World*. London: Allen Lane.
Linder, Staffan Burenstam. 1970. *The Harried Leisure Class*. New York: Columbia University Press.

Leonard, Tom. 2015. Could Humans One Day Live to 500? That's What a Group of Eccentric Billionaires Believe—and They're Spending Fortunes on the Research they Hope Will Make it Possible. *Daily Mail*, April 2.

Lorey, Isabelle. 2014. The 2011 Occupy Movements: Rancière and the Crisis of Democracy. *Theory, Culture & Society* 31 (7–8): 43–65.

McCracken, Grant. 1988. *Culture and Consumption: New Approaches to the Symbolic Character of Consumer Goods and Activities*. Bloomington: Indiana University Press.

McGoey, Linsey. 2018. Bataille's Compromise: Reassessing Gifts, Debt and Economic Surplus. *Theory, Culture & Society.*

McKendrick, Neil, John Brewer, and John Harold Plumb. 1982. *The Birth of a Consumer Society: the Commercialization of Eighteenth-Century Century England*. London: Hutchinson.

McNay, Lois. 2009. Self as Enterprise: Dilemmas of Control and Resistance in Foucault's the Birth of Biopolitics. Special issue on Michel Foucault. *Theory, Culture & Society* 26 (6): 55–77.

McRobbie, Angela. 2011. The Los Angelisation of London. In *Critique of Creativity: Precarity, Subjectivity and Resistance in the 'Creative Industries'*, ed. G. Raunig, G. Ray, and U. Wuggenig. London: May Fly Books.

Miller, Daniel. 2008. *The Comfort of Things*. Cambridge: Polity Press.

Miller, Michael. 1981. *The Bon Marché: Bourgeois Culture and the Department Store 1869–1920*. Princeton, NJ: Princeton University Press.

Mirowski, Philip, and Dieter Plehwe. 2012. *The Road from Mont Pelerin: The Making of the Neoliberal Thought Collective*. Cambridge, MA: Harvard University Press.

Moses, Kara. 2013. China Lead the Waste Recycling League. *Guardian*, June 14.

Mythen, Gabe. 2013. Ulrich Beck, Cosmopolitanism and the Individualization of Religion. *Theory, Culture & Society* 30 (3): 114–127.

Nava, Mica. 2002. Cosmopolitan Modernity: Everyday Imaginaries and the Register of Difference. *Theory, Culture & Society* 19 (1–2): 81–99 In Cosmopolis, Special Issue, eds. M. Featherstone, H. Patomäki, J. Tomlinson and C. Venn.

Neilson, Brett, and Ned Rossiter. 2008. Precarity as a Political Concept, or, Fordism as Exception. *Theory, Culture & Society* 25 (7–8): 51–72.

OECD. 2014. Inequality Hurts Economic Growth, Finds OECD Research. December 9. http://www.oecd.org/newsroom/inequality-hurts-economic-growth.htm.

Oyama, Shinji. 2011. *The East Asian Brandscape: The Globalization of Japanese Brands in the Age of Japanization*. PhD thesis, Goldsmiths, University of London.

Papastergiadis, Nikos, and Charles Esche. 2014. Assemblies in Art and Politics: An Interview with Jacques Rancière. *Theory, Culture & Society* 31 (6): 27–41.

Pels, Dick, and Aya Crebas. 1988. Carmen or the Invention of a New Feminine Myth. *Theory Culture & Society* 5 (4): 509–610.

Peck, Jamie. 2012. *Construction of Neoliberal Reason*. Oxford: Oxford University Press.

Peck, Linda Levi. 2005. *Consuming Splendour: Society and Culture in Seventeenth-Century England*. Cambridge: Cambridge University Press.

Peretti, Jacques. 2015. What I Learnt About Inequality After Spending Time with Some of the Richest People in the World. *Independent*, February 1.

Pieterse, Jan Nederveen. 2006. Oriental Globalization. *Theory, Culture & Society* 23(1–2):411–413. Special Issue. In Problematizing Global Knowledge, eds. M. Featherstone et al.

Piketty, Thomas. 2014. *Capital in the 21st Century*. Cambridge, MA: Harvard University Press.

Pine, B. Joseph, and James Gilmore. 2011. *The Experience Economy*. Cambridge, MA: Harvard Business School Press.

Pleij, Herman. 2003. *Dreaming of Cockaigne: Medieval Fantasies of the Perfect Life*. New York: Columbia University Press.

Pomeranz, Kenneth. 2000. *The Great Divergence*. Princeton, NJ: Princeton University Press.

Pomeranz, K. 2009. 'Putting Modernity in its Place(s),' Special Section on Jack Goody on Occidentalism and Comparative History, Theory, Culture & Society 26(7–8).

Reno, Joshua Ozias. 2014. Toward a New Theory of Waste: From 'Matter out of Place' to Signs of Life. *Theory, Culture & Society* 31 (6): 3–27.
Ritzer, George. 2014. Automating Prosumption: The Decline of the Prosumer and the Rise of the Prosuming Machines. *Journal of Consumer Culture* 15 (3): 407–424.
Roberts, John Morris. 1985. *The Triumph of the West*. London: BBC Books.
Rosen, Marjorie. 1972. *Popcorn Venus: Women, Movies and the American Dream*. New York: Coward McCann & Gergeshan.
Ruppert, Evelyn, John Law, and Mike Savage. 2013. Digital Devices: Reassembling Social Science Methods. Special Issue on the Social Life of Methods. *Theory, Culture & Society* 30 (4): 22–46.
Sample, Ian. 2014. Coastal Communities Dumping 8m Tonnes of Plastic in Oceans Every Year. *Guardian* (February 12).
Schiermer, Bjørn. 2011. Quasi-objects, Cult Objects and Fashion Objects: On Two Kinds of Fetishism on Display in Modern Culture. *Theory, Culture & Society* 28 (1): 81–102.
Schivelbusch, Wolfgang. 1986. *The Railway Journey: The Industrialization of Time and Space in the 19th Century*. New York: Berg Publishers Ltd.
Schulze, Gerhard. 1992. *Die Erlebnisgesellschaft: Kultursociologie der Gegenwart*. Frankfurt am Main/New York: Campus Verlag.
———. 1997. From Situatedness to Subjects: Moral Discourse in Transition. In *Constructing the New Consumer Society*, ed. Pekka Sulkanen, John Holmwood, Hilary Radner, and Gerhard Schulze, 22–46. New York: St Martin's Press.
Schwarz, Ori. 2012. The New Hunter-gatherers: Making Human Interaction Productive in the Network Society. *Theory, Culture and Society* 29 (6): 78–98.
Seigel, Jerrold. 1986. *Bohemian Paris*. New York: Viking.
Serres, Michel. 1982. *The Parasite*. Baltimore and London: John Hopkins University Press.
Serres, Michel (Bruno Latour). (1995). Conversations on Science, Culture, and Time. Ann Arbor: University of Michigan Press.
Simmel, Georg. 1991. The Berlin Trade Exhibition. *Theory, Culture & Society* 8 (3): 119–123.
———. 1997a. The Concept and Tragedy of Culture. In *Simmel on Culture*, ed. David Frisby and Mike Featherstone. London: Sage.
———. 1997b. The Future of Our Culture. In *Simmel on Culture*, ed. David Frisby and Mike Featherstone. London: Sage.
———. 1997c. The Conflict of Modern Culture. In *Simmel on Culture*, ed. David Frisby and Mike Featherstone. London: Sage.
Sloterdijk, Peter. 2013. *In the World Interior of Capital: Towards a Philosophical Theory of Globalization*. London: Polity Press.
———. 2014. *You Must Change Your Life*. London: Polity Press.
Smith, Adam. 1776. *An Inquiry into the Nature and Causes of the Wealth of Nations*. London: W. Strahan.
Sombart, Werner. 1967. *Luxury and Capitalism*. Ann Arbor: Michigan University Press.
Steiner, George. 1971. *Bluebeard's Castle: Some Notes Towards the Re-definition of Culture*. London: Faber and Faber.
Sugg, Zoe. 2014. *Girl Online*. New York: Simon & Schuster.
Tamari, Tomoko. 2006. The Rise of the Department Store and the aestheticization of Everyday Life in Early Twentieth Century Japan. *International Journal of Japanese Sociology* 15: 99–118.
Taussig, Michael. 2008. Redeeming Indigo. *Theory, Culture & Society* 25 (3): 1–15.
Thompson, Edward. 1967. Time, Work-Discipline and Industrial Capitalism. *Past & Present* 38 (1): 56–97.
Toffler, Alvin. 1980. *The Third Wave*. New York: Bantam.
Toscano, Alberto. 2013. Gaming the Plumbing: High-Frequency Trading and the Spaces of Capital. *Mute* 3 (4): 1–11.
Turner, Graeme. 2004. *Understanding Celebrity*. London: Sage.

Urry, John. 2010. Consuming the Planet to Excess. Special issue on Changing Climates. *Theory, Culture & Society* 27 (2–3): 191–212.
———. 2014a. The Problem of Energy. Special Issue on Energy & Society. *Theory, Culture & Society* 31: 3–20.
———. 2014b. *Offshoring*. New York: Wiley.
Venn, Couze. 2001. *Occidentalism*. London: Sage.
———. 2006. *The Postcolonial Challenge*. London: Sage.
Virilio, Paul. 2006. The Museum of Accidents. *International Journal of Baudrillard Studies* 3 (2): 81–85.
Walsh, Bryan. 2013. The Surprisingly Large Energy Footprint of the Digital Economy. *Time Magazine*, August 14.
Weber, Max. 1981. *General Economic History*. New Brunswick, NJ: Transaction Books.
———. 2001. *The Protestant Ethic and the Spirit of Capitalism*. Trans. S. Kalberg. New York: Routledge.
Williams, Raymond. 1976. *Keywords*. London: Fontana.
Williams, Rosalind H. 1982. *Dream World: Mass Consumption in Late Nineteenth-Century France*. Oxford: University of California Press.
———. 2009. Putting Modernity in its Place(s). Special Section on Jack Goody on Occidentalism and Comparative History, Theory, Culture and Society 26: 7–8.
Mike Featherstone, (2016) The Heroic Life and Everyday Life. Theory, Culture & Society 9(1):159–182. Reprinted in Featherstone, M. (1995). Undoing Culture: Globalization, Postmodernism and Identity. London: Sage

"You Are a Socialist Child Like Me": Goods and Identity in Bulgaria

Evgenia Krasteva-Blagoeva

Introduction

The world of goods and commodities, framed by the theory of person-object relations (established by Thorsten Veblen's theory of conspicuous consumption of luxury goods as status symbols- Veblen 1899), is still not studied in the context of Bulgarian socialist and postsocialist culture. Having a biography and a social life of their own (Appadurai 1986), goods carry cultural meaning; they are indicators and maintainers of cultural categories and social relations. A consumer's objective is to create an intelligible universe by choosing goods (Douglas and Isherwood 1979: 59, 60, 65). Societies construct the world of things and the social world

> "simultaneously and in the same way … constructing objects as they construct people" (Kopitoff 1986: 90).

Despite economic specificities (lack of "real market" and private ownership over "the means of production"; a centrally planned economy; deficits, etc.) and ideological premises (propaganda), the socialist world was also constructed as a meaningful entirety through goods, just as the capitalist West was. Consumption was at the core of the socialist culture of modernization, yet consumer culture as such was in fact not established (Slater 1997) because of specificities of the local cultural milieu.[1] In this context the social genesis of value seems even more important than exchange as a source of value (Appadurai 1986: 56). In this chapter

[1] "To state the obvious, consumer culture is capitalist culture. Historically it develops as part of the capitalist system. *It does not arise in non-capitalist societies*: in the case of both actually existing socialism and religiously fundamentalist societies, for example, political control over consumption and the suppression of its 'decadent' culture are crucial. Conversely, when either regime slackens its control or breaks down, capitalist entrepreneurialism linked to expanded consumer markets does indeed arise" (Slater 1997: 26).

E. Krasteva-Blagoeva (✉)
Department of Anthropology, New Bulgarian University, Sofia, Bulgaria
e-mail: eblagoeva@nbu.bg

E. Krasteva-Blagoeva (ed.), *Approaching Consumer Culture*, International Series on Consumer Science, https://doi.org/10.1007/978-3-030-00226-8_2

I will argue that during socialism certain types of goods (especially Western ones) were significantly *overvalued*—treated with extreme care, creatively reused, collected as a hobby, displayed at home to gain prestige, and so on. I will try to outline and analyze socialist and postsocialist consumption patterns in Bulgaria through people's attitudes towards goods, including ways of acquisition, usage, and consumption (practically, symbolically, visually, etc. (Featherstone 2007); social messages of consumption; cultural peculiarities encoded in attitudes towards goods; and, in general, goods usage in the process of individual and collective identity construction. Continuities and discontinuities of these tendencies in the period after 1989—i.e., after the fall of communism—are outlined as well.

The methodology used in this research is varied. It consists of my long-term observations and participant observations over the last 30 years; in-depth interviews with 19 people of different ages and social status (3 elderly, 12 middle aged, and 4 young men and women from the capital Sofia, the city of Pleven, the towns of Vratsa, Kărdžali, Kozlodui); and media data—newspapers, radio, television, social media, etc.[2]

Socialist Consumption: Coping with Shortages

In socialism consumption was ideologically constructed as satisfying collective needs rather than personal necessities. Socialist doctrine promoted collective principles at the expense of individual needs, whose satisfaction was ideologically perceived as "capitalist greediness." This state "messaging," however, contributed to the existing deep alienation of the people from the state and its official ideology. Habitually ignoring and undervaluing propaganda messages were mixed with collective schizophrenia—a constant discrepancy between words and deeds (Roth 2000; Creed 1998). This ambivalence relates to other discrepancies of socialist society: between ideology and practice, between official and everyday discourse, etc. In this context, goods preserved their communicative function and new meanings of their acquisition, distribution, and exchange were introduced.

As a result of mass repression, nationalization campaigns, confiscation of property of the bourgeoisie, and practice of legal theft, an entirely new ownership discourse appeared as a popular interpretation of official ideology. What was private became common and stealing it was no longer seen as a sin. Habitualized theft from cooperatives was driven by the following logic: "This belongs to the cooperative, it is common, it belongs to the people. We are the people, so it is ours. We are not stealing, we are simply taking what belongs to us." In Gerald Creed's words

> "if common property is not being respected by all, then all must take their share."

He interprets theft as an example of

> "how one could, if not beat, then at least manipulate it and make use of the system" (Creed 1998: 199).

[2] I would like to express my gratitude to Mike Featherstone and Iskra Velinova for their valuable comments and to Peter and Barbara Black for language editing of this text.

Mass pilferage from factories, state firms, offices, etc. was similar. Workplaces were perceived as the source of deficit products. All kinds of goods were available to be taken for free—whatever was produced or sold there: from printing paper, office consumables, and chocolates to small machines, clothes, fuel, and rarely even TV sets and commodities falsely declared as waste. Free access provided at the workplace was an opportunity for people to steal goods and later exchange them for something else needed. As brilliantly shown in a sociological analysis of the so-called "second net," in socialist society there were strict rules of exchange of goods and personal favors. Civil society itself was considered a specific totality of exchanges—exchanges of goods for goods, statuses for goods, and statuses for statuses (Raichev 2003). Having access to such goods was key social capital ensuring social actors with access to the second net. Thus they not only were able to meet their own consumer needs but also to communicate actively with other members of the second net. The deficits of the socialist goods supply system were compensated and complemented by gift exchange; people had to rely much more on personal contacts and to give something more than money to get necessary goods or services (Dichev 1999). Social actors were much dependent on each other and as a result they were much more sociable.

Velinova argues that socialist consumption was primarily different from "capitalist" consumption on account of the practices associated with shopping. Shopping was not a habitual, banal activity—it was incidental, unpredictable, and time consuming. In everyday language, there was a tendency to abandon economic concept of shopping and replace it with euphemisms showing more clearly how exactly the product was obtained—*"where did you get this from," "I provided a TV set," "I queued for bread," and "we were given an apartment"* (Velinova 2004: 74). People queued for everything, sometimes even standing in line without knowing what was on sale—if others were in line, there was something worth waiting for.[3]

Production and distribution in socialism were planned, although plans were frequently unrealistic and rarely fulfilled. Nevertheless all kinds of enterprises, factories, and cooperatives proclaimed that they had carried out a 5-year plan for 4 years. This was an ideological illusion, propagated by the media—people were aware of this and apprehended it as they did with all other everyday discrepancies between words and deeds. Consumer needs in socialism were dominated by a bureaucratic machine—Fehér et al. call this *dictatorship over needs* (Fehér et al. 1983). In the absence of a real market system this dictatorship (based on economic, political, and ideological power) satisfied consumer needs to a certain extent and in a way was presupposed by state and party.[4] Consumption patterns were constituted by political or quasi-political organizations such as the Bulgarian Communist Party,

[3] On the shortage economy under socialism see Kornai (1980) and Verdery (1996: 19–38).

[4] Most indicative is the case of a deficit of sanitary napkins: "*They were produced in one paper factory only and were almost inaccessible for women. Whenever they appeared in a few specific drug-stores in Sofia instantly queues appeared too and people were given two packages only. I remember a man saying 'I have a wife and two daughters – how can I have only two packages – whom am I supposed to give them to?'*"—E.K., born 1970 in Sofia.

the Young Communist League, and other cultural organizations invading the private sphere in an unprecedented way. Via propaganda and various means of surveillance (including secret and anonymous reports to the authorities) communist rulers strove to control all aspects of everyday life and to establish an entirely new socialist way of life (Brunnbauer 2008; Koleva 2017). Yet these efforts met serious resistance from below. Thus the lack of political freedom in socialism was directly connected to suppressed consumer freedom. Yet socialist customers were not passive objects of a centrally planned economy—they chose what to buy, sometimes refused to consume, and ascribed their own meaning to consumables through active appropriation and bricolage (Reid 2002: 214).

In official socialist ideology, especially in the 1950s, Western consumer culture was branded as decadent. On the other hand "rising satisfaction of people's needs" was defined as a supreme aim of communism. As mentioned above, these needs were defined as common, not individual. In other words, consumption was constructed as an ideal but consumer culture was discarded as associated with the West. In Velinova's words, socialist ideology constantly transformed material codes into political ones and thus converted the social style of living into an ideology in sharp contrast to the Western one (Velinova 2004: 80).[5]

Socialist consumption had a structural defect—instead of possessing products, the consumer was enslaved by them. Dichev calls this *natural leasing*—you buy something cheap but then you must invest your time and personal competence in repairing it (Dichev 2005).[6] Mass production kept prices low but the quality was also low. Since the early 1960s the quality of consumer goods was a principal concern of Bulgarian communist officials—satisfying people's material needs was the basis of their legitimacy (Guentcheva 2012: 141). Only in the 1980s after long ideological disputes did the category of luxury goods appear. For the first time differences in quality and thus in social categories were implied. Before then quality and prices hardly varied. If somebody dared to complain that his/her apartment was full of technical defects the answer was "If you do not like it, give it back." There were many people on the list eager for it. So, the only option left was to repair everything oneself. Creed registered how many types of activities were practiced by Bulgarian men in order to avoid paying for them (Creed 1998: 201). Finally "given an apartment" after waiting for years, people then spent years repairing and reorganizing it. Buying a car was also an exceptional type of purchase—the typical waiting time was between 3 and 10 years. There was a joke, "I am waiting for my car to be produced in the USSR next year, so maybe in two years I'll get it."

In socialism customers had limited rights, but they were active agents, not passive victims of the goods deficit. They had to be constantly alert for what was about to be put on the market (when and where) and to belong to broad social networks in

---

[5] Here is a quotation from a famous lady's magazine "Woman today": "*British 'Women' magazine deals only with beauty, cosmetics, how a widow can find a new partner. It does not say a word about unemployment, strikes, high rents, bad schools and low wages in England …*" (Krasteva-Blagoeva 2003: 184).

[6] In the 1970s and 1980s in Bulgarian cities there were the so-called "Do it yourself" shops providing materials and tools so that people could produce or repair their goods themselves.

order to have access to scarce products. Very typical was the impersonal phrase *"they released bananas"* or *"they let off oranges."* It implied that some impersonal collective embodiment of power released products to the market and distributed apartments to its citizens: in fact it took care of the people. Years and decades after 1989 people continued expecting the state to keep fulfilling this role—it was considered entirely responsible and obligated to them for their well-being.

In this context, "do it yourself" ideology (presupposing that consumers should prepare their commodities themselves by buying tools and materials from special shops under the same name) blurred categories in a specific way. Production and consumption were mixed—consumers were active agents not only in consumption but also in production—specifically in elaboration of their own goods, constantly repairing and taking care of them. "Do it yourself" resembles customization and craft consumption in particular: the consumer should be directly involved in both design and production (Campbell 2005: 31). Gaining wide currency in socialist Bulgaria "do it yourself" led to a transformation of concepts of working time and spare time. Instead of entertainment, free time was frequently occupied with informal economic activities (Creed 1998: 184–219) and working time was not used for work only. A range of home produce activities are included in the "do it yourself" pattern—making preserved food, using fruits and vegetables from personal gardens in the villages and villas (Krasteva-Blagoeva 2005, Stroe this volume), home sewing and knitting to avoid standard shop clothing (Krăsteva-Blagoeva 2015), etc.

Overvaluation of Goods in Socialism: "Be Mine Forever"

Due to these characteristic features of socialism's socioeconomic pattern, goods failed or only rarely were able to become real commodities. The process of commoditization was partial and incomplete[7]; something more then money was needed to have access to goods. According to Simmel value is not an inherent property of objects but it is a result of people's judgments about them; a unique constitutive element of value is

> "the difficulty in acquisition, the sacrifice offered in exchange" (Simmel 1978: 100).

Thanks to personal efforts, social actions, and time invested in their acquisition and proper usage, goods in socialism were not emotionally neutral. They became *sensitive objects* (Frykman and Povrzanovic Frykman 2016) able to trigger affect and maintain different emotions—and thus became instruments in identity formation processes, i.e., "biographical objects" (Hoskins 2013). As a result certain goods were significantly *overvalued*. Overvaluation may be seen as a process of transformation

[7] "The process of commoditization is the transformation of objects into commodities, which occurs when things (products, activities, services, etc.) become exchangeable goods on the market"—Babcicky Philipp, THE BIGRAPHY OF OBJECTS, www.babcicky.com, June 27, 2012, accessed April 14, 2018.

of goods from ordinary articles into “objects with history.” Overvaluation is a specific socialist and partially postsocialist set of ideas about and practices associated with objects (certain goods and commodities) significantly exceeding their “normal” or “habitual” value and expressed in the extreme care of objects, new hobbies of collecting goods packaging, extraordinary prolongation of usage, creative re-usage practices, etc.. Not every kind of good has the potential to be overvalued. As we shall see in the empirical examples described below, in most cases extraordinarily scarce products were overvalued—their scarcity was enough to transform them into luxury products and sources of personal prestige in socialism. Thus, the distinction between primary and secondary commodities—i.e., necessities and luxuries (Appadurai 1986: 16)—was blurred and both objective systems were constructed in a specific way: a banal pair of jeans was cherished as a luxury item.[8] In other words, shortages create luxuries. Rationing, typical of the first decades after the Second World War, also led to overvaluation of goods—especially food items—and related corruption too. Contrary to the general assumption that

> “commodities by virtue of their exchange destinies and mutual commensurability tend to dissolve the links between persons and things” (Appadurai 1986: 24)

the overvalued objects become highly personalized and even (in some cases) animated—in Benjamin’s terms. In this sense, animation is a spiritual injection of life or human qualities into goods. For Benjamin his reading box was more than an object—it was the repetitive movement of his hand in using it (Benjamin 2006). Animation can occur with restricted supply as in our case—but also via customization—e.g., Paul Willis’s motorbike boys fetishize Buddy Holly records (Willis 2014).

> “As a person identifies with a commodity item, he or she faces the possibility of NOT identifying with other people … and alienate himself/herself of the company of other living beings finding solace in having ‘a relationship’ with the commodity item” (Benjamin 1999: 7).

In the socialist context, such alienation from other people via overvalued rare and deficit products was due to the desire to demonstrate self uniqueness in a standardized and homogenized “grey” cultural milieu. In a specific way overvalued goods were able to reflect the most typical personal features of their owners. Overvaluation is typologically close to customization, prosumption, remixing, bricolage, and other elements of consumer tactics, to follow de Certeau, through which people are able to build their own worlds and identities by using industrially produced objects creatively and individualistically (de Certeau 1984).

Overvalue may be defined as a kind of category such as and similar to the classic concepts of use value, exchange value, non-use value, and sign value. It is most close to symbolic value. Basically it may be seen as a specific combination of use value and symbolic value. As a subject of research in its own right in sociology and anthropology, these disciplines emphasize that products carry a functional (or utilitarian)

[8] What is more, Western jeans imported not via “regular” ways discussed below, i.e., CORECOM, were faultlessly identified by people on the street as even more precious, so they did not hesitate to stop a person and ask a normal question of the time, “Where did you get these jeans from?” (personal communication with Iskra Velinova).

and a symbolic (or expressive) value. In other words, individuals value goods both because they perform practical functions and because they can be used to signal social identity and status (Ravasi and Lindova 2004). Overvaluation of goods combines elements of these two concepts. Use value of goods (1) locally produced; (2) produced in other socialist countries within *the Council for Mutual Economic Assistance (COMECOM)*; (3) produced in the West and imported officially; and (4) produced in the West and typically imported illegally, mainly through the neighbor countries of Greece and Yugoslavia, was evident in all cases. Their exchange value was partially evident, because, as mentioned above, some of them were not entirely commoditized—they were not considered solely as exchange objects of economic value. The symbolic value of the four groups of goods (according to their place of origin) was different and progressively higher—i.e., Western goods were imbued with the highest symbolic value and prestige—yet all of them were used to define a specific set of social and cultural meanings, which enabled consumers to communicate information about their identity (Ravasi and Lindova 2004). According to Paul duGay, products are "meaningful" insofar as they are a part of a certain "cultural universe" and have been incorporated into a system of "shared social knowledge" (du Gay et al. 1997). In addition to concrete use value a more latent (probably individualized) use value may be present. For example, the obvious use value of a teacup may be its use for drinking tea, but its signifying value or symbolic value may be tied to the fact that it was a gift from a precious friend or family member.[9] In our case this additional symbolic value is related to the difficulty of access to goods, their overvaluation, and their subsequent transformation into sensitive objects and objects with history. Being imbued with an individualized history—perceived as unique and personal, but in fact typologically common—goods were invested with uncommon new meanings due to which their life was prolonged disproportionately to their purpose. They were treated with extreme care untypical of ordinary objects in consumer culture. Thus the meaning of overvaluation is close to that of concepts such as sacralization and singularization. According to Kopytoff, usually commodities are singularized by being pulled out of their usual sphere—i.e., the West, in this case (Kopitoff 1986: 74). Circulating in different regimes of value in space and time things can move in and out of commodity states depending on the commodity context (Appadurai 1986: 13, 15; Kopitoff 1986: 83). In our case overvaluation of goods might also be seen as well as a phase in an object's biography, close in some cases to terminal commoditization (when further exchange is precluded). Non-use value was also evident in some cases (types of goods) and in some phases of their biography as commodities. A good example of this was the case of guest rooms in socialist village houses—furnished lavishly and always with a big doll sitting on a nicely covered bed. These rooms were in fact rarely or never used; they served as an impressive display of the owner's prestige.

[9] Babcicky, Philip. Use value, exchange value, and symbolic value. www.babcicky.com, June 16 2012, Theory, accessed March 31, 2018.

Overvaluation of goods in socialist Bulgaria is evident in empirical data in two main dimensions—very high estimation of rare Western goods and extreme care of some local deficit goods. Entering a socialist culture

> "objects from the West ... stripped from their original social context, served different cultural functions" (Merkel 1998: 284).

Their overvaluation may be interpreted in this context, as a culturally specific form of localization (Robertson 1995). The penetration of goods from the other side of the Iron Curtain was different in different sub-periods of socialist rule and in different parts of the country as well. As R. Guentcheva points out,

> "in 1950s western goods were perceived officially as containers and transmitters of decadent bourgeois influences. In the 1960s, there was a marked ideological change that made their appearance in Bulgaria acceptable. Roughly at that time, socialist countries accepted the challenge of defeating capitalism on its own ground, i.e. in the field of consumption. This is a radical ideological change that opened the gates for the West, and especially for western goods, to come to the East and serve as gauges of socialist development" (Guentcheva 2009: 15–16).

Certain elements of Western culture were perceived as useful and desirable (especially machines because they served the public good) while others such as Western consumer goods were considered carrying significant ideological connotations. They were problematic because they served individual ends and could still be regarded as capitalist—that is why they needed to be isolated and their penetration into socialist Bulgaria had to be prevented (Guentcheva 2008: 373, 377). Channels of illegal penetration of Western goods into Bulgaria—mainly through Greece and Yugoslavia—were perceived as giving a serious advantage to Bulgarian consumers in comparison to their Soviet comrades who had no such channels in the USSR. On visiting the Soviet Union many Bulgarians have reported experiencing unpleasant encounters with local people aggressively insisting on buying something from them:

> "We were on a school excursion to Moscow and almost everywhere on the streets local boys stopped us demanding to buy things from us – no matter what: jeans, bottles, cigarettes, cassettes etc. Some of our friends were prepared for this: they had brought such items with them from Bulgaria for the purpose of selling them – and they made big money. But my friend and I had nothing to sell and we were annoyed by this."[10]

The availability of goods supply was a leading principle in demarcating the status of the capital city, the cities, the towns, and the villages in socialist Bulgaria (Dichev 2003: 43–50). There were several social groups permitted to travel abroad—high officials of the Bulgarian Communist Party, diplomats, trade representatives, pilots, sailors, international drivers, sportsmen, and people working in countries then considered less economically developed, mainly doctors, nurses, and builders.[11] Among these groups drivers were the most active in importing and reselling goods bought during their constant journeys: jeans, albums and tape-recorder cassettes of

---

[10] E.K., born 1970 in Sofia.

[11] In the mid-1980s in Libya only 10–12,000 Bulgarians worked—engineers, doctors and nurses, geologists, agricultural specialists (Guentcheva 2009: 12).

pop and rock music, chocolates, etc. Such items were also sold in the hard-currency enterprise of socialist Bulgaria "CORECOM." Founded in the 1960s, its name was an abbreviation of the French **Co**(mptoir de) **re**(présentation et de) **comm**(erce) or management of representation and commerce. CORECOM accepted hard currency only. Goods sold there were not released into the internal market. Some brands of alcoholic drinks such as Scotch whiskey, Marlboro cigarettes, electronics, cosmetics, magazines, and even chocolate eggs, which were unofficially labeled as "CORECOM eggs,"[12] could only be found in these shops. Some Bulgarian commodities designed for export and scarce in the internal market were also sold there. These shops were officially accessible to everyone but in fact each customer there was subject to investigation of the source of his/her currency. With the exception of foreigners hard currency in Bulgaria was only available to the high-ranking members of the Bulgarian Communist Party and people who had the right to travel or work abroad. In 1964 the Bulgarian state introduced special coupons for shopping in CORECOM. All customers, even foreigners, had to be strictly identified by showing their passports at the counter and by signing receipts—that is, how anonymity in the modern act of buying was destroyed (Guentcheva 2009: 20).

This is how G.K. managed to buy a tape recorder from CORECOM for his son's graduation:

> "It was impossible for ordinary people to go and shop there. "CORECOM" was like a window display of the West inaccessible to us. I was lucky that I had a friend married in France. When he came to Bulgaria I asked for his help. I wanted to buy a tape-recorder for my son – he had just finished high school and he was going to the army for the obligatory military training for 2 years. So we went there – my friend and I. I was like a cat on hot bricks. I felt very uneasy because I expected that we will be checked and interrogated. He was very calm, he asked me to choose which one I liked – and I chose by instinct, I had no idea which one was better. He paid with his money and we went out. I paid him back in Bulgarian leva and I was very happy. It was a Japanese tape recorder "Hitachi" – something unseen, not many people in Bulgaria at that time could have such a thing."[13]

CORECOM clients were frequently surprised by sudden police raids (Guentcheva 2009: 23), and that is why G.K. was so nervous. In the 1980s state control was not so strict—people used to go to CORECOM at the end of the working day—between 4.30 and 5.00 p.m. because then such raids ended. Some respondents suspect that this was deliberately done to let people buy what they needed and to avoid social discontent.[14] Selling cars produced in the West or in socialist countries was a main CORECOM activity according to the archives (Guentcheva 2009: 9). During my fieldwork, however, only a few cases of people working abroad who officially bought Western cars from CORECOM were registered. Such was the case of L.S., born in 1963 in Sofia. His father was a military doctor working in Ethiopia. He made so much money that after his death his widow did not know how to spend it. This situation was

[12] Among some of the activities of CORECOM were the selling of fixed property (apartments, houses, and land for the construction of summer houses) as well as the selling of building materials—a permanent deficit in socialist Bulgaria (Guentcheva 2009: 8).

[13] G.K., born 1934 in Sofia.

[14] E.M., born 1964 in Sofia.

typical of the 1980s, a time of economic well-being: many people in Bulgaria (even those working in the country) had plenty of money but investing options were scarce. So L.S. bought the first Audi in Sofia—it was so unusual that his car was even shown on TV. He drove so fast that the police could not measure his speed.

The original meanings of Western goods were dissolved and were replaced by new meanings, thereby entrenching them in a socialist system of consumption (Guentcheva 2009: 27). Possessing such objects was a sign of prestige and a reason for pride—that is why Coca Cola, original jeans, etc. had the halo of extremely valued objects. Their original packaging and plastic bags with the logos and names of Western brands were very fashionable; they imbued their owners with unique individuality. Western consumption was a symbol not only of material success and personal pleasure but of personal freedom as well. A key characteristic feature of the fetishism of Western goods was the fact that those goods were very carefully tended. Their regular and practical consumption was mixed with symbolic consumption—they were consumed visually and symbolically. The above-mentioned packaging materials were reused many times because of their high symbolic value:

> "I remember I was in fifth grade at school when my father got something small from CORECOM, but it was put in an incredibly big plastic bag, glossy and thick, with an inscription. I was so proud of having it that I used it as a schoolbag for years. All the other children were envious. From the first moment I came in carrying it, all their eyes were on me and they all asked me where I got it from. I was very proud. This made me feel special. To understand this properly you have to know that there were no plastic bags like this in Bulgaria in the 1980s. People used string-bags for shopping and even ordinary plastic bags were very precious, CORECOM bags even more so."[15]

Later on, going to school with CORECOM plastic bags instead of schoolbags became a fashion—pupils, especially teenagers, used to put their textbooks in such branded plastic bags and carry them folded under their arms like portfolios. Some girls even had such bags of different colors and changed them every day to match their clothes.

Possessing Western toys was also very prestigious. If parents were able to travel abroad (a rare case) their children received precious gifts. Some of them grew accustomed to having such presents and they did not value them as high as did their friends not lucky enough to have such toys:

> "My friend on the 5th floor had many foreign toys because her father travelled a lot on business. I remember an incredible doll she got from Athens – she was a Barbie doll but we did not know the name at this time. She was absolutely real, she had many costumes so we could change her clothes. And the most amazing was that she had real tits. She was not comparable to our socialist dolls – they were all sex-less, with no sign of tits at all. It was great but soon my friend D. got bored with it and even threw it from the window! I was so confused – I brought it back to her and I told her that she really did not understand how lucky she was having such a doll."[16]

[15] K.G., born 1972 in Sofia. Plastic bags with the CORECOM logo were a peculiar type of deficit object. They were produced in sufficient quantities and were free, but they were often used as gifts and even sold outside the shop (Guentcheva 2009: 25).

[16] E.K., born 1970 in Sofia.

G.B., born in 1967 in Sofia, remembers how his schoolmate whose father was an international driver constantly had cases of Coca Cola at home. The boy showed off a lot about it and "*it was a great honor if he treated his friends to a drink.*" Western goods were so valuable that people started collecting their empty packages and new types of hobbies appeared:

> "One never deposits such things wishing to have them forever."[17]

> "All bottles of shampoo, deodorant and perfume were not thrown away after use – we kept them because they were beautiful. Of course, they weren't very many because getting one was a piece of rare luck. Their design was not comparable to our socialist stuff. Some of them continued smelling nicely for a long time."[18]

Collecting is a creative process, a form of craft consumption providing new meanings and significance to industrial products and presupposing a considerable investment of "the self" of the collector (Campbell 2005: 34). In socialist Bulgaria the hobbies of collecting empty packets of Western cigarettes, empty or full bottles of alcoholic drinks and beer, bottle labels, posters of rock bands, boxes of matches, badges, chocolate packages, toys of chocolate eggs, etc. were very popular. These collections illustrate most clearly the overvaluation of goods on the one hand and the aesthetics of commodity diversion and de-contextualization on the other (Appadurai 1986: 28). Parts of products considered rubbish and thrown away right after opening by Western consumers were diligently collected by socialist customers. Instead of ordinary use value, these parts of products were loaded with symbolic meanings. Thus people expressed their deep attitude towards these goods. They also gained prestige in their local community by showing how many deficit items they had consumed. Finally they used to put these collections into albums and display cases or to arrange them in a special place at home as a visible sign of their pride. For example, N.K.[19] was not a smoker but he collected cigarette packages when he was young. He liked them a lot because they were "Western and glittering." He used to take them from his friends and acquaintances who were smokers. In some of them there were two or three cigarettes left. He displayed them in special boxes on the wall of his room. Others collected matchboxes with images of Western football players and movie stars. Small black-and-white photographs of actors and rock stars given as rewards and sold on shooting grounds in amusement parks were also collected. Their quality was very bad. Sometimes it was not easy to identify who was in the photograph but they were expensive because traders knew that they were in fact selling a dream of the West and the normality people were longing for. A very widespread hobby among girls in the 1980s was collecting Western paper serviettes. They were diligently put into albums and exchanged according to strict rules. For example, one "silk" serviette, almost transparent and similar to a cobweb, was very precious and if exchanged it would bring in ten "regular" serviettes. Those advertising Western establishments were also very popular.

[17] N.K., born 1964 in Sofia.

[18] A.P., born 1965 in Pleven.

[19] N.K., born 1964 in Sofia.

A very typical example of overvaluation of goods is the case of a 78-year-old woman from a village near Vratsa, North West Bulgaria. According to her granddaughter:

> "All objects are extremely important to my grandmother. With each object, no matter its type and rank, she makes an effort to keep and use it as long as possible. That is why she repairs things many times instead of binning them. When we were children in socialist times, she used to take the toys from our chocolate CORECOM eggs and put them in the cupboard next to her crystal glasses. All of them are still there."[20]

Such a display of plastic toys next to crystal glasses in a visible place implies that these items are imbued with equal value. At first glance, this may be interpreted as a lack of "taste". In fact it is an expression of the overvaluation of goods and the aesthetics of de-contextualization:

> "... value is accelerated or enhanced by placing objects and things in unlikely contexts" (Appadurai 1986: 28).

On the one hand, this personal attitude and care of small and (from an adult's point of view) insignificant children's toys are due to the culture of poverty typical for this part of Bulgaria in all historical periods and even today (northwestern Bulgaria is known as the poorest region in the EC) and on the other it is also due to the specific fetishism of Western goods. The fact that these toys are still there today, almost 30 years after the fall of communism, reveals the cultural conservatism of this particular person-object relation. Goods overvaluation has become *habitus* (Bourdieu's terms) and that is why it remains unchanged despite the socioeconomic and political evolution of the country.

Another characteristic feature of goods overvaluation was the ingenious repurposing of objects, especially Western ones. They were creatively reused and new functions were attributed to them mainly because of their beauty. Aesthetics was almost lacking in local products and the contrast with the artistic beauty of Western objects was the reason for inventing new ways to use them. For example, A.K. chanced to receive as a gift some luxury soap "Nina Ricci." For 3 or 4 years she used the empty package as a jewelry box. This is instructive in two ways. First, the fact that soap was given as a present is very unusual because according to traditional Bulgarian beliefs donating soap is tabooed.[21] Apparently this soap was so extraordinary and highly esteemed that it was excluded from the rule. On the other hand, its use as a jewelry box indicates a lack of such exquisite objects on the local market. Similarly, E.M.'s mother used face cream boxes as jewelry boxes. Even today, 10 years after her death and 29 years after the fall of communism, E.M. still keeps them in memory of her mother. She preserves as well a set of fantastic paints bought from CORECOM in 1984:

---

[20] Data by Stefani Handjiiska, born 1998, Bachelor student, Anthropology, New Bulgarian University—Sofia.

[21] This is a very old belief. The taboo is still observed in contemporary Bulgaria. Long ago soap was used for magic. According to some new interpretations if you make such a gift your friendship will be washed away.

> "It is still usable, although I do not use it. I gave half of my salary for it then and it was worth it. I got the dollars from a friend who was a tinsmith repairing cars—he had dollars and gave them to friends at different rates depending how close friends they were. It was a great palette with two levels, lots of brushes and two glosses. It was absolutely impossible to find such a thing in Bulgaria. Even today it is not an object, it is history to me. History and the memory of my youth …."[22]

The famous Neckermann magazines, free catalogues of West German shops, were imported by drivers and sold in Bulgaria. They were useless as catalogues because none of the products could be found in the country but yet people paid for them. They satisfied the romantic desire for Western goods—in Ivan Evtimov's[23] words:

> "We had no consumer culture but we had a dream of it. It was a lovely romantic dream."

Rock music was a lively expression of this dream. Access to it was also complicated. In the late 1970s in a special place at Sofia center, so-called *haifars* (from hifi—high-fidelity technics) started gathering. Rock albums, mainly imported from Yugoslavia, Hungary, Poland, and the West, were exchanged and illegally sold there. The police was aware but took no measures against it because the authorities reduced the pressure and the control over everyday life at this time. Also, it was possible to order a record of a specific album. This was an expensive informal service. The price of a record and a cassette was very high. Accordingly, if someone obtained a long-playing record, it was quickly circulated by recording it from one tape recorder to another many times. Circles of friends were very active in this respect. Initially those records were made on tape recorders and from the second half of the 1970s on cassette recorders. Cassettes also were hard to find. No new blank cassettes were sold except for the worthless Orwo cassettes imported from East Germany. That is why inventive repurposing was practiced as well. People bought Bulgarian fairy-tale cassettes. These tapes were of very good quality, so they were used to record rock music. Funny situations occurred as young people frequently bought lots of fairy tales. They were careful to choose the longest tales so that a whole album could be recorded. The price was one and the same but some of the tales were shorter and so people soon found out that they had to avoid those shorter tales. Obtaining a cassette recorder and nearly 10 years later, a video player, was not easy either. Respondents use to call it "the fight for recorders" (see Bankov, this volume). In the late 1980s big circles of friends (20–30 in number) used to gather in one's flat with a video and watched two or three films from the West. The same thing had happened almost 30 years earlier with their parents' generation. Crowds gathered in the houses of people with television. Scarcity made people more sociable and reinforced their solidarity.

Many specialized objects needed for specific activities were also unavailable in Bulgaria. Decent painting materials were hard to find. Sports goods were rare too, so people had to buy them from CORECOM which imbued them with the aura of a luxury despite the fact that they were not that special. That is why the first Western

---

[22] E.M., born 1964 in Sofia.

[23] Ivan Evtimov is a Bulgarian sociologist, born 1942 in the city of Varna.

companies to gain access to the local market had great success although their products were not particularly high grade. Such was the case with Italian Romika, importer of the first sneakers into Bulgaria.

The second trend of goods overvaluation is seen in the extreme care of deficit products, either locally produced or imported from other socialist states. Because they were rarely accessible people used them very carefully. After finally having bought a new TV set, people would cover it with a centerpiece to protect it from the dust and cold; others did not unwrap the remote, using it with the nylon wrapping still on to protect it. In an extreme case that became a well-known anecdote, a family from the town of Gotse Delchev after waiting for years to buy a car did not go inside it with shoes. Instead, mother knitted special slippers and everyone put them on before getting into the car. Although this was a unique case and it was interpreted in the larger society as an example of utter ignorance and impact of the "rural" culture into the cultural milieu of small towns (resembling villages in many ways), this practice reflects the extraordinary care of goods on the one hand and the symbolic perception of a car as a mobile house on the other (Baudrillard 1996; Urry 2004). Traditionally people take off their shoes at doorsteps and entrance halls, so the same was when entering a car as well. Furthermore this practice continued in the postsocialist period as well when this family's son bought a car. Buying a car was not a problem anymore, but the specific cultural habit persisted.[24]

The extraordinary care of goods is registered in many different examples both before and after 1989. Many families discard practically nothing. All items are cleverly and diligently reused as many times as possible. An extreme example of this respect is an old woman from the town of Vratsa who keeps even the plastic packages from yellow cheese and all the small jars she buys every day. She finds ways how to reuse them again and again. Stockpiling food may be seen as a kind of expression of goods overvaluation as well. During socialism preparing winter supplies was quite widespread. Every autumn urban and village families used to prepare an enormous quantity of vegetable preserves in jars—tomatoes for cooking, chutney, pickles, fruit syrups, and jams.[25] The only difference between city and village was in their quantity (Smolett 1989; Yung 2009). A great many jars were sent from villages to towns. An exchange within the so-called neo-extended family (Konstantinov 2001) was carried out: young urban migrants would actively help their parents in villages to cultivate land and in return they received part of the crop preserved in jars. Because of active food exchange and movement of a large quantity of food in jars all over the country, Elinor Smolett called socialist Bulgarian culture "an economy of jars" (Smolett 1989).

[24] B.A. thesis by Hristo Tzenov, Department of Anthropology, New Bulgarian University, Sofia, 2008.

[25] The same holds true for other Balkan countries as well. For the Romanian case see Stroe in this volume.

Postsocialism: The Unusual Consumers

In the context of the upsurge of neoliberal capitalism in Bulgaria, concepts of common and private property are mixed and intertwined. Witnessing the unprecedented plundering of the socialist state property by politicians of all parties, ordinary people continue excusing the pilferaging of common property. Appropriation practices in the workplace still occur although they are decreasing. They are directed towards either an unidentified owner (the state, which in the past was considered an alienated institution, detached from ordinary people and their needs[26]) or a private owner (perceived as a potential criminal, because wealth in postsocialist Bulgaria, especially in the first 20 years after democratic changes, was presumably culpable). In both cases pilferage is seen as an act of mundane justice by ordinary people, expressed in rituals of grabbing what they believe they deserve. In the 1990s stealing toilet paper from public lavatories, restaurants, and workplaces was widespread, not because it was scarce or expensive, but because it was seen as pleasant sponging hard to resist. According to a TV journalist, today such practices are typical of lavatories on a particular floor of the assistant personnel in the television—toilet paper, liquid soap, napkins, etc. vanish right after stocking. Even scholars working at an institute of the Bulgarian Academy of Sciences are known to do the same. According to E.M., a regular full-time employee, she and her colleague paid to repair the lavatory because in the institute's budget there was no money for this for years. They started putting soap and toilet paper bought with their own money in the toilet but the scientists, coming to the institute once a week for a couple of hours, used them. E.M. and her colleague put a note asking people using the toilet to pay a small amount for these items, but only two of the scientists responded. Soap regularly disappeared only hours after stocking. They deliberately put out a quite unpleasant old soap, but it was taken too. At last the two women understood that their efforts were in vain and they started keeping toilet paper and soap in their room even though it was very far from the toilet and carrying these items back and forth several times a day was inconvenient. This case is interesting in two ways. Firstly, it reflects the postsocialist tendency (although not widespread) of people uniting in a common cause and compensating for institutional deficits. These women used money from their very low salaries to repair the toilet. There are other examples, for instance people who asphalt their streets because the local administration refuses to do this for years and villagers who pay security firms to protect them from criminals instead of the police, who are always missing in Bulgarian villages. Secondly, this type of appropriation is different because the people providing the items are known; it is not an anonymous common property. What is more, there is a considerable (and well-known) difference in salaries of scientists and other employees. When scientists tried to cheat their lower status colleagues, this is an expression of the

[26]This is a tendency dating back to the period of Ottoman rule (1396–1878), which continued after the Liberation of Bulgaria. It was intensified in socialism because of the aggressive penetration by the state into the private lives of people and the attempt to create an entirely new socialist way of life (Brunnbauer 2008; Koleva 2017). This intensification continued during the crisis of postsocialism as well because the state failed to fulfill its main functions and Bulgaria became known as the most corrupt state in the EU.

cultural habit to scrounge by all means and not to lose a single chance of obtaining insignificant banal items for free. Such practices are perceived by many as a normal reaction against the hardships of the constant economic crisis Bulgarians have lived through over 30 years[27] now. In fact, their origin can be traced back to socialist pilfer-aging and maybe even further.

Because of rapid economic and political changes in the period after 1989 and penetration of Western consumer culture patterns, overvaluation of goods as a widespread social phenomenon has been gradually decreasing. However, some expensive products are still overvalued. Some habits of thought that exaggerated the value of goods and some practices of extreme care are still typical, mainly of middle-aged and old people, i.e., those generations who survived communism. The example given above of special car slippers worn by the second generation is an illustration of such cultural continuity. Reusing objects as long as possible is another characteristic feature of postsocialist consumer culture in Bulgaria. Y.K., 50 years old, used to reuse disposable nappies when her children were born in the 1990s, a period of harsh economic crisis. She found a way to wash and dry them even though they were made of paper, not because she was poor (as were many others) but because she was taught by her parents to economize. Practical re-usage of packaging (jars, plastic boxes, plastic and glass bottles, plastic bags, and even, though rarely, plastic milk and yellow cheese packaging) are frequently accompanied by a significant change of contents.[28] This reflects de Certeau's argument about the difference between the production of an image and the secondary production hidden in the process of its utilization, and re-usage in this case (De Certeau 1984: XIII). This widespread tendency is reflected in a witty Facebook post. Under the images of a Coca Cola bottle full of a white liquid and a plastic ice cream box there is an inscription: "Only Bulgarians know that *rakia* (traditional brandy) is on the left and *sarmi* (stuffed cabbage) is on the right."[29] When I shared on the net my intention to use the post in this chapter I received several critical notices that I should not do so, because *"we will be shamed before the world."* These comments clearly illustrate the connection between consumption and identity—both personal and collective. Sharing a "secret knowledge" about the way packaging is reused is in fact a cultural competence governed by notions of "honor" and "shame." It is an element in the construction of postsocialist discourse of *unusual consumers* and, in fact, *craft consumers* (Campbell 2005). It serves to reconcile the shame of being the poorest EU country with the honor of being inventive, practical, thrifty, and clever. This discourse is evident most clearly in clothing practices.

---

[27] A highly indicative illustration of the system as a force driving decent people to become thieves is presented in the low-cost film "Lesson" based on the real story of an honest woman teacher who robbed a bank to pay her husband's debt and to save their house.

[28] Another option is what Campbell calls subversive customization (Campbell 2005: 31), i.e., the creative repurposing of an object. An illustrative example in this respect is the clever usage of a plastic bottle as a joint container and dispenser of water from both faucets of a British sink to mix hot and cold water together. The lack of this option in British sinks is a great problem for Bulgarians living in the UK. That is why this invention is proudly displayed on Facebook with a picture and caption—"Bulgarian genius in England. I know the guy personally"—Filmi online, 20.03.2018, accessed March 23, 2018.

[29] www.kaldata.com—accessed December 27, 2017.

In the last 20 years wearing second-hand clothes has become normal consumer practice for many Bulgarians. An important factor in their popularity is the opportunity to dress differently every day at low cost. Home sewing, an ancient practice in Bulgaria, was reactivated during socialism as one of its "do it yourself" practices. It continued today as women refashion, improve, and decorate second-hand clothes at home without the services of a tailor.[30] This also occurs in Western societies (Campbell 2005: 32). After the fall of communism home sewing became a core of a specific compensatory discourse setting women up as sophisticated consumers despite their lower social status vis-à-vis other women in the European Union:

> "We are unusual consumers. Women in the West simply go to the shop and get everything ready. We can sew, we can knit, we can do something from nothing … so we are better"[31] (Krăsteva-Blagoeva 2015: 240).

The notion of unusual Bulgarian consumerism is a way of compensating them for their reputation as "the repressed," "the excluded," or even "the failed consumers" (Bauman 1998) who cannot freely decide upon their consumption due to economic restraints. The unusual consumerism of Bulgarian women is found in their combination purchases. The low price of second-hand clothes is a good reason to buy them for possible future use even when there is no immediate need.[32] They think through their choices, keeping in mind their existing wardrobe and what might go with it. Such combinative ability is of course typical for the lower social strata of other nations as well, given their lack of enough resources to buy whole ensembles brand new. In the Bulgarian case it is applicable to the majority of women, because that majority is (and self-identifies) as poor. This is why big piles of clothing are bought. But, stocking up is also an element of the culture of survival. For this reason having more clothes is seen as providing security and even wealth. The fact that these clothes are second hand is almost pushed down into the subconscious. Through acquiring them, the feeling of normality is reconstructed and revitalized. This feeling is crucial for freedom to consume. By becoming free to consume again (even second-hand clothes) women vindicate themselves in their own eyes as ladies of decent, "normal" social status, not as second-hand persons. That is how in a peculiar way second-hand clothes contribute to the identity construction of people wearing them as "first-hand" individuals (Krăsteva-Blagoeva 2015: 240).

[30] This is generally a typical desire of women in countryside in many countries. Modern trends to produce handmade clothes and home objects appeared in the USA and Europe in the 1970s and 1980s. It started with the famous TV show of Martha Stewart (http://www.fashion-lifestyle.bg/success_broi24http://en.wikipedia.org/wiki/Martha_Stewart). Housewives wishing to have a unique home and trying to escape consumer culture's uniformity were her followers. Bulgarian women do not suspect that such trends can appear in wealthier societies, too. The difference is that in one case it is a survival strategy, in the other—a way to escape boredom.

[31] Informant M.M. 53 years old, Bulgarian, hairdresser.

[32] "My mother always shops for the future. For instance, she bought me a office shoes, second hand shoes, very elegant. I do not wear such shoes but she said—'you will need them when you graduate next year when you will start looking for a job,' and she bought them." Y.B., 17 years old, Bulgarian from the town of Kurdzali.

As demonstrated above, in postsocialism overvaluation of goods is not preserved in a clear form, but remnants of it can still be observed and recorded. These remnants may be considered cultural relics coming from the recent past and still active in particular cases and conditions. They are most visible in the consumption practices of the poorest people interviewed in my research. For example, that old woman from Vratsa mentioned earlier is interesting in this respect because she is inclined to save, stockpile, preserve, and very slowly consume all types of goods, even food:

> "If somebody gives her chocolates as a present she puts them in the fridge and treats her visitors with them for months. The same holds true for the exotic food items my cousin brings her from Germany. She even puts bread in the fridge and eats it very slowly. She was very happy when my boyfriend and I bought her a birthday cake. She cut it in small pieces and treated her neighbors for weeks with it. When we started living together she offered us as a gift a new microwave, in its original packaging, bought 13 years previously. When my grandfather died she presented us with a golden edged porcelain dinner set. It became apparent later that it was part of my parents wedding gifts. According to my mother set disappeared right after the wedding. Obviously granny had kept it intact for years in its original packaging. She also keeps my grandfather's and my dad's things, they passed away some time ago. From time to time she offers me something which belonged to my father. She believes this is a great honor for me."[33]

Such patterns of relation with goods refer not only to the level of poverty and to socialist deficits but also to the cultural practices (typical for other Balkan countries too[34]) of grabbing and extra care of what is seen as valuables. Keeping the possessions of those who have died appears to be traditional but in fact it is not entirely so. According to tradition these objects, especially clothes, are to be given away to friends and relatives on the 40th day after death. The continual use of these objects ensures a symbolic presence of the dead in the life of their heirs. Such objects attain affective value and serve as

> "the focus of narrations and as starting points for a return to past worlds" (Frykman and Povrzanovic-Frykman 2016: 19).

For instance, that old woman proposed that her granddaughter use an old sunshade belonging to her dead father. This is valid practice for old objects belonging to living people as well. Children are frequently given toys, fairy-tale books, clothes, knitted pullovers, hats, gloves, etc., belonging to their parents when they were young and carefully retained by grandmothers for years. Such practices, traditional in origin, exceed the parameters of overvaluation because these goods ensure the symbolic continuity of family relations. Old people are convinced of the high value of these objects solely because they belonged to a close person, dead or alive. This is not always comprehensible to their grandsons and granddaughters. Having many

[33] Data by Stefani Handjiiska, born 1998, Bachelor student, Anthropology, New Bulgarian University—Sofia.

[34] There is an interesting parallel between the hiding of the porcelain wedding set and a scene depicted in "Zorba the Greek" by Nikos Kazandzakis: old village women robbed all the valuables from a Western woman's dead body. The disappearance of such objects immediately after a ritual occasion—wedding or death—reflects the strength of the cultural impulse to grab valuables no matter the temporal and cultural context.

more options to buy and consume, children cannot understand why should they play with the old-fashioned socialist toys of their parents:

> "watching Mickey Mouse and many other movies every day they cannot realise what was "Ну погоди" to us—a Russian animated kids series, very well done. It was, in fact, the only animated series we were able to watch on TV in the 1970s. That is why my mother kept a figurine of the famous wolf of this series and gave it to my children. They did not throw it away because they are well-mannered but they were not impressed at all."[35]

Yet, some children adopt their parents' attitudes towards goods. Among young people, especially those raised by their grandparents (a very widespread practice which the socialist state tried to restrict in various ways (Iliev 2001)), overvaluation of goods or remnants of it are evident. For example, E.M.'s nephew, 23 years old, raised by his grandmother, adopted from her the habit of not throwing away anything. He is convinced that all objects, even old and damaged ones, "*may serve a purpose*." A young couple with a new second home at the seaside wanted to use an old cooker, inherited from a dead relative even though they barely knew him. He had no children, his home was sold, and the cooker was the only thing of his left. Their decorator tried to convince them that a new cooker would fit in their kitchen better with no success.

> He told me, "This old cooker irritates me, it does not match the other furnishings. I told him I will be the one looking at it every day, not him. It is not about money, it is about using something which is still usable and about honoring a dead man."[36]

Objects from the socialist past are preserved and still used for practical reasons as well. Recently, years after the fall of communism it has become apparent that not all socialist products were of bad quality. This is especially true for some Soviet machines and for some food items as well, at least in memory.[37] According to experts in repairing electric devices, some Soviet washing machines, refrigerators, etc. are still working and are even better than new products which are deliberately made with plastic parts so that whenever a part is broken it cannot be repaired. This is done to force customers to buy a replacement. Soviet machines can be repaired using spare parts and that is why they still work. According to P.P., an all-around expert, this is because

> "the Soviets produced everything once for a lifetime – they were poor and could not afford to buy new machines."

[35] G.T., born 1967 in Sofia.

[36] E.K., born 1970 in Sofia.

[37] The quality of food products made during socialism is strongly preferred to contemporary foodstuff. Even though there was no diversity in the market (for example, there were only two types of cheese, cow's milk and goat's milk, and there were few brands), food products are remembered as being of high quality and very tasteful. These qualities were completely lost after 1989 according to many consumers who remember those products as being "real." Tomatoes were "delicious," cheese was "milky," yoghurt was "sour" and because it was "natural" "spoiled quickly," and sausages and bread were "very tasty." Shkodrova explains because Bulgarian food production was not completely industrialized, its raw materials were of higher grade, there were almost no additives, control was stricter, and in general pre-industrial production practices prevailed (Shkodrova 2014: 44–45).

He has regular clients who are quite attached to their old machines:

> "There is an incredible Soviet refrigerator "Zill" entirely made of metal, with an American compressor. I have repaired it several times and finally I had to tell the owner it was impossible to repair it any more. He almost cried as if it was a real family member and not an inanimate object. This was because not only they were poor pensioners, but also because they had become accustomed to it and did not want to change it at all. They were not able to understand that the new one would be energy saving and therefore cheaper."[38]

This inability to approach items practically and the related predomination of symbolic value of objects are also a result of socialist overvaluation of goods. Yung recorded similar attitudes towards residential properties at the beginning of the 1990s. Many old people living alone in big apartments in the center of Sofia did not even consider the possibility of selling their home for a smaller one and living on the money from the deal, or of renting a room which could be an income to supplement their low pensions.[39] This is due to the perception of "my house is my fortress" attitude towards lodging of many Bulgarians. The possession of a home is a primary life goal, and renting is considered suitable of young people only. The high symbolic value of home ownership prevents them from perceiving it as a source of income.

After 1989 goods became commodities, they were routinely accessible and freedom to consume was experienced as a primary form of freedom from communism in the early 1990s.[40] After a transitional decade of "carnival" unrestrained consumption, known in Russia as *the frantic 1990s*, a period of normalization and habitualization of consumption practices followed. In recent decades, social media have become full of practical advices about how to avoid industrial products by producing them at home. These products include homemade food items—because the food sold in shops generally are rejected as unhealthy and of poor quality. Homemade cosmetics, alternative medical practices, and traditional Bulgarian and exotic herbs are also part of this phenomenon. This topic needs further research. Here it is worth mentioning that these tendencies reflect global anti-consumer cultural practices and culturally habitualized socialist "do it yourself" practices and discourses, circulated in a new way. Some precious goods are decommoditized because of the emotions they arouse in their owners. After socialism these emotions are not due to scarcity, as earlier, but are a result of affordability or of the emotional value of things which are the first of their kind obtained. Consequently, people hardly part with these goods—they neither can throw them away nor sell them. These items are singularized and hardly ever

---

[38] P.P., born 1949 in Sofia.

[39] Personal communication with Yuson Yung.

[40] Right after the Berlin wall came down, Easterners started shopping frantically in West Berlin. The taste of freedom was inseparable from the newly gained freedom to consume equally to the Westerners.

recommoditized.[41] Such is the case of I.I.[42]—a young and rich businessman who travels a lot and makes thousands of photographs of each journey. He has a collection of cameras because he always wants to have the best camera available on the market. He finally decided to sell his first camera bought in the early 1990s. He had not used it for years even though it still makes nice pictures. They are just not good enough for him anymore. He found a client ready to pay a good price for it, but at the last moment I.I. cancelled the deal:

> "I realized I was not able to sell it. It was too much for me. I will always remember how I saved up the money for this camera. I am not using it but I am not ready to say good bye to it either."

The reaction of the client was revealing. Instead of being angry, he paused and said:

> "**You are a socialist child like me**. We know the real price of things. That is why we cannot part with them."

This "real price" is not measured in money but reflects the active relation between laboriously acquired goods and self-construction of postsocialist Bulgarian consumers, which inevitably calls upon cultural attitudes and consumption practices originating in the socialist past. This case may also be interpreted by reference to McCracken's divestment rituals as well:

> "when an individual is about to dispense with a good either by giving it away or selling it … divestment rituals are used to erase the meaning associated with the previous owner. Individuals fear the dispossession of personal meaning, a phenomenon that resembles "the merging of identities" that sometimes takes place between transplant donors and recipients" (McCracken 1988: 87).

Here a divestment ritual is actually not performed because the actors are afraid of losing the personal meaning invested in the goods. They resist losing items, useless but precious, which have become symbols of their lives and personalities. Their attitudes towards such goods has become an infallible indicator of them as people raised in times of deficit. It has been interiorized and transformed into habitus (Bourdieu 1984), which is why it is so difficult and even impossible to overcome, even when the person has become wealthy enough to afford more "precious" goods.

---

[41] "Imagine purchasing a dog on the market. The dog is an exchangeable good, ascribed with an exchange value and sold as a priced good. Once the dog enters the family, over time, it becomes part of the social fabric of the family and eventually ceases to be a commodity. A process of *decommoditization* has begun. The dog has now its very own place and becomes *singularised.* Through a singularisation of the dog, it becomes less likely to be *recommodified* at a later stage again. Later, the dog may have puppies and some of them may be sold (becoming commodities) while one puppy may be kept by the owners. Chances are, that this puppy will never actually become a commodity and thus will be kept away from the spheres of exchange entirely. In terms of commoditization, quite different trajectories of objects are conceivable. A biography of an object may be marked by a single or recurring commoditization process, or by perpetually avoiding marketisation. Every object has its own biography which is partially determined by the spheres of exchange it falls into." Babcicky, Philip The Biography of objects. June 27, 2012—www.babcicky.com, accessed April 4, 2018.

[42] I.I. born 1972 in the town of Kozloduy.

After 1989 the identity functions of overvalued goods are still evident. The difference with the previous period is that their messages are targeted in a much more inward direction towards the person himself/herself rather than outwards to the social environment. Overvalued goods are individualized in many ways. E.M. was really heartbroken when her new television got out of order. Living alone, she had a real "relationship" with it. She talked to it and jokingly called it "her husband." The high symbolic value of overvalued products is reflected in specific naming practices. For example, in postsocialist period cars are not scarce any more, but they are expensive and hardly accessible, especially new ones. That is why a considerable percentage of cars in Bulgaria are second-hand, air-polluting old machines contrasting with the extremely expensive cars of the elite. Many people give a name to their car, especially if it is a new one. This is predominantly typical of women drivers. Such personal names as *Pierre, Barco*, and *Mitiobishito* (a transformation of Mitsubishi) are reported.[43] This last deserves attention. The first part of the name is the diminutive of the personal name Dimitar (Mitiyo). The suffix "to" is a gender-neuter definite article. This is how a Bulgarian sounding personal name transforming the original brand name is made. It conveys three levels of information: (1) this is Mitsubishi vehicle, (2) this is the car of Mitiyo, and (3) it is "almost alive," even though it has no gender, because it is personalized and its name carries an article. Naming unanimate objects with personal names reflects a high level of anthropomorphization. They are so overvalued that they are treated almost as family members. Traditionally, Bulgarians used to name cattle this way. It is not an accident that only cars are named this way in the postsocialist era. Naming a car reflects the specific cultural perception of an automobile as "a dwelling in movement" (Urry 2004). It is an object consumed, experienced, and treated in many different ways by family members. Compared to other goods and commodities cars are the things that express most clearly individual identity of the owner. His/her personal qualities are embodied in a car. In this context many visual signs are used in decorating cars and endowing them with the personal characteristics of the driver. For Bulgarians this tends to mean Christmas decorations—mainly antlers put over the front windows transforming a car into a "Santa Claus reindeer"; binding *martenitsa*—twined tasselled red and white thread, symbol of spring and health, with which the first of March is celebrated in Bulgaria, and even in isolated cases images of the prime minister Borissov as a sign of approval of him and his policies. Conspicuous consumption practices with cars are widespread. Aggressive and illegal driving, also typical of other Balkan countries, is considered a sign of machismo, which is a very important element of individual identity formation. Right after they buy a new car, many men retune the engine in order to be able to accelerate very quickly. Even though this is illegal, it is a main activity of many Bulgarian service stations. To check if this has been done, the police must disassemble the car, which is practically impossible.[44] This is one of the reasons for the carnage carried out on Bulgarian

[43] Data by Konstantin Georgiev, BA anthropology student, New Bulgarian University, Sofia.

[44] According to an anonymous worker in just such a service station, even the car of the chief of the traffic police was transformed this way. This illustrates the level of corruption in Bulgaria.

roads, with the number of victims increasing every year. Specialty license plates, those with six identical or consecutive digits, or personal names, nicknames, names of football teams, etc., are very expensive, costing six times the minimal salary. Purchasing one is a typical example of personalization. Doing so is to engage in the possession ritual enabling one to engage in conspicuous consumption (Campbell 2005: 30). But this practice is also seen as a lack of taste:

> "I would not put such a registration number on my car. I think people do it to demonstrate their exclusive social status and to enjoy themselves, because they have money. It is nice if there are four consecutive figures or if there is some other symbolism in the numbers but I would not put anything written– this is bad taste to me."[45]

Interest in such *golden registration numbers* dates back to the socialist period, when only "special people" were given access to them. They are considered a symbol of wealth, personal success, and prestige. According to police officers some people choose such numbers due to superstition or other personal reasons, but in the last few years this fashion has declined. Perhaps this is because rich businessmen and people with dubious fortunes now prefer not to demonstrate their well-being so conspicuously in order to avoid troubles.[46] According to Chief Inspector Vladimir Gerassimov in the Vidin region, the most expensive numbers are rarely bought but there are people who wait for months for a particular consignment of registration plates to be finished and plates with other numbers to be produced.[47] Waiting for a car (so typical of the socialist past) is rare nowadays but waiting for a license plate does happen, not because of deficit or economic restraints but out of superstition and fashion.

Conclusion

In this chapter I've tried to show different aspects of specific "socialist" object-person relations coded in ways people deal with goods and their connection to processes of self-construction and collective identity formation. The state deconstruction of former bourgeois ownership relations and proclamation of legal mass appropriations of urban property and forcible land cooperation as the rightful government activity "in the name of the people" presupposed the blurring and mixing of concepts of private and common property and gave birth to a specific culture of justified violation of somebody else's—especially common—property. Thus socialist individuals came to neglect and partially even reject common property, either cooperative or state, to aggressively and furtively follow their personal interest and profit.

---

[45] R.I., born 1959, Vidin.

[46] Tsvetanov, T., Yoncheva, M. What is the cost of a "golden" registration number?—Bulgarian National Radio. Radio Vidin, November 28, 2016—www.bnr.bg.

[47] Ibid.

Once acquired (due to formal and informal practices such as "do it yourself," queuing, knowing the right people, years of waiting, pilferage, etc.) some goods were decommoditized. They were given additional worth; that is, they were overvalued and became "objects with history." Both Western and local deficit products were treated with extreme care, and for as long as possible creatively and practically reused with their primary purpose kept or transformed according to the owner's needs. Overvaluation of goods is a cultural practice typical of socialism and partially preserved after 1989. It is a specific combination of use value and the symbolic value of products and as such it is able to generate meanings related to the social identity and status of the user (McCracken 1988). It reflects the identity construction of Bulgarians as "non-normal" consumers—not free to consume "properly" in socialism and not able to consume "properly enough" in the postsocialist era, living as they do in the poorest EU country. Traces of overvaluation are habitually kept alive even in the few cases where the social identity and financial status of the users are significantly improved—so that "normality" has been externally achieved. Yet, internally these "socialist children" remain the same.

References

Appadurai, Arjun. 1986. Introduction: Commodities and the Politics of Value. In *The Social Life of Things. Commodities in Cultural Perspective*, ed. Arjun Appadurai, 3–63. Cambridge: Cambridge University Press.

Baudrillard, Jean. 1996. *The System of Objects* (trans: James Benedict). London: Verso.

Bauman, Zigmunt. 1998. *Work, Consumerism and the New Poor*. Buckingham: Open University Press.

Benjamin, Walter. 1999. *The Arcades Project* (trans: Howard Eiland and Kevin McLaughlin). Cambridge, MA and London: Belknap Press.

———. 2006. *Berlin Childhood Around 1900* (trans: Howard Eiland). Cambridge, MA and London: Harward University Press.

Bourdieu, Pierre. 1984. *Distinction. A Social Critique of the Judgement of Taste*. Cambridge, MA: Harvard University Press.

Brunnbauer, Ulf. 2008. Making Bulgarians Socialist. The Fatherland Front in Communist Bulgaria, 1944–89. *East European Politics and Societies: and Cultures* 22 (1): 44–79.

Campbell, Colin. 2005. The Craft Consumer. Culture, Craft and Consumption in a Postmodern Society. *Journal of Consumer Culture* 5 (1): 23–42.

Creed, Gerald W. 1998. *Domesticating Revolution. From Socialist Reform to Ambivalent Transition in a Bulgarian Village*. University Park, PA: The Pennsylvania State University Press.

De Certeau, Michel. 1984. *The Practice of Everyday Life*. Berkeley: University of California Press.

Dichev, Ivaylo. 1999. *Darut v epohata na negovata tehnicheska vuzproizvodimost [The Gift in the Epoch of its Technical Reproduction]*. Sofia: LIK.

———. 2003. Usiadaneto na nomadskia komunizam. Sotsialistichaskata urbanizatsia I krugovete na grazdanstvo [Sedentation of Nomadic Communism. Socialist Urbanization and the Circles of Citizenship]. *Sotsiologicheski Problemi [Sociological Problems]* 3–4: 33–63.

———. 2005. *Prostranstva na zelanieto, zelanija za prostranstvo. Etjudi po gradska antropologija [Spaces of Desire, Desires for Space. Studies in Urban Anthropology]*. Sofia: Iztok-Zapad.

Douglas, Mary, and Baron Isherwood. 1979. *The World of Goods: Towards and Anthropology of Consumption*. London: Allen Lane.

du Gay, Paul, Stuart Hall, and Linda Jones. 1997. *Doing Cultural Studies: The Story of the Sony Walkman*. London: Sage Publications in association with the Open University.

Fehér, Ferenc, Ágnes Heller, and György Márkus. 1983. *Dictatorship Over Needs. An Analysis of Soviet Societies*. New York: St. Martin's Press.

Featherstone, Mike. 2007. *Consumer Culture and Postmodernism*. London: Sage.

Frykman, Jonas, and Maja Povrzanovic-Frykman. 2016. Affect and Material Culture. Perspectives and Strategies. In *Sensitive Objects. Affect and Material Culture*, ed. Jonas Frykman and Maja Povrzanovic Frykman, 9–31. Lund: Nordic Academic Press.

Guentcheva, Rossitza. 2009. Mobile Objects: CORECOM and the Selling of Western Goods in Socialist Bulgaria. *Etudes Balkaniques* XLV (1): 5–28.

———. 2008. Images of the West in Bulgarian Travel Writing During Socialism. In *Under Eastern Eyes. A Comparative Introduction to East European Travel Writing on Europe*, ed. Wendy Bracewell and Alex Drace-Francis, 355–378. Budapest, New York: Central European University Press.

———. 2012. Material Harmony. The Quest for Quality in Socialist Bulgaria 1960s–1980s. In *Communism Unwrapped. Consumption in Cold War Eastern Europe*, ed. Mary Neuburger and Paulina Bren, 140–163. Oxford: Oxford University Press.

Hoskins, Janet. 2013. *Biographical Objects: How Things Tell the Stories of People's Lives*. London: Routledge.

Iliev, Iliya. 2001. Familie, Ideologie und Politik: Die Grossmutter in der stadtischen Familie nach 1945. In *Vom Nutzen der Verwandten. Soziale Netzwerke in Bulgarien 19 und 20 Jahrhundert*, ed. Ulf Brunnbauer and Karl Kaser, 89–114. Wien: Bohlau Verlag.

Koleva, Daniela, ed. 2017. *Negotiating Normality: Everyday Lives in Socialist Institutions (Memory and Narrative)*. New York: Routledge.

Konstantinov, Juljan. 2001. Nahrung vom Dorf, Beziehungen durch die Stadt: Über den gegenwärtigen Charakter des bulgarischen Land-Stadt-Haushalts. In *Vom Nutzen der Verwandten. Soziale Netzwerke in Bulgarien (19 und 20 Jahrhundert)*, ed. Ulf Brunnbauer and Karl Kaser, 43–68. Wien: Bohlau Verlag.

Kopitoff, Igor. 1986. The Cultural Biography of Things: Commoditization as Process. In *The Social Life of Things. Commodities in Cultural Perspective*, ed. Arjun Appadurai, 64–91. Cambridge: Cambridge University Press.

Kornai, Janos. 1980. *Economics of Shortage*. Amsterdam, New York, Oxford: North-Holland Publishing Company.

Krasteva-Blagoeva, Evgenia. 2003. Obrazi na bulgarkata v epohata na sotsialisma [Images of Bulgarian Woman in Socialism]. In *Sotsialismut: realnost i iluzii. Etnologichni aspekti na vsekidnevnata kultura [Socialism: Reality and Illusions. Ethnological Aspects of Everyday Culture]*, 182–190. Sofia: Ethnological Institute of Bulgarian Academy of Sciences.

———. 2005. Country House Ownership: A Rural-Urban Phenomenon in Bulgaria. *Ethnologia Balkanica* 9: 169–184.

Krăsteva-Blagoeva, Evgenija. 2015. Clothing and Fashion in a Time of Crisis. The Case of Kărdžali. *Ethnologia Balkanica* 18: 227–249.

McCracken, Grant. 1988. *Culture and Consumption: New Approaches to the Symbolic Character of Consumer Goods and Activities*. Bloomington: Indiana University Press.

Merkel, Ina. 1998. Consumer Culture in the GDR, or How the Struggle for Antimodernity was Lost on the Battleground of Consumer Culture. In *Getting and Spending: European and American Consumer Societies in the 20th Century*, ed. Susan Strasser, Charles McGovern, and Matthias Judt, 281–299. Cambridge: Cambridge University Press.

Ravasi, Davide, & Lindova, Violina. (May 2004). Creating Symbolic Value: A Cultural Perspective on Production and Exchange. *SDA Bocconi*, Milan, Case No. 111/04. Electronic copy retrieved from http://ssrn.com/abstract=1265021

Raichev, Andrej. (2003). Vtorata mrezha [The Second Net]. Newspaper "Sega"—19.07, 26.07 and 02.08 2003.

Reid, Susan. 2002, Summer. Cold War in the Kitchen: Gender and the De-stalinization of Consumer Taste in the Soviet Union Under Khrushchev. *Slavic Review* 61 (2): 211–252.

Robertson, Roland. 1995. Glocalisation: Time-Space and Homogeneity-Heterogeneity. In *Global Modernities*, ed. Mike Featherstone, Scott Lash, and Roland Robertson, 25–44. London: Sage.
Roth, Klaus. 2000. Managing Everyday Life in a Village in Socialist Bulgaria: Practices and Strategies. In *Bulgaria. Social and Cultural Landscapes*, ed. Christian Giordano, Dobrinka Kostova, and Evelyn Lohmann-Minka, 179–194. Fribourg: University Press Fribourg.
Shkodrova, Albena. 2014. *Sotz gurme. Kurioznata istoria na kuhniata na NRB [Socialist Gourmet—the Curious History of the Cuisine of National Republic of Bulgaria]*. Plovdiv: Zhanet 45.
Simmel, Georg. 1978. *The Philosophy of Money*. London: Routledge and Kegan Paul Ltd..
Slater, Don. 1997. *Consumer Culture and Modernity*. Cambridge: Polity Press.
Smolett, Elinor. 1989. The Economy of Jars: Kindred Relationships in Bulgaria—An Exploration. *Ethnologia Europea (Journal of European Anthropology)* 19 (2): 125–140.
Urry, John. 2004. The "System of Automobility". *Theory, Culture and Society* 21 (4–5): 25–39 London: Sage.
Veblen, Thorstein. 1899. *The Theory of the Leisure Class. An Economic Study of Institutions*. London: Macmillan Publishers.
Velinova, Iskra. 2004. Za potrebnostite, potreblenieto i konsumatsijata pri sotsializma [On Needs and Consumption During Socialism]. In *Anthropologichni Izsledvanija [Anthropological Studies]*, vol. V, 71–81. Sofia: New Bulgarian University Press.
Verdery, Katherine. 1996. *What Was Socialism and What Comes Next?* Princeton: Princeton University Press.
Willis, Paul. 2014. *Profane Culture*. Princeton: Princeton University Press.
Yung, Yuson. 2009. From Caned Food to Canny Consumers. Cultural Competence in the Age of Mechanical Production. In *Food and Everyday Life in the Post-socialist World*, ed. Melissa Caldwell, 29–57. Bloomington: Indiana University Press.

Consumer Culture from Socialist Yugoslavia to Post-socialist Serbia: Movements and Moments

Ildiko Erdei

Widespread narratives on consumption mostly connect it with capitalism and (Western) modernity. That is the main reason why most of the scholarly and popular writings on consumer culture and consumption practices after the fall of the Berlin Wall and in the context of post-socialist transformation tend to paint the process as a *discovery*, wherein former *socialist subjects* learn how to consume in new, Western, individualistic, materialistic, and hedonistic ways.[1] The German film "Goodbye, Lenin" represents a suggestive visualization of this discourse. In its plot, the main character's mother experiences a stroke as the Berlin Wall is torn down and falls into a coma. During the following few months she spends in the coma, Eastern Germany goes through paramount changes, and she wakes up in a country that has in the meantime changed dramatically. We see how visible signs of capitalism penetrate ordinary life on a daily basis: Coca-Cola banner stands on a nearby high-rise building, family apartment goes through refurbishing, and Ikea furniture arrives in Eastern Berlin with the "Wessies" who relocate. Supermarket shelves are full of new products, resembling the capitalist vision of plenty. Nevertheless, doctors suggest that her fragile heart can't bear any strong excitement, so the family decides to simulate the ordinary life of socialism, with all the minutiae of everyday things, objects, habits, rituals … in order to keep her undisturbed and—alive. In other words, the family tries to soften the effect of the presumed overwhelming change and her exposure to it. I believe that this narrative about the change of consumer culture—from socialism to post-socialism—as a cultural shock is exaggerated, and that it is probably used to strengthen the drama of the profound social change the

[1] It seems that the trope of the "discovery" tended to paint the experience of consumption for "post-socialist subjects" at the same time when, according to Don Slater, the latest "discovery" of consumption as the object of research in humanities and social sciences occurred (Slater 1997).

I. Erdei (✉)
Department of Ethnology and Anthropology, School of Philosophy, Belgrade University, Beograd, Serbia
e-mail: ierdei@f.bg.ac.rs

E. Krasteva-Blagoeva (ed.), *Approaching Consumer Culture*, International Series on Consumer Science, https://doi.org/10.1007/978-3-030-00226-8_3

movie presents. Furthermore, existing literature on consumption and consumer culture in socialism and post-socialism enables us to go for more subtle explanations and understandings that reveal a picture of interweaving continuities and discontinuities in the development of consumer culture (or its rise in some times, and decline in others) in a longer term, more than radical "offs" and "ons" as the above-mentioned narrative suggests.[2] Therefore, it is necessary for any understanding of the consumer culture of post-socialism to offer at least a brief description of "what was before," an outline of consuming culture in socialist times. Even more so, recently it has been suggested that some institutions and structures of the socialist order were, during the last period of socialism, used for articulation of discourses and practices that were alternative to the official ideology, and some of them in opposition to it. In that way light was shed on the processes of continuity between social currents in socialism and "what came next."[3] It is my intention in this chapter to present the continuities and discontinuities in development of consumer culture in socialist Yugoslavia in a longer time frame, from its beginnings in mid-1950s up to today.[4] I will trace the most important movements and decisive moments affecting the changes and transformations of consumer culture in post-socialist period, arguing that consumer culture should be understood as a process, whose current manifestations always develop in longer time frames, and are embedded in local historical, political, social, economic, and cultural contexts.

[2] Writings on consumption in socialism including former Yugoslavia abound after 2000. See Katherine Verdery 1996; Crowley, Reid (eds.) 2000; Reid 2002; Bartlett 2010; Crowley and Reid 2010. For the Yugoslav context: Marković 1996, Marković 2007; Švab 2002; Patterson 2003, Patterson 2011; Duda 2006, Duda 2010; Erdei 2006, Erdei 2012; Luthar 2006; Velimirović 2008; Grandits (ed.) 2010; Vučetić 2012; Malešević 2012; Dimitrijević 2016.

[3] For this, see particularly Yurchak 2006.

[4] For the reader unfamiliar with the particularities of historical context of socialist Yugoslavia, it has to be pointed that the historical path of Yugoslavia differed from the rest of the Eastern European countries. It was due to the fact that its leader and president Josip Broz Tito parted with Stalin in 1948, establishing closer relations with the West. In the decades that followed, Tito further developed a specific branch of Yugoslav socialism, which was considered "softer" than its "Soviet" counterpart. It resulted in improved standard of life, relative openness toward Western influences, consumer items and lifestyles, increased mobility and travelling abroad, and—in general—more liberal social and cultural atmosphere compared with other countries behind the "Iron Curtain." Yugoslav branch of socialism was renowned for its specific political and social features. Policies of self-government were introduced in economy and nonalignment politics has led to the establishment of the Non-Alignment Movement during the 1950s. The founding Conference was held in Belgrade in 1961, in which Yugoslavia played a prominent role. The Non-Alignment Movement aimed to gather the newly independent countries of the third world, advocating a middle course for states in the developing world, trying to avoid the antagonisms and imperialistic legacies of both Western and Eastern Blocks during the Cold War. Therefore, Yugoslavia was often depicted and represented, both in academic and popular discourses, as a country that is "between" East and West, in many respects. This "in-betweenness" is considered to be an older historical legacy, but it has also found its materializations and cultural representations in the period of socialist rule. In regard to consumerism, consumer culture and practices of consumption, this gave way to the notions as "market socialism," "Coca-Cola socialism," and "Yugoslav Dream," which served to describe this peculiar historical experience.

From Scratch: Affirming Consumption in Socialist Yugoslavia

The beginnings of establishment of consumer culture in socialist Yugoslavia can be traced back to about the same time after Stalin's death in 1953 which came to affect other Eastern and Central European socialist states (cf. Crowley and Reid 2000). In 1955, Yugoslav authorities and the President Josip Broz Tito himself made a decision about the reorientation of the state economy, from its former emphasis on heavy industry toward production of consumption goods. The aim of this political and economic shift was to make the life of socialist citizens easier and more appealing, and to bring the promised "better future" closer to everyday life. With the economic reform in 1965, a tight planned economy was abandoned in favor of looser economic structuring, and elements of market economy were introduced as the so-called standard of living policy was proclaimed to be a new political and social goal, which undoubtedly helped foster development of consumer culture. Different sources indicate that the period between 1955 and 1965 could be described as a time of "economic miracle," with an unprecedented rise of about 10% in GDP and annual earnings (Duda 2006; Čalić 2013). Since the end of the 1960s all the "ingredients" important for the existence of consumer culture were present: intensive modernization of society (urbanization, industrialization, social emancipation projects on a mass scale, including public education, women entering the workforce, and the subsequent forming of new family relations) and rise in production of consumption goods, together with purchasing power, resulting in the rising standard of living of the population. In two decades between 1952 and 1972, Yugoslav society adopted many institutions and features of Western consumerism: advertising, consumer credits, fashion and entertainment magazines and popular media, cult of celebrities, and culture of leisure. When the 42-h workweek was introduced in 1965, the institution of the weekend was gradually established, and the extension of annual leave—considered as a right and not a privilege—further stimulated development of tourism, as a specific venue for consumption. Nevertheless, all of these remained strongly anchored in the dominant frame of socialist values and norms—hard work, earnestness, care for others and for society, and modest materialism, as parts of socialist modernity they were expected to reproduce.

During the 1970s, consumer culture was still developing and diversifying. That was due to the rising purchasing power, shopping expeditions to nearby Western cities known as "commercial meccas" for Yugoslav consumers—Trieste above all, but also Graz and Vienna for those living in Croatia and Slovenia—and novel consumer items brought in by guest workers from their "temporary" workplaces: Germany, Austria, Italy, Sweden, and Switzerland.[5] Duda calculated that the peak of the rising living stan-

[5] On shopping tourism, and particularly shopping excursions to Trieste, more in Velimirović 2008; Švab 2002; Luthar 2006. On the role of the guest workers, "*gastarbajteri*" (from German "Gastarbeiter") for inflows of cash into Yugoslav economy and for introducing novel consumer items and consumer habits into society, Marković 2007; Duda 2010; Patterson 2011; Dimitrijević 2016, Bratić and Malešević 1982; Kovačević 1985.

dard and the Yugoslav "good life" was in 1979, when the salaries and the purchasing power combined reached their highest point since the end of WWII. The 1970s were a time when Yugoslavs further refined their consumer skills and deepened knowledge of the processes of social and cultural differentiation that lie at the root of consumption as a technique of modernity. Consumption was recognized to lead to production of different lifestyles, although in the 1970s it still operated as a cultural weapon in the hands of the socialist middle class, reflecting both its relative prosperity and a distinctive aesthetics of (socialist) modesty, contrasted with the supposed capitalist opulence. The average middle-class apartment was entirely furnished and decorated with products of Yugoslav industry, from furniture to home appliances. Famous was furniture from "Meblo," "Sloveniales," "Simpo," stoves and refrigerators from "Gorenje," "Rade Koncar," "Milan Blagojevic," "Obodin," TV sets from "EI Nis," "RIZ," "Rudi Cajavec," or "Iskra" phones, all of which contributed to the aesthetic homogenization of Yugoslav middle-class tastes and made their homes look rather similar to each other (Dajić 2014). Subtle differences in incomes and tastes could be noticed through the choice of drinks in home bars (domestic, maybe even homemade plum brandy vs. imported whiskey or gin), technological properties or brands of TV sets and other home appliances, presence or absence of a home library and its contents, and quality of art and decorations on the walls and shelves (cf. Erdei 2015: 110–12). Apart from the "home front," consumer culture had been burgeoning in the field of fashion and celebrity. New, Yugoslav fashion had been established, and Aleksandar Joksimović, "Yugoslav Dior," who was the official stylist of the Yugoslav first lady Jovanka Broz, became one of its heroes (Velimirović 2008). Magazines and TV helped launch the carriers of many actors and media personalities who quickly rose to the status of national celebrities, and from that point on they were led to lend their popularity to an array of Yugoslav _industrial products, using their fame and glamour to advertise not only consumer goods, but also a new way of life in socialist Yugoslavia and "the Yugoslav dream" itself. In the 1970s and the 1980s, common Yugoslav market facilitated the creation of an imagined community of Yugoslav consumers, connected through consumption of iconic Yugoslav products, belonging mainly to the area of consumption at home (food and candies, hygiene and cosmetic items, home appliances, TV shows), but also to a growing repertoire of pop-cultural forms, such as movies, music bands, concerts, youth press .... At the same time, Western goods were available on the market, and were also acquired by travelling abroad, on shopping expeditions to Italy (Trieste) and Austria, and through guest workers' cultural import of the items of material culture of Western modernity (see: Antonijević 2013: 203–205). Influence of the American style of consumption and allure of particular consumption items that held iconic status, such as blue jeans, nylon stockings, chewing gums, Coca-Cola, jazz records, cartoons, and movies, was at its most intensive during the 1950s and the 1960s (Vučetić 2012). Eastern European consuming goods were also on offer, like the famous rose perfumes from Bulgaria, Winter Salami and animated TV series "Gustav" from Hungary, camping appliances and animated TV series "Lolek and Bolek" from Poland, Czech and Eastern German cars ("Skoda" and "Wartburg"), and great works of art, like films by Andrzej Wajda, Jiří Menzel, or *Péter Bacsó*, and literature by Czesław Miłosz, *Sławomir Mrożek*, Bohumil Hrabal, Milan Kundera, or *Václav Havel* (to mention but a few). Thus, tastes and sensibilities of Yugoslavs were built around not only consumption of "made in YU," domestically produced goods, but also consumables from Western Europe and the USA, exemplifying Western capitalist modernity, and from Eastern and Central Europe, following an older stream of cultural influences that preceded socialism and Cold War antagonisms. Adding goods and commodities originating from non-European, non-Western parts of the world, which were present in Yugoslavia due to its membership and economic ties with countries belonging to the Non-Aligned Movement in Asia, Africa, and Latin America a picture of openness and rather cosmopolitan consumer tastes available to Yugoslavs in socialist times appears.[6]

"One Step Forward, Two Steps Backwards": Continuities and Discontinuities

At the same time, the notion of a consumer society was used in public discourse both to describe and explain the changes Yugoslav society was going through, and to engage in critical debates about the nature of these changes. Critical examinations of the concept of consumer society and its practices were performed within official state and party structures (Patterson 2011: 197–224; Dimitrijević 2016: 61–64). At the same time, intellectuals raised their voices echoing the post-1968 anti-materialism discourse of the Western political left (critical accounts of the superficiality of consumer society and the inauthenticity of mass culture originating from the West).[7]

The decade after the death of state and party leader Josip Broz Tito in 1980 was marked by the economic decline and return of shortages and rationed provision that was not seen in Yugoslavia since the mid-1950s. It was a period in which, as Čalić suggests, the contradictions of modernity in crisis came into full visibility, in Yugoslavia as well as in Western Europe (Čalić 2013: 364–366) which contributed to more intensive social diversification and rise of social inequality. That means that shortages and restrictions in the provisioning of basic goods, such as flour, sugar, coffee, and washing powder, along with blackouts and limited usage of cars within so-called even-odd ("par-nepar") system (in which individuals were allowed to use their cars every other

[6] Here I primarily mean a potential for developing "vernacular cosmopolitanism" in a sense that Mica Nava 1998 and 2000 suggests for nineteenth-century England. Whether it was really achieved or not is open to debate, and Ivana Spasić already warned us not to go too far with this assumption, Spasić 2007: 51–70.

[7] See, for example, a critical review of a popular TV series "Theatre at Home" ("Pozorište u kući") from the beginning of the 1970s. This series was the long-lasting TV series in Yugoslavia (aired through five seasons, from 1972 to 1985), and was characterized at the beginning as a routinely, "industrially" produced (and thus "inauthentic") and contrasted to older popular TV shows, which were described as "authentic." In words of an influential critic, while former TV shows have engaged in serious social critique and therefore grasped the "real life," "Theatre at home," with its "superficial humor," missed that opportunity: "A quality show program should put forth important social commentary, valuable ethical concepts, generalizations about human destiny that will be of significance," in Igor Mandić, "Obitelj je šou," Vjesnik, 20.4.1974. (cf. Erdei 2017 (in print).

day, depending whether their license plate ended in an even or odd number), went together with visible signs of further development of consumer society, contributing to more intensive social diversification and the rise of social inequality. It was hard to get coffee, "real" chocolates, or washing powder in the market until the mid-1980s, but at the same time children could enjoy eating "kinder eggs" and playing with miniature toys found inside. They could also taste what was considered to be the epitome of American fast food, "Big Mac" burgers from McDonald's, when this food chain opened in Belgrade in 1988, being the first of its kind in Eastern Europe.

When Yugoslavia disintegrated in the 1990s five independent national states emerged with their own nationalized consumer markets. Nationalization of markets belonging to particular Yugoslav republics was evident toward the end of the 1980s, when the first economic boycott was performed in Serbia related to consumer goods and services from Slovenia, due to political disagreements between the republics (cf. Erdei 2006, 2007). Further decline of consumer culture as it developed in the socialist period was followed by a radical adaptation to the new political and social context in 1992, when the International Community introduced economic sanctions against Federal Republic of Yugoslavia (FRY, consisting of Serbia and Montenegro) for its involvement in the war in Bosnia. Therefore consumer culture in Serbia in the immediate aftermath of the disintegration of Yugoslavia fell back into the mode of operation from the early post-WWII years. And while the rest of the former Eastern Block was turning its back to the constraints and limited supply of planned economies, consumers in Serbia and Montenegro revisited the experiences of rationed provisioning, queuing, extreme scarcity of basic items, blackouts, and poor central heating, which fostered revival of almost forgotten consumer skills needed for survival. Along with queuing for basic items such as bread and milk, people started to buy whatever was offered, whether they needed it or not, and hoarding of items developed as a practice. Different strategies of acquiring scarce goods were activated, ranging from "amateur" market analyses to information obtained through informal networks and connections and bribing the salesman to put the desired goods "under the counter" for someone. Tactical skills, such as hanging around shops around delivery times and always carrying elastic or plastic bags in case something hard to obtain pops up, were also sharpened during this decade, particularly among the older generation which already experienced post-WWII scarcity.

As much as the 1990s could be seen as a great step backwards and a discontinuity with consumer experiences, consumer practices, and consumer culture from previous decades, it was during that time that the foundations of important social and economic currents that would continue, evolve, and fully develop after 2000 were laid. Here, three features of the changing consumer culture in post-socialism are outlined, from the 1990s to the present day: profound transformation of society, from one with strong collectivist culture and ethos of social solidarity to a global "society of individuals"; changing attitudes toward materiality, materialism, and money as the objectification of value; and atomization of previously common market and imaginary community of consumers. The following periods are taken into account to mark the most important moments of the transformation: 1992/1993 (period of hyperinflation), 2000 (moment of the change of regime and stronger orientation toward the West), 2008 (when the world economic crisis started), and 2012 (after which strong neoliberal policies in economy and society were pushed further), and their respective influences on the transformations of consumer culture are shown.

Changing Society

Major sociologists who have studied the 1990s agree that during this decade society had been thoroughly "destroyed" (Popović et al. 1991; Bolčić 1994, 1995; Lazić 1994; Prošić-Dvornić 1994). Values and norms of the socialist period were eradicated, nationalism was enthroned as the new ideology, wars waged but never officially declared militarized the culture, and economic sanctions imposed by the International Community for involvement of the FRY in the war in Bosnia devastated the formal economy, led to hyperinflation, and made informal economy, with its muddy schemes and illegal activities, to flourish. It seemed that the whole system was turned upside down: majority of hardworking, common people lost their ground and were disoriented within the vanishing order, while the minority quickly adapted to the chaotic situation, grabbing the opportunity and making enormous profits, giving way to social stratification according to new criteria of resourcefulness, moral indifference, and financial success.[8] It was the nucleus of the future dividing of consumption modes into different registers, which would develop in the following years: a small section of luxury consumption, reserved for the "new rich," a slightly wider section of the consolidating middle class whose tastes are built around middle-range branded products, and the majority of the population that barely make ends meet and whose consumer choices are mostly influenced by the affordable prices of the consumables. The society that was broken in the 1990s was never pulled together in the same way people knew it, not even after the so-called democratic turn in 2000. In the following period, differently designated as "unblocked transition" (Mladen Lazić), or "second transition" (Ivan Kovačević), Serbia entered the global world and global economy that had, too, profoundly changed during the 1990s. "The society of individuals" (Norbert Elias) in its neoliberal form put the figure of self-centered *sovereign consumer*, exercising freedom of choice, at the heart of the new order (Elias 1987; Giddens 1991). The role of state in regulation of economic and social life was minimized, including its former palliative actions in cases of social crisis and loss, and principles of social justice and solidarity became issues of second interest, replaced with social competitiveness and the idea of individual success. The consumer culture Serbia was facing after 2000 was significantly different than the consumer culture that had developed in socialist Yugoslavia during 1960s and 1970s, in the same way in which the figure of the consumer has changed from *modest* in socialist modernity to *sovereign* in late capitalist modernity. As Bauman puts it, speaking about contemporary consumerism:

[8] For the majority of people socialized in the previous system that was confusing and hard to cope with. By the majority, society was seen as a generator of insecurity, fear, and uncertainty, contrary to its presumed role to bring the sense of order, predictability, and safety to its subjects. Renowned sociologist Silvano Bolčić wrote in 1994, in the midst of the "transitional times," in an article that sounded as a personal lament as well as a sociological comment, that "withdrawing from the society" (in the meaning of stepping back from the social situations and arrangements we found unacceptable, into private sphere, I.E.) was one of the possible ways to handle the situation. "People have to disengage with the society in order to exist" (Bolčić 1994: 142).

"What sets the members of consumer society apart from their ancestors is the emancipation of consumption from its past instrumentality that used to draw its limits—the demise of 'norms' and the new plasticity of 'needs', setting consumption free from functional bonds and absolving it from the need to justify itself by reference to anything but its own pleasurability. In the consumer society, consumption is its own purpose and so is self-propelling" (Bauman 2001: 12–13).

Therefore Serbia, after stepping out of the period of "blocked transition," entered into fully developed global consumer society, obsessed with "consumerist syndrome," which"implies more, much more than the fascination with the pleasures of ingesting and digesting, with pleasurable sensations and 'having a good time'. It is truly a 'syndrome', a variegated bunch of attitudes and strategies, cognitive dispositions, value judgments and prejudgments, explicit and tacit assumptions of the ways of the world and the ways of walking them, visions of happiness and ways to pursue them" (Royek 2004: 293).

Consumer culture in the post-2000 Serbia was shaped by transformative powers of the elements of the so-called transitional package (Chriss Hann), whose economic elements included liberation of market and privatizations of former state-owned enterprises. Proliferation of commercial activities resulted in changing geographies of consumption, particularly in capital cities. As in other Eastern and Central European states, public spaces were more increasingly used for promotion of private interests through marketing campaigns and their advertising images and slogans that saturated cityscapes. Supermarket chains and shopping malls modeled after their American counterparts, built in the hearts and on the peripheries of cities, involved consumers into a new kind of consumer behavior and experience. Malls soon became a favorite place for spending free time, apart from actual purchases: people were visiting cafés and restaurants in malls, went to the cinema and computer game parlors, and even came just for a walk in the cool space of the mall during the unbearably hot summers. Due to the fact that consumption was popularly understood as a natural expression of "freedom of choice," people were drawn to it. This was used by the political elite that promoted consumer choices as shortcuts to democracy, personal freedom, and success.[9] In many cases the openings of new supermarket chains or shopping malls at the beginning of the 2000s were framed as important social events, caught the public eye, and were attended by politicians and prominent public figures. It was clear that these openings brought into play something more than only marking the beginning of a commercial enterprise, and that other meanings must have been at stake, beyond strictly economic. The character of consumption was often frantic. When the Slovenian supermarket chain "Merkator" opened its first postwar commercial establishment in Serbia, Belgrade, in 2002, that commercial event triggered a variety of hidden (and suppressed) emotions, needs, and desires that were part of complex relations between Serbia and Slovenia, which

[9]While in socialism the state had a decisive role in the production of discourses on happiness, in the world of (neoliberal) capitalism it is the individual who is held responsible for his/her own personal happiness, and the pursuit of happiness is directly connected with the world of consumable objects, goods, and services cf. Erdei 2004, 2006, 2012.

both parties had to reconfigure in the post-Yugoslav context. "Merkator" was eagerly awaited, the hypermarket was overcrowded at the opening, and in the following days it recorded the highest commercial turn of all the "Merkator's" operations.[10] It was like Belgrade consumers were caught by *Merkator fever*,[11] in the similar way as *Intersparmania* was shaking Slovenia, transforming commercial places into spectacular spaces for social imagination and for staging of "particular forms of public dramas of late modernity" (Luthar 1998: 126).[12]

Although it is tempting to interpret such an intensive relation toward consumption in terms of postmodern "liberation" paradigm (individualization, self-expression, self-identity, lifestyling), and although there surely could have been those impulses included as well, there were some reasons for this craving for consumer possibilities in the early 2000s that had to do with collective identification. As it was already stated in several writings on post-Yugoslav societies, there was a strong desire to reclaim the sense of "normalcy," the idea and practice of "normal life," the way it was before the Yugoslav wars (Jansen 2014, 2015; on the notion of "yearning for normal life" in scholarship on Bosnia and Herzegovina, see Jansen et al. (2017): 13). In the same vein, "yearning for normalcy" could be said to echo, in greater or lesser degree, in various consuming practices, from purchasing in Belgrade "Merkator" hypermarket (sign of quality in former Yugoslavia, and symbol of pre-war common market) to educated urban youth in Novi Sad mimicking "Western" consumer styles in order to situate themselves "above" the social milieu that is not changing at the desired pace, and to sustain the sense of themselves as being "cosmopolitan" (Simić 2017) and to awaiting for IKEA, interpreted as bearer of lifestyle that will transcend extremes of relative poverty and excessive wealth, and be in tune with "normal order of things" as people remember it (Erdei 2012, 2014).

However, one of the paradigmatic impressions of the changing consumer culture in post-socialist transformation was the inscription *akcija* (action, in English) written in bold red capital letters, mushrooming on the posters and banners throughout shopping areas, mostly in supermarkets. The word indicates lowering of prices, and is similar to the term "sales," but the former is loaded with more potent meaning that calls for immediate action (purchase), and relates mostly to special offers.[13] It is interesting how the ascending commercial culture has absorbed and transformed the meaning of the term "action," which was connected with the field of production, hardworking efforts, and particular institution of voluntary youth work ("omladinska radna akcija") in socialism. Recently, the notion of "action" has served to unlock

---

[10] http://www.vreme.com/cms/view.php?id=329914 (accessed 24.7.2017).

[11] See more on this in Erdei 2007.

[12] Although consumers in Belgrade (and in the rest of Serbia) were also led by desire to retain "normality" in the arena of consumption practices, after the decade in which they were deprived of all the consumer places, objects, and activities they were previously used to.

[13] There was an institution of seasonal sales in socialism, though they were never on such scale as in capitalist markets, but in this case the new term was invented to indicate the new nature of the consumption process ("rasprodaje", meaning "sales", was replaced with "action", which was sometimes dramatically underlined with an exclamation mark, "Akcija!").

the entirely new domain of inciting consumers through advanced sales techniques (weekend actions, seasonal actions) and persuasive discourse of favorable purchase ("super opportunity," "three for two," "best buy," "final sale"), which could connect, as Miller shows, with cultural valuation of thrift (Miller 1998). Paradoxically, it simultaneously reveals the opening of a world of possibilities and a vision of plenty, which stand at the core of neoliberal consumer culture, and the low purchasing power of the majority of population, who are mostly interested in chasing "special offers," "discounts," "seasonal sales," and altogether operate within still dominant low registers of consumption. Today this discrepancy is the source of a significant disillusionment with the fruits of liberal capitalism in Central and Eastern Europe, including Serbia.

The period of economic relief was short-lived and was soon interrupted by the global economic crisis in 2008. This brief interlude was insufficient for significant consolidation of the middle class, impoverished, and disempowered during the 1990s, which is a paradigm of modern consumption and traditional base of modern consumer culture. Thrifty consumption again overcame lifestyle consumption, and the two categories of consumers, widely recognized as *transitional losers and winners*, took up entrenched positions. While the former drew back to fulfilling their basic needs and making ends meet, the latter were gradually developing conspicuous lifestyles around consumption of luxury goods and services. Social stratification and social differences became evermore pronounced and visible. According to data from the Statistical Office of the Republic of Serbia from October 2016, the average household in Serbia consists of three members, and its monthly expenditures exceed the average salary of 14,000 dinars,[14] and more than one-third of the family budget is spent on food.[15] At the same time, the most expensive cars at the Belgrade Car Fair 2017, several hundred thousands of Euros worth, were the most sought after, and luxury yachts priced as much as 30,000 Euros "were being sold like hotcakes."[16] This situation, in which further solidification of middle class was interrupted, and the two extremely polarized consumption registers were stabilized instead, could be compared (albeit within much less differentiated community of consumers) to two other moments in the history of Yugoslav economy and consumption: at the end of the 1960s and then at the beginning of the 1980s, due to declining foreign aid and international loans, the economic growth slowed down and with it the purchasing power and standard of living decreased. Therefore, we could argue that continuity in the development of consumer culture has existed from the 1950s to the present. Nevertheless, the continuing strengthening and diversifying of consumer society were obstructed every few decades (in almost regular 20-year cycles, closely related to the political situation) with significant fallbacks to what were almost economies of survival, particularly outside urban areas.

---

[14] http://www.blic.rs/vesti/ekonomija/nesklad-plata-i-troskova-fali-nam-100-evra-mesecno-da-bismo-preziveli/lp5573g (accessed 17.4.2017).

[15] http://www.politika.rs/sr/clanak/352862/Za-hranu-dva-evra-dnevno (accessed 17.4.2017).

[16] http://www.alo.rs/jahte-od-30-000-evra-prodaju-se-kao-alva/98859 (accessed 17.4.2017).

Changing Attitudes Toward Materiality, Materialism, and Money

Consumer practices and experiences in the 1990s were decisively shaped by two events: hyperinflation at the beginning of the decade (1992/93) and two rounds of economic sanctions (1992–1997 and 1998–2000). Hyperinflation had extremely dramatized the economic context of consumption. Money had been devaluing on daily or even hourly basis toward the end of the period. "Inflation in FR Yugoslavia reached the point of 19,810.2%. National Bank of FRY issued the 500 billion dinar banknote with the portrait of national poet Jovan Jovanović Zmaj at the end of 1993, when inflation reached its peak. Prices were doubling every 16 h. German mark became the unofficial currency. Some salaries went down as low as two German marks. The price of a pack of cigarettes would be one billion dinars in the morning, and by the afternoon it doubled. Statisticians recorded that a simple envelope in December 1993 sold for 3.5 billion dinars. Shops were empty, for a jar of pickled cucumbers one would pay 2.100, while 2 L of milk or 200 g of mustard were sold for as much as 500 billion dinars worth."[17] In bars, prices rose even between ordering a round and paying for it. Black market flourished for all sorts of goods, including exchange of devaluing dinars into "solid" currency—German marks. Money dealers were operating on the street corners and along open markets, where deficit items could be bought as well. Their way of discretely differentiating themselves from the ordinary passersby was by making a characteristic sound "dvze, dvze, dvze …" (shortening of the Serbian term "devize," used for foreign currency in general) through their teeth (cf. Ljuboja 1994). There were dealers who specialized in selling gasoline, which was in short supply and was also sold at open markets in small quantities packed into plastic bottles. It was a fertile ground for Ponzi schemes, organized by new "bankers" Dafina Milanović and Jezdimir Vasiljević, to pump out the remaining cash from desperate and gullible citizens. As newcomers to the world of financial operations, they were ignorant of financial calculations and unaware of possible frauds, and thus many were caught short after the schemes suddenly disappeared. There was no doubt that these financial schemes were tolerated by the state because they were partly used to finance the war and soften the consequences of the economic crisis, but, as Verdery (1996) has shown for Romania, they simultaneously lend themselves to an unintended consequence: discovery of the new importance and meanings of money. The new understanding of the value of money was achieved through learning the terms of participation in financial operations, such as taking risks with money investments, calculating interests, and developing specific relation toward the growing amount of cash that sometimes resulted from them. That gave a new boost to materialistic orientation, which was not unknown during socialism but had been driven either by scarcity of goods or by their relative availability, and tamed by socialist virtues of humanism, anti-materialism, and

[17] http://www.kapitalmagazin.rs/hiperinflacija-u-jugoslaviji-1992-1994/ (17.4.2017).

modesty (cf. Berdahl 1999, in Simić 2017, manuscript). On the other hand, discovery of the new aspects of dealing with money and the role it played in social differentiation has served as an embryo of the neoliberal economic agenda, as a "political project to re-establish the conditions for capital accumulation and to restore the power of economic elites" (Harvey 2005: 19). Basic postulates of neoliberal economy were embraced through reception of the so-called transitional package immediately after 2000, but they were fully embraced by the political elite only in the late 2000s. During the 1990s, foundations were laid for a stratification within consumer culture, which was once more homogeneous. Two registers of consumption were clearly differentiated: *a mode of survival*, based on scarce resources, making ends meet, sharing and relying on the network of kin or friend support, buying low-quality items in downgraded places of consumption (open markets, car boot sales, cardboard sales on the streets …), and *conspicuous consumption*, practiced by social climbers, whose new wealth was gained through profiteering on illegal activities related to sanctions and the war, and who needed to put their new social statuses on display. Between those two mostly exposed positions, there was also a space for individuals and certain sections and portions of society (parts of middle class still holding jobs in public sector, young professionals, beginners in new professions, students, all of them self-consciously claiming to have more cultural than economic capital) who tried to escape both registers of consumption described above. Today, they seek to distance themselves both from the perceived "taste of necessity" connected with the crisis and socioeconomic devastation of the 1990s, and from the "vulgar" tastes of the nouveau riche, and make efforts to situate themselves into a position they imagine they should occupy, and which is closest to the middle-class relation to consumption that stresses individuality, originality, creativity, measure, style, and—very importantly—ethics and aesthetics (cf. Simić this volume; Erdei 2014).

Changes in the Imaginary Community of Consumers

Until the end of the 1980s, the imaginary community of Yugoslav consumers was built on the common Yugoslav market and its various products, which during the 1970s and the 1980s counted more for the creation of the feeling of belonging to the country than official ideology of "brotherhood and unity" did. That was particularly apparent among the generation of children growing up after Tito's death, whose childhood was influenced more by the growing offer of consumer items for children (sweets, toys, magazines, movies, literature, music, popular culture) than with the ideological role of the pioneer (cf. Erdei 2006, 2012). During the 1990s, former Yugoslav market had gone through nationalization and finally dissolved into several closed-off and mutually antagonized economies. In Serbia, the process of market nationalization started at the end of the 1980s, through the 1989 boycott of Slovenian goods, followed by the boycott of commodities from Slovenia during the 1990s and of McDonald's during the NATO bombing in 1999. Boycott campaign "Buy domestic, renew Serbia," initiated by the

Ministry of Trade, Tourism, and Services in 2004, was short-lived but nevertheless provided for the articulation of economic nationalism and economic patriotism that were notable discourses in the first decade of the twenty-first century in Serbia, but also in Croatia and Bosnia.[18]

The former imagined national community of consumers, created through the consumer boycotts from the end of the 1980s to today (boycott of Slovenian goods, 1988/1989, 2008; boycott of McDonald's, 1999) and positive campaigns, "bajkot" ("Kupujmo domaće," 2004), diversified itself throughout the past years to groups of smaller communities of consumption, which are becoming consumers of local and regional cultural differences, objectified in food and music festivals. This simultaneously signifies the altered path of economy, deindustrialization, and transformation of economy to an economy of services, in which local traditions, culture, entertainment, and tourism bind together in a new way, and in one unique package offer themselves to the emerging market of newly established (a posteriori) cultural diversity.[19] From the ethnological and anthropological point of view, the most interesting are the examples of food festivals throughout Serbia and music festivals initiated in a few smaller places in Vojvodina (2007–2009), which celebrate heroes of global pop culture, such as Rocky Balboa, Bob Marley, Johnny Weissmuller, Tupac Shakur, or Pamela Anderson. Ivan Kovačević (2007) coined the term "gastronomske tradicijade" to indicate the invented and constructed character of food festivals, which play with the notion of tradition both in its older—cultural—and newly discovered, market-valued capacities. Today there are around 50 officially registered "tradicijadas" in the Serbian festival calendar for the year 2017, and they are dedicated to pretty much every foodstuff you can imagine: cabbage, paprika and eggplant, bacon, sausage, prosciutto and cracklings, fruit brandies (rakija), wine and beer, strudel, and other cakes, but also specialty goodies such as "pihtije" (traditional kind of a jelly dish, made from pig's ears, tail, or legs) and "beli bubrezi" (pork testicles in garlic sauce). These food festivals gradually developed from local events to parts of a burgeoning field of manifestational tourism. Classified as economic-cultural festivals, they unite both the function of entertainment and the rudimentary tourist offerings and aspirations of local communities in that respect. In the municipality of Pančevo, city near Belgrade, every village boasts at least one of those festivals, the oldest being Slaninijada in Kačarevo, which first opened in 1987. The second example of "consumption festivals" is the small music festivals organized in a few towns and villages in Vojvodina, based on the "magical attraction" that icons of pop culture hold, which are supposed to attract audiences and bring to

---

[18] In the state-sponsored "buy domestic" campaigns, the notion of *domestic* relates to the national state whose borders delineate the community of producers and consumers. *Domestic* thus comprehends whatever is produced within national borders, and consumption that takes place within same territory. That notion of domestic prevailed in the first decade of 2000s, while later, in contrast with that, the notion of *domestic* was more closely related to local, small-scale, autochthonous, deindustrialized, sustainable modes of production and consumption, particularly in the area of food growing.

[19] For the notion of *a posteriory cultural diversity* and authenticity in a modern society, more in Miller 1995: 3. On cultural (re)production in capitalist economies, see Clifford 1988.

life the dormant economies of the small communities. In 2007 in Žitište, close to Zrenjanin, the young townsfolk erected a statue of Rocky Balboa, the movie hero. They found parallels between their marginal position in the overall economy of Serbia and the position of the aforementioned character, who ascends due to his own power and prowess, achieving victory over himself and his enemies, changing his fate. Conducting a sort of "rationalized magic," they used the global media attention that found their initiative "bizarre" enough to give them exclusive media coverage (indeed the largest media houses were reporting from the opening of the Rocky monument, such as CNN, BBC, New York Times, Washington Post, and numerous Internet sites worldwide) and managed to initiate a whole set of activities that kick-started the economy of the small place they live in—above all, a music festival, and then the smaller investments of foreign investors, Italians and Americans, who were neatly tied with the ethnic affiliations of Rocky himself (Erdei 2011).[20] Similar attempts were made in Banatski Sokolac, where the statue of Bob Marley was erected, and reggae music festival established, while in Medja, the small village where popular actor Johnny Weissmuller, best known for his role of Tarzan, was allegedly born, monumentalization was only debated. Toward the end of the 2000s, rumors said that actress Pamela Anderson and hip-hop artist Tupac Shakur would also be memorialized. Since the earlier production capacities on which small towns founded their economy and cultural identity declined during the 1990s and the beginning of the new millennia, the aforementioned festivals participated in changing their identities, and helped them find their place in the new economy and labor division (Erdei 2011).

The case of "Rocky made in Serbia" and also the mentioned cases of using pop culture heroes to attract attention and other resources from outside to the local community bring us to the characteristic of global economy which in Serbia came to prominence remarkably after 2012 when the new government took the strong course toward further neoliberalization of society. Ever since SPS (Serbian Progressive Party, originally SNS, Srpska napredna stranka) came to power, having secured the parliamentary majority, the government, and the president, the neoliberalization of the economy and society has been mainstreamed in the national politics. Tightening the belt, not spending, became the crucial word, and the decaying standard of life continued to drop. The elusive nature of financial capital and its speculative ways and results, together with its fetishization and reinvestment of the magic capacities in economic plans and activities, gained new visibility. This constitutes the context in which the neoliberal consumer society and capitalism of spectacle currently operate in many societies on the periphery and half-periphery of the world system. The new utopia is shaped through the dramatization and performativity of economy (cf. Comaroff and Comaroff 2001; Tsing 2005). It consists of large new modernization narratives, through stories of "economic wonders," "foreign investments," through mantras of "opening of new workplaces." The narrative of economy is structured through the mobilization myth, and the imagination of consumer possibilities represents its integral part. The story of "Belgrade Waterfront,"

[20] On the phenomenon of monumentalization of pop-cultural heroes in post-2000 Serbia and Western Balkan, more in Mijić 2009.

a grand government-promoted development project in the capital city, advertised as the "investment of the century" and the pledge of economic and social development of Serbia in the twenty-first century, is a good example of this tendency. As Ana Tsing (2005) singles out, many economic political actors are interested in "conjuring business" today, seeking to extract a significant profit, or just collateral gains, from making "spectacular dramatizations" of the economic projects, staging them in the best manner of Hollywood productions—with their carefully constructed sets, well-chosen casting, skillful directors, disciplined crew, and above all efficient PR and media services—long before their realization starts.

Both popular and expert opinions in the last 2 years have pointed to the intricate shadiness of the "Belgrade Waterfront," indicating that a variety of collateral gains were already won while the core of the business enterprise was still an empty shell. As Tsing had learned from her Indonesian case, companies are not "alone in the conjuring business in these times." Countries, regions, and towns follow their example and join in dramatizing their potential as places for investment. Tsing concludes:

> "It seems likely that successfully conjuring the globe is possible, at least now, only in thick collaborations with regional and national conjurings; certainly, financial conjuring has been deeply implicated in promises of making regional and national dreams come true" (see in Erdei 2016).

Besides material goods, the consumption of culture, information, and new technologies is taking precedence in the new generation of Millennials (instead of the luxury and status goods that were important in the first years of "normalization" of consumption in early 2000), provoking moral panic among the older generation and producing contemporary discourses of technophobia, which resemble the older anti-consumption discourses that treated consumption as an erosion of culture.[21]

Conclusion

In this chapter, it was shown how consumer culture has been evolving and transforming from the moment of its initial incitement in socialist Yugoslavia in the mid-1950s to present day. It is argued that consumption has not been "discovered" in post-socialist transformation, except in its latest disposition—as the all-embracing activity of late modern capitalism and its cultural-ideological legitimization. The Yugoslavs had developed and sharpened their consumer skills through decades of living in socialist society that witnessed periods of high prosperity (the 1960s and the 1970s) and deep crisis (beginning of the 1980s, the entire 1990s). This had brought into almost parallel existence both modes of survival and tastes of necessity and more developed and sophisticated tastes and consumer practices paired with social differentiation. After the severe economic downgrading during the 1990s, it could be

[21] On the notion of consumption as an "erosion of culture", see in Miller 1996, particularly section on the myths about consumption.

said that consumers in what then was FR Yugoslavia (Serbia and Montenegro) were overjoyed to be able to approach "normal" environment for consumption as they were used to in the past, but it could not justify the view that they were newcomers to the world of consumption, as is sometimes suggested. As I hope I succeeded in presenting, an elaborate consuming culture had developed in socialist Yugoslavia, albeit this development was never quite successfully paired with the development of equally functioning consumer society, for the state never abandoned controlling the economy until its very end (cf. Dimitrijević 2016). Therefore, it could be said that in socialism, consumer culture existed without consumer society as its (back)ground. The similar cultural inconsistency exists in today's Serbia, when society has made its breakthrough toward consumerism as a guiding principle, but, due to decreasing purchasing power of the ever-larger parts of the population, the very base of the modern notion of consumers and consumption has been put into question, for it could end as a "consumer society without consumers." It means that, due to comprehensive and all-pervasive infrastructure and discourses of consumer culture, consumer desires remain in full capacity, but consumer possibilities are gradually declining for the most part of the population, and the processes of social stratification and differentiation are becoming more and more pronounced. Disappointment is fueled with unfulfilled expectations that were set up both through the promises of liberal elites in Serbia and from the West and that the application of the "transitional package" would bring the fruits of liberal democracy to Serbia, and the almost naive and impatient belief of the majority of Serbian population that this will happen immediately, and with almost no social and cultural consequences. The post-2000 opening of the Serbian market to forces and commodities of the neoliberal-market-gone-global has presented the Serbian citizens and consumers of the new millennium with many paradoxes. One of them was the fact that the "capitalist modernity" that was looked up to and which was embraced by post-socialist societies at the end of the twentieth century was epitomized not in high-quality, high-end, nicely designed and widely affordable Western goods (as it was desired and awaited for), but in a cheap, poorly manufactured goods coming from the East, mainly from China. As Simić writes, relying on Caroline Humphrey and Ivan Szelenyi,

> "it seemed that capitalist modernity has arrived to post-socialist societies in its 'trash' modality instead in its high register" (Simić 2009: 247).

In many ways, consumption as a discourse, set of practices, and amounting almost to a contemporary "way of life" has been mainstreamed, and presented as having no alternatives. However, as much as it appears inevitable, and despite how hard it could be today to imagine a society which wouldn't be consumerist, for it embraces the widest specter of activities, relationships, and values, even those that oppose it, or try to limit it in some way, as ethical consumption, consumer boycotts, or sustainable living, it should not be left at large too easily. Many consumption theorists and critical thinkers with different theoretical and ideological inclinations and affiliations have been warning about the effects of the consumerist society on democratic values. It has been voiced that if the pursuit of pleasure and individual fulfillment prevails over ideals and values of democratic society—if the philosophical, ideological, and social limits of consumption completely disappear, and consumption becomes its own goal—it will bring upon a state of democratic deficit. In it, connecting private choices with public virtues would be impossible, unlike in the era of solid modernity when it was still possible to associate consumption with both individual freedom and social change. A vision of such society, in which the democratically ensured freedom of choice exhausts itself in selections of cooking chocolate or maxi-pads, is simultaneously a symptom of the "new banality" (Miller 1994: 398) which we are subjected to today, and terrifying and dangerous for society and its inhabitants. If the freedom of choice focuses on the subject of the thousandth new flavor of biscuit, or shampoo aroma, if the ideological and political frames of the economy that makes it possible become disregarded, and the conditions and ways of production are put aside, then, in the end, both the products and the contexts in which they gain meaning will be compromised. By this I have in mind not only the immediate contexts for and communities of consumption, but also the broader political and social horizon of liberal democracy whose promises are now put to the test. Having a million choices within a badly constructed system to which it is claimed there is no alternative isn't much of a choice. It seems that this idea resounded in today's Serbia, at least, founded its way to one of the protest signs during the post-election student protest in the spring 2017. Among many original, witty, brave inscriptions and drawings on the posters, criticizing the prime minister and his cabinet for their politics, one peculiar and seemingly banal message singled itself out (and soon provoked a lot of media attention), reading "No to salty plazma," referring to the newest taste of the enormously popular "Plazma" biscuit, once produced in Yugoslavia and today in Serbia. Having been used as baby food and a delicacy for young children, its sweet taste became an inextricable part of "food memories" for many generations. Nevertheless, the production (which today is privately owned) is obviously adapting to the changing economy, and started to differentiate its products to remain competitive, which eventually brought about the unthinkable—"plazma" that tastes salty. "Plazma" and its transformation (from economic status of the factory to the changing organization of production and the mostly cherished products with strong identity value) thus stands as an epitome of political and social changes that created the rather bitter present of not only the post-Yugoslav societies, but the rest of the world as well. Following this young man through the streets of Belgrade, I later approached him by social media where he has built a strong visibility in arguing his case against "salty plazma." I wasn't sure if I was reading too much into his efforts, assuming that he somehow, by creating that slogan, touched into the heart of "democratic deficit," until one day he appeared on TV, explaining his inscription, commonly accepted as funny and eccentric. Unexpectedly, the nexus of politics, economy, and identity came out, and the feeling of "democratic deficit"—that even though consumer choices abound, or exactly because of it, democratic values are abandoned in favor of the authoritarian rule, which passes unnoticed, because people are obsessed with their choices in the commercial arena—was there. Asked about the future of the unfolding protest, and his personal attendance, he told a reporter that he would stay on the streets "until the end," until the situation has been settled and new elections are announced. To her question, if it really is that bad, he replied: "It's disgusting. Like salty 'plazma.'"

References

Antonijević, Dragana. 2013. *Stranac ovde, stranac tamo. Antropološko istraživanje kulturnog identiteta gastarbajtera [Stranger Here, Stranger There: Anthropological Exploration of Cultural Identity of Migrant Workers]*. Beograd: SGC.

Bartlett, Đurđa. 2010. *Fashion East: The Spectre That Haunted Socialism*. Cambridge, MA: MIT Press.

Bauman, Zygmunt. 2001. Consuming Life. *Journal of Consumer Culture*: 9–29.

Berdahl, Daphne. 1999. *Where the World Ended. Re-unification and Identity in the German Borderland*. Berkeley: University of California Press.

Bolčić, Silvano. 1994. *Tegobe prelaska u preduzetničko društvo [Difficulties of Transition Toward an Enterpreneur Society]*. Beograd: ISI FF.

———. 1995. *Društvene promene i svakodnevni život: Srbija početkom devedesetih [Social Change and Everyday Life: Serbia at the Beginning of the 1990ies]*. Beograd: ISI FF.

Bratić, Dobrila and Miroslava Malešević. 1982. Kuća kao statusni symbol [House as a Status Symbol]. In *Etnološke sveske IV*, 144–154. Beograd.

Čalić, Mari Zanin. 2013. Istorija Jugoslavije u 20. veku. Beograd: Kilo.

Clifford, James. 1988. The Pure Products Go Crazy. In *The Predicament of Culture: Twentieth Century Ethnography, Literature and Art*. Cambridge: Harvard University Press http://www.writing.upenn.edu/~afilreis/88/clifford.html. Accessed 23 July 2017.

Comaroff, Jean, and John Comaroff, eds. 2001. *Millenial Capitalism and the Culture of Neoliberalism*. Durham: Duke University Press.

Crowley, David, and Susan Reid, eds. 2000. *Style and Socialism. Modernity and Material Culture in Post-War Eastern Europe*. Oxford, New York: Berg.

———, eds. 2010. *Pleasures in Socialism. Leisure and Luxury in the Eastern Bloc*. Evanston, Illinois: Northwestern University Press.

Dajić, Ana. 2014. *Estetika socijalističkog stana: analiza enterijera u jednoj stambenoj zgradi na Sajmu u Beogradu [Aesthetic of the Socialist Apartment: Case Study of a Building in Staro Sajmiste, Belgrade]*. B.A. Thesis. Belgrade: School of Philosophy.

Dimitrijević, Branislav. 2016. *Potrošeni socijalizam, kultura, konzumerizam i društvena imaginacija u socijalističkoj Jugoslaviji (1950–1974) [Consumed Socialism, Culture, Consumerism and Social Imagination in Socijalist Yugoslavia (1950–1974)]*. Beograd: Fabrika knjiga.

Duda, Igor. 2006. *U potrazi za blagostanjem [Quest for Abundance]*. Zagreb: Srednja Europa.

———. 2010. *Pronadjeno blagostanje [Abundance Found]*. Zagreb: Srednja Europa.

Elias, Norbert. 1987. The Society of Individuals (Translated by Edmund Jephcott). In *The Collected Works of Norbert Elias*, ed. Robert van Krieken, vol. 10. Dublin: University College Dublin Press.

Erdei, Ildiko. 2004. "The Happy Child" as the Icon of Socialist Transformation: Yugoslavia's Pioneer Organization. In *Ideologies and National Identities – The Case of Twentieth-Century Southeastern Europe*, ed. John Lampe and Mark Mazower, 154–179. Budapest, New York: CEU Press.

———. 2006. Odrastanje u poznom socijalizmu – od "pionira malenih" do "vojske potrošača" [Growing up in Late Socialism – From "Little Pioneers" to "Army of Consumers"]. In *Devijacije i promašaji, etnografija domaćeg socijalizma*, ed. Lada Čale Feldman and Ines Prica, 205–240. Zagreb: Institut za etnologiju i folkloristiku.

———. 2007. It Takes Two to Tango: Encounters of "East" and "West" in Everyday Economies in Postsocialist Serbia. In *Places of Encounter, In Memoriam Borut Bruman*, ed. Rajko Muršič and Jaka Repič, 151–168. Ljubljana: Zupanjčeva knjižnica.

———. 2011. "Rocky Made in Serbia": globalne ikone i lokalni razvoj ["Rocky Made in Serbia": Global Icons and Local Development]. In *Horror, Porno, Ennui: kulturne prakse postsocijalizma*, ed. Ines Prica and Tea Škokić, 273–298. Zagreb: Institut za etnologiju i folkloristiku.

———. 2012. *Čekajući Ikeu, potrošačka kultura u postsocijalizmu i pre njega [Waiting for IKEA, Consumer Culture in Postsocialism and Before it]*. Beograd: SCG.

———. 2014. IKEA in Serbia: Debates on Modernity, Culture and Democracy in the Pre-Accession Period. In *Mirroring Europe*, ed. Tanja Petrović, 114–134. Leiden: Brill.

———. 2015. Kombinirana Soba. In *Made in YU*, ed. Jernej Mlekuž and Tanja Petrović, 107–117. Ljubljana: ZRC SAZU.

———.2016. Misty Gains from Outside: Economic Enterprises and Their Magic. *Perspectives. Political Analysis and Comentary* (2): 42–44.

———. 2017. *Fragmenti jugoslovenske socijalističke modernosti 1970-ih u TV seriji "Pozorište u kući" [Fragments of Yugoslav Socialist Modernity During Seventies, Seen in TV Series "Theatre at Home"].* Etnoantroploški problemi (in print).

Giddens, Anthony. 1991. Modernity and Self-Identity. In *Self and Society in the Late Modern Age*. Palo Alto: Stanford University Press.

Harvey, David. 2005. *A Brief History of Neoliberalism*. Don Mills: Oxford University Press.

Jansen, Stef. 2014. On Not Moving Well Enough. Temporal Reasoning in Sarajevo Yearning for "Normal Lives". *Current Anthropology* 55 (9): S74–S84.

———. 2015. *Yearnings in the Meantime: "Normal Lives" and the State in a Sarajevo Apartment Complex*. New York, Oxford: Berghahn.

Jansen, Stef, Čarna Brković, and Vanja Čelebičić, eds. 2017. *Negotiating Social Relations in Bosnia and Herzegovina: Semiperipheral Entanglements*. London: Routlegde.

Kovačević, Ivan. 1985. *Socijalno-emfatička funkcija monumentalnih grobnica [Socio-Emphatetic Function of Monumental Burial Places]*, Etnološke sveske VI, 81–87. Beograd.

———. 2007. *Antropologija tranzicije [Anthropology of Transition]*. Beograd: SGC.

Lazić, Mladen, ed. 1994. *Razaranje društva: Jugoslovensko društvo u krizi 90-ih [Devastation of Society: Yugoslav Society in Crisis of the 1990ies]*. Beograd: Filip Višnjić.

Luthar, Breda. 1998. Ne tako visoka kultura: prepovedani užitki nakupovanja. [Not so High-Brow Culture: Guilty Pleasures of Consumption]. *Časopis za kritiko znanosti* 189 (XXVI): 117–130.

———. 2006. Remembering Socialism. On Desire, Consumption and Surveilance. *Journal of Consumer Culture*. 6 (2): 229–259.

Ljuboja, Gordana. 1994. Etnografija haosa - Beleška o dileru [Ethnography of Chaos – Note on a Dealer]. In *Kulture u tranziciji*, ed. Mirjana Prošić-Dvornić, 161–166. Beograd: Plato.

Malešević, Miroslava. 2012. Iskušenja socijalističkog raja – refleksije konzumerističkog društva u jugoslovenskom filmu 1960-ih [Temptations in Socialist Heaven – Reflections of Consumerist Society in Yugoslav Film in the 1960ies]. *Glasnik Etnografskog instituta SANU* 57 (2): 107–123.

Marković, J. Predrag. 1996. *Beograd između Istoka i Zapada [Belgrade Between East and West]*. Beograd: Zavod za izdavanje udžbenika.

———. 2007. *Trajnost i promena. Društvena istorija socijalističke i postsocijalističke svakodnevice [Continuity and Change. Social History of Everyday Life in Socialism and Postsocialism]*. Beograd: Službeni glasnik.

Mijić, Emilija. 2009. *Spomenici posvećeni ikonama popularne kulture na prostoru Zapadnog Balkana [Monuments Dedicated to Popular Culture Icons in Western Balkans]*. Manuscript of the M.A. Thesis. Belgrade: Library of Department of Ethnology and Anthropology. School of Philosophy.

Miller, Daniel. 1994. Artifacts and the Meaning of Things. In *Companion Encyclopedia of Anthropology*, ed. Tim Ingold. London: Routlegde.

———. 1995. *Worlds Apart – Modernity Through the Prism of the Local*. London and New York: Routledge.

———. 1996. Consumption Studies as a Transformation of Anthropology. In *Acknowledging Consumption. A Review of New Studies*, ed. Daniel Miller, 1–57. London and New York: Routledge.

———. 1998. *A Theory of Shopping*. Cambridge: Polity Press.

Nava, Mica. 1998. The Cosmopolitanism of Commerce and the Allure of Difference: Selfridges, the Russian Ballet and the Tango 1911–1914. *International Journal of Cultural Studies* 1 (2): 163–196.

Patterson, Patrick Hyder. 2003. Truth Half Told: Finding the Perfect Pitch for Advertising and Marketing in Socialist Yugoslavia, 1950–1991. *Enterprise and Society* 4: 179–225.

Patterson, Patric Hyder. 2011. *Bought and Sold. Living and Losing the Good life in Socialist Yugoslavia*. Ithaca: Cornell University Press.

Popović, M., et al. 1991. *Srbija krajem osamdesetih: sociološko istraživanje društvenih nejednakosti i neusklađenosti [Serbia at the End of the Eighties: Sociological Exploration of Social Inequalities]*. Beograd: ISI FF.

Prošić-Dvornić, Mirjana, ed. 1994. *Kulture u tranziciji [Cultures in Transition]*. Beograd: Plato.

Reid, Susan. 2002. Cold War in the Kitchen: Gender and the De-Stalinization of Consumer Taste in the Soviet Union Under Khrushchev. *Slavic Review* 61 (2): 211–252.

Royek, Chris. 2004. The Consumerist Syndrome in Contemporary Society. An Interview with Zygmunt Bauman. *J Consumer Cult* 4 (3): 291–312.

Simić, Marina. 2009. *"Exit to Europe": State, Travel, Popular Music and "Normal Life" in a Serbian Town*. Manuscript of Ph.D. Thesis (Courtesy of the author).

———. 2018. *Consuming 'Others': Postsocialist Realties and Paradoxes of Appropriation in Postsocialist Serbia*. this volume.

Slater, Don. 1997. *Consumer Culture and Modernity*. Cambridge: Polity Press.

Spasić, Ivana. 2007. Smrt Bricea Tatona i uslovni kosmopolitizam socijalističke Jugoslavije [Death of Brice Taton and Provisional Cosmopolitanism of Socialist Yugoslavia]. In *Horror, Porno, Ennui: kulturne prakse postsocijalizma*, ed. Ines Prica and Tea Škokić, 51–70. Zagreb: Institut za etnologiju i folkloristiku.

Švab, Alenka. 2002. Consuming Western Image of Well-Being – Shopping Tourism in Socialist Slovenia. *Cultural Studies* 16 (1): 63–79.

Tsing, Lowenhaupt Anna. 2005. *Friction: An Ethnography of Global Connection*. Princeton and Oxford: Princeton University Press.

Velimirović, Danijela. 2008. *Aleksandar Joksimović, moda i identitet [Aleksandar Joksimović, Fashion and Identity]*. Beograd: Utopija.

Verdery, Katherine. 1996. *What was Socialism and What Comes Next?* Princeton: Princeton University Press.

Vučetić, Radina. 2012. Koka kola socijalizam [Coca Cola Socialism]. In *Službeni glasnik*. Beograd.

Yurchak, Alexei. 2006. Everything was Forever Until it Was No more. In *The Last Soviet Generation*. Princeton and Oxford: Princeton University Press.

Overview of Consumer Culture in Bulgaria: From Perestroika to Facebook

Kristian Bankov

Before 1989

The end of the regime has been described with countless hypotheses, models, and variants. For the purposes of this outline, the most appropriate approaches come from Castells, who sees the advent of the information society as the main reason behind the collapse, and Chavdarova, who explains it as an internal revolution of the economized *nomenklatura* (Castells 1996; Chavdarova 2001).

According to Castells, the centralized planning of the socialist states had produced impressive results for the industrialization of all Eastern Bloc countries. Moreover, the state monopoly over all phases of the economic cycle predicted enviable stability (which does not mean prosperity) of those economies. There is no reason to think that the industrial socialism of the Eastern Bloc would have retreated into the Cold War if the race had been left on this front. It is clear that if isolation and "big enemy" rhetoric had been preserved at their early-1960s levels, even the obvious differences in consumer standards would not have been the cause for any substantial erosion of socialism. However, major developments in information technology did begin and transformed the fetishism for Western goods from the early decades of the regime into a new type of social dynamic that spiraled out of the communist government's control. The battle between the two blocs had started even earlier than this technological phase, on a miniaturized scale, when the sounds of Western radio began to penetrate the East—mostly in the form of music and propaganda. The influence of these channels continued to increase and, as Markov (1990) quite aptly described, predetermined a mass appetite for radios and tape recorders. Consequently, foreign media became the bearer of lifestyles that had been severely

K. Bankov (✉)
New Bulgarian University, Sofia, Bulgaria
e-mail: kbankov@nbu.bg

E. Krasteva-Blagoeva (ed.), *Approaching Consumer Culture*, International Series on Consumer Science, https://doi.org/10.1007/978-3-030-00226-8_4

sanctioned by the regime.[1] During the next decade, the trend developed even more, owing to intensified exchange between East and West, and this occurred most prevalently through tourism and the export of specialists. Along with consumer goods in the Eastern Bloc, and in Bulgaria in particular, large quantities of vinyl records, tape recorders, magazines, and piles of other information made their way across borders. However, the real "blow" information delivered to socialism was strengthened by the *imagery of the West*. In the mid-1970s, video tape recorders appeared. Only a few years later it had become inconceivable that somebody would travel abroad (mostly in northern Africa) for work without bringing a recorder with them. Through video, for the first time, Western consumerism became visible on a massive level. In addition to porn and karate, there were many films unacceptable according to the regime's censorship, and an endless musical hit parade recordings and hypnotic commercials. In a mere decade, information technology would make it possible and inexpensive to privately reproduce and store all of these media. One of the most dynamic unofficial networks was dedicated to the exchange of recordings, films, concerts, etc.

Bulgarians found tourism's lure irresistible as a result of this exponential penetration of Western lifestyles through imagery. Markov describes how in this period contraband goes to a mass level. We know that in the 1980s this became the profession of many future Bulgarian mafia "entrepreneurs," but apart from them there were hundreds of thousands of Bulgarians on the trip to the West. The dam of the regime cracked under the pressure of these people's ingenuity and of the increasing amount of Western currency available from illegal commerce. In those years, mixed marriages were also on the increase. I do not know a single young (or not-so-young) person in Bulgaria who in the late 1980s was not oriented towards the fashion of Western pop music and styles, nor anyone whose dreams were not heavily associated with the West.

The regime lost its control over the spread of information, and with it—in the information age—its overall control over society. Of course, all this was made possible by favorable macroeconomic circumstances. The union between Reaganomics and the internal economical *nomenklatura* within the fertile environment of perestroika was victorious. "Money for Democracy" became the dowry of many economic mixed marriages. As the party collapsed, its far-sighted members rode the revolutionary wave of consumerism and took up privileged positions in profitable sectors of the future free market; others plunged into the plunder of infrastructure and formed organized crime networks; and some party outsiders remained faithful to the communist ideals. But this is not the main point. We are more interested in the mass consumer drivers that marked the beginning of the transition and their present-day legacy, with Bulgaria increasingly following the tracts of the globalized consumer society.

---

[1] Emblematic is the short story "Private radio receiver" by Anatoly Teofilov, published by Geneva and Gospodinov (2006: 59-65).

Bulgaria's Transition to Consumer Society

With the transition began the social development phase when consumption started to dominate. According to a widely accepted view, the revolutions of the late 1980s were revolutions of consumers (Dichev 2007). As evidenced above, all the prerequisites for this had been generated in the preceding decades, but after the regime's fall and the short-lived enchantment with democracy, a collapse occurred for the strong, unified conceptual schemes which had once explained Bulgarian society. In this pluralistic context, the standards of consumption became the only tangible reference point.

This chapter is nothing more than a very brief introduction to the sociology of consumer society in Bulgaria that is just waiting to be written. That is why it will end exactly where the extended research should begin. In the remaining few pages, I will try to describe its basic movements with the support of statistics and expert summaries, as well as with my own participatory observations.

The V-Like Structure of the Consumer Revolution from 1989 to 2008

It will hardly ever be possible for all the data about the Bulgarian transition to be arranged in a single human mind, nor for such a privileged mind to gather us and in simple words explain "This is what happened …." Of course, this does not mean that many have not placed themselves in such a position, and we do listen to such *super interpretations* in all possible narrative forms. Without this disclaimer, my version would sound the same way—how to explain everything about the transition within the consumer culture perspective.

If it is sufficiently obvious that 1989 was a consumer revolution; the paradox is that communism played the role of a school for these consumers, turning them into individuals "ready to propel the capitalist machine—submissive politically, plastic socially, ready for the new global order of eternal *transition*" (Dichev 2007). This thesis, which has proven more than valid in the long run, does not seem to pay enough attention to the first, economically unfortunate, transition phase. The idea of the "V"-shaped structure serves to emphasize that it departs from a certain level, and then steadily decreases down to the bottom before beginning steady new growth. This precisely reflects graphic representations of the most important statistical data, e.g., income, GDP, and consumption. The 1996–1997 crisis came across not only as a political and financial shock, but also as a sort of catharsis of consumption, the tabula rasa of savings, and a new beginning for society's propensity to consume.

Strong attitudes towards consumption at the end of the regime should not be confused with the authentic propensity for consumption that led Western economies out of the Great Depression. No matter how much social energy was invested in the socialist years via the attainment and consumption of Western goods, their social importance has always been distorted by the economy of deficit (Kornai 1980). From this proposal's point of view, the school of consumerism was closed in 1998–1999. We can also utilize the metaphor of a pendulum—artificially retained by the deficit in one direction, drawing on an uncritical consumer element in the other, and then forced to an end by the collapse of the post-socialist economy. The emblem of the initial wave of the consumer revolution became the "banana eaters"—the East Germans, who had found themselves in the well-stocked shops of Western Germany, stumbling upon never-before-seen quantities of goods that in the pre-1989 era had been given to them in only tiny increments. In Bulgaria, these were the years of mass *trade tourism* of low-quality apparel and other gaudy items from Turkey, as well as rattletrap cars from Western Europe. Then, the invisible hand of the market began to shape some streams in the element, with the following goods and information services—interpreted in a Bulgarian manner—standing out: huge quantities of audio cassettes being sold without any regulation or copyright; many people obtaining satellite dishes (which had been previously disallowed), and then launching the signal to their neighbors (a trend which led to the no less pirate-like business of the local cable TV networks); and the practice of video cassettes being exchanged among friends turned into family-run movie rental businesses. With consumer habits in music, the *cultural hunger* for Serbian pop-folk not only developed a whole sector of audio piracy but also inspired local production, ushering in a new era of Bulgarian pop culture—an entirely new pop-folk style, *čalga*, which prevailed over all other forms of cultural production in the decades that followed. In general, *čalga* became the emanation of the entire cultural climate of the period, and alongside the new style of yellow journalism is a fully authentic source that can help describe the value system of Bulgaria's consumer culture (see Dimov 2001; Gehl 2011).

The consumer element of the early transitional years put into circulation long-saved and tucked-away money that, due to the general institutional crisis and level of lawlessness, instantly made its way into the shadow economy. There is no clear correlation between the shadow economy's revenue component and the severely exposed abuse of the Yugoslav embargo, let alone the draining of the banks through the syndication of the so-called *credit millionaires*, but it is most directly related to the experience of consumer euphoria. The only conclusion that can be made is that precisely the people with economic-criminal "street smarts," immersed in free market conditions, were the ones to harvest the fruits of the initial consumer element rather than the official economy. The capitalist machine could not take full advantage of this new consumerism, in so far as it could work only in benign principle as a "first" or "official" economy.

This period was characterized by such a level of economic chaos that even in her tailor-made study of the shadow economy, Chavdarova cannot point to an unambiguous statistic on its share of GDP. However, it is widely accepted that even the boldest hypotheses of 50% are difficult to rebut (Chavdarova 2001: 167 ff.). In an in-depth study entitled "End Household Consumption as a Factor of Bulgaria's Economic Development" (Nestorov 2002), the author considers data from the first decade of the transition. In particular, he compares GDP, income, consumption, and savings: "All these figures show that throughout the period under review we have literally eaten up our GDP and have not used it for accumulation and growth in the future." The exception is the period from 1998 to 2000 (Nestorov 2002: 135). A more comprehensive analysis shows that although the absolute values are not very low, the structure of expenditure—the ratio between food costs, short-term and durable goods, savings, etc.—is characteristic of typically poor countries. This analysis is important to take into account, as it provokes stark contrast with the symbols of prosperity among the powerful elite observed around the mid-1990s. The icons of this prosperity quickly became Mercedes-Benz, mobile phones, and offices equipped with new computers. Perhaps it was not by accident that the system of automobility took on this *elite distinction*, while at the same time the insurance business (managed by mafia groups) filled the vacuum between the two extremes and entrenched its infinitely effective network. Rarely in the sociology of consumption have examples of such symbolic significance been encountered—expensive cars and mobile phones were rapidly acquired in those years at the expense of unprecedented social polarization.

To a great extent, we can explain this phenomenon with the completely ruined confidence in institutions and the devaluation of social capital (Chavdarova 2001: 274 ff.), which, under normal circumstances, are the conventional markers of social status. That is why such "mobile" status symbols have assumed this function and become imperative in those years. It is no coincidence that the first large-scale campaign of the new Minister of Internal Affairs, Bogomil Bonev—called *Komar* (Mosquito)—after the 1996–1997 state collapse consisted of checking the documents of expensive car owners. The campaign's implicit meaning was "The State Strikes Back" and, whether they were proven innocent or not, men from the muscular elite dressed in dark clothes and sunglasses being removed from their dark limousines under the watchful eye of the hooded special police forces had a very strong effect on the general public. Here begins the next phase.

The Bulgarian New Deal (1999–2008)

Perhaps from a financial point of view, it's most appropriate to point to the 1997 adoption of the currency board as a turning point in the "V" graph of consumption. The results of this were felt quickly, although the endless debate since its introduction has given rise to the most varied of estimations. In the history of the transition, whose main protagonist is consumption, a key point was the banks' stabilization after the board. The statistics from that point on have been "flawless," though as we shall see shortly this in no way translated to mass prosperity (Table 1):

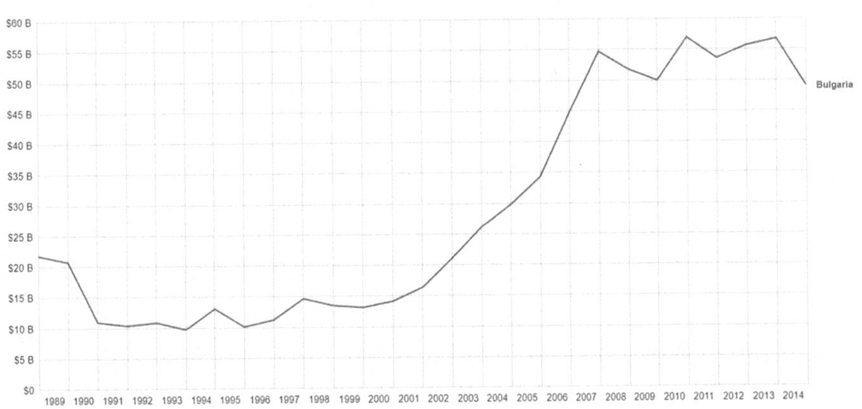

Table 1 With data from the National Statistics Institute

GDP growth rates

1992	0.0	1993	1994	1995	1996	1997	1998	1999	2000	2001	2002	2003	2004	2005	2006	2007	2008
1993	−1.5	0.0															
1994	0.3	1.8	0.0														
1995	3.2	4.8	2.9	0.0													
1996	−6.5	−5.1	−6.8	−9.4	0.0												
1997	−11.8	−10.4	−12.0	−14.5	−5.6	0.0											
1998	−8.2	−6.8	−8.5	−11.1	−1.8	4.0	0.0										
1999	−6.1	−4.7	−6.4	−9.0	0.4	6.4	2.3	0.0									
2000	−1.0	0.5	−1.3	−4.1	5.9	12.1	7.8	5.4	0.0								
2001	3.0	4.6	2.7	−0.2	10.2	16.7	12.2	9.7	4.1	0.0							
2002	7.2	8.9	6.9	3.9	14.7	21.5	16.8	14.2	8.4	4.5	0.0						
2003	12.2	14.0	11.9	8.8	20.1	27.2	22.3	19.6	13.5	9.7	5.0	0.0					
2004	19.5	21.4	19.2	15.9	27.9	35.5	30.2	27.4	20.9	16.9	11.9	6.6	0.0				
2005	26.6	28.6	26.2	22.7	35.4	43.5	37.9	34.9	28.0	24.1	18.8	13.2	6.2	0.0			
2006	34.6	36.7	34.2	30.4	43.9	52.5	46.6	43.4	36.1	31.9	26.3	20.3	12.9	6.3	0.0		
2007	43.1	45.3	42.7	38.6	53.0	62.1	55.8	52.4	44.7	40.1	34.1	27.8	19.9	12.9	6.2	0.0	
2008	51.5	53.9	51.1	46.8	62.0	71.7	65.0	61.4	53.2	48.5	42.1	35.5	27.1	19.7	12.6	6.0	0.0

These data reflect the statistical laws of an economy that traces the rails of normality, albeit with a slow start. The table shows growth in gross domestic product and consumption that is faster than the norm in advanced economies. Still, raw statistics leave out a great deal of information. It is common knowledge that in socialist times they were used quite manipulatively to maintain a desirable, but unrealistic, picture of living conditions.

In order to avoid the inaccuracies of official statistics and to measure the real stratification processes in Bulgaria, Mediana Agency launched a large-scale study, lasting nearly 10 years and covering17,000 respondents. The survey was based solely on *consumption* and not as a self-assessment, but as a report on the actual consumption during that period (Mediana 2008: 8). The findings from the latest edition of the study are quite indicative. Here are some of them:

- Over a period of 8 years, extreme poverty has declined seven times, with overall poverty declining two and a half times.
- Well-integrated people have increased four times over that period.
- For the first time in a decade, by 2008 more than half of the people surveyed did not report their basic material concerns as strongly affecting their everyday lives.
- The employment structure of the *state-private sector* of the economy is already practically indistinguishable from a number of Western European countries. This shows that the transition (in terms of economic transformation) is now complete.
- Increased inflationary pressures are seen as a result of the sharp rise in wages. Currently, wage growth significantly outpaces that of GDP. Somewhat reassuring is the fact that this above all applies to the salaries of the highly qualified workforce.

Expressed in concrete figures, the "Bulgarian Consumer Revolution" looks like this (Fig. 1):

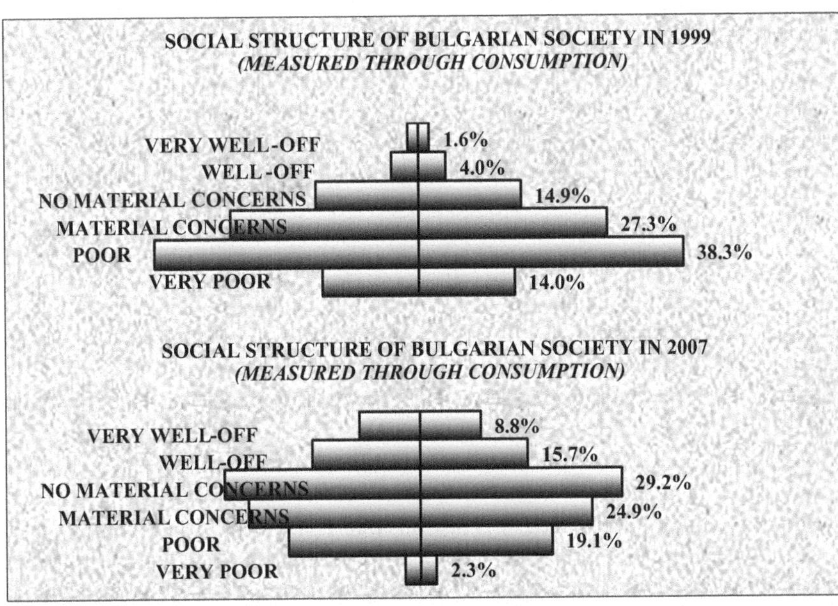

Fig. 1 With data from Mediana agency

Since I attended the presentation of the results of this study, I know that at this point most people are deeply dissatisfied with the data. However, the study also responds to this discrepancy, which still serves as a qualitative indicator of Bulgaria's new consumer culture. The very respondents whose actual consumption this picture draws upon were asked to directly self-assess their situation, answering whether or not they found it worse than before. It turns out that the evaluation of living standards has almost entirely been directed towards the upper strata, just as Simmel describes in his theory of the trickle-down effect (Simmel 1957). In 2007, 32.9% of these same people identified themselves as having "material concerns," 28.6% as "poor," and 12.6% as "very poor," or, in other words, 74.1% of Bulgarians considered themselves to be living below average living standards! (see also Yossifov and Naumov 1998). Obviously, in Bulgaria the acculturation of new standards of consumption has been quick and the classical scheme of the "democratization of luxury" has imperceptibly transformed from mere aspirations to the estimation of what is necessary.

The report repeatedly uses the expressions "way of life" and "lifestyle," although the leading word in it is the description of social strata with mostly quantitative parameters. Perhaps the most immediate application of the sociology of consumption in Bulgaria would be a definition of "lifestyle groups," using methodologies such as those used by the VALS project in the USA and RISC in Europe. Similar attempts, though on a more limited scale and for marketing purposes, have been made by the GfK Marketing Research Institute and MMD Partners. But before we look at one of the most visible testimonies to the existence of commercial lifestyle segments in Bulgaria, I will offer a few words about the credit euphoria of 2001–2008.

In fact, this euphoria was *consumer euphoria* because all the credits were immediately transformed into material prosperity. For many, this practice conceals something vicious, as it contrasts the traditional Bulgarian wisdom of saving money for an uncertain future. But beyond this ethno-cultural resistance, the growth of consumption—whose final outcome will be revealed at some future time—awakens even more anxiety in experts. One of Bulgaria's foremost financial historians comments:

> Even closer to the present day, the credit restriction following the introduction of the Currency Board in 1997 has retreated from 2001 onwards to a new expansion. Growth in financial intermediation has picked up momentum that is reminiscent of the most turbulent credit inflation. Although it starts at a very low base and the banking system has been structurally healed, this type of processes cannot completely evade the logic of familiar historical precedents (Avramov 2007: II: 600).

The first half of the twentieth century brought with it severe, and sometimes catastrophic, financial crises. Notwithstanding pessimistic attitudes, however, banks are currently making tremendous efforts to encourage credit withdrawals. Consumer loans in recent years have grown between 50 and 70% annually (with the exception of 2005, due to restrictions on the part of the National Bank of Bulgaria). Even the US mortgage loan crisis of 2008, which led Bulgarian banks to raise interest rates, did not stop this trend.

From my position (still laic), it is obvious *that consumer euphoria has boosted the Bulgarian economy*, and was made possible thanks to the aggressive banking policy which followed the strictly disciplined constraints of the currency board.

Either way, the common good indicators of the economy evidenced here mean that its overall functioning has improved, but the initial impetus still came from consumption. To make an analogy with US President Roosevelt's New Deal, a strong, stabilizing effect in Bulgaria after 1997–1998 was played by the positive signals from the EU and NATO that preempted Bulgaria's real membership. I emphasize the *psychosocial* effect of these signals, which certainly had a stronger impact than the official messages coming from the government. The combination of a comfortable EU integration climate with a bank lending policy encouraged by the government of Simeon II created the necessary long-term propensity for consumption that we still find today.

There is another factor that distinguishes the apocalyptic scenarios of credit euphoria from the past and today's situation. Some call it a *tax revolution*, making it adequate for prosperous Western economies: value-added tax (VAT), inspired by France in the 1950s, is rapidly being accepted by most other European countries as the basis for the EU's overall tax policy. VAT is an indirect tax charged on final consumption. It is quite normal for VAT revenues to make up over 40% of total state revenues. Although VAT does not reverse the need for an economy to produce, it largely mitigates the effect of the trade deficit—ultimately increasing the impact of where the product is purchased and consumed. If credit is spent on imported goods, it does not have the damaging effect that such a trend once did. The fact that the main share (around 70%) of today's prosperous economies is comprised of the service sector, owing only 25% to industrial production, further detracts from the unfavorable scenarios of the past. If this were not the case, then today's China—the global consumer goods factory—would enjoy the world's highest standard of living.

All this concerns the context of consumer culture in Bulgaria. The faces, or protagonists (those which are visible), are elsewhere. Advertising, the "armed wing" of consumer culture (Ferraresi 2005: 93), is one of its most intrusive visible media. In some highly competitive sectors, such as bank lending, telecommunications, and sales of beer, sausages, and hard liquor, there is an increasing trend which resorts to authentic messages tailored to Bulgarian new lifestyles. Logically, messages with narratives closer to everyday reality are easier to perceive and identify with than with those sterile, anesthetized images of global consumerism. Some companies like Vivacom have created a rich imagery of the new Bulgarian and his/her family in the information age. Mastika Peshtera (a brand of anise liqueur) has become permanently entrenched in the *čalga* lifestyle, not only with it as a musical background but also as an authentic source of attitudes and viewpoints. Many local beer brands exploit the mythology of Bulgarian football, just as Heineken and Carlsberg do elsewhere around the world.

Worthy of particular study is the extremely successful commercial copywriter Gencho Genchev. More than anyone else, he has been able to associate many different brands with important moments from Bulgaria's past, traditions, and present. The video for Macedonian-style sausages by Leki brand[2] will surely remain a gold standard in Bulgarian advertising, just like his other cult commercial hit "Oh,

[2] https://www.youtube.com/watch?v=CigtbB_5kxM (last accessed 12/08/2017)

Pepi!"[3] With no less mastery, Genchev has managed to circulate some rather simple messages into Bulgarian consumer culture, such as "That's the banging I was waiting for."[4] But Genchev's most intriguing and intuitive feat, for the purposes of our study, is his exploitation of the strongly charged meanings from the socialist past. A whole series of commercial videos, including "Oh, Pepi!" were inspired by Bulgarian cult movies of the 1960s and 1970s. One *lukanka* salami commercial staged a real slice of socialist life, with a typical deficit economy problem and final resolution—with the help of a member of the Communist Party *nomenklatura*.[5]

New Forms of Consumption After the Rise of Social Media

What makes the study of consumer culture in Bulgaria interesting is its rapid progression. Until 2008, there was an accelerated transition from deficit economy to consumerism, economically supported by the EU integration process of the country. After 2008, "conventional" consumer culture continued to develop, encompassing larger and larger shares of society. At the same time, the global advent of social media began to provoke changes in consumer culture (Close 2012: xii ff.) and Bulgaria is no exception to this trend. A still immature consumer culture, combined with the impact of social media, created interesting ritualized forms of symbolic consumption whose semiotic mechanisms for using brands are essential to understanding present-day consumer culture in Bulgaria.

The Rise of Brands

In the 1970s and 1980s the companies with the biggest and most recognizable brands became the main semiotic mechanism for attributing symbolic value to goods and services. If traditional marketing paradigms started from the position (1) that there are objective consumer needs and (2) that companies using the marketing mix compete to better satisfy them, then after decades of market development in certain product categories it became clear that the traditional approach was not enough. *Brand management* comes in as a common practice in the systematic creation of distinctive value of brands when the conventional tools of marketing are no longer enough. There were many remarkable brands in the past, but the major innovation of brand management is not so much that the product works for the brand; but the brand, loaded with strong, unique, and favorable associations, rather works for the product's success. In the new phase, brands begin to function as an autonomous cultural institution and begin to circulate within the collective imagination of various themes and messages that raise

[3] https://www.youtube.com/watch?v=XnjF0ECiC9A (last accessed 12/08/2017)

[4] https://www.youtube.com/watch?v=dtzVIVqYsfw (last accessed 12/08/2017)

[5] https://www.youtube.com/watch?v=I4opdifPBfE (last accessed 12/08/2017)

consumption to the spiritual sphere (but, with the same success, we can say that the reverse is true—throwing spirituality into the field of consumption). Consumption began to be stimulated with messages that associate it with love, freedom, creativity, adventure, faith, madness, euphoria, etc. A*dvertising* during those years began to transfer meaning and messages from those sociocultural areas previously occupied by religion, nationalism, history, literature, and cinema, among many others, and onto consumption. Thus, Western brand fetishism, in which some brands have become icons of mythological value for their consumer-worshippers, was born; the attitude towards them is "religious"—suffice it to mention only Apple, Harley Davidson, and Chanel, although the list could go on and on (Vincent 2002). And that phenomenon does not occur visibly to cultural analysts only. During the 1980s, the financial evaluation of brand equity began, completely independent from both the fixed assets of companies and their actual capital in the banks and stock markets. For example, in 2016 the mere Apple *symbol* was estimated by the agency Interbrand at about 178 billion (!) dollars, followed by Google, Coca-Cola, and Microsoft, respectively, in order of their values. Contrary to classical marketing logic, this fact means only one thing: the symbol is more important than the product.

The extraordinary power of brands in the last decades of the twentieth century has overturned the interdependencies between brands and lifestyles. Previously, companies had lifestyle or psychographic segmentations of the market in order to formulate their messages according to values and attitudes. Later, the encouragement of culturally significant consumption began to form a new type of values and attitudes—new lifestyles already patterned by companies. The very notion of "lifestyle," as far as it means the long-term belonging to a stable social group, entered a crisis. These new patterns of behavior presupposed the simultaneous combination of many styles. In this period, new and more sophisticated academic models were developed which reflected a much more dynamic social reality. For example, the model of *microtrends*, introduced by Mark Penn (and brilliantly applied to Bulgaria by Mila Mineva 2009), which captures the emergence of small groups, is destined to have a growing influence on society. If the number of lifestyles in the first VALS model is 9 and in general this approach had reached no more than 15 or 16, Bulgarian microtrends according to Mineva amount to 40.

Another equally important approach to the analysis of the new forms of consumer society comes from the Italian sociologist Egeria Di Nallo (Di Nallo 1998, Bankov 2009: 175). She remains entirely in the sociological paradigm and her contribution is based on an observation of Gerd Gerken that marketing cannot rely on stable consumer groups alone. It needs to rely on consumers, grouped around certain consumer practices that could be permanent. Di Nallo suggests that a more appropriate research orientation would be not to see people as belonging to a lifestyle, but rather to identify *styles of consumption*, a unifying (albeit temporarily so) form of social interaction. This is based on many observations of postmodern identity, and thus likens the social function of consumption with *meeting points* (or bubbles of demand), which in any case are more durable than the individual whims of the modern consumer. Di Nallo's contribution mainly refers to the new consumer practices in Western Europe, but is today also valid in Bulgaria, after the rise of the giant malls and shopping centers—real cathedrals of the big brands. Undoubtedly, cyberspace and especially social media also fall under the umbrella of this logic of consumption.

Practices and Rituals

With the contribution of Di Nallo, the panorama of the evolution of consumer culture meets the evolution of consumer practices. We may observe that the available literature on consumer practices and its fieldwork is infinite, while the writers who construct theoretical models based on those practices are few. In an in-depth review of these authors (Bankov 2009: 103–104, 177–178) I refer to Michel de Certeau, Mary Douglas, Colin Campbell, Bernard Cova, and Grant McCracken. All these authors have patterned the consumers' invention of everyday life; the subject of a separate study would be tracking the evolution of the practices described by them in social media. For the purposes of this study, I shall base my analysis on one of their models—Grant McCracken's typology of consumer rituals.

What makes McCracken's model particularly suitable for the analysis of consumer rituals on Facebook is its starting point, namely how exactly the transfer of meaning comes to pass from the goods or services to their consumer (McCracken 1988: 76 ff.). According to my preliminary hypothesis, that process is growing at an unprecedented rate in the age of social media.

McCracken lists four main types of rituals present in real life in many varieties and combinations. These rituals are *possession, exchange, grooming, and divestment.* But in order to have the potential to emit meaning, goods and services are subject to another, more centralized transfer—that is, onto them from the cultural space. Although not limited to them, the most emblematic "machines" for this stream of significance are advertising and the fashion industry. The huge daily cultural resource that these two institutions emit in the cultural space is intended to fight the entropy of consumer culture. Entropy comes from the endless creative invention of everyday life, in which each of us uses the meaning of the components of our own shopping cart for our own identity or for the micro-strategies of self-affirmation in the social environment. Left only to those processes, consumption would have taken unpredictable directions of development, elusive from the control of the production system. Therefore, in the highly competitive and hypermediatized social space, it is evident that the basic effort of corporations is the transfer of discernible meanings onto their brands (Rifkin 2000), which introduces fresh, creative images/ideas which serve as ready-made patterns for the market of identities. These images/ideas (or mimes), in the initial phase after their launch, compete with the existing meanings in popular culture, already out of the control of the corporations. They in turn influence consumer choice, and this cycle seems frenetically repeated after each semiotic "wearing out" of the new images/ideas.

Consumer rituals reflect precisely this phase—how in practice we *capitalize* the meanings (images/ideas) on behalf of our identity, inscribed by the companies in their goods and services. The first, and perhaps most important, ritual in McCracken's system is *possession*. He carefully distinguishes it from the actual legal ownership of goods, which does not transfer any meaning. The ritual consists of the communicative act of publicly announcing ownership—a stop at the restaurant with the brand-new car, inviting friends over to show them the new home theatre system, sporting the just-purchased sexy outfit in the shopping mall, and so on. Complementary to the ritual of possession is that of grooming. Tuning the car to refine some detail in front of the condo, upgrading the home stereo in such a way that the neighbors understand thereto, excessively cleaning one's pipe, having previously attracted the entire cafeteria's attention with the smoke of the branded tobacco, and thousands of other practices with which we "declare" our relationship with the goods all result in the *gain*, at least temporarily, of their *symbolic value*.

The ritual of *exchange* is based on the fundamental archetype of possession. Following the classic work of Mauss on the gift (Mauss 1954), a whole research program has been opened, an important part of which is the exchange of gifts in consumer society (McCracken 1988: 85). The gift is an extremely powerful tool for interpersonal influence and it is based entirely on the complex transfer of meanings which connect the product to the giver and the recipient. One such ritualized gift is the engagement ring—whose act sanctions extremely important relations, but even the giving of a garment projects a vision of a lifestyle for the recipient which is imposed in an oblique way. Giving services as gifts is another inexhaustible semantic universe. People who have developed the art of the gift can practically "say" everything through this consumer ritual, not to mention that since Mauss' time, the feast also belongs to this practice.

The last and least relevant of McCracken's rituals for the purposes of this study is *divestment*. It reverses the direction of the transfer of meaning, or rather it is the ritual with which we weaken the already established relations between the user and the good. For example, functional reasons often bring us to change part of our home furnishings. When it comes to pieces of furniture towards which we feel a kind of affection and on which we have experienced important moments of our lives, it is normal that a person cannot easily separate from them in spite of rational reasoning to do so. Rituals happen when we bring the respective item to the basement or the attic, and so maintain our possession, albeit without use. Thus, a cooling of our relationship with the object arrives and after varying periods of time we already see this piece of furniture as unnecessary and therefore acceptable to throw away. Another example of symbolic divestment is when, before we sell it, we take away all the customization we have done to the car, as if we do not want the new owner to gain access to the part of our life which took place in it.

E-Consumption on Facebook

I will not dwell on the list of reasons for the phenomenal success of the social network Facebook, which helped assign the label of media to this category of Internet platforms and which has brought such concepts as "society" and "human relations" to acquire a whole new meaning for new generations. For us, it is important that the whole evolution of consumer culture touched on so far leads to an extended integration of the symbolic role goods and services play on interpersonal relations. For this reason, a new phase inevitably begins with the rise of FB. *The aim of the remaining part of the study is to bring some level of systematic patterning of the processes of meaning transfer from goods and services to consumers* on FB in Bulgaria, by way of an analogy with McCracken's consumer rituals.

We academic scholars are hunters of invariants in any spiritual and social reality, and we cannot remain indifferent to a universe such as FB. Although there are no studies on the consumer rituals of FB so far, there are many on digital virtual consumption (see Denegri-Knott and Molesworth 2010). There is one interesting study on the rituals of possession on Pinterest (Schiele and Hughes 2013) and another on FB rituals in the new forms of romantic/intimate relationships. The latter was based on seven semi-structured, in-depth interviews among Irish students (Mod and Bowe 2010), but this did not prevent the authors from drawing a typology of the rituals and some important generalizing conclusions. The analogy with McCracken's rituals is visible at first glance, although there is no reference to his book. For example, the act of changing the publicly announced relationship status is analogous to the ritual of possession. In the debriefing of the interviews, it becomes clear that for the partners in the relationship, the act of public disclosure of the commitment has a lot in common with the fencing of one's own territory (Mod and Bowe 2010: 69). Following this act, public flirting or sexual advances by third parties acquire quite another meaning. FB also gives conditions for the ritual of public displays of affection, completely analogous to the ritual of grooming in consumption. The ritual can be fulfilled verbally with written messages and with images of the couple's tender moments, as well as through countless applications.

One of the authors' most important conclusions is related to how the specifics of FB's publicity differ from life off-line. The fact that after the communicative actions of the ritual there remains lasting evidence makes the disclosure of an engagement much more efficient than the usual ceremonies, which, in the words of the author, would hardly reach 150 people (Mod and Bowe 2010: 67). Efficiency is not expressed in the momentary impact, which is certainly stronger through live interaction, but it is far more effective at a quantitative level, insofar as the act becomes known to thousands, and mostly because of the registered public feedback, which can visualize the scale of the impact and record countless nuances of human relations—accounting for the range of cultural and social capital of friends and relatives, taste, lifestyle, and so on.

These findings make us propose a strong semiotic hypothesis on the consumer practices derived from the comparison of verbal speech and written text. Elsewhere, I have developed a detailed theory (Bankov 2015), but here I would only stress that the difference in the structure of the building of possible worlds is radically different. Therefore, the structure of consumption rituals in their off-line version, as described by McCracken, coincides with the statements of verbal speech, while the same rituals carried over FB become carriers of the structure of the written text. As in the case of an engagement, just as in the conspicuous display of the new car, it would be difficult to find a place that could gather all friends (and significant others), while posting an image to FB notifies the acquisition of the item to a wide audience and opens up a platform for the inevitable ritual greetings, wishes, and all sorts of comments. So begins the "novelty" of this remarkable event, which later everyone will be able to find in the archives of the profile.

Therefore, we can conclude that *the degree of semioticity of the FB-mediated consumption is higher than that of the standard off-line practices*, being that this process is partially offset by the supersaturation of updates about all sorts of consumer acts which, at some point, we cease to have the physical ability to respond to adequately.

Another important conclusion at this phase of the research is that the narrative form of the feedback makes it impossible to typologize FB rituals. We can certainly find samples identical to the types described by McCracken (such as publishing a photo of the receipt from the first iPhone 5 purchased in Bulgaria), but generally speaking social media, mobile communication, and the entertainment industry have erased the clear boundaries separating consumption from work, communication, and entertainment. By contrast, however, we can find semiotic invariants on the platform that concern the way it provides conventionalized tools for ritualized consumption. The list that follows is in order of the power of the "semiotic" impact of each item.

Names

In light of the case of a football fan from the Bulgarian city of Svishtov who after 15 years of legal proceedings was able to change his name from Marin to Manchester United, undoubtedly a taboo has fallen. This fact draws attention to how huge the potential is for the transfer of meaning that a person's name can have. It's true that this is a pathological case, as evidenced by the same man having tattooed the logo of Man United on his forehead. But this event directs us towards another practice—replacing personal name on FB profile with a brand, product, or service name, without resorting to court proceedings. Many people in Bulgaria did this during political protests in a sporadic way through political messages: the efficacy of this communicative act of individual identity has been proven. The strong semiotic effect is based also on the unusual nature of the change of this field of the FB profile, unlike that of the profile photo, cover, status, and so on. In my research, I came across a classical case from Sofia: a male, working at Hewlett-Packard, with Harley David in the place of his real name. In another case, a person from the village of Peturch (near Sofia) wrote *Мерцедес Бенз* [Mercedes Benz] as his name. Actually, there is more than one profile with different variations of the legendary German brand, as well as *Тихомир Беемвето* [Tihomir the BMW], *Пламен Ауди Стефанов* [Plamen Audi Stefanov], *Ники Найка*[Nikki the Nike], *Виктория Сикрет* [Victoria Secret], *Ваня Версаче* [Vania Versace], and *Мис Диор* [Miss Dior]. The correlation between the gender of the users and the product category of the chosen brands is very interesting and might be subject of a separate study since here I am focusing just on the semiotic mechanism of the transfer.

Profile Pictures

Unlike the name, the profile picture is very actively used by a large number of users for acts of strong identification with all sorts of things, including brands. Perhaps the automotive industry holds the championship among male users, but football is not far more inferior. Among female users, it was anticipated that lingerie and shoes would be in first place, but in the actual search brand references among women were balanced across all sectors and in relatively much lower numbers than among men. The profile picture is a communicative medium that makes possible the transfer of meaning not only of the classic rituals of possession and grooming, but also of various forms of worship, lifestyle, parody, and more. The simplest form of ritual identification is when the user posts the logo of the brand without any modification. This way, the transfer of values is complete and entirely in line with the corporate identity. However, a profile picture may explore the brand's value in its capacity to represent a certain lifestyle: playing golf with Lacoste; riding a beloved motorcycle (as in the aforementioned profile of Harley David); or self-ironic representations, e.g., with a cheap bottle of Ariana beer amongst the ultra supporters at the football stadium. Profile pictures among Bulgarian FB users are almost never used entirely for consumer practices, but at the same time they are seldom completely independent from them.

Family and Relationships

One possible manipulation of the platform which I was alerted to by students of a culture and semiotics course is registering a fake profile of your favorite brand and entering into marriage, engagement, kinship, love, or friendly relations with it. Like the use of the name, such a trick can have a strong impact if used successfully. This is a rarely used semiotic resource whose creativity makes it difficult to be classified. Yet anyone would be impressed by the marital status "married to Manolo Blahnik" or "in love with Christian Dior!"

Cover Photo

This communicative attribute of FB was barely adopted after its introduction 3–4 years ago, due to the unusual proportions of the image, but then started to be successfully integrated into profiles. From the many examples reviewed, I have noticed that the cover is a space used to express the aesthetic attitudes of the users on the axis nature-culture. This means that in 90% of cases, there are natural landscapes or tourist attractions, architecture, or a work of art. In the few cases in which the cover is used for ritual homage to a brand, product, or service, the latter is represented in a design or an aesthetic light. If, for example, the logo of Mercedes Benz is used as a profile picture, then on the cover one of the German corporation's magnificent models is represented (this example comes from the account of a colleague at New Bulgarian University).

Timeline/Status

Any change to our profile gets sent automatically as a live feed to the profiles of our friends; this is the purpose of the timeline, but still the most semiotic tool within our control is the status. Statuses most approximate FB to verbal speech communication—but with the great advantage that instead of words any media can be integrated. We share our lives in real time precisely through the status. Therefore, in it one finds the whole phenomenology of Bulgarian consumer practices, of course with a much lower impact factor than the previous examples because of the high turnover of information. Food and drinks consumption, led by the relentless regularity of physiological needs, motivate millions of status shares; likewise, posting food pictures has become a trend, comparable, and partially overlapping with *selfie mania*.

Likes

"Like-ing" is the most common FB ritual for universal use. That is why its semiotic potential is quite limited. Meanwhile, "Likes" have become a marketing industry in the e-economy and companies pay those who can guarantee them a large number of likes. Companies also pay for databases of people who have liked goods and services similar to theirs. This fact further devalues the semiotic impact of the ritual. Something that increases the importance of "Likes" for consumer practices even more is the sum of everyone's likes, which is a separate heading of each profile's information (after photos, music, places, films, books, etc.). As one usually "Likes" a large number of things, this section typically has a commercial orientation. If one bothers to check how his or her likes are presented to other users, one might rethink whether or not to "Like" commercial pages.

Albums

In a study of the influence of FB rituals on intimate relations, it turns out that old albums with images from previous relationships are a strong premise for jealousy and discord in couples (Mod and Bowe 2010: 72). However, all photos with consumer practices that are simply somewhere in the photo albums of users, in the logic of this review, are semiotically the weakest medium for ritualized consumption.

Conclusions

Observing the lightning social transformation in Bulgaria from the perspective of consumer culture studies offers many advantages when trying to understand the whole picture. It is too early for there to be an acceptable historical account of the last several decades, but certainly one of the most observable areas of social life for theoretical patterning is consumption. It emerged so immediately after the fall of the Berlin Wall and it continues today with the expansion of social media, where new technologies have made it possible for everyone to share his or her experiences in real time with practically everyone around the globe. The way young Bulgarians transfer meaning from brands and construct their FB identities bears the traces of peculiarities in the development of consumer society in Bulgaria.

References

Avramov, Roumen. 2007. *Komunalniyat kapitalizŭm:Iz bŭlgarskoto stopansko minalo. [Communal Capitalism: From the Bulgarian Economic Past].* Vol. 1-3. Sofia: Tsentur za liberalni strategii, Fondatsiya "Bulgarska nauka i kultura".

Bankov, Kristian. 2009. *Konsumativnoto obshtestvo. [Consumer Society].* Sofia: LIK.

———. 2015. Udovolstvieto ot hiperteksta [The Pleasure of Hypertext]. In *V gradinata s rozite III. Lekcii i Slova (2007–2014)*, ed. Vesselina Vassileva, 50–77. Sofia: NBU Press.

Castells, Manuel. 1996. The Information Age: Economy, Society and Culture. In *The Rise of the Network Society*, vol. I. Cambridge MA/Oxford UK: Blackwell.

Chavdarova, Tanya. 2001. *Neformalnata ikonomika [The Informal Economy].* Sofia: LIK.

Close, Angeline G. 2012. *Online Consumer Behavior: Theory and Research in Social Media, Advertising and E-tail.* New York: Routledge.

Denegri-Knott, Janice, and Mike Molesworth. 2010. Concepts and Practices of Digital Virtual Consumption. *ConsumpMarkCult* 13(2): 109–132. https://doi.org/10.1080/10253860903562130.

Di Nallo, Egeria. 1998. *Quale marketing per la societácomplessa?* Milano: Franco Angeli.

Dichev, Ivaylo. 2007. Komunisticheskata shkola na konsumatora ["The Communist School of the Consumer"]. *Kultura* 7 (2446): 22.

Dimov, Ventsislav. 2001. *Etnopopbumat. [The Ethnopop Boom].* Sofia: Bulgarsko muzikoznanie.

Ferraresi, Mauro. 2005. *La società del consumo. Lessico della postmodernità.* Roma: Carocci.

Gehl, Katerina. 2011. Čalga as a desired cultural pattern in post-communist Bulgaria. *Bulg Ethnol* XXXVII (2–3): 72–93.

Geneva, Yana, and Georgi Gospodinov. 2006. *Inventarna kniga na socializma [Inventory Book of Socialism].* Sofia: Prozorets.

Kornai, Janos. 1980. *Economics of Shortage.* Amsterdam, New York, Oxford: North-Holland Publishing Company.

Markov, Georgi. 1990. *Zadochni Reportaji za Bŭlgaria. [In Absentia Reports for Bulgaria].* Sofia: Profizdat.

Mauss, Marcel. 1954. *The Gift: Forms and Functions of Exchange in Archaic Societies. (Ian Cunnison,Trans.).* London: Cohen and West.

McCracken, Grant. 1988. *Culture and Consumption: New Approaches to the Symbolic Character of Consumer Goods and Activities.* Bloomington: Indiana University Press.

Mediana. 2008. *Socialnata stratifikacia v Balgaria 1999–2007 [Social Stratification in Bulgaria 1999–2007].* *The reference is to the official document of the agency.

Mineva, Mila. 2009. *Patevoditel 2020.* Sofia: Ikonomedia.

Mod, Greg, and B.A. Bowe. 2010. Reading Romance: The Impact Facebook Rituals Can have on a Romantic Relationship. *J Comp Res Anthropol Sociol* 1 (2 (Fall 2010)): 61–77.
Nestorov, Lydmil. 2002. *End Household Consumption as a Factor of Bulgaria's Economic Development*. 2nd ed. Sofia: Economic Research Institute.
Rifkin, Jeremy. 2000. *The Age of Access: The New Culture of Hypercapitalism, Where all of Life is a Paid-for Experience*. New York: Penguin/Putnam.
Schiele, Kristen & Hughes, Mine Ucok. 2013. Possession Rituals of the Digital Consumer: A Study of Pinterest. E-European Advances in Consumer Research (10). Gert Cornelissen, Elena Reutskaja, Ana Valenzuela. Duluth, MN: Association for Consumer Research. 47–50.
Simmel, Georg. 1957. Fashion. *Am J Sociol* 62: 541.
Vincent, Laurence. 2002. *Legendary Brands: Unleashing the Power of Storytelling to Create a Winning Marketing Strategy*. New York: Dearborn Trade Publishing.
Yossifov, Assen, and Iliya Naumov. 1998. Poverty-Cultural Models and Mass Attitudes. In *The Bulgarian Transition: Challenges and Cognition*, ed. Peter Emil Mitev. Sofia: LIK.

Consuming "Others": Post-socialist Realities and Paradoxes of Appropriation in Serbia

Marina Simić

Introduction[1]

In this chapter, I want to address the impact of the specific understanding of choice (in this case "consumer choice"), that is central to "Western" ideologies of "individualism" (see Strathern 1992; Cronin 2005), on the understanding of consumption in Eastern Europe. The majority of literature on consumption in post-socialist Europe that emerged immediately after the fall of Communism tends to see consumption as a political act in choosing between Western goods and their

> "less sophisticated" Eastern European versions, to put it rather crudely, which lead some authors to conclude that consumption in the post-socialist countries was actually consumption of the images of the West. However, today almost 30 years after the fall of the Berlin Wall, "brands are no longer metonyms of the 'Imaginary West'" (Crăciun 2012, 853; cf. Yurchak 2006)

and a variety of Western branded consumer goods are available in shopping malls, retail oases, and supermarkets (Crăciun 2014). The same is true for contemporary Serbia. I argue that in Serbia Western brands were not simple metonyms for the West even in the early period of post-socialist transition,[2] but rather that shopping

[1] This paper was originally presented at the conference *New Consumer Practices of XXI-st Century: Anthropological Perspectives,* held at the New Bulgarian University in Sofia in April 2015. I am grateful to the conference participants for their critical and useful comments. The paper is published as the result of the work at the project No. 47021, financed by the Ministry of Education, Science and Technical Development of the Republic of Serbia.

[2] I am aware of the difficulty of using the term "transition" (cf. Burawoy and Verdery 1999a, 1999b; Humphrey 1999) for post-socialist transformation in Europe and I use it here as a technical period denoting term. Moreover, for most of the people with whom I worked in Serbia in the last 10 years, this process was not really a "transition," as the term implies—between imagined socialism and imagined capitalism—but rather "the situation" (*situacija*)—the state of affairs as it is, which not

M. Simić (✉)
Faculty of Political Science, University of Belgrade, Belgrade, Serbia
e-mail: marina.simic@fpn.bg.ac.rs

E. Krasteva-Blagoeva (ed.), *Approaching Consumer Culture*, International Series on Consumer Science, https://doi.org/10.1007/978-3-030-00226-8_5

for Western and other goods served as some kind of the "ordering" tool through which people understood and created their (mostly ambiguous) social position.

I offer an ethnographic study of the specific group of people with whom I worked in the northern Serbian town of Novi Sad, and Belgrade from 2005 onwards.[3] At the time I first met them, some of them were young professionals, while others were students who were about to become young professionals. Most of them had left the country in the last 10 years. These people do not form a "community" or a coherent group; my interest in them lies in the discursive practices of positioning through which they made sense of the current "Serbian situation" and emerged from these practices as individuals of a certain kind (cf. the ethnographic approach of Jansen 2005).[4] They had a relatively high social status with high cultural and social capital and their identification strategies were directed towards "cosmopolitan" practices that also include shopping. These practices required them to negotiate both the space and time scale—between Serbia and the imagined (and real) West and East, and between socialist past and imagined (and real) capitalist futures.[5] My analysis also combines these two scales. My initial fieldwork study was a year-long "extended stay" in the mid-2000s, supplemented with the "back-and-forth model" of Eastern European anthropologies/ethnologies (cf. Brković and Hodges 2015) in the subsequent years which enabled me to track continuity and change in the local community. This approach allows for observing the situation in its dynamic transformation as it takes into account the flow of time helping us to avoid the frozen picture of the "situation" in the time of rapid changes. In addition, combination of the time and space scale allows us to avoid the pitfalls of two usual approaches in the consumption studies, one that Carrier and Heyman call "epochal" and another that is reduced almost to the "non-time" of "wanting and acquiring" (Carrier and Heyman 1997: 359). I will first introduce the historical emergence of consumer society in Eastern Europe and socialist Yugoslavia in particular and will then proceed with the ethnographic account of the contemporary consumption practices in Serbia.

---

only applied to the circumstances of the Serbian state (corruption or inefficiency, for example) that people found themselves in, but also denotes a certain "state of mind" and "moral and cultural degradation," as my informants called it, that developed during the 1990s and continued today in the various guises (Simić 2016: 94).

[3] I have concealed the identities of the people I have worked with and all names are pseudonyms.

[4] As Cronin writes, following Judith Butler, "'the individual' is not an entity formed prior to an engagement in discourse. There is not a preconstituted, core self to be expressed or communicated in acts of consumption and display. The self is constituted performatively in the very action of acting, mediated through discourse" (2005: 36). However, as it will be clear later in the chapter—the practices of shopping that my informants were engaged in did not enable them to emerge from them as individuals they wish to be.

[5] I am aware of the possible difficulties in dividing the real and imagined, but that is the distinction which proved to be rather important for my informants as it will be clear in the course of the chapter.

Consumption in European Socialist Countries and the Yugoslav Experience

Carrier and Heyman explain that the so-called epochal type of literature on consumption describes the historical emergence of modern consumption as occurring in certain politico-economic conditions in Western Europe (Campbell 1987; McKendrick et al. 1982; Williams 1982): the rise of capitalism (Mintz 1985; Miller 1987) and its intrusion into "non-Western" societies (see for example Worsley 1970). Contrary to that, the socialist modernist experience is seen as some kind of deviation, as socialism did not fulfil its promise to produce enough goods for consumers (see for example Smith 2003). Following on that, it seems that many authors understand socialist consumption to be similar to its capitalist counterpart, albeit "deficient." Hence, socialist economies are frequently dubbed "economies of shortage" (the term introduced by Kornai 1980), while some authors argue that the inability of socialism to meet the consumption needs of its citizens was the main reason for its fall (Verdery 1996; cf. Gellner 1994, 1995 who argues that the "attraction of consumer society" actually overthrew socialism). However, as Berdahal warns "the 'consuming frenzy'" that stroke Eastern Europe after the fall of the Berlin wall was just an extension of a "commodity fetishism" that "was an integral part of daily life in 'actually existing socialism'" (Berdahl 1999: 105).

Availability of goods and "level of consumption" in the few years immediately after the Second World War in socialist Europe were similar to those in Western Europe (Szalai 2000), while after the late 1940s, different socialist countries followed different paths with occasional shortages and "consumer booms" like that in Poland in the late 1950s (Crowley 2000), or in the 1970s in Yugoslavia (Erdei 2006a), the German Democratic Republic (Bryson 1984), and Hungary (Szalai 2000). Unlike the situation in other socialist countries, the Yugoslav economy was not controlled in the way that was the case in the Soviet Union and a variety of consumer goods with their accompanying advertising practices were not unknown to people in the former Yugoslavia (Švab 2002; Patterson 2003). Yugoslavia's relative openness towards the West after Tito's break with Stalin in 1948 enabled people in the former Yugoslavia to enjoy relative prosperity. Many people in Serbia believe that their lives were as good as (or almost as good as) those of the people in European capitalist countries of that time, despite some internal difference that made some parts of the country more "Western" than others (see also Erdei 2006b). Lack of visa requirements from the mid-1950s onwards made it easy for most people to go on the now (in)famous shopping tours in Italy, notably in Trieste, that many of my middle-age informants remember with nostalgia (cf. Švab 2002; Erdei 2006a, Luthar 2006; according to Szerbhorvàth 2002 in 1979 10,000 Yugoslavs traveled there daily).[6] This obviously signalized a desire for "Western" Italian

[6] On the other hand, in the 1950s Hungarians were going to Romania to buy consumer goods, while in the 1970s and 1980s goods smuggled from Hungary and Yugoslavia had high value in Romania (Chelcea 2002).

commodities, but to the participants in my research, they seemed much more easily available "back then" in the socialist period. Furthermore, for many people in their 20s and 30s, certain commodities like clothing brands, chocolate, or sticker albums that were common on the Yugoslav market were regularly seen as markers of a shared Yugoslav identity and usually invoked in talk about "good old times" of the 1980s (see Erdei 2006a).

However, this is not to say that socialist Yugoslavia was some kind of "consumer paradise." There were several economic crises in Yugoslavia (see Woodward 1995) which propelled trips abroad (mostly to Italy and Austria) in search of "Western" goods (see Švab 2002; Erdei 2006a; Luthar 2006). Thus, when some of my informants referred to the socialist times as the time of "normality," they did not really claim that socialism was a time when the difference between them and the "West" did not exist; rather, it only seemed that the difference was smaller and more contested, or even that *difference* was a kind of "normal" and easily manageable. The last crisis before the breakup of the country happened in the 1980s when most of my informants were teenagers or children. However, for them, as well as for other people I met, the major point of disruption was the crisis of the 1990s when Serbia was under a UN embargo. This lasted for almost 10 years, with different degrees of intensity from 1991 to 2000, making the legal import of goods impossible and nourishing the proliferation of black markets in almost everything. Consequently, all previous crises looked minor, while most people saw the current period as a period of "normalization."

After the NATO bombing of 1999 and the collapse of Milošević's government in 2000, the embargo was lifted and production somewhat restored, with stores once again full of goods. This was, of course, welcomed by most people. During my initial time in Novi Sad most of my informants, both women and men, spent a considerable amount of time searching through newly opened shopping malls, or just window shopping. Many times I was not only engaged in conversations about goods, but due to my apparent lack of any obvious job and abundance of free time (as well as supposed knowledge of Western goods), I was seen as a good companion for shopping expeditions undertaken as part of everyday activities on any day of the week, at any time of the day (some of my informants were self-employed or worked in shifts). However, this initial "consumer frenzy" calmed down in the recent years. Most of the local boutiques had vanished and the initially too expensive shops have been supplemented with less expensive variety. Most of thc people with whom I have been working left the country for the USA and Western Europe, while some of them traveled between Serbia and the West.

In this chapter I will follow a part of their trajectories, trying to understand how certain ways of shopping serve simultaneously as sources for the understanding of social life itself and as an important element for building the proper moral self. In that process, I will try to avoid the language of the "lifestyle" in the way that the term is widely used in academic writing on Western European and North American consumerism that Featherstone unfavorably describes as denoting "individuality, self-expression, and a stylistic self-consciousness" (Featherstone 2000: 83). This was rightly criticized for understandings of consumption that seem to emphasize the "individual" and what has often been described as "postmodern" subjects, who are free to construct themselves as they wish, while at the same time treating "consumption in markedly intellectualist and even aesthetic ways" (Carrier and Heyman 1997: 356; cf. Featherstone 2000; Kellner 1983).[7]

Little has been written on the possibilities of "stylistic self-consciousness" in post-socialist part of the world. This line of reasoning probably builds on a specific understanding of "consumer-citizenship" (Cronin 2005) on the one hand, and Baudrillard's writings on consumer society under capitalism, on the other. According to Baudrillard, consumption under capitalism leads to the endless reproduction of commodities as a self-referential system, which makes the current capitalist societies of the "West" postmodern (Baudrillard 1981; see also Baudrillard 1983, 1993). It is commonly assumed that this kind of "development" was not intrinsic to the socialist societies in the way it was to the capitalist ones. This makes people in Eastern Europe appear either as the victims of "Western commodity fetishism" or as rebels against their socialist states (cf. the critique of Lampland 1995, which argues that "commodity fetishism" was a consequence of socialism insomuch as it was also the consequence of capitalism). I will not talk much about "commodity fetishism" in strictly Marxist terms, but I shall make a few points about what some of the people with whom I worked in Novi Sad know about the "power of goods," questioning the simple dichotomies of capitalism and socialism, capitalist originals, and post-socialist copies. In that sense, I will use Taussig's (1993) concept of mimesis and alterity so as to explain my informants' relationship with the West that was built through certain goods. Taussig (1993) developed those concepts in order to explain religious figures of Cuna Indians that serve in healing practices and resemble the images of the Spaniards. Taussig (1993: xiii) writes that "the *wonder* of *mimesis lies* in the *copy drawing* on the *character* and *power* of the *original*, to the *point whereby* the representation may even assume that character and that power." However, arguing against simple interpretation of those figures as the consequence of the contact between Cuna and Europeans, Taussig writes that although mimesis seems primarily to make the mimic similar to the mimed, it nevertheless reproduces the difference between the two. Paradoxically, difference is made by making oneself similar to something or someone else by mimetic imitation. Similar can apply to the situation of my informants. For people with whom I worked, Western brands, and I focus particularly on goods closely connected with bodies and self, like clothes, cosmetics, and jewelry (cf. Rollason 2008 for a similar analysis applied to clothing), served as a medium between them and the specific others they wanted to become. However, Western brands were not simple tools of appropriation. Shopping for Western brands made the position of my informants ambivalent, placing them out of cosmopolitan circles to which they wish to belong. This seems paradoxical, taking into account that specific understanding of "choice" is a central element of Western

[7] Instead, most of the anthropological literature on consumption that started to emerge in the 1970s (for an overview see Miller 1995) aimed to focus "upon a relationship between an individual and a larger context understood as 'society' or a social space, within which the possibilities for individual expression may derive their meaning and potential" (Miller 1998: 140).

concepts of consumption, individualism, and citizenship. As Cronin (2005) writes "'choice' comes to mediate the terms in which certain subjects have access to the politically validated categories of 'the individual' and 'the citizen'" (ibid, 32). She further argues that

> actualizing one's potential as individual and citizen of a national community becomes intertwined with "consumer choice", which comes to be seen as a right and a duty in order to express one's "inner, authentic" essence (Cronin 2005: 32).

In that sense, my informants' inability to express their "inter, authentic essence" through consumer choice was a direct *consequence* of their inability to be recognized as "citizens" (of a certain kind), which means that choice of goods was not enough for them to be recognized as people they wish to be. In the following sections, I will introduce some ethnographic material in order to show how complex and often contradictory tactics[8] of shopping employed by my informants, which were supposed to produce individuals of certain kind, inevitably failed, as those tactics were conditioned by the very *location* that my informants had to negotiate.

Local Boutiques: The Dolls from Hell

During the 1990s, most socialist shops were closing down or were full of outdated and expensive clothes, and most people were forced to shop in open markets. Open markets with smuggled goods or locally produced fake brands were flouring all over Serbia. In Novi Sad, there were several outdoor markets including *Riblja pijaca* (Fish Market) in the very center of the town and several others; one in every district. As it was the case in other European post-socialist countries, these places were seen as a disgrace (cf. Crăciun 2014) and most of my informants were rarely shopping there, unless they were searching for specific homemade garments that slowly started to become chic in the last few years.[9] These places were later supplemented with China shops and locally owned boutiques that sold clothes "that were just a little bit finer, but still from China," as Kaća, who used to work in one of the boutiques, put it.[10] In many towns all over Serbia they did not only replace old socialist shops, but many new outlets were opened on the ground floors of the houses of the preserved,

[8] Here I refer to de Certeau's (1988) concept of tactics and strategies, where tactics are understood as everyday activities which people use in order to create a space for themselves in the setting of imposed strategies. In my understanding of de Certeau's work, it does not mean that in these "acts of creating" people necessarily subvert meanings that are imposed on them from above, but they find different ways of using them (sometimes to their own benefit, but not necessarily).

[9] It is important to stress that for people in Serbia these places were part of the collective disgrace—fall from grace that comes with the fall of socialism, while in some other European countries, like Romania, this places denoted broken promises of capitalism and Westernization (Crăciun 2014).

[10] There was a clear and well-known hierarchy in "non-Western" garments—those from Turkey were considered of better quality than those from China (cf. Crăciun 2012 for the same situation in Romania) and they were even considered as goods of medium quality.

old-style town centers, transforming them into shopping zones. The same thing happened in Novi Sad, where all the streets around the main square were full of boutiques of all kinds that were surrounded with newly opened foreign shops and framed with two open markets at their ends. These shops were usually small and crowded, sometimes consisting of only one room. In the last few years, these shops have been mostly pushed out by newly open foreign shops and although my informants sometimes did shop in them, they are mostly considered as cheap remnants of the 1990s when they were the only shopping option, apart from open markets. My informants usually did not pay any special attention to them, as these shops were found all over town. Only specific encounters with more concrete "others" made me aware of their importance for my informants' social positioning. Let me illustrate.

In late fall and early winter 2005, Martina and Vesna—my key informants—had visitors from Russia and the USA—Nataša, a young Russian woman studying Serbian in Moscow and Mike, an American from New York, whom Vesna met when she was studying in Canada. Nataša showed great enthusiasm for the town taking part in our shopping expeditions. She told us that Novi Sad had wonderful architecture and that she liked it very much. On one occasion, some friends who were with us asked Nataša if she had traveled to other countries and Nataša confessed that she had not, "only to Ukraine," and that was when she was a child. My friends answered in one voice: "That's why you like it." Nataša was somehow not a "proper other," being Eastern European which together with her poor travel experience meant that she was not really considered to be a good judge of Novi Sad's qualities. On the other hand, Mike did not show any excitement about the town, grumbling about its poor lighting and dirty streets. He joined us shopping, looking for a jacket in the newly opened diesel shop. The shop was placed in one of the streets leading from the main square between some fashionable shops and some boutiques from the 1990s. While we were walking down the street, Mike was taking photos and he stopped in front of a boutique with two worn-out mannequins (one female and one male) without noses, dressed in winter coats, and chained by their necks to a metal stick. Vesna and he found the image hilarious. Mike added that the dolls look like prisoners of war. Laughter and camera flashes provoked the lady who was the owner of the boutique to come out and explain to us that it was not nice to laugh at her dolls. Vesna and I passed by this boutique frequently, but never before had we felt the need to stop and comment on its dolls. Vesna explained to Mike that these dolls were probably leftovers from the 1990s, adding that poor taste and lack of means probably saved them to the present day. Empty shop windows with naked and broken dolls were a common sight in the state shops in the 1990s—and a point of mockery. However, these ironic enjoyments that enabled us to distance ourselves from a state we disapproved of, but also to keep our "insiderhood" (Herzfeld 1997), were usually played out in a circle of friends who were always "ours." Even when they were not, as it was the case when Vesna went to have her key cut for Mike in a small private shop and came back without the job done as the seller was talking on the phone and ignored her for several minutes, the subject of the ironic exposure was something that people could place "outside" themselves, like shop assistants whose ignorance of proper selling behavior[11] could be exposed and our own "superior" knowledge confirmed, even if "we" and shop assistants belonged to the same "culture."

In my example above, Mike's presence made me feel as if I was looking at the familiar shops through someone else's eyes, and the "cultural intimacy" (Herzfeld 1997) that Vesna and I, as well as the owner of the boutique, shared was broken. When I later talked to Vesna about the particular event, she did not see anything particularly problematic in Mike's presence; she was very unhappy about "the situation in Serbia" and Novi Sad in particular, where she was working as an editor in a private TV company, and was ready to go to the USA, finally leaving for New Jersey a year after my initial fieldwork. This is not to say that Vesna identified with the USA more than she did with Serbia, but rather that she was trying to distance herself from both, while seeing the USA as a place of better opportunities. Thus, Vesna did not mind shopping in different places, including second-hand shops, although she avoided open markets apart from buying a woollen scarf and gloves. She used to be very critical about "cheap clothes and food" even if they were of "Western" origin, and she told me once that she "refused to be duped by this trash that our people think is great."

Skeggs (2004: 136) writes that in "Western societies," a great flow of goods made "knowledge of new goods, their social and cultural value, and how to use them appropriately" crucial for establishing social "distinction" (cf. Featherstone 2000). Or, as Sassatelli puts it, "stress is put on the ability of the consumer to recognize the value of things and it is by instructing them on the value of things that consumption can be governed" (Sassatelli 2007: 33). Similarly, Appadurai writes that "commodities represent very complex social forms and distributions of knowledge" (Appadurai 1986: 41). Consequently, "as distances increase, so the negotiation of the tension between knowledge and ignorance becomes itself a critical determinant of the flow of commodities" (Appadurai 1986: 41). The question of the imagined "distance" was especially important for my informants and their ability to adequately appropriate different goods, both those sold in "Western" shops and those sold in local boutiques with foreign goods.[12] Thus, Vesna's shopping practices were not simply *mimesis,* or imitation (Taussig 1993) of the imagined West through certain goods, even if that required specific knowledge that not all people in Serbia possess. Thus, it could be said that my informants saw "mimicry"

[11] Shop assistants were important part of the shopping experience and my informants paid special attention to them. It is usually assumed that in socialism they were generally considered rude and disinterested (cf. Humphrey 2002), a practice that was supposed to have changed after its fall (cf. Simić 2012).

[12] Specific knowledge, required to distinguish between "counterfeits" and "originals," was especially important during the 1990s and people used to employ very sophisticated techniques in order to do so. Slight differences in the seam of a pocket in a pair of jeans could be used in order to distinguish between "original" and "fake" Levis, for example. In recent years the knowledge necessary for distinguishing between "counterfeit" and "originals" has ceased to be important, but it is still important to be able to distinguish among the goods available in order to be able to "appropriate" available fashion into "style."

in a similar way to that described by Deleuze and Guattari, as a "very bad concept, since it relies on binary logic to describe phenomena of an entirely different nature" (Deleuze and Guattari 2004: 12). However, although my informants did try to negate the binary logic of the "West versus Serbia" discourse, they did not see Serbia and "the West" as phenomena of an entirely different nature. Consequently, my informants could not follow the logic suggested by Deleuze and Guattari (2004) to "deterritorialize" their relations with their imagined others and form a surplus "value of code" (ibid) which would enable them to cancel the dichotomy.

Vesna did not see herself as particularly different from Mike, but rather more different from the people who used to buy in the local boutiques. Even if local boutiques were not selling counterfeit clothes of the famous brands, as was the case in open market, the goods sold in local boutiques were still "copies" of "the real fashion." "Real fashion," for my informants, was obviously unachievable through the goods sold in the local boutiques—although, according to my informants, some "ignorant people" might think that it was. Still, this *internal* distinction was supposed to be achieved through the contested relation that my informants established with the imagined West through the goods acquired. My informants believed that they should be wearing "original" clothes, both in terms of clothes that are not counterfeit and in terms of the "individuality/originality" created through the particular styles they chose. In the case of "non-original" goods from local boutiques, or those worn-out boutiques' mannequins, the distinction was not that difficult to make, but the problem remained: Is it possible to achieve this "originality" in a non-original context? This question of "originality" turned out to be the question of *location* that was not that simple to solve through the appropriation practices available to my informants. In the following sections I will discuss how even Western shops and original goods bought in foreign shops might not be able to generate this originality for my informants.

The Case of Dorothy Perkins: The Deceit of Goods

Visits to shopping malls, alongside window shopping and browsing, was a regular activity and as Novi Sad's center is relatively small with the mall and shops within a slow 20-min walk I was included in those activities almost on a daily basis. Some of the newly opened shops, like Dorothy Perkins, had existed only in Belgrade.[13] They were located in a newly opened shopping malls in the area called New Belgrade (mostly built after the Second World War on previously agricultural land). On one occasion, I joined Tanja on her shopping trip to the new mall. Tanja is a young medical doctor who works for a foreign pharmaceutical company in Belgrade and she commuted daily between Novi Sad and Belgrade in the company's new and rather posh car. She used to give me a lift between the towns on a couple of times.

[13] In the meantime, Dorothy Perkins closed down and so did some other British shops like Marks and Spencer and Lush that I will mention later in this chapter.

She told me that it was not that easy to find nice things in Novi Sad and that she shopped in Belgrade.

On our first trip to the new Belgrade mall, we went to Dorothy Perkins; at that time, I did not even know that it had opened in Belgrade. Tanja was really surprised by that and said something like "Where on Earth do you live?" She managed to spend more than 2 h in what was a fairly small shopping mall, but my frustration escalated when I was refused entry to the Dorothy Perkins shop, as the alarm went on when I entered. After some negotiations, the shop assistant checked my bag guessing that it contained some cosmetics from a boutique that had not been checked out properly and this was triggering the alarm. However, it turned out that the alarm was caused by the small notebook that I bought several years ago in Belgrade's IPS, one of the first "Western-style shops" that was opened in Serbia. Embarrassed by this, I left the shop and joined Sanja, Tanja's friend from Belgrade, who was taking a break in one of the mall's bars. She had come to the store with her mother, but later left her mother to shop with Tanja, when she decided to take a break. Sanja was a quite well-known graphic designer and she used to travel a lot. I complained to her about my experience in Dorothy Perkins and she comforted me with the explanation that all these shops were not "real Western shops," but only the most commercial ones (as I, living in the UK, should have known) that basically sold cheap clothes to ignorant Serbs and were staffed by ignorant shop assistants who "do not know how to behave." This time, I became the "other" of sorts and our shared "experience in the West" enabled us to reveal the thin layer of modernity, or "incomplete modernity" of Western shops—Serbian style.

At the end of her shopping tour, Tanja joined us for a quick drink. As we were heading back to Novi Sad she commented on her shopping. She bought a plastic necklace that was around 12.5 Pounds Sterling at that time, something she considered expensive, a t-shirt at Top Shop, and ballet shoes in Dorothy Perkins. She was not really happy with the things she had bought, commenting that they were actually not of that great value. She told me, "If you live like this, the only pleasure you have is to spend the money you earn." Like many young professionals in Serbia, she was very unhappy with her working hours and the amount of work she had to put in. She felt that "the Western way" understood as a formal dress, a lot of work, and not enough time "for higher activities" like reading was not really a good idea. The worst of all was that she had to meet very different kinds of people that she would never dream of knowing, but what was even worse was that she had to work with them, which she found quite different from the "aristocratic" job her boyfriend was doing at the Novi Sad University. She felt that she needed to apologize for her spending and she said that she saw it as a "substitute" for the life she lost when she started the job.

This attitude is similar to what Miller describes as "an abiding sense in this literature [on consumption more generally] that pure individuals or pure social relations are sullied by commodity culture" (Miller 2001: 227). And further,

> "indeed the central plank of the colloquial term 'materialism' is that this represents an attachment or devotion to objects that is at the expense of an attachment and devotion to persons" (Miller 2001: 227).

Similar ideas were frequently used to describe the official socialist position on consumption that resembles what Miller (2001: 227) calls "the historical sense" of consumption as "a wasting disease," repeating the well-known assumption that "while production creates the world, consumption is the act whereby we use it up." Following that line, some authors argue that, apart from the "consumer frenzy" after the fall of socialism, there was also a tendency among Eastern Europeans to refuse Western goods, which some authors connect with the socialist legacy and its condemnation of the "superficial bourgeois practice of consumption" (Crowley 2000). The usual critique in the former Yugoslavia was addressed to "conspicuous consumption" attributed to *Gastarbeiter* (guest workers, most often working in Germany) under socialism and the nouveauriche in the 1990s and condemned by both state officials and academics writing on the topic (cf. for example Malešević and Bratić 1982; Kovačević 1985; Szerbhorvàth 2002).[14] However, most of my informants' critique of consumerism, including that of Tanja, was not nostalgia for the socialist "time of innocence." For Tanja, as well as for other people with whom I worked, it was important to distinguish themselves from the "conspicuous consumption" of the new rich and Western goods played an important part in establishing this difference. Here, the distinction is made through a difference in knowledge/technique. Namely, it is established in the awareness that the "West" contains both "trash" (stuff imported from China that is sold in open markets and is made of nylon and plastic, and has no aesthetic value at all) and "high-culture" artifacts that take a lot of knowledge and experience, as well as money, to recognize. For my informants, people who go for conspicuous consumption are the ignorant nouveau riche with no aesthetic sensibilities. In other words, it is more about what people from Serbia *know* and do not know, rather than what they are able to buy.

Thus, my informants were not naive believers in the "consumer paradise" of the "West," but were also sophisticated critics of it. Or more precisely, the very critique of "the West" enabled them to position themselves if not completely as "Westerners," than at least not as easily duped "Eastern Europeans." It is not to say that my informants simply "see through" the "commodity fetishism of Western goods" but most of them thought that they needed to "belong" to some kind of "capitalism" in order to be able to criticize it while that critique would be the ultimate proof of belonging. Žižek (2008) writes, following Sloterdijk, that today's political ideologies (of capitalism and communism alike) operate despite/because people see "through" them, but continue to behave as if they do not (Žižek 1992, 2008). He further argues that people agree to follow ideology, because they believe that they are actually expressing their free subjectivity through their critique of it (in cynicism) (Žižek 2008: 241–245; cf. Žižek 1992 for the same argument). Thus, Tanja did not "appropriate" Western goods, remaking them in a "Serbian way," as is usually argued in the academic literature on the appropriation of "Western" goods in

[14] These practices included monumental tombstones, excessive weddings (wedding parties/receptions), huge houses, or guest rooms that are actually not used, or clothes which are not worn, but displayed.

non-Western contexts. Instead, her critique of Western goods that she nevertheless shopped for made her position ambiguous.

My informants were very aware that this kind of irony is the ultimate proof of belonging to the "system" (of capitalist production) that they would have rather criticized. Thus, although Tanja was critiquing "consumerism" that was also common in "the West," her critique did not come from "the West" itself. Consumption of "Western goods" regardless of the critique that it was exposed to still makes an insolvable dilemma for most of my informants. That paradox can be crudely put like this: buying "Western" goods with the awareness of their "Western-ness" actually confirms our own "non-Western" position, and that is actually the very distinction we want to get rid of. The more of "the West" we consume, the further away from it we are and our "non-Western-ness" becomes more and more visible. The very imitation (mimesis) of the "West" actually creates the separation and the uniqueness of the "other." Shopping in different shops for different kinds of goods made people aware of the ambiguous position they felt themselves to be in—simultaneously placed in and outside the "West." Thus, the question of relative location became crucial for the positioning of my informants, posing a paradox. On the one hand, the shopping practices in this chapter created a clear spatiotemporal ranking between Serbia and the West(ern Europe), while on the other, research participants constantly tried to undermine this ranking. For most of my informants the only way to undermine this ranking was to emigrate to the West and many of them did. Let me illustrate with some final ethnographic examples.

Pandora's Box

Tanja moved to Denmark, where her husband obtained a position at a university. We met in Novi Sad where she was visiting her parents several years after my initial fieldwork. We were sitting in the main street, near Tanurdžićeva palace—one of the city landmarks, built just before Second World War, drinking coffee with Voja and some other mutual friends, talking about the political situation in Serbia and in the West. Tanja mentioned Danish Pandora shop that was located centrally in the building's ground floor, commenting that local shops were gone and that everything was replaced with foreign shops of "all kinds" (meaning of low and high quality) that still sold not-so-great goods to "our stupid people." Tanja explained that those shops, like Pandora, just resemble "real" foreign shops, but that products made for Eastern European markets are not of the same quality as those made for the Western market. Tanja explained those practices as the "cynicism" of the "Western political correctness" that speaks of equality, but constantly produces difference, and told us that we should just discount them. However, Voja, one of a few of my informants who did not leave the country in the last few years, but remained working in a local NGO, disagreed rather furiously that it is not about "political correctness" because "here, nobody is politically correct anyway" asking us what would be the shopping alternative to Pandora, since we did not have our own jewelry industry anymore and pointing to the cheap American Claire's shop nearby as the only alternative.

Socialist Yugoslavia had developed jewelry production. The most famous one was Zlatara Majdanpek, from a small industrial town in Eastern Serbia, whose name still resonates with my informants' memories/ideas about socialist times. There are other jewelry shops in Novi Sad today, including Rogaška—Slovenian, formerly socially owned company,[15] and Crystal Ambience from the USA, but their presence in Novi Sad did not counter Voja's argument. For my informants, in order to dismiss empty promises of "political correctness," they first needed to be in the position to be politically correct and that is impossible from the position people occupy in Serbia. In that sense, domestic shops can never replace the foreign one and it was impossible to imagine them as places of resistance to dominant shopping culture that my informants sometimes call for.

In the last few years, some state shops were sold out and started to reopen, refurbished and new clothes on offer, but their prestige was not very high, although some people believed that they represented good value for money. Still, most of my fashion-consciousness informants would not shop there. Thus, I was a passionate shopper in the last remaining Belgrade YUmco shops, one of a very few remaining Yugoslav textile industry companies, but my informants were not very enthusiastic about them. Similarly, once I spotted a jacket in a state shop Progres (Progress—the name indicates its socialist legacy) that was about to be closed down, but a friend of mine told me that it was far too much money for Progres, "for that money I could buy a jacket from a foreign firm," he added. I objected that Dorothy Perkins was of the same quality as Progres, or even worse, and as proof I displayed my very much worn-out 2-year-old Dorothy Perkins jumper that I was politely told was not good enough to be worn in public. However, that was taken as a bad joke, and Voja remained persuaded that the foreign firms were better than domestic ones. In a similar vein, in one of our usual meetings in the bar called Cuba Libre, a friend of mine said that she recently managed to finally find a pair of shoes she liked in Mango that cost one-third of her salary. She justified her choice by explaining that it was very hard to find something nice to buy in Novi Sad and that if you were lucky enough to find something of good quality you should get it immediately. People were usually proud of Novi Sad for many reasons, but when it came to keeping up with fashion, they found themselves disadvantaged compared to the (imagined) "West." This is a specific understanding of backwardness, or some kind of incomplete version of a modernity unachievable through consumption. And it was unachievable not because these people were unable to consume it in the way they wished to, but because whatever they consumed they could not achieve it. Thus, when on another

[15] Following the introduction of the so-called Yugoslav self-management in 1950, the vast majority of the enterprises, factories, firms, and institutions were socially owned, unlike in other East European countries where the state ownership was a dominant model. In the Yugoslav case and self-management theory, the firms were communally owned and controlled by the employees via elected councils and ruling boards (*društveno vlasništvo*).

occasion, Svetlana and I went to shop in the newly opened Lush store in Novi Sad, and I mentioned that I did not usually shop there, Svetlana told me,

> "Probably, they [Lush] are nothing really special, but here we think they are great—we are so pathetic."

At that moment, I was the "other," taken as an expert on 'Western' goods, even when I explained that I did not shop there because I thought it was too expensive. But Svetlana added, "You know, we don't really have a choice [if we want to keep up with 'Western' fashion]. If we had a choice, we would choose not to shop here."

Similarly, Voja once told me that the limited choice of Western consumer goods in Serbia makes people uncritical and "unethical" in their shopping habits. In other words, if there was a choice, people would be able to criticize certain shops or "excessive spending" and through that very critique they would be able to become what they criticize.[16]

Conclusion

My informants end up being located in an uncomfortable position in terms of shopping in Novi Sad: whatever they are offered, they assume that it is not quite the "real thing," or that if it is it does not have a really very high value in the West. Therefore, it is all about location, e.g., social and political context: Novi Sad is not London or Paris, and for that simple reason, there is no possibility that the shops or the people will be of a similar quality or status to those that exist in London and Paris. The fact that all the same things, both the "nasty goods" of open markets and Lush shops, also exist in some parts of London and Paris is irrelevant: the issue, it seems to me, is that this is Serbia, and in Serbia it is hard for these people to be recognized as being the people that they wish to be, or feel themselves to be. For my informants, in order to be regarded as "performed subjects" who "apply individual agency in acts of consumption" (Cronin 2005: 10), they *first* had to be recognized as individuals of certain kind. In that sense, performativity embedded in the act of consumption, through which citizens are supposed to be consumers, was not enough. My informants had to be recognized as citizens in order to perform/build themselves as consumers they wish to be.

My informants' attempts to be recognized as average cosmopolitan persons was based on the Western model of the individual that has as its imperative the recognition "of each individual for their unique identity—for their difference from others, rather than for their equality with others" (Cronin 2005: 22). For my informants, this

[16] This is their recognition of their inability to "catch up" with the West that is also an appreciation of their inability to "pass" for Western and "middle class." And this inability was different from that of the *nouveau riche* who are also unable to "pass." The difference is that my informants think that the *nouveau riche* are not aware of their incapacity.

difference is achievable in a *local context* with variously defined internal others (like previously mentioned shop assistants, or local boutique owners), but it is unachievable in the "*global*" *one* through which they measure themselves. The difference of location between them and the imagined others of the West is the difference that *disables* their *potential for difference* which should be achievable through consumer choice. The consumer choice they were presented with seemed not to be a choice at all—their "authenticity" was unachievable through shopping, as the very discourse of shopping disabled them to build themselves as the people they wish to be. Of course, this applies only if someone believes in the distinction of West/non-West in the first place. If there is no such belief, then there is no reason to avoid or to choose "Western goods," as they are not different from the ones that are not "Western." Furthermore, the distinction may actually be useful to people in some contexts and less useful in others. Finally, even if people take the distinction seriously, there could also be some variations—some things that are "non-Western" could occur in the "West" and some things that are "Western" could occur in places that are not clearly "Western." So long as those distinctions are understood to be ideological, where they occur can be entirely flexible. There is no essential or automatic link between certain people, certain parts of the world, and a stereotypical, idealized "West." However, there *is* an economic, political, and media-dominated link between them. With that in mind, my research participants were free to try and generate whatever aspects of the "West" they liked, but they did not necessarily have the power to make themselves "Western." In that sense, my informants—young, well educated, and Serbs having a relatively high social status—feel dislocated, and are attempting to distinguish themselves from everything they consider to place them in a position of being different from any average cosmopolitan person, a status that seems impossible to attain.

Acknowledgments I would like to thank my informants for their continued patience with my work and especially Nikolina Nedeljkov for her help and hospitality. I would also like to thank my mother Slavica Simić and my aunt Slobodanka Andrić for taking care of my baby daughter, which enabled me to write this chapter.

References

Appadurai, Arjun. 1986. Introduction: Commodities and the Politics of Value. In *The Social Life of Things: Commodities in Cultural Perspective*, ed. Appadurai Arjun, 3–63. Cambridge: Cambridge UP.

Baudrillard, Jean. 1981. *For a Critique of the Political Economy of Sign*. St. Louis, MO: Telos.

Baudrillard, Jan. 1983. *In the Shadow of the Silent Majorities*. New York: Semiotext(e).

Baudrillard, Jean. 1993. *Symbolic Exchange and Death*. London: Sage.

Berdahl, Daphne. 1999. *Where the World Ended: Re-unification and Identity in the German Borderland*. Berkeley: Univ. of California Press.

Brković, Čarna, and Andrew Hodges. 2015. Rethinking World Anthropologies Through Fieldwork: Perspectives on "Extended Stay" and "Back-and-Forth" Methodologies. *Anthropol Noteb* 21 (1): 107–120.

Bryson, J. Phillip. 1984. *The Consumer Under Socialist Planning: The East German Case*. New York: Praeger.

Burawoy, Michael, and Katherine Verdery. 1999a. *Uncertain Transition: Ethnographies of Change in the Postsocialist World*. Lanham: Rowman & Littlefield Publisher.

———. 1999b. Introduction. In *Uncertain Transition: Ethnographies of Change in the Postsocialist World*, ed. Michael Burawoy and Katherine Verdery, 1–17. Lanham: Rowman & Littlefield Publisher.

Campbell, Colin. 1987. *The roMantic Ethic and the Spirit of Modern Consumerism*. Oxford: Basil Blackwell.

Carrier, G. James, and Joslah McC. Heyman. 1997. Consumption and Political Economy. *J Roy Anthropol Inst* 3 (2): 355–373.

Chelcea, Liviu. 2002. The Culture of Shortage During State-Socialism: Consumption Practices in a Romanian Village in the 1980s. *Cult Stud* 16 (1): 16–43.

Crăciun, Magdalena. 2012. Rethinking Fakes, Authenticating Selves. *J Roy Anthropol Inst* 18: 846–863.

———. 2014. *Material Culture and Authenticity: Fake Branded Fashion in Europe*. London and New York: Bloomsbury.

Cronin, M. Anne. 2005. *Advertising and Consumer Citizenship: Gender, Images and Rights*. London and New York: Routledge.

Crowley, David. 2000. Warsaw's Shops, Stalinism and the Thaw. In *Style and Socialism: Modernity and Material Culture in Post-War Eastern Europe*, ed. Susan E. Reid and David Crowley, 25–47. Oxford and New York: Berg.

De Certeau, M. 1988. *The Practice of Everyday Life*. Berkeley, Los Angeles, London: Univ. of California Press.

Deleuze, Gilles, and Felix Guattari. 2004. *A Thousand Plateaus: Capitalism and Schizophrenia*. London and New York: Continuum International Publishing Group.

Erdei, Iidiko. 2006a. Odrastanje u poznom socijalizmu – od "Pionira malenih" do "vojske Potrošača"[Growing Up in Late Socialism – From "Little Pioneers" to "Army of Consumers"]. In *Devijacije i promašaji. Etnografija domaćeg socijalizma*, ed. Lada Č. Feldman and Ines Prica, 205–240. Zagreb: Institut za etnologiju i folkloristiku.

Erdei, Ildiko. 2006b. It Takes Two to Tango: Encounters of "East" and "West" in Everyday Economies in Post-Socialist Serbia. In *Places of Encounter*, ed. Rajko Muršič and Jaka Repič, 151–168. Ljubljana: Filozofska fakulteta, Oddelek za etnologijo in kulturno antropologijo.

Featherstone, Mike. 2000. *Consumer Culture and Postmodernism*. London, Thousands Oaks, New Delhi: SAGE Publications.

Gellner, Ernest. 1994. *Conditions of Liberty: Civil Society and its Rivals*. London: Hamish Hamilton.

________. 1995. *Anthropology and Politics: Revolutions in the Sacred Grove*. Oxford: Basil Blackwell.

Herzfeld, Michael. 1997. *Cultural Intimacy: Social Poetics in the Nation-State*. New York and London: Routledge.

Humphrey, Caroline. 1999. Traders, "Disorder", and Citizenship Regimes in Provincial Russia. In *Uncertain Transition: Ethnographies of Change in the Postsocialist World*, ed. Michael Burawoy and Katherine Verdery, 19–52. Lanham: Rowman & Littlefield Publisher.

———. 2002. *The Unmaking of Soviet Life: Everyday Economies After Socialism*. Ithaca, N.Y. and London: Cornell UP.

Jansen, Stef. 2005. *Antinacionalizam: Etnografija otpora u Beogradu i Zagrebu. [Antinationalism: Ethnography of Resistance in Zagreb and Belgrade]*. Beograd: Biblioteka XX vek.

Kellner, Douglas. 1983. Critical Theory, Commodities and the Consumer Society. *Theory Cult Soc* 1 (3): 66–83.

Kornai, János. 1980. *Economics of Shortage (Vol. A and B)*. Amsterdam: North-Holland.

Kovačević, Ivan. 1985. Socijalno-emfatička funkcija monumentalnih grobnica [Monumental Tombs in the Function of Social Emphasis]. *Etnološke sveske* 6: 82–94.

Lampland, Martha. 1995. *The Object of Labor: Commodification in Socialist Hungary*. Chicago and London: The Univ. of Chicago Press.
Luthar, Breda. 2006. Remembering Socialism: On Desire, Consumption and Surveillance. *J Consum Cult* 6 (2): 229–259.
Malešević, Miroslava, and Dobrila Bratić. 1982. Kuća kao statusni simbol [House as the Symbol of Social Status]. *Etnološke sveske* 4: 144–152.
McKendrick, Neil, John Brewer, and Johan H. Plumb. 1982. *The Birth of a Consumer Society: The Commercialization of Eighteenth-Century England*. London: Europa.
Miller, Daniel. 1987. *Material Culture and Mass Consumption*. Oxford: Basil Blackwell.
———. 1995. Introduction: Anthropology, Modernity and Consumption. In *Worlds Apart: Modernity Through the Prism of the Local*, ed. Daniel Miller, 1–22. London and New York: Routledge.
———. 2001. The Poverty of Morality. *J Consum Cult* 1 (2): 225–243.
Mintz, Sideny W. 1985. *Sweetness and Power: The Place of Sugar in Modern History*. New York and London: Sifton.
Patterson, Patrick H. 2003. Truth Half Told: Finding the Perfect Pitch for Advertising and Marketing in Socialist Yugoslavia, 1950–1991. *Enterp Soc* 4: 179–225.
Rollason, William. 2008. Conuter Parts: Clothing, Value and the Sites of Otherness in Panapompom Ethnographic Encounters. *Anthropol Forum* 18 (1): 17–35.
Sassatelli, Roberta. 2007. *Consumer Culture: History, Theory and Politics*. London: SAGE Publications.
Simić, Marina. 2012. When Money is Not Enough: Selling and Shopping in Novi Sad. *Ethnologia Balkanica* 16: 73–91.
———. 2016. Moral (Dis)Order and Social Anomie: Concepts of Community and Society in Post-Socialist Serbia. *Glasnik Etnografskog instituta SANU* 64 (1): 93–105.
Skeggs, Beverly. 2004. *Class, Self, Culture*. London: Routledge.
Smith, Jeff. 2003. From Házi to Hyper Market: Discourses on Time, Money, and Food in Hungary. *Anthropol E Eur Rev* 21 (1): 179–188.
Strathern, Marilyn. 1992. *After Nature: English Kinship in the Late Twentieth Century*. Cambridge: Cambridge UP.
Švab, Alenka. 2002. Consuming Western Image of Well-Being – Shopping Tourism in Socialist Slovenia. *Cult Stud* 16 (1): 63–79.
Szalai, Julia. 2000. From Informal Labor to Paid Occupations: Marketization from Below in Hungarian Women's Work. In *Reproducing Gender: Politics, Publics, and Everyday Life After Socialism*, ed. Susan Gal and Gail Kligman, 200–224. Princeton, NJ: Princeton UP.
Szerbhorvàth, György. 2002. Suffering and Legitimacy. *Cult Stud* 16 (1): 127–144.
Taussig, Michael. 1993. *Mimesis and Alterity: A Particular History of the Senses*. London and New York: Routledge.
Verdery, Katherine. 1996. *What was Socialism, and What Comes Next?* Princeton, New Jersey: Princeton UP.
Williams, Rosalind H. 1982. *Dream Worlds: Mass Consumption in Late Nineteenth Century France*. Berkeley and Oxford: Univ. of California Press.
Woodward, L. Susan. 1995. *Socialist Unemployment: Political Economy of Yugoslavia 1945-90*. Princeton: Princeton UP.
Worsley, Peter. 1970. *The Trumpet Shall Sound: A Study of 'Cargo' Cults in Melanesia*. London: Paladin.
Yurchak, Alexei. 2006. *Everything Was Forever, Until it Was No More: The Last Soviet Generation*. Princeton and Oxford: Princeton UP.
Žižek, Slavoj. 1992. *Enjoy Your Symptom!: Jacques Lacan in Hollywood and Out*. New York and London: Routledge.
———. 2008. *For they Know Not what they Do: Enjoyment as a Political Factor*. London: Verso.

The Meanings and Practices of "Consumer Activism" in Postsocialist Bulgaria

Yuson Jung

Introduction

Back in 1999 when I was just starting my research about consumer culture after socialism in Bulgaria, my Bulgarian teacher took me to a resort by the Black Sea near Varna: "this is how you can understand Bulgarian culture and mentality!" This trip proved to be memorable for several reasons, but especially in terms of introducing me to key consumer phenomena in postsocialist Bulgaria, namely the notion of "*mente*" (fake, fraudulent, or counterfeit in the local parlance), and the prevailing sense of distrust (vis-à-vis the merchants, the stores, the consumer experts, the state, etc.) in the everyday consumption practices.

During our stay at the resort, predominantly occupied by Bulgarians (as opposed to foreign tourists), my teacher and I would often pick up drinks such as bottled water, soft drinks, or wine from the stores in the resort. One morning I noticed that my water tasted a bit unusual with an unpleasant aftertaste and asked my teacher to taste it. After a sip, she shrugged her shoulders and replied: "*mente* (fake/fraudulent/counterfeit)!" It seemed that she was not even surprised by this incident. At that time, I did not fully understand her reaction (in other words, how common this experience with *mente* was among Bulgarian consumers) other than thinking this must be a typical case of deception with fraudulent goods in touristy areas. In my subsequent experiences for almost two decades of studying Bulgarian consumer culture, however, I was often brought back to this cultural expression of "*mente*." In fact, it was not difficult to notice how *mente* was deeply embedded in Bulgarians' everyday experiences of consumption.

When state socialism collapsed in 1989 and a capitalist market economy started in postsocialist Eastern Europe, everyday consumption practices became central in people's experiences with the rapidly transforming society. The stereotypical con-

Y. Jung (✉)
Wayne State University, Detroit, MI, USA
e-mail: yuson.jung@wayne.edu

E. Krasteva-Blagoeva (ed.), *Approaching Consumer Culture*, International Series on Consumer Science, https://doi.org/10.1007/978-3-030-00226-8_6

trast between consumption under socialism and capitalism often manifested itself as shopping under scarcity of goods with long queues, versus shopping in the abundance of goods but with little money. In consumption studies since the call to overcome the productivist bias (e.g., Douglas and Isherwood 1979; Miller 1995, 2012; Featherstone 1991), everyday consumption practices have often been analyzed as expressions of creative individual agency, identity politics, or economics (Humphrey 1995). In my study about postsocialist consumption practices in Bulgaria, however, I realized that consumption was not always about creative expressions of one's identities or manipulating the larger structure by means of individual agency. Such approaches are premised upon the idea that consumption practices are essentially matters of individual choice. In postsocialist Bulgaria ordinary consumers grappled with a market environment which was flooded with *mente* (fake) goods which included goods that were of inferior quality and possibly unsafe. It is important to note that "fake" in this context implies a range of things such as counterfeit, knock-off, and simply lower quality things (trying to be like the originals). Thus, discerning "fake stuffs" when shopping was one of the consumers' main agonies, and these agonies were often perceived as something beyond individuals' choice matters. Everyday practices in such an environment cannot be understood adequately if viewed merely from the perspective of "consumer choice."

I start with this anecdote of *mente* not because I want to highlight some Bulgarian peculiarities or exoticize the Bulgarian context. On the contrary, the problem of fake or counterfeit goods has been commonly observed and documented in many different countries in different times of their histories, and is not unique to Bulgaria (Hilton 2009; Craciun 2014; Lin 2011). The idea of consumer protection has historically developed from the idea of how to protect consumers from the abuses of the market such as fraudulent products and services (Hilton 2009; Cohen 2003). More importantly, I suggest that the phenomenon of *mente* in Bulgaria raises a number of critical questions that have preoccupied many postsocialist consumers regarding consumer activism and accountability. My Bulgarian interlocutors have often expressed ambivalence about life under democracy and capitalism:

> "There is an abundance of nice goods in the market economy, but can we all afford them?"

Even if they could afford to buy products and services, many asked themselves who would protect their rights as consumers that they could get the "decent" quality of goods and services. They pointed to the ordinary Bulgarians who feel anxious to buy stuff that might not be safe and healthy for them because they could not be certain of its quality. They frequently asked:

> "What choice do I really have—even if I have the money, how can I make sure that I am not being cheated [of *mente* products]?" "Who will be accountable for all these *moshenitzi* (thieves and bandits) who take advantage of the vulnerable consumers? How can Bulgarians have an 'anxiety-free' (*spokoen*) and 'normal' life?"

Everyday consumption practices since the collapse of state socialism have revolved around these questions, even as consumption practices also expressed one's creative self as well as individual and group identity (Caldwell and Patico 2002;

Krasteva-Blagoeva 2014, Patico 2008). And various responses to these consumer agonies and demand for accountability reflect the ways in which consumer activism is understood and practiced in postsocialist Bulgaria. Over the transition from a socialist state to a EU member state (1989–2007), Bulgarian consumers have tried to understand and exercise their rights as consumers. This process included cultivating a consumer identity seeking rights, especially because the consumer identity during an economy of scarcity (socialism) did not revolve around the idea of a right-seeking individual. Unlike consumption studies in the past where rights were understood as something to be advocated for (Hilton 2009), postsocialist consumers in Bulgaria have questioned the meaning of consumer rights, how they ought to be practiced, and who should facilitate the process of exercising rights and fulfilling responsibilities in a globalized consumer society. What seems most significant in this context is how the structural changes from a centrally planned economy to a market economy informed consumers of the role of the state—*real and perceived*—as well as other social agents such as merchants/stores and consumer experts in the economic activities of production, distribution, and consumption. The role of these different social agents is important in understanding the meanings of consumer activism in postsocialist Bulgaria.

In my study on Bulgarian consumer culture after state socialism (Jung 2014, 2009, 2019), I have noticed that the context of postsocialist consumption practices is often marked by a strong sense of distrust vis-à-vis the merchants/stores, the consumer experts, and the state. What this context is ultimately demanding is accountability by these various social agents who are expected to address and ease consumer anxiety. Thus everyday consumption practices become fascinating sites for understanding consumer activism. The relationship between consumers and social agents such as merchants, consumer experts, and in particular the state is an aspect that has not been given much attention when discussing everyday consumption practices (cf. Dunn 2008; see also Jung 2009).

By consumer activism, I refer to consumers' practices that seek rights and justice from the abuses of the marketplace, which is a common understanding in the context of consumer movements since the 1930s (Hilton 2009). Consumer activism in this sense can be facilitated by organizations such as consumer advocacy NGOs but they can also be practiced without formal organizations. Ultimately consumer activism demands social responsibility by consumers and accountability by social agents. Many consumption studies thus far have approached consumption in terms of individual choices based on ideas of desires (aspiration) within the capitalist market system (see also Hart 2012; Graeber 2011; Klumbyte 2010). Thus consumption practices in different sociocultural contexts—be they in advanced capitalist societies such as the USA, UK, or Japan, or in developing societies such as Nepal, Zambia, and Barbados—are primarily discussed in regard to identity politics and how consumption provides a rich site for expressing individual agency (Hansen 2000; Freeman 2001; Sheldon and Maclachlan 2005; Liechty 2002). But what about the larger political economy that implicitly and explicitly influences individual consumer choices (or the lack thereof) and the ways in which these choices interact with ideas on accountability?

Understanding consumption from the perspectives of consumers as merely individual shoppers who choose things and assign meanings on their choices offers an incomplete picture of modern consumption practices in the era of globalization where goods and services travel around the world in more rapid and intense ways. I argue that the postsocialist experiences offer a productive vantage point where the tension of the politics of consumption—namely, the often contradictory questions of "access" and "choice"—is reflected. And it is in this sense that the postsocialist Bulgarian case provides a significant perspective regarding consumer activism. According to historian Matthew Hilton, consumer movement across the world has started as questions of social welfare (i.e., access to basic needs) and moved towards questions of the satisfaction of individual desires (i.e., satisfaction of good life) in the past century (Hilton 2009). From the perspectives of postsocialist consumption practices in Bulgaria, the aspect of social welfare plays an important role in the meanings and practices of everyday consumption because many citizens believed that "access" was related to protection that was achieved during socialism. Hence, when the *mente* phenomenon became prevalent, many Bulgarian consumers felt that the country was "going backwards" and demanded accountability in the capitalist marketplace. Yet, there is seemingly a lack of organized collective actions or an indifference to become due-paying members of a consumer advocacy organization, for example, as a means of consumer activism in postsocialist Bulgaria. This perhaps points to the enduring conundrum of distrusting the multiple social agents (such as merchants/consumer experts/the state) that are engaged in everyday consumption practices on the one hand, but also expecting protection and accountability from them on the other hand.

In this chapter, I focus on this conundrum by examining the meanings and practices of consumer activism in postsocialist Bulgaria, and show how postsocialist consumption practices provide a productive site to understand the tension of the politics of modern consumption between "access" and "choice," and how multiple social agents (merchants, consumer experts, the state, and consumers) navigate these tensions that present themselves as moral dilemmas over abundance in the contemporary world. In the following, I will discuss two illustrative ethnographic examples, one regarding the practices of "consumer activism" vis-à-vis the merchant, and another vis-à-vis the consumer experts to tease out my arguments. Before delving into the concrete examples, I will start with an ethnographic vignette to situate my argument in the larger historical and ethnographic contexts of postsocialist Bulgaria.[1]

---

[1] This chapter is based on my long-term ethnographic research on consumption practices after state socialism, conducted over the span of 1999 and 2013 in Sofia, Bulgaria. In addition to extended periods of fieldwork (13 months in 2001–2002 and 5 months in 2008–2009), I have collected ethnographic data over the summers of 1999, 2000, 2007, 2012, and 2013. I would like to express my gratitude to Evgenia Krasteva-Blagoeva for inviting me to present an earlier version of this paper at the conference entitled "New Consumer Practices of 21st Century: Anthropological Perspectives" in Sofia, Bulgaria, in April 2015. Some of the arguments in this chapter are examined more extensively in my book, *Balkan Blues: Consumer Politics in Post-socialist Bulgaria* (2019, Indiana University Press).

Consumers Between "Access" and "Choice" in Postsocialist Bulgaria

In the years of 2000–2002, it was easy to notice a similar "odd normality" in downtown Sofia. When the work hour was coming to an end and people hurried to return home for dinner one could witness a busy crowd, donned with clothes made of modest polyester fabric moving against a backdrop of new flashy neon signs of various cafes, restaurants, and stores with Western brands and logos. While Sofia appeared relatively "emptier" in the summer months as many Sofians took off for the Black Sea for a vacation, the cafés, bars, and restaurants maintained a busy clientele. It was not uncommon for customers not to be able to find seats in the afterwork hours in popular bars and restaurants. While I was waiting with a friend for a table in front of a popular pizza restaurant of Vitoshka (a main boulevard in Sofia) in 2000, I could not help thinking how ironic it was that every Sofian I had met would complain about the poverty of Bulgarians and lament the increasing number of Bulgarians going through the garbage bins, while the cafés and restaurants seemed always full.

In fact, my friends themselves would joke about this phenomenon and taught me the local expression of "*burkan bank*" (jar bank) which was a pun of the Bulgarian National Bank "Bul Bank" undergoing a controversial privatization process then. *Burkan* referred to a glass jar where Bulgarians traditionally put pickled vegetables and fruit preserves. During the turmoil of the social changes of the first decade of transition with dramatically fluctuating currency rate and ever-increasing inflation rate, Bulgarians supposedly started to put their money in this glass jar and/or under their mattresses. Although the name of their national bank was "Bul Bank," it was in fact in the "*burkan bank*" the story went, where Bulgarians actually saved their money. My friends explained that "Bul Bank" had no money and was bankrupt, but "*burkan bank*" was not. Consequently, they laughingly added that although Bulgarians were poor, they could still hang out in these social venues thanks to their *burkan bank*. The joke possibly offered an explanation to this discrepancy between the official statistics of a monthly average salary of 132 Lev and the successful (!) business of these cafés, bars, and restaurants then. But could there be other explanations why my friend and I had to wait for half an hour to get a table? I did notice over time during my stays and visits to Sofia that the primary customers in these busy social places tended to be younger, such as college students who lived with and were still supported by their parents. Or they were young adults who often lived with their parents but had disposable income even if it was small. The older crowd in those places could be more often seen having only a cup of coffee or a soft drink which did not cost much.

While Bulgaria's living standards have improved over the following decade as they joined the European Union in 2007, the rising inequality between the haves and have-nots continued to influence the way ordinary consumers viewed themselves as consumers. When Bulgarians refer to "ordinary consumers" they are the ones that are considered "have-nots" in comparison to those "haves" who are called "the rich," referred often as those who accumulated sudden wealth during the transition period.

The wealth was often believed to be from shady privatization of previously state-owned properties and other business deals that used legal loopholes. According to my interlocutors, all of whom considered themselves as "ordinary," they still aspired to be "normal" consumers who do not have to feel constantly anxious about their everyday purchases. This is an important context through which one can understand postsocialist consumption practices: namely, how everyday consumption is not only a matter of individual "choice" to fulfill desire, but also a matter of "access" to fulfill needs. Access here is not simply about access to "basic needs" such as food, clothes, and shelter, but access to "normal-quality" stuffs and services so, as an ordinary consumer, one does not need to feel anxious or deceived when engaging in daily consumption practices. In other words, consumption for ordinary Bulgarians in the aftermath of state socialism often entailed the question of "access" because it was related to a sense of normality they were used to (such as a seaside vacation at the Black Sea), or aspired to (such as hanging out in bars and restaurants like during socialism (e.g., in an unassuming neighborhood bar (*kruchma*) or a sweet house (*sladkarnitsa*)).

While consumption studies about the Western societies with capitalist systems tend to take "individual choice" for granted in discussing consumption practices, historian Matthew Hilton observes that the history of consumerism in the Western societies had a turning point in the 1980s when the meaning of consumerism changed from *access* to *choice* (Hilton 2009). This suggests that the idea of "consumer" is also subjected to historical and sociocultural contexts. This change from seeing the consumer as the agent for "access" to the agent of "choice" was significantly influenced by the antiregulatory agenda of neoliberal capitalism and globalization. Before that when modern consumerism developed since the eighteenth century, the consumer was considered as someone who needed protection, especially from the abuses of the market. The important question here is who should protect the consumer? In many capitalist societies, consumer movements have mobilized individual consumers to protect themselves through consumer boycott (e.g., Ralph Nader in the 1960s against the automobile companies). More recently, ethical consumerism such as fair trade (as opposed to free trade) or organics (as opposed to chemical-laden conventional production) is increasingly engaged as a mean to address unfair labor practices and inequities within the globalized neoliberal market regime. Here too the agent of protection is the individual consumer (as shopper) who exercises one's rights and responsibilities as a consumer to protect not only one's own well-being but also the well-being of others (such as the less privileged and the disadvantaged). This suggests how the meanings and practices of consumer activism cannot be taken for granted, and requires them to be situated ethnographically to understand the complex aspects of consumers' practices in the era of post-Cold War and neoliberal capitalism. The Bulgarian case offers an interesting vantage point to think about consumption practices in a more nuanced and complex ways.

Distrust vis-à-vis Merchants/Stores

As I settled more into my extensive fieldwork routine in 2001–2002, I began to notice frequent and bitter commentaries by my Bulgarian interlocutors concerning their purchases and consumer experiences. Consumers' daily complaints, for example, varied from poor-quality yogurt and meat products (*kolbasi*) to batteries, shoes, cell phone services, heating bills, salespeople, and restaurant and dry cleaning services. At first, I thought they were perhaps complaining because a foreign researcher was there to listen. Yet, my interlocutors in the consumer advocacy NGOs[2], as well as Bulgarian talk shows on TV and newspaper reports, identified two elements to the common agony of Bulgarian consumers: deception and low purchasing power. During my fieldwork at the consumer NGO in 2001–2002 and in 2007, I was also able to see the written consumer complaints filed with the consumer organizations. They were very similar to the daily complaints one could hear in the Bulgarian everyday practices and persisted into the 2010s. Such consumer complaints were important in understanding postsocialist consumption practices because they reflected consumers' intimate engagements with the larger social changes and highlighted the issues of accountability in the context of everyday consumption. As Geertz has insisted, analyzing social change requires an understanding of the passions and imaginings that provoke and inform it (Geertz 1984). Daily consumer complaints offer a great window to such passions and imaginings of social changes. It also animates discussions on why, despite the social discontent reflected in the complaining practices, there has been little collective resistance (one typical form of activism) involved.

In 2007 several months after Bulgaria became a member of the European Union, I was catching up with a friend in Sofia, a working mom in her early 50s who was eager to share her recent experience with a dry cleaner in her neighborhood. Her pants suit got damaged but her dry cleaner refused to admit the fault and compensate her. She was very frustrated that her neighborhood dry cleaner to whom she regularly brought her cloths would not take responsibility. In a very animated fashion she said:

> "I was so mad that I thought to myself, I will not let this go in this way. Not this time. Enough. So I went to the 'Agency for Consumer Protection' and explained to them the situation. A friendly man there told me that I could write a 'petition' marks and file a formal complaint so the agency could look into the matter. My husband and friends all told me that I was wasting my time. But I was determined that I would do something about this immoral people. I am lucky that I have a job and the damaged suit will not ruin me, but as a consumer, don't I have rights now? Could these merchants be so dumb to cut a regular in this way and risk their reputation in the neighborhood? In any case, I wrote the petition in much detail and took it first back to the dry cleaner. I told them I would file the complaint

[2] Consumer advocacy NGOs were established in Bulgaria after the collapse of state socialism as part of the EU accession requirement. Hence, the consumer NGOs in Bulgaria were more of a top-down project rather than a grassroots organization. As of 2017, there were over two dozens registered consumer advocacy NGOs although some of them are not very active. For my research, I have been following the most active consumer NGO which was established in 1999 when new consumer law was passed in Bulgaria's parliament. See more in Jung (2010, 2019).

> with the government agency if they would continue to refuse to admit fault. I was nice to them—I did not raise my voice. I was civil. But guess what? I could not believe that they were the same people I dealt with in the past years. They bluntly told me—'Go ahead. Do whatever you want Ma'am.'"

After a deep sigh my friend said that she filed the complaint with the Agency. She checked with them every month for 3 months. Nothing happened. But she was determined to see an end to it. After another 3 months, she was finally told that the merchant (dry cleaners) refused to cooperate to appear in a mediation session with the consumer, and there were no other complaints filed against the same merchant so there was essentially nothing that the Agency could do any further. My friend looked at me and slowly said:

> "So … not that I was terribly disappointed that nothing got resolved … it would have been actually a big surprise if something did happen. But I have to admit, it nevertheless left me with a bitter sense that there is *nothing* I can trust as a consumer—even my neighborhood dry cleaner … Merchants—they are all *mente* and don't care about their customers."

My friend expressed a deep sense of distrust to merchants but stopped short of raising the question of who could fix the problems of the vulnerable consumers. Her final comment that "merchants, they are all *mente*" meant that they did not think they had a responsibility vis-à-vis their customers and were not interested in keeping the business going. As she also added:

> "these people, they are just interested in making money quickly—long-term interests are not important to them …."

This sentiment was echoed by numerous consumers in Sofia with whom I talked. As these interlocutors often asked:

> "if I buy a *mente* and waste my money, and even jeopardize my health, is this my fault? Who is responsible?"

According to the public talks by consumer experts[3] who have often embraced themselves with the discourse of the EU's consumer policy (reflecting the neoliberal turn of the global economy), each consumer ought to be responsible for oneself. To claim one's consumer rights, the consumer has to be better informed and make better choices. "Protection" from the abuses of the market, therefore, was to be done by consumers themselves with better information about the products and services. Consumer advocacy organizations were there to help *inform* consumers and ease discontent. Note here that the notion of "protection" is absent. Many of my Bulgarian interlocutors across different age groups and gender, however, believed that such an approach would only make sense if a "normal" system was in place. If one had to worry about food safety when purchasing daily groceries such as cheese and milk, my informants insisted then one knew the system was abnormal. In "normal" countries, they continued, consumers did not need to be afraid of purchasing "garbage"

[3] In Bulgaria, professionals who work at consumer advocacy NGOs refer themselves to "consumer experts" rather than "consumer activists" which is a more common way to describe these professionals in the Western societies.

products. Granted, the "normalcy" they invoked was often an imagined one, based on their normative ideal rather than based on actual realities of "Western countries," as postsocialist citizens increasingly learned the setbacks of Western liberal democracy. With little trust for the merchants, however, their form of "consumer activism" for now was to rely on their own experiences and those of their friends and families to avoid engaging with *mente.*

My Bulgarian interlocutors' uneasiness about creating a viable consumer sector by means of consumer activism as proposed by the EU model stemmed from their distrust of their "abnormal" system and people. As a result, consumer complaints were rarely channeled through formal Western-influenced consumer activism and consumer advocacy organizations (NGOs) in the postsocialist context. This meant that ordinary consumers did not believe that the civil organizations ("consumer experts") could fix the problem with the system.

Another interlocutor reported a similar incident in the fall of 2008. She bought a carton of milk from a supermarket chain and got sick. The milk's expiration date had not passed. When we gathered together with two other friends at her house, she complained first how such milk could even be on the shelf for sale. Then, she remarked sarcastically that during socialism you never had to look at the expiration date because there would be nothing left on the shelf due to the limited amount and irregularity of supply. I asked her whether she went back to exchange her milk. She shrugged her shoulders and said she doubted that they would do anything. One time in 2002, I pointed out to my former landlady (who was at that time in her 80s) as she was buying a pack of yogurt that she should look at the dates. This happened in one of those old-style neighborhood stores where the salesperson gave the desired item over the counter when the buyer asked for it. My landlady explained to me that she had been shopping in that store for a long time and they never gave her anything bad. Moreover, she added that was why she preferred to go to this store where she knew the salesperson, rather than to go to Western-style supermarkets or other stores where a personalized relationship between the buyer and the seller did not exist. Hence, one did not have to bother looking at the expiration date of the product. It is interesting to note, however, that the seller of the store that my landlady frequented did not really have a personalized relationship with her. She recognized her face, but rarely did they exchange any personal greetings or engage in pleasantries. Nevertheless, for my landlady, the same familiar face she saw regularly was more assuring than the unfamiliar faces she would encounter by going to Western-style supermarkets where sellers rotated and took shifts because ultimately it was about "trust." Regardless of the expiration date, my interlocutors mentioned that without the "trust" relationship, you are more prone to buy "*mente*."

I asked my landlady whether the personal relationship with the salesperson was such a decisive factor in shopping. I wondered whether she did not enjoy the right to choose directly from the shelves among various items in the supermarkets. Neither my landlady nor my other friends whom I asked seemed to regard such "choice" (or way of choosing) as a big deal in daily grocery shopping. More important was the fact that they could trust the products they bought from the stores. My friend who bought the spoiled milk explicitly stated that she felt less vulnerable to deception under such familiar circumstances. This indicated that in both my friend's and former landlady's experiences, the consumer asked to be "protected" by a trusted agent or system. And the protecting parties included the newly emerged group of consumer activists to whom consumers turned with the expectation of protection and fixing the "abnormal" system.

Distrust vis-à-vis Consumer Experts: Credible Consumer Information Should Be Free?

In 2009, I was invited to observe two focus group interviews organized by a consumer NGO, BNAAC (Bulgarian National Association Active Consumers),[4] which I had been following for my research since 2001. BNAAC was conducting a study to figure out how their consumer magazine could sell better. Similar to the consumer magazines in the Western countries such as *Consumer Reports* (USA), *Which?* (UK), *Que Choisier* (France), and *Test* (Germany), BNAAC argued that Bulgarian consumers needed to be better informed in order to make better choices, and it worked hard to start an independent consumer magazine in Bulgaria. Essentially, these consumer magazines were based on independent comparative testing of various commodities and services in the marketplace ranging from food items to electronics and banking services. BNAAC managed to get seed funds from the EU to roll out the magazine. It put a lot of resources in conducting the independent testing and offering credible information to consumers. It also became a member of the ICRT (International Consumer Research and Testing), an international, independent, and reputable organization that ran comparative testing on global products. As a subscribed member, BNAAC had access to the test results and could publish the relevant ones in its magazine. For products that were available only in the domestic markets (e.g., Bulgarian food products), they contracted independent labs affiliated with BAN (Bulgarian National Academy). In order to make the consumer magazine sustainable, they needed to increase the subscription base and sell more magazines. This study came about in this context.

Collaborating with a market research consulting firm which specialized in focus group interviews, two of the consumer NGO staff, one of the firm's staff and I listened in to the focus group discussion in the adjacent room which had a large window that enabled us to see and hear the discussion. As is the case with a standard focus group setting, the moderator and participants of the focus group could not see us. The moderator who was a trained sociologist and an experienced focus group leader started the discussion by asking the participants how they generally obtain information about products when they shop. The ten participants appeared to be on the younger side, in their 20s and 30s, but there were also a couple of people in their 40s

[4]This organization changed its name from BNCA, Bulgarian National Consumer Association, in 2010.

and 50s. To the first question by the moderator, several participants said that they looked up information on the Internet. The moderator probed how they determined the credibility of the information they found in the Internet. One of them answered that he would look at the rating and reviews on the commercial websites where they sell the products. Another mentioned that he relied on a website called BG-Mamma where users share information about products.[5] One woman mentioned that she asked her sister and friends when she needed information about products. When the moderator asked how they knew to trust the information they found either from the Internet or from friends, several participants shrugged their shoulders and one man responded:

> "well, you don't just rely on one piece of information but read through several opinions on the Internet and make up your mind. I think I am pretty good at knowing what to trust and what not to trust—I'm unable to explain better, but I just know."

The woman who said she relied on her sister and friends mentioned that word-of-mouth information tends to be accurate because it is usually based on first-hand experience with the product from people you trust. The discussion continued for a little while about how one could not trust fully what the stores sold or what the sales people said. Needless to say, several *mente* (fake stuff) experiences were shared during the discussion accompanied by a commonly observed frustration about the state (*durjavata*) unable to control the *mente* products.

Then, the moderator showed several issues of the recently published consumer magazine by BNAAC. She passed them around the table. The magazine had been in the market for about a year and half at that point. She first asked whether the participants had seen the magazine. In that particular focus group, nobody had actually seen it although some of them recognized the name of the consumer organization. The group dynamic was collegial and quite engaged and nobody seemed aloof or bored. The moderator gave them a little time to look through the magazine and then continued to ask what they thought of the magazine and the information it offered. One man raised his hand and said,

> "it looks very professionally done—who funds these tests?"

The moderator explained how the tests were done and how the consumer organization received the results (as explained earlier in this section). Another man noticed that the magazine had a price printed on the front page: 3 leva (about $1.70). The magazine's price belonged to the lower-medium range among the popular magazines available in the newsstand around the city.

> "Hmm … 3 leva …," the man said, "I like the way it looks with nice quality pictures and no advertisement … it seems that the magazine is a serious one …. But I don't think I would pay 3 leva because I can get this kind of information on the Internet for free."

[5] Over the years, BG-Mamma (www.bg-mamma.com) has become an influential information portal site where ordinary consumers exchange information on products as well as parenting and other everyday matters, but in 2009 they were just becoming popular and were not frequented by a lot of people yet.

A woman asked where one could find this magazine and why the consumer organization did not publicize it better so more people knew about it. More participants chimed in with their thoughts about the magazine as they flipped through the pages. What struck me as the most interesting message that the focus group participants expressed was the idea that they did not think they should pay for this kind of consumer information, even though they recognized that the information in the magazine seemed serious (not paid by commercial interests) and reliable. Instead, they repeatedly mentioned that this kind of information should be offered by the state for free since all consumers were vulnerable by the rampant abuses of the Bulgarian marketplace. At one point, the moderator went back to the man's commentary earlier about how the Internet provided similar information for free. When she asked how he knew whether the Internet offered credible information, he responded: "well, there is no guarantee, but how can you guarantee that *paid* information is better and more objective? Shouldn't the state provide this kind of information for free? As consumers, we have the rights to access credible information, or?"

As described earlier, the participants of the focus group were a mix group of people in terms of ages and professions. The hesitation about accessing reliable information by paying for it (i.e., buying the consumer magazine) was related to the expectation they had from the state in terms of its role in responding to consumers' needs ("access"). Namely, the state is (and *ought to be*) responsible for protecting ordinary consumers from the rampant abuses of the marketplace. This included providing credible information for free. Even though one can hear daily complaints about the state (it doesn't function normally, it is corrupt, it doesn't care about citizens, etc.), many consumers still identified the state as a key social agent that could (and should) address consumer anxiety and take accountability. This is not to say consumers will just wait for the state to take action, but in many consumers' minds it is the normative ideal they hold for a "normally functioning" state (*normalna durjava*). Here, "the protection by the state" is not simply an abstract notion in the patronizing sense as during state socialism, but in the sense that the state is accountable to enforce the laws properly to protect its citizen-consumers. Even after a decade of joining the EU, Bulgaria's judicial system continues to be criticized for corruption and this is partly why consumers continue to carry a sense of distrust and frustration in their everyday consumption practices.

This expectation of the state by consumers who did not feel confident about the "choices" that were available to them (i.e., they are unsure of the quality of products and services even if they could afford them) also explained partly why Western-style consumer organizations were having a hard time to engage ordinary citizens as members of the organization and to represent their interests. To my interlocutors, the basic rights of the consumers were associated with the protection by the state as the normative ideal, in that the state is obliged to take care of the abuses of the marketplace. If the contemporary consumer movement revolved around the idea of providing better information to consumers, then in my interlocutors' minds, this ought to be done for free by the social agents such as the state or the consumer organization. For many consumers, the credibility of the information was to be guaranteed ultimately by the state, even if the information was gathered by consumer organizations.

This kind of expectation of the state is premised upon a cultural logic in which "choices" are not considered "real" choices (you cannot be guaranteed of the quality you paid for) and it was more important that "access" was guaranteed and protected (the state could enforce the laws so basic quality and safety standards were not compromised). While the mission of this kind of consumer magazine in Western capitalist societies has changed over the years reflecting the larger changes from an emphasis on "access" to "choice" regarding consumer politics, this logic did not resonate much among postsocialist consumers, despite the continued consumers' frustration regarding various *mente* products: even if they were to focus on their "choices," those choices had to be enabled foremost by access to credible information provided for free by the state because it was considered one of the state's fundamental responsibilities towards its citizens.

Concluding Remark: The Conundrum of Consumer-State Relations After State Socialism

Consumer activism is a form of consumer politics that originated historically within the nation-state boundaries to protest against market abuses in the Western world (Hilton 2009). Consumer campaigns such as product and corporate boycotts have promoted alternative moral economies and politicized the act of consumption, thereby giving ordinary people a chance to organize themselves as "citizen-consumers" (Cohen 1998, 2006). While consumers' leagues through which consumers could mobilize themselves started in the late nineteenth century, the establishments of modern consumer rights advocacy organizations came about when the consumer society reached a certain level of maturity measured by a prosperous marketplace (Cohen 1998: 2–4, Cohen 2006). Prominent consumer activists such as Ralph Nader became synonyms for the so-called consumer movement in the Western world in the 1960s. Consumer movements expanded gradually worldwide in the second half of the twentieth century as marketplaces in the developing world matured and consumers there likewise participated in the global world of goods. During this process, the meaning of "consumer rights" evolved from *rights to access* to *rights to choice*, and there was a tremendous growth of consumer protection systems all over the world through grassroots initiatives (Hilton 2009: 11–13). Given such a historical trajectory of consumer activism which was mostly organically grown out of consumers' need in the daily market activities, a top-down approach to a national consumer sector required by the EU in the postsocialist context constitutes an interesting comparison for understanding global consumer movements and consumption practices in the globalization era.

As discussed in this chapter, the meaning of consumer activism and how it ought to be practiced in postsocialist Bulgaria are particularly noteworthy in regard to how "trust" vis-à-vis different social agents (merchants, consumer organizations, the state) was a key notion in consumers' everyday experiences. My discussion in this chapter has not focused on whether Bulgaria does or does not have consumer activism. Rather, my argument is that it is important to understand the different social and cultural contexts in which ordinary consumers try to deal with the abuses of the marketplace, by seeking both better choice and access. During this process, they developed their respective consumer competence as individual consumers to make better choices and not buy *mente* for example, but if they fail with their consumer competence, they also demanded the state to fix the abuses of the marketplace. This is how postsocialist Bulgarian consumers think consumer activism ought to be practiced by demanding the state to provide consumers with a sense of normalcy and anxiety-free everyday life through building up trust that the system works (laws are enforced, judicial system functions without corruption, etc.). While consumption practices show many interesting aspects of individualized desires and identity politics, and how agency is exercised in the world of goods, they also reflect other social relationships such as between the individuals, the state, and various civil organizations. Everyday consumption practices in postsocialist Bulgaria offer a productive vantage point to understand how ordinary consumers articulate their rights and responsibilities while coping with the vagaries of the globalized world that increasingly demand contradictory aims between greater individual choice and greater collective access (Hilton 2009: 97). For many postsocialist consumers in Bulgaria, the most fundamental thing that could normalize everyday consumption experiences with less agonies about purchasing *mente* is the rebuilding of trust with different social agents including the state. In its most concrete level, this means that the merchants, the consumer organizations, as well as the state ought to recognize how this issue of trust is not a taken-for-granted matter, but at the heart of how they can connect with the consumers, combat abuses in the marketplace, and ultimately seek justice in the globalizing consumer society.

References

Caldwell, Melissa L., and Jennifer Patico. 2002. Consumers Exiting Socialism: Ethnographic Perspectives on Daily Life in Post-Communist Europe. *Ethnos* 67 (3): 285–294.

Cohen, Lizabeth 1998. à 2003. A Consumers' Republic: The Politics of Mass Consumption in Postwar America. New York: Vintage Books.

Cohen, Lizabeth. 2003. *A Consumers' Republic: The Politics of Mass Consumption in Postwar America*. New York: Vintage Books.

Cohen, Lizabeth 2006. "The Consumer's Republic: An American Model for the World?" In The Ambivalent Consumer: Questioning Consumption in East Asia and the West, edited by Sheldon Garon and Patricia Maclachlan, 45–62. Ithaca, NY: Cornell University Press.

Crăciun, Magdalena. 2014. *Material Culture and Authenticity: Fake Branded Fashion in Europe*. London: Bloomsbury.

Douglas, Mary, and Baron Isherwood. 1979. *The World of Goods: Towards and Anthropology of Consumption*. London and New York: Routledge.

Dunn, Elizabeth 2008. Postsocialist Spores: Disease, Bodies, and the State in the Republic of Georgia. American Ethnologist 35(2): 243–258.

Featherstone, Mike. 1991. *Consumer Culture and Postmodernism*. London: Sage Publications.

Freeman, Carla. 2001. *High Tech and High Heels in the Global Economy*. Durham: Duke University Press.
Garon, Sheldon, and Patricia L. Maclachlan. 2005. *The Ambivalent Consumer: Questioning Consumption in East Asia and the West*. Ithaca: Cornell University Press.
Graeber, David. 2011. Consumption. *Curr Anthropol* 52 (4): 489–511.
Geertz, Clifford 1984. "Culture and Social Change: The Indonesian Case" Man, Vol 19 (4): 511–532.
Hansen, Karen T. 2000. *Salaula: The World of Secondhand Clothing and Zambia*. Chicago: University of Chicago Press.
Hart, 2012. à Hann, Chris and Keith Hart, 2011, Economic Anthropology: History, Ethnography, Critique. Cambridge, UK: Polity.
Hilton, Matthew. 2009. *Prosperity for All: Consumer Activism in an Era of Globalization*. Ithaca: Cornell University Press.
Humphrey, Caroline. 1995. Creating a Culture of Disillusionment: Consumption in Moscow, a Chronicle of Changing Times. In *Worlds Apart: Modernity Through the Prism of the Local*, ed. Daniel Miller. London: Routledge.
Jung, Yuson. 2009. From Canned Food to Canny Consumers: Cultural Competence in the Age of Mechanical Production. In *Food and Everyday Life in the Postsocialist World*, ed. Melissa Caldwell, 29–56. Bloomington, IN: Indiana University Press.
———. 2014. Ambivalent Consumers and the Limits of Certification: Organic Foods in Post-Socialist Bulgaria. In *Ethical Eating in the Postsocialist and Socialist World*, ed. Yuson Jung, Jacob A. Klein, and Melissa Caldwell, 93–115. Berkeley: University of California Press.
———. 2019. *Balkan Blues: Consumer Politics After State Socialism in Bulgaria*. Bloomington, IN: Indiana University Press.
Klumbyte, Neringa. 2010. The Soviet Sausage Renaissance. *Am Anthropol* 112 (1): 22–37.
Krasteva-Blagoeva, Evgenia. 2014. *Vsichko za prodan. Konsumativnata kultura v Bulgaria [Total Sale. Consumer Culture in Bulgaria]*. Sofia: New Bulgarian University Press.
Liechty, Mark. 2002. *Suitably Modern: Making Middle-Class Culture in a New Consumer Society*. Princeton: Princeton University Press.
Lin, Yi-Chieh Jessica. 2011. *Fake Stuff: China and the Rise of Counterfeit Goods*. New York: Routledge.
Miller, Daniel. 1995. Introduction: Anthropology, Modernity and Consumption. In *Worlds Apart: Modernity Through the Prism of the Local*, ed. Daniel Miller. London: Routledge.
———. 2012. *Consumption and its Consequences*. Cambridge: Polity Press.
Patico, Jennifer. 2008. *Consumption and Social Change in a Post-Soviet Middle Class*. Washington, DC & Stanford, CA: Woodrow Wilson Press & Stanford University Press.

Preserves Exiting Socialism: Authenticity, Anti-standardization, and Middle-Class Consumption in Postsocialist Romania

Monica Stroe

"We make preserves ourselves in order to dodge all the poison that *they* put in our food," says Luminiţa,[1] a woman in her late 50s, as she turns off the stove top under a boiling pot with sterilizing jars of plum compote, which she has just prepared. The culprit, a vague, unnamed "they" (the public authorities? the food companies? immoral food scientists?), is presumed guilty of cheating the consumer of his or her right to health and safe products. It is early August and her pantry is already filling up with homemade preserves. Although there is still time until the intensive preserving activity in the fall, most jams and compotes in this year's campaign are already sitting on pantry shelves, in mismatched, reused jars, which once contained tomato paste, mustard, or last year's batch of jam. The supermarket chain catalogs have already started to advertise preserve-making tools and accessories (vegetable mashers, jars, lids, cauldrons) and to designate special shelves, with special offers for utensils, vinegar, jars, and spices on display. Luminiţa has intensified her preserving work since the birth of her granddaughter, in an attempt to protect her from the risks associated with the mass-produced foods available.

At roughly the same time, the Facebook group of a middle-class residential neighborhood of detached homes just outside Bucharest, which I have been following over the past months, was hosting regular posts by two of the residents selling their homemade preserves to their neighbors. The naive, amateur pictures posted show stages of the making-of process (the fruits or vegetables in the garden before picking, the boiling and the sterilization process) while orders and enthusiasm were pouring in the comments.

---

[1] The names of my informants have been changed.

The title is a direct reference to "Consumers exiting socialism: Ethnographic perspectives on daily life in post-communist Europe," an article by Jennifer Patico and Melissa L. Caldwell (2002).

M. Stroe (✉)
National University of Political Studies and Public Administration (SNSPA),
Bucharest, Romania
e-mail: monica.stroe@politice.ro

E. Krasteva-Blagoeva (ed.), *Approaching Consumer Culture*, International Series on Consumer Science, https://doi.org/10.1007/978-3-030-00226-8_7

One year ago, at a summer party fueled by several cases of bottled Grolsch beer, I seized the opportunity to ask my friends, the hosts, if I could save the empty, swing-top bottles so I could send them to my mother. Over the last years, she had been using them to store homemade tomato juice for the winter. I was surprised to have to negotiate the division of the empty beer bottles with my host, whose mother also had the same project and had claimed the bottles for her own preserve-making campaign.

The postsocialist abundance of consumer goods, including preserves, has projected the consumer into a universe of choice, which is a challenge to navigate. Supermarket shelves and Internet orders provide the typical urban consumer in present-day Romania with around-the-clock year-round opportunities to buy fresh or frozen fruit and vegetables as well as fruit or vegetable preserves from anywhere from France to Greece or Lebanon. However, shopping and preserve-making sessions with my informants were consistently marked by expressions of mistrust and precaution or resignation regarding the "honesty" of the products. They were pointing out the "E"s on the labels[2] or making comments about the "foreign" origin of common ingredients, comparatively deploring the neglect of Romanian agriculture and the lack of a market for the Romanian-grown fruit and vegetables.

In a food system regulated by the European Union, with several institutions tending to food safety and a free European market offering a wide range of shopping possibilities, suspicions regarding untraceable, unverifiable food products push certain consumers to adopt various strategies of sidestepping the conventional, formally regulated supply of convenience foods and of transitioning to alternative ways to authenticate and control the quality of their food. As the above three ethnographic episodes suggest, after the consumerist spree of the 1990s, there seems to emerge a new consumer culture, which draws a more reflexive consumer towards a reappraisal of self-provisioning. I examine the transformations in the culture of preserve consumption of Romanian middle-class consumers emerging from postsocialist Romania as a shift in meaning from necessity and shortage to the sphere of quality products. I read the jar as a metaphor of broader transformations in Romanian consumer culture.

In Romania, pantries used to stock fruit and vegetables preserved in various ways. The typical domestic stocks of fruit and vegetable preserves included fruit syrups, jams, *dulceață*, compote, sour soup seasoning, vegetables (and sometimes fruit) pickled in brine and vinegar, jarred boiled vegetables, tomato sauce, sauerkraut, and *zacuscă*. The task of translating the Romanian fruit preservation universe in English is intimidating, as, in addition to syrups and jam, there are several preservation methods, which notably include *dulceaţă* (whole or large pieces of fruit preserved in clear syrup) and *magiun* (plum jam reduced on a slow fire, with no added sugar),[3] *Zacusca* is a savory vegetable spread present in different versions and

[2] The artificial food additives that act as colorants, preservatives, stabilizers, jellifying agents, acidity correctors, flavor enhancers, or sweeteners, and are codified by the European Union with a capital E, followed by a three- or four-digit number on the labels.

[3] A blog account by British-based anthropologist and travel writer Anna Colquhoun (2008) attempts

denominations throughout the Balkans, made of a base of red peppers and onions; variations can also include eggplants, beans, mushrooms, or even fish.

For the scope of this chapter, I have followed the development of three alternative preserve-provisioning strategies, which I consider to stand as modes of resistance, or counter-reactions, of middle-class consumers to the Romanian contemporary foodscape dominated by convenience, mass-produced goods. Firstly, I examine a tendency to reconsider the quality of socialist-era foods in a positive light, as more authentic, wholesome products. Secondly, I follow and discuss the emergence of the local market for artisan preserves under the frame of "quality products," where producers and middle-class consumers negotiate new meanings and new sources of value for the preserve jars. Thirdly, I examine the revival of homemade preserves as a practice that cuts ties with its functionalist, shortage-driven version of the socialist era and becomes repositioned as a modern, empowering, and creative domestic activity of self-provisioning. My attempt is to better understand practices and meanings attached to preserves under the various spheres: the mass market, the artisan market, and the domestic self-provisioning, respectively.

Following the three coordinates described above, I will focus on preserves to examine present-day consumer culture, in an attempt to explain consumer strategies in connection to socialist and postsocialist transformations, with my focus placed on the cultural politics of self-provisioning. The research is built around the following questions:

How does preserving associate with the postsocialist transition away from the culture of shortage? How does a market for (highly deregulated) artisan jars develop? Why is this market integrated in the quality product scene? What cultural competences do consumers use to authenticate them and to establish trust? Why do middle-class consumers in an affluent postsocialist consumer society come to appreciate the food-preserving techniques associated with the socialist shortage economy? What are the new cultural meanings of domestic self-provisioning?

---

to explain post-Ottoman fruit preservation, as found during a food study trip to Romania: "[W]e seem to have identified no fewer than seven different kinds of Romanian 'jam', each with its own word, most of which seem to come from different roots. There's a clear set (but pectin-free) jelly called pelte (from a Turkish word); a thick opaque paste made of rosehips called pasta (from Latin roots); marmelada (from the Portuguese), a thick fruity paste containing apple or quince for their pectin; magiun, a very thick plum paste (also from Turkish); and gem, from the English, er, 'jam' (and, like that, a sort of mush of fruity bits). [...] Things got more interesting with dulceaţă, though—partly as Eduard makes his own quince version, by preparing little strips of quince and boiling them in syrup (it's a bit more complicated than that, of course, but you get the basic idea). It's an old traditional method, and used to be made with ingredients that we'd consider strange now—green walnuts, aubergines and tomatoes. But whatever you use, the point is to end up with something made of clear, runny syrup with whole intact fruit pieces. The look of the dulceaţă therefore becomes almost as important as the taste, and in days gone by, this said something about the household which produced it. When guests came to visit, you might serve them little bowls or spoonfuls of dulceaţă which they would admire and eat on their own (possibly with coffee, but not spread on bread or anything which would detract from their perfection)" http://www.culinaryanthropologist.org/to-romania-in-a-spoon/#more-117, accessed on July 5, 2017.

Scholarship on consumer culture often relies on the concept of authenticity associated with quality foods. Alternative food chains associated with artisan foods, constructed in opposition to the industrialized food system, are invested with authenticity, precisely based on values derived from this opposition (Pratt 2008). Pratt claims that alternative food chains are based on attempts to reconnect the worlds of production and consumption:

> "Some connections are organisational: self-provisioning, the preference given to small farmers and producers whose supply lines are "direct" or "fair", and the embedding of market relations. Others are more "discursive", the conversations about how and where the food was produced, elaborating knowledge and expertise which may be based on direct experience, or crucially on labels […]" (Pratt 2008: 67–68).

Arnould and Price speak of authenticating acts to argue what facilitates authentication during processes of construction of self and community (Arnould and Price 2000). To describe authenticating acts, the authors show.

> "specific ways in which consumers effectively appropriate individual meanings (e.g. create agency) from products and services" (Arnould and Price 2000: 148)

> "including the story of an informant making homemade horseradish paste from garden to jar. They illustrate two types of authenticating acts, where "the consumer works creatively with products or consumption experiences to obtain self-authentication" and where "a consumption object or experience is transformed into an individuated possession or experience by linking it to self-narrative" respectively" (Arnould and Price 2000: 149).

In order to explore the authentication of preserves, I look at how consumer competence operates with an understanding of preserves' qualia. "Qualia" are defined as "pragmatic signals (indexes) that materialize phenomenally in human activity as sensuous qualities" (Harkness 2015: 573). An account on the "qualia of comestibles" is offered by anthropologist Anne Meneley, who uses the term "quali-signs" to explore how the different physical qualities of olive oil (namely luminosity, liquidity, spreadability, durability, etc.) are "potentially the material basis for a sign" (Meneley 2008: 305). She stresses the particular contemporary discourses of distinction, in which "the positive qualities of olive oil are not those primarily registered by the ordinary senses of taste, touch, and smell, but rather those that are established discursively by expert opinions of various kinds, which attest to olive oil's 'healthful' qualities" (Meneley 2008: 303).

Authentication strategies can be seen as responses to a growing consumer anxiety, recorded by sociologist Claude Fischler and attributed to the role of the food in enhancing the "omnivore's paradox"[4] (Fischler 1980). The paradox captures the tension between neophobia, the diffidence about new foods as potentially dangerous and neophilia, the curiosity towards new foods, which is necessary in order "to adjust to new situations and maintain a wide enough range of diet" (Fischler 1980: 945). To explain the consumer demand for symbols of nature, which he records, Fischler interprets it as "a response to, a reaction against, the increasingly serious problems we face in identifying our food" (Fischler 1980: 945).

---

[4] The term is attributed to psychologist Paul Rozin (1976).

In a study on British consumers, geographer Peter Jackson analyzes the roots of contemporary food anxieties (Jackson 2010, 2015). He looks at the social determinants of anxiety, which he defines as "a social field that can be occupied by many different social actors, including those who are caught up in discourses of anxiety even if they are not themselves anxious" (Jackson 2010: 154). He attributes a key source of anxiety to the increasing gap between food producers and consumers and to "the disproportionate power of food retailers and corporate agri-business" (Jackson 2015: 14).

In an anthropological account on the consumption and self-provision of preserves among Bulgarians in Sofia, Jung finds an increasing acceptance and normalization of buying factory-produced preserves and argues that "a growing consumer competence enabling people to execute their own control over the food they consume is a significant aspect of changing attitudes toward standardized food" (Jung 2009: 33). She associates this finding with the consumers' rationalizing tendencies based on modernization associated with the socialist period and further developed in the neoliberal context. Jung argues that her informants resort to store-bought jars because of lower costs and their growing consumer competence, "the ability to choose certain brands that produce reliable and affordable products that taste good" (Jung 2009: 51).

My research will focus on a different facet of the growing consumer competence displayed by postsocialist consumers in Eastern Europe, central to Jung's article: an anti-standardization resistance shaped as a positive reevaluation of pre-convenience food products. Preserves that are perceived as outside the spectrum of the contemporary convenience system, due to their modes of production, such as artisan production, domestic self-provisioning and, to a certain extent, locally produced "heirs" of socialist era preserves, materialize the middle-class consumers' quest to mitigate consumer anxiety and to regain control over their food supply. For this objective, I am following the discourses and practices employed to authenticate alternative production of jars and to shape it as a reliable, controllable consumer experience, by contrasting it with the standardized product category.[5]

I have researched the topic by employing a number of directions and methods of research. In an ethnographic pursuit, I have followed the consumption activity of eight middle-aged, middle-class women in Bucharest and in the Transylvanian city of Brasov, whom I observed and interviewed, as well as seven artisan producer families, roughly corresponding to the membership of the Slow Food Presidium of Saxon Village Preserves (located in southern Transylvania, close to the city of Brasov). During the research, I participated in preserve-making sessions with domestic makers, as well as artisan producers, and I joined domestic consumers on shopping expeditions, and artisan producers to farmers' markets and food festivals. I have also examined older and newer cookbooks and my informants' recipe notebooks, and documented storage spaces. Additionally, I drew data from farmers'

[5] Similar to Jung's (2009) terminological option, I will also use the term "jar" instead of "can" to refer to the fruit and vegetable preserves, as they are always stored in jars and glass bottles.

markets, local food blogs and social media, and discussions and observations among recipients of food parcels containing preserves. The ethnographic data is based on the experience of middle-class consumers.

Eating (in) Socialism: Shortage, Depositing, and Thrift

One of the iconic scenes in the cult movie "Good Bye, Lenin!" (Arndt and Becker 2003) is Alexander's febrile attempt to satisfy the wish of his mother—a recovering stroke victim whose temporary coma had prevented her from witnessing the fall of the Berlin Wall and had to be led to believe that she still lived under socialism—to eat Spreewald pickled cucumbers, the East German state brand of cucumbers whose production had in fact been discontinued after the reunification. A supermarket attendant, vexed by Alex's request for a product associated with an unpleasant past, directs him to choose from an abundance of new, Western preserves from the fully stocked shelves of the supermarket. After failing to find as much as an empty jar of the desired brand, Alex reports to his mother that there was a supply shortage of Spreewald cucumbers. The news of the pickle shortage does not arouse the mother's suspicions; she takes it as a casual fact of life, with no further questions.

During the socialist period, Romania's food landscape was likewise shaped by the planned economy under a culture of shortage: "a special management of consumer goods in households" (Chelcea 2002: 32–33). This included hoarding, rationing, affective investment, and recycling (Chelcea 2002: 37). As food was increasingly harder to come by in the centralized distribution system of the 1980s,[6] various responses and means of resistance emerged, at individual, household, and collective levels. They were common throughout the Eastern bloc and involved queuing strategies, systems of informal exchange networks which permitted the circulation of unavailable food products (Ledeneva 1998; Smollett 1989), stocking food, or reliance on small garden plots that allowed the production of crops that were then transformed into stocks of preserves (Caldwell 2007, 2011).

The ideology of rational food and eating was central to the organization of the Romanian food system. Devised in the 1960s and revised in the 1980s under the frame of public health, it allocated each citizen a fixed amount of calories and nutrients, which were calculated by scientific methods, according to gender, age, and profession. The Program for Scientific Eating, alongside the Program for the Self-governance and Territorial Self-administration for the Good Provisioning of the Population with Agricultural and Food Products, provided the basis for the food rationing put in place in the 1980s, which limited the amount of food staples a citizen could buy. The quantity of bread was fixed at half a loaf per person per day, while sugar, flour, and oil were limited to 1 L/kg/month. Meat, eggs, and cheese were also rationed. The allocated ratios were marked on a card that granted access to specified products. The shortage of food was masked by the introduction of fillers

[6] As the government had set out an economic plan to pay the external debt of Romania.

or substitutes, such as mock coffee made with chickpeas and barley, cold cuts (salami) made with soy,[7] and sodium bicarbonate added to cooked dishes.

Rational (scientific) eating also included a particular policy of supplying the population with frozen oceanic fish, as a result of the attempt to substitute meat, which was being exported to pay off the country's external debt. As other instances of food shortage, this too was masked as a nutritional and public health measure. The slogan "*Nici o masă fără peşte*"/"No meal without fish" was coined by state authorities. A recurrent visual representation of shortage in my informants' memories is that of the canned fish that was allegedly spread out on store shelves, in order to conceal the lack of other food products available for purchase.

Certain luxury goods, such as Western-brand cigarettes, instant coffee, and alcohol like whiskey or cognac, suffered a process of terminal commoditization (Kopytoff 1986): they were never consumed but saved and circulated as trading items to secure access to other goods or services (educational or health services in particular). The acquisition of unavailable or insufficient commodities relied on networks of connections, on gifts and exchanges, or on appropriation of state factory production.[8]

A key resilience strategy of the urban household in the face of hardship and shortage was the reliance on the food resources produced in the households of rural relatives. As industrialization and urbanization advanced, it was common for newly urbanized families to entertain a diffuse household (Mihailescu 2000, 2014) or neo-extended family (Konstantinov and Simić 2001) with their relatives (often elderly parents) in the countryside, cooperating for the common pooling of resources such as labor and goods.[9] Reciprocity had a decisive impact on the urban household, allowing the procurement of agricultural and food resources (poultry and pork meat, vegetables, wine, and brandy).

Acquiring food from abroad was also a strategy some categories of the population employed, in order to stock up on unavailable staples or desirable luxury foods.[10]

---

[7] A critique of not only the quantity but also the quality of available products resulted in the popular branding of disparaged products: *nechezol* (a derisive vernacular branding based on the root "a necheza" ("to neigh"), for coffee replacement based on chickpea and barley, suggesting horse fodder), "*adidasi de porc*" (pig sneakers) for pig hoofs or *Fratii Petreus* (Petreus Brothers) for the two small chickens packaged together, which consumers compared to a popular duo of folk music singers.

[8] These strategies have been documented by anthropological research throughout the Eastern socialist bloc (Verdery 1996; Mateescu 2005; Zerilli 2004; Mars and Altman 1987; Berdahl 1999a, b; Ledeneva 1998; Lampland 1995; Sampson 1984 etc.).

[9] Children with urban residence would typically use their vacation from remunerated job (often in industry) to help with the seasonal agricultural labors (hay cutting, plowing, harvesting). Creed (1998) in Bulgaria and Kideckel (1993) in Romania elaborate on such instances of domestication of industry.

[10] Petty border traffic and trader tourism with neighboring Yugoslavia and Hungary (Chelcea 2002) allowed families in Western Romania to bring home particularly the "exotic" foods that Romania had ceased to import in the 1980s, such as cocoa and coffee, but also staples, like butter and oil.

At household level, depositing products and creating food reserves was so important that it shaped the residential environment. The domestic space was reorganized and its functions sometimes altered to enable food deposits. Owning an apartment with larder space and a balcony was a particularly prized advantage in terms of domestic space design. One of the reasons that pushed many urban inhabitants to risk fines for the illegal closing of balconies (Iancu 2011), aside for the need to thermally insulate the apartment, was the need to compensate for the lack of designated storage spaces. After enclosure, the balconies were fitted with shelves that stored full jars, bottles, or sacks of potatoes (Poenaru 2008). Some of the apartment buildings' common areas also became attractive storage opportunities: the buildings' (limited) basement space was extremely sought after. It was divided between neighbors and equipped as a cellar, allowing for the long-term food storage of jarred and bottled fruit and vegetables or for the wintertime storage of fresh potatoes, onions, apples, or ubiquitous barrel of pickled cabbage.[11] Even communal spaces such as laundry rooms were appropriated as extra food storage space.[12]

Food deposits, as well as eating and cooking habits were also shaped by other factors. The communist government's aim for the energetic independence of Romania, as well as the state's prioritization of industrial versus domestic consumption, limited access to and usage of electricity, hot water, natural gas, and petrol. This meant that refrigeration was subject to limited availability. The refrigerators that one could purchase included a small-volume freezer,[13] which meant that freezing as a domestic means to preserve food was largely unavailable.

Disruptions to the supply of electricity, gas, and heating also impacted the organization of domestic temporalities and geographies. Household cooking was often pushed into the late night or the very early morning (before dawn), when the gas pressure was high enough to allow the thermal preparation of food. Shortage (of radiator heating) turned the kitchen into a family room, which concentrated many of the daily indoor activities in wintertime, when the members of the household would gather around the heat of the gas stove.

Outside the home, prepared food was available at factory canteens and restaurants.[14] Restaurant food was cooked in a standardized manner, according to a set of

---

[11] Typically in autumn, a family would buy up to 100 k of potatoes to last them through the winter. The last batches of potatoes needed to be cleaned of their growing sprouts, as winter drew to an end. The emptying and cleaning of the sauerkraut barrels in the spring, using the limiting facilities of apartment buildings, created a very specific seasonal smellscape that permeated the communal spaces and the domestic space of apartment building dwellers.

[12] Aside from the long-term storage of food, families would intensify the saving up of food before family feasts or important Orthodox holidays (Easter and Christmas), when eggs, butter, and other ingredients available as rationed products were saved up for several weeks in advance, as they were required for the rich festive cooking and cakes.

[13] Big enough to fit two chickens, as one informant estimated.

[14] Mistrust and diffidence of the public food catering were diffuse. In the 1980s, the food shortage was also manifest in the restaurant's offer, with many dishes (especially meat-based ones) missing from the menus. Additionally, the decreasing quality of dishes, with cooks increasingly resorting to inferior, substitute ingredients and the lack of standard enforcement, made consumers wary of using the public eating infrastructure and the grocery stores.

fixed recipes collected in the 1957 General Recipe Book for Culinary Dishes (*Rețetar general de preparate culinare*), it too an expression of the rational (scientific) eating ideology. Fixed quantities of each ingredient had to be used in a fixed number of recipes in each restaurant, thus enforcing a gastronomy focused on thrift and standardization.

Notwithstanding the ideologically driven effort of the socialist state to create gender equality (through the inclusion of women in the labor force or the creation of childcare infrastructure (8-h crèches and kindergartens)), domestic work was clearly the woman's domain, as attested by the numerous educational materials and self-help literature of the epoch. Titles such as "Sfaturi gospodărești"/"Household Advice" (1960) reinforced traditional gender roles and contributed to the normalization of the "double burden" (Hochshild 1989; Miroiu 2004). The figure of the virtuous female householder (*buna gospodină*) was a typical trope of the era.[15]

The domestic principles—or "practical advice," as they were often dubbed—communicated via this popular literature included nutritional advice (and even dedicated books), as well as elements of home economics focused on thrift[16] and limiting food waste. Of this, reusing leftovers and making preserves were key focuses.[17] A recurring presence in recipe notebooks and in my informants' recollections of socialist-era homemade preserves is aspirin. Aspirin, a preservative, seemed to be a key ingredient in just about every recipe: for sour cherries in syrup, tomato juice, and jams. Also recurrent were indications to sterilize the jars in bain-marie and then wrap them in blankets in order to slowly cool them down. The lack of many prized ingredients shaped a domestic gastronomy characterized by improvisation and awkward alterations of the dishes, with creative innovations such as omelet with fried mortadella or schnitzel made of canned, spam-like Chinese pork meat.[18] Such instances of ingredient substitution arguably added to a creolized (Wilk 2006) cuisine of shortage, which mirrored the failure of the state food production and distribution systems. Cookbooks and recipe notebooks, including my informants',

[15] The name *Gospodina* (the good housewife) was given to a chain of public groceries of the time, which sold semi-prepared foods in the 1980s. The initiative, towards which women recall being ambivalent, was an attempt to relieve the women from cooking chores.

[16] The cult cookbook of twentieth-century Romania, Sanda Marin's "Carte de bucate/Cookbook," first published in 1936, was reedited several times during communism, beginning with 1954, when it was rewritten to erase high-class bourgeois elements, such as references to Western elites and heritage (Napoleon cake or béchamel sauce were renamed to be stripped of their connotations). It was also rescaled to fit the shortage economy: quantities of eggs, butter, and meat in recipes were halved.

[17] In the abundant literature of practical advice of the epoch there are also preserve cookbooks (e.g., "Conserve de legume și fructe"/"Fruit and vegetable preserves" (1954), "Îmi reușesc toate conservele de legume"/"All my vegetable preserves are successful" (1969).

[18] As recalled by foodie and food writer Alex Baciu interviewed by Marius Chivu (2016): http://dilemaveche.ro/sectiune/tema-saptamanii/articol/statul-mult-timp-in-bucatarie-e-marca-celor-nascuti-in-comunism, accessed on July 15, 2017.

contained recipes such as "economic cake," "mock caviar," and "cake with tomato puree."[19]

Preserving food during socialism was one of the keys of household resilience in the face of the unreliability of food provisioning within the centralized distribution system. The memory of preserves during socialism enjoys a negative top-of-mind representation among my middle-aged and older informants; to them, finding oddly spaced cans of fish and, sometimes, canned beans on the store shelves equaled empty stores. The material expression of scarcity consisted of canned fish, canned beans casserole, jarred fruit in syrup, and biscuits sold by the kilo.[20]

There is a consensus among my informants that preserves very widely unavailable in the 1980s. Cornelia resents many of her food memories of socialism. Hailing from a working-class family in Eastern Romanian city, she moved to the industrialized city of Brasov, in a mountain region of Transylvania, to work as an engineer at a truck factory. She vividly recalls the absence of basic foodstuff and the hard domestic labor needed for provisioning her family with food. With no relatives in the countryside and no network of connections in her new town, she was cut off from the main modes of informal provisioning:

> "Back then, we would jar everything, because you couldn't find anything to eat. It was such hard work, such a struggle."

Looking westwards, to the desired branded world of capitalist goods, was also embedded in the self-provisioning culture. The West, as Fehervary notes,

> "is a continuing presence in imagination, conversation, and local systems of distinction, and embodied in images as well as materialized in select consumer goods" (Fehérváry 2009: 436)

Cornelia, my informant, recalls that everyone in her social network was preparing and preserving homemade Florio, originally a classic Italian brand of Marsala wine, prized as a premium, difficult-to-acquire alcoholic drink. They would improvise it at home from wine, distilled alcohol, cherry syrup, and almond flavoring. She recalls it as extremely fashionable; she and her friends would save it for poker nights that they organized in turns in their apartments. A materialization of the desired West is *Bradola*, translatable as "Fir Tree Cola," the name that Marina had coined for her homemade fir tip syrup, which families would routinely make in spring, with foraged fir buds. When consumed, sparkling water was added and the result was a minty, sweet fizzy drink, which could—indulgently—be likened to the highly desired Coca-Cola. A recipe notebook also included a recipe for homemade Garrone, wherein the classic Italian vermouth was made from raisins, rice, lemon, and cinnamon, fermented together and then stored.

---

[19] An in-depth radiography of cooking under shortage (in the USSR) is Anya von Bremzen's (2013) "Mastering the Art of Soviet Cooking: a Memoir of Food and Longing."

[20] The wide availability of biscuits and waffle-like baking sheets as opposed to primary desert ingredients such as eggs, butter, or flour was reflected in the adaptations of bakery and cake recipes, to substitute the classic dough with a replacement dough of crumbled biscuits or waffle.

As far as politics of memory go, recollections of sensorial repulsion, hunger, fillers, substitutes, blandness, and unfulfilled cravings associated with the personal experience of the socialist food system abound. A phenomenology of shortage can be traced through the post-revolution anti-communist memoir literature and journalistic writing, where personal accounts of food shortage experiences are a key theme.[21] But there is also another face to memory, as socialist-era food also reemerges after 1989 as an expression of Ostalgia: a playful commoditization of socialism, for touristic and other consumption contexts, as will be illustrated further on throughout the chapter.

To the West and Back: The Winding Aspirational Road of the Postsocialist Consumer

Postsocialist transition swept through Eastern Europe with massive privatization, deindustrialization, and layoffs in the state-owned enterprises. Many of the urban households were affected by persistent unemployment and loss of eligibility on the labor market, as it shifted from production activities to the service sector. Labor reconversion (typically de-professionalization) and low-skilled labor migration to mainly Western European countries developed into economic survival strategies. Another significant occupational outcome of deindustrialization was the re-peasantization of the industrial labor force: part of the peasants-turned-workers of the socialist industrial project, middle-aged or unemployed, returned, either fully or seasonally, to their parents' rural household and took up agricultural labor as a semi-subsistence project, benefitting from a controversial process of land restitution.[22]

Production-based identity, as documented by Berdahl in the socialist GDR, fell into crisis with the fall of socialism (Berdahl 1999a, b, 2005). State production began in a complex path towards the emergence of a postsocialist consumer-citizen (Merkel 1998).

Partaking in the global capitalist market allowed the postsocialist consumer to experience belonging to a transnational community of consumers; it emancipated them into a revelation of normality, which consumers attributed to capitalist, Western shopping experiences, retail practices, and lifestyles (see Fehérváry 2002; Rausing 2002). The cultural significance of the globalization of shopping and

[21] The collective volume "Intelectuali la cratiţă: amintiri culinare şi 50 de reţete"/"Intellectuals in the kitchen: culinary memories and 50 recipes" (Pârvulescu 2012) is a particular case in point. The social history of East German and Soviet cuisine and cooking is likewise subject to this type of memory. For reference, see bestsellers such as Anya von Bremzen's (2013) "Mastering the Art of Soviet Cooking: a Memoir of Food and Longing," Olga Syutkin's (2015) "CCCP Cook Book: True Stories of Soviet Cuisine," or Hans and Barbara Otzen's "The GDR Cookbook" (2012) and "The GDR Baking Book" (2014).

[22] For literature on postsocialist transformations in Romania (see Verdery 1996; Kideckel 2008; Chelcea 2006; Micu 2012; Horváth and Anghel 2009; Anghel 2013; Diminescu 2009).

consumption in postsocialist societies (in Eastern Europe and elsewhere) was captured by a wide body of anthropological literature, much of which described specific strategies of localization or domestication of the consumption experiences of foreign foods (Patico and Caldwell 2002; Lankauskas 2002; Caldwell 2004; Watson 2006; Yan 2000).

As foreign capital entered Romania, it opened the way to new forms of food production and consumption. Privatization and deindustrialization rendered most of the socialist food industry obsolete. Some production units, especially from the milk and meat industries, were successfully integrated into the capitalist production system. In 1991, Coca-Cola had already opened a production unit in Romania. Kraft Foods followed in 1994. Supermarket chains, as well as food and cafe chains such as McDonald's, KFC, and Starbucks, developed their commercial networks in Romania, making Western food products widely available to the population. From the economy of shortage, consumers abruptly plunged into a consumer society, governed by the myth of abundance (Baudrillard 1998), to which they responded with "symbolic bulimia" (Mihăilescu and Iancu 2009). Taste became aligned with global trends, the consumer experience became enthusiastically westernized, and the United States became the ultimate reference of desirability and emulation. Consumption in the 1990s and early 2000s was decisively configured by the magnetic attraction to mass production and mass retail, Western brands, and goods.[23] "*Acum şi în România*"/"Now also available in Romania" became a slogan of the early postsocialist years (Dumitrescu 2015).

Capitalist modernity entered the domestic kitchens as well, through an inflation of kitchen gadgets: coffee filters, blenders, and new refrigerators with larger (or detached) freezers became the norm in aspiring middle-class Romanian kitchens. Convenience foods and cooking "shortcuts" were part of the desired modernity: instant powders, artificial flavorings, soft drinks, and bouillon stocks. Domestic preserve-making was "upgraded" with preserving gelatins (Gelfix, Pikantfix) and spice mixes with monosodium glutamate, which were, intuitively, positioned as liberating ingredients, which decreased cooking time and effort, and promised a more predictable end result: the promise that the preserves will look attractive, will be seasoned consistently, and will not spoil.

Domesticity and store-bought modernity would meet each other in unexpected ways, as the reciprocal appropriations between mass-produced brands and homemade or "traditional" products marked the food culture of the 1990s. Marina, the author of the previously described Bradola, integrated Prigat,[24] one of the new brands of soft drinks that emerged on the market in the 1990s, into her domestic production: she "created" Mirabelle Prigat, by giving the name to the bottles of sour mirabelle paste that she preserved as soup seasoning.

---

[23] See Berdahl for an account on the Eastern Germans' fascination with bananas (Berdahl 1999a, b) and Caldwell for the Muscovites' initial awe of McDonald's (Caldwell 2004).

[24] Prigat is one of the first international brands of non-carbonated soft drinks to arrive in the Romanian market, in 1993, and is still very popular today, holding a large share of the Romanian market.

The nicely designed and convenient packaging of capitalist products was soon revamped into containers for the storage of domestically produced foods: plastic bottles of soft drinks became moonshine wine and brandy recipients, while jars and glass bottles were reused for jams or compotes. Cecilia's most treasured tomato juice containers, which she keeps reusing year after year, are a few bottles of Prigat syrup bought in the early 1990s.

Pizza was one of the new additions to the range of convenience-oriented, westernized taste of the Romanians. Many families promptly took to adapting the mix of Western taste/convenience to their home cooking: homemade pizza was a frequent memory of the pre-home-delivery 1990s, with domestic cooks typically replacing the time-consuming dough with a base of bread slices softened in milk. In connection to the appetite for homemade pizza, my respondents integrated homemade ketchup into the fall preserve-making campaign. The trend and the acquisition of knowledge circulated via social networks: Cornelia's recipe notebook records two versions of ketchup recipes, shared by two different friends.

The cultural logic of stocking up food as a means of autonomy during the turbulent postsocialist transition is explained in a study by Ries on the central role of domestic production and stocking of potatoes in postsocialist Russia (Ries 2009). She considers the mass-scale organization of such self-provisioning practices a way of legitimizing and celebrating "the population's ability to feed itself autonomously, 'no matter what'," "while the collective wealth of nations is privatized and concentrated" (Ries 2009: 183, 185). Ries describes a "potato system," in which self-provisioning legitimates and stabilizes the inequalities characteristic of postsocialist Russia. Storing potatoes and shelving homemade preserves—even when they are not required by economic and nutritional necessity—is a culturally meaningful strategy to produce "a semblance of food security" in postsocialism, and the activities employed are "fetishized, aestheticized, and celebrated" (Ries 2009: 187).

A culture of frugality lingers in the Romanian as well as in other state-socialist societies, in contrast to the Western postwar throwaway societies:

> "goods were kept for long periods of time and well-cared for, while disposable items were rationed out in full consciousness of their value. An example is the common practice of peeling two-ply paper napkins apart and refolding them for use, something not explained by a shortage of paper napkins (they were plentiful) but by the relative imbalance between rising norms for modern lifestyles and limits on disposable income" (Fehérváry 2009: 435).

Recycling containers and an adamancy to recycle food waste are practices my informants still observe. Thrift is still haunting the memories of Eugenia, currently a well-off woman: she ferments the uneaten jams of the previous years into moonshine brandy.

A sociocultural divide arose and shaped the mass of consumers by the tradition—modernity divide, wherein nostalgics of the past (including those that yearn for the Soviet or socialist foodways) contrast with enthusiastic adopters of Western food and foodways. This divide is embodied in the alcohol versus soft drink consumer choice in an account of a Lithuanian wedding by Lankauskas (2002), or in the contrast between consumers of Soviet versus "European" sausage brands in

Lithuania. In Lithuania, Europe is seen as a marker of high class and high prices and has come to represent a type of modernity from which many Lithuanians feel excluded (Klumbyte 2009). A preference for food products from the socialist era versus products perceived as European stands for an ideological division and a boundary of exclusion. This fuels certain intellectuals and politicians to label citizens who are nostalgic for such foods "turnips":[25] backwards and anti-modern (Klumbyte 2009: 147–148). Melissa Caldwell's similar—but perhaps more nuanced—account of post-Soviet Russia describes the shaping of a consumer culture that reflects tensions between local and foreign food products, in which choices reflect the broader political attachments of consumers. Identifying a nationalistic orientation to consumption in Moscow, Caldwell writes that

> "domestic food producers, store clerks, and customers collaborate to classify foods and other products as either 'Ours' (*Nash*) or 'Not Ours' (*Ne nash*) and describe local goods as superior to foreign goods in terms of taste, quality, and healthfulness" (Caldwell 2002: 295).

Cosmopolitan consumerism is tempered by local-centric attachments to food, which becomes more ideologically nuanced and less related to education and wealth, as well as to class belonging in general. Equating the West with modernity and normalcy, professed particularly by the younger, urban, emerging middle-class consumers, becomes more blurry, as consumers grow more skeptical of Western food practices and more preoccupied with issues of food safety and quality. The "modernization" of the food offer brought about by globalization and the European market lies at the origin of a food anxiety, which finds consumers fearful of potential unknown consequences of techno-food features that they cannot fully understand. The fear of artificial additives and other synthetic ingredients of the mass production associated with capitalist modernity as well as the lack of traceability, accountability, and "origin" increasingly raise alarm over globalized foods. This paves the way for a counter-reaction of concerned consumers seeking to regain control over what they ingest, increasingly turning to shorter food chains and more local production, as a strategy to mitigate uncertainty.

The particular configuration of postsocialist food nationalism—as shaped by consumer preferences and marketing—has been observed in Russia by Caldwell (2002), in East Germany by Berdahl (1999a, b) and Merkel (1994), and in Georgia by Manning and Uplisashvili (2007). In Romania, it has been discussed by Mihăilescu and Iancu (2009) and Dumitrescu (2015). Caldwell, as well as Mihailescu and Iancu, describe the appeal of "made in Russia"/"made in Romania" marketing claims and "buy domestic" campaigns. Caldwell notes that postsocialist spaces have been characterized by the "commercialized appropriation of the past and the traditional" (Caldwell 2002: 307).

Food nationalism is shaped by quests for more authentic, locally meaningful, and convincingly wholesome alternatives. Under this generous category, in the following

[25] To this classification, Elizabeth Dunn provocatively opposes the term "mangoes," to emphasize how dichotomizing discourses about class have become and how they are fueled by discourses and practices of distinction through taste and culinary choice (Dunn 2009: 218).

sections, I am going to refer to three responses to standardized capitalist production, shaped in Romania roughly after it joined the European Union in 2007: the Ostalgic recuperation of the socialist preserve industry, the emergent market for non-serial artisan jars, and the positive revaluation of the domestic self-production of preserves.

The Artisan Feel of Socialist Preserves

Various preserves "from the old days" were retrospectively bestowed with qualities related to taste, as well as health and safety. Often the favorable image of wholesomeness, control, and accountability was bestowed on the local industrial food production. In Romania, the socialist food industry has become the unlikely object of appreciation and nostalgia, through a process of selective memory, where past products are invested with a memory of pre-modern trustworthiness. These recent trust credentials, several of my informants argue, are based on the perceived absence of for-profit pressure in the former state-planned economy. This perception projected the memory of socialist food-processing units into a horizon of perceived morality: the socialist production is recalled as part of a "clean," "pure," pre-modern, pre-"E" era. Dumitrescu describes another dimension that encouraged the activation of the nostalgic taste: the products also had an effectively artisan feel to them, of basic, unsophisticated processing, due to "the incapacity of the socialist consumer goods industry to ensure a constant quality and to supervise the observance of product attributes, as well as the precariousness of packaging, labels and merchandising" (Dumitrescu 2015: 20).

My informant, Eugenia, sarcastically remarks that socialist preserves were delicious so long as you could find them. She holds a positive memory of the wholesomeness of socialist preserves in comparison with capitalist ones: "I've recently bought a jarred ratatouille, because I was craving the old ones. There used to be a pretty delicious jar preserve in the time of Ceausescu, I think it was made in Tecuci. This was nothing like the old one. I couldn't eat more than two spoonfuls." One of Cornelia's fondest food memories is marmalade:

> "It came in 10-kilo carton crates; they would disassemble the crate and be left with a huge chunk. You would buy it in bulk. It was really good, I could eat half a kilo in one sitting! You would find the occasional apple or pear seed. You could feel the chunks of fruit. It was divine! I recently saw it again and I bought some, but it is not the same recipe. It is probably made by modern methods and its taste is disappointing."

In her reply, Cornelia uses quaint imperfections such as discarded seeds and chunky texture as symbolic means to authenticate the honest, minimal processing of the socialist product.

This consumer interest fueled the rebranding and sometimes repositioning of various socialist-era production sites, now turned into brands (such as the Topoloveni, Râureni, or Tecuci fruit and vegetable-processing units, or the Albalact and Napolact milk- and dairy-processing units).[26] Perhaps the most remarkable success of a former produce-processing plant is that of the Topoloveni preserve factory in Southern Romania. It was bought in 2001 by an entrepreneur, who successfully continued the production of sweet and savory preserves (jams, compote, *zacuscă*, etc.). More notably, it was one of the first enterprises with Romanian capital to put together a product line of certified organic products and even made Romanian food history through its 2011 certification, in 2011, of the Magiun[27] de Topoloveni as the first Romanian Protected Geographical Indication (PGI), the consecrated EU quality scheme that attests to the value of agricultural and food products based on their geographical origin. The fruit and vegetable preserve factory in Râureni, also in Southern Romania, was privatized in 1994 to local entrepreneurs, who grew it into a successful brand. Both the entrepreneurs in Topoloveni and in Râureni grew their business by transforming the toponimical reference of the factory location into a brand, thus capitalizing on the continuity of the two factories' socialist-era prestige.[28]

The quest for food traceability and authenticity in the postsocialist world makes some consumers reevaluate the socialist state production under a nostalgic horizon, where the products of the socialist industry are seen as more reliable. Fueling this perception is a shared conviction among Romanian consumers that international companies treat them as second-rate consumer-citizens, as foreign products destined for Eastern European markets are made with cheaper ingredients and are of a general lower quality compared to the same product destined for Western markets.[29] This perceived dishonesty of international companies[30] adds to the mistrust against global brands and paves the way towards a positive reappraisal of locally produced goods.

---

[26] As documented by Berdahl (1999a, b, 2005), in her account on Ostalgia, the nostalgic consumption of Eastern German brands after the fall of the Berlin Wall current consumer culture in Romania integrated Ostalgia under a re-interpretative consumption frame, where common socialist-era consumption or production venues such as "alimentara" (grocery store), "gostat" (state farmhold), "cantina" (canteen), "fabrica" (the factory), or "atelierul" (the workshop) are reinvented into cool or exclusive brands. Various brands of consumer goods from socialism, such as Dacia (cars), Pegas (bicycles), and Farmec (cosmetics), have also gained a consumer basis by capitalizing on Ostalgia.

[27] The plum *magiun* is a thick, no-sugar-added plum jam that used to be made traditionally in rural households by a labor-intensive process that necessitated 6–9 h of mixing in a typically open-fire large pot.

[28] Even if socialist production was centralized and standardized, consumers would discriminate between the various production units. They knew that products originating from certain production units (such as the factories located in Râureni, Topoloveni, or Tecuci) were tastier, or of higher quality.

[29] Because of the perceived quality difference, it is common for consumers to attempt to acquire certain brands of goods, such as cosmetics or coffee, during trips to Western European countries, or to request them from relatives or friends living or traveling abroad, even if the same brands are available to buy in local stores.

[30] Circulated for a long time as an urban myth, this suspicion prompted an investigation in 2017 by the Romanian Ministry of Agriculture (so far with inconclusive findings). For a discussion about how the distribution of food quality is geographically overlaid onto the map of Europe, according to the geopolitics of taste, see Dunn (2009).

Preserving Authenticity: Quality Products and the Value of Artisanship

Aside from the globalization of consumption, another key structural factor that triggered a counter, nationally oriented consumer turn in the postsocialist foodscapes is the European Union member status of Central and Eastern European countries in the millennium. Europeanization, with its inherent standardization, brought about the revelation that EU regulations can constitute a threat to national foods and foodways. This becomes an additional incentive for consumers to reevaluate the local food repertoire in a positive light and to reflect on it under the looking glass of collective (national) identity. Gille (2009) makes a compelling account of how quality and hygiene standards paradoxically affect the quality and safety of the Hungarian national spice, the paprika. Mihăilescu and Iancu (2009) describe the "cheese crisis" that occurred in Romania because of the misinterpretation of an EU law that would have forbidden the distribution of the national *telemea* cheese.[31] Mincyte recalls how EU regulations created an informal market for illegal raw milk, sought by consumers skeptical to food safety regulations, who considered raw farm milk healthier and safer (Mincyte 2009).

Standardization associated with Europeanization is experienced as a loss of taste and of an ineffable "soul" of the food. This, in turn, urges consumers to seek authenticity and the emotional comfort they associate with tradition and belonging. The need for belonging to a community and for cultivating a national identity, for "finding" one's roots and performing authenticity, is part of the consumers' requisites in relation to the foods they ingested. They have become part of the marketing strategies of domestic food producers. The consumer arguments that favor an option towards local products invoke health, taste, food safety, or social responsibility.[32]

The clandestine small producers of socialism were left to fend for themselves in Romania's postsocialist informal economy, while postsocialist authorities favored large, international producers (the figure of the "foreign investor" was regarded by the authorities as a deus ex machina). In a foodscape where tradition as a food category could not be claimed by small, rural producers, as they lacked the capital to comply with regulations, it was claimed as a rhetorical construct by the food industry and mass retail, under a process for which Dumitrescu coined the term "the

[31] The cheese crisis was rivaled by another food identity scandal in 2013, concerning a popular urban dish of grilled minced meat ("*mici*"), whose classical preparation with sodium bicarbonate, a conservative and an antioxidant, risked becoming illegal, as the use of these ingredients was forbidden by the EU food safety regulation. Romania then applied for—and was eventually granted—an exemption from the ban, by invoking cultural tradition.

[32] A particular vegetal declination of this food trend is the establishment, in Romania, of a metonymic relation between the "Romanian tomato" and nationalist taste attachments and food identity. In a market saturated by the new "efficient" (productive and resistant) but tasteless tomato varieties, the demand for a so-called Romanian tomato, which is implicitly tasty, embodied, at the beginning of the millennium, an idyllic quest for taste authenticity, roots, heritage, and a reappraisal of the moral purity of a peasant-producer, generally deemed to be honest and naive.

supermarketization of traditions": a means through which tradition and artisanship were appropriated via commercial communication as branding and marketing strategies (Dumitrescu 2015).

Preserving and selling fruits and vegetables arose as a half-informal entrepreneurial opportunity for disenchanted peasants, pushed towards the subsistence economy by the dissolution of state farms, the failure of agrarian reforms, and the lack of a viable rural development strategy. Consumers were targeted particularly via agritourism and by direct, farm-door sales, as well as through mouth-to-mouth reach. Jars of pickles, *zacusca*, or jams could be seen and bought (informally) at urban farmers' markets, displayed discreetly as additional merchandize on the (legal) fresh produce stand, as a strategy for producers to create added value to their raw produce.[33]

While this informal model survives to the day, roughly after Romania became an EU member state, in 2007, the consumer culture increasingly welcomed the figure of the peasant-producer into the formal economy. The return was supported by a parallel inflation of occasional or weekend farmers' markets in large Romanian cities,[34] which provided the distribution venues for processed or manually preserved local foods, made with pre-industrial recipes and techniques. The establishment of the Slow Food network in Romania was a decisive event for the configuration of the artisan foodscape, and for fruit and vegetable preserves in particular, as will be detailed below.

The configuration of the alternative market of quality products was captured by anthropologists Mihailescu and Iancu, who describe its emergence as counter-reaction to the alienation caused by the inflation of delocalized, a-temporal, and ultimately depersonalizing consumer society global foods. Quality products are defined as follows:

> "they have a tradition, opposed to the absence of history from the mainstream market, they can take the face of identity (our traditions) as well as otherness (their traditions) [...], they have a personal history, attached to an identifiable producer, or at least imaginable, opposed to the industrial anonymity; inscribed into a personal history of the buyer, as they constitute a recognition of an assumed childhood paradise lost [...], they are local or localized, as opposed to the delocalized supermarket products and, not least, they have taste, unlike serial products, which all share the same taste" (Mihăilescu and Iancu 2009: 42).

The consumer and producer rhetoric of "quality products" is structured under a "generic polarity industrial/present/abundance – domestic/past/rarity" (Dumitrescu 2015: 143) and ultimately on the opposition artificial—authentic. The "human face"

---

[33] For some village economies, post-1989 local conditions worked against the development of informal trade of fruit and vegetable products. For an account of the failure of the informal postsocialist trade of apples and palinka and a discussion on how a local economy became autarchic, see Anghel (2004).

[34] Most likely, the first regular farmers' market, named The Peasant Fair, was initiated, not without symbolism, by the Museum of the Romanian Peasant in Bucharest. Other notable actors who configured the scene were the National University of Agricultural Sciences in Bucharest, the Museum of Rural Civilization in Sibiu and the various local Slow Food chapters, as well as a few nonprofit organizations (see Stroe 2016).

of food is an important attribute that feeds the search for authenticity and meaning. Iancu zooms in on a consumer trend that captures the image of grandmothers as a powerful metaphor of taste[35] (Iancu 2014). A noticeable proportion of the Romanian artisan jar producers with greater visibility have an explicit reference to authorship inserted into their brand: *Gemuri de la Rozi* (Jams from Rozi), *Cămara lui Matei* (Matei's Larder), *Saveurs d'Yveline, Dulceața lui Răzvan* (Răzvan's *Dulceata*), and *Ograda lui Luca* (Luca's Yard). This communication of authorship achieves a symbolic traceability and humanizes the product and the connection implied by the familiar, informal use of the artisan's given name.

The consumer quest for counter-mainstream foods as well as the domestic production of food are linked to the consumer aspiration to the construction of an authentic self.

A significant founding moment for the food artisanship market in Romania was the arrival of the Slow Food organization. Significantly, Slow Food's presence in Romania began with jam: the first local structure was the Presidium[36] of Saxon Village Preserves: it was created in 2005, registered by the British co-founder of a local development NGO based in Southern Transylvania. It reunited a handful of local rural residents from a few villages in Southern Transylvania. NGO experts were guided by Slow Food experts in selecting a set of producers (not necessarily occupied in agriculture) with a reputation of good cooks, to engage them in a coordinated operation of making preserves (jam, *dulceata*, compote, but also pickles and *zacusca*) for the market.[37]

I have conducted multi-sited ethnographic work on a network of producers in southern Transylvania, who corresponded roughly to the membership of the Slow Food Presidium of Saxon Village Preserves. Over a period of 2 years, I joined the various producers (seven families) in their jam-related activities: fruit and vegetable harvest and procurement, preserve-making (cooking the fruit and vegetables, jarring, labeling), and selling the products (or assisting them), especially at food festivals and farmers' markets in Bucharest and Transylvania, where I could interact with potential consumers.

Through the following account, I seek to describe how domestic producers project and transfer their self-provisioning jarring onto the market, what attributes and values sought in the consumption of artisan jars create a market of quality products,

[35] In another analysis of how the homemade food category is appropriated by the branded marketplace, the authors classify homemade as "a material objectification of a domestic moral order" (Moisio et al. 2004: 379).

[36] The Presidia represent a format created by the international Slow Food organization to protect local agricultural varieties, local dishes, and food preparation techniques. It reunites a group of producers committed to protect endangered plant varieties, animal breeds, and preparation techniques.

[37] The name of the Presidia was meant to invoke the local cultural heritage of German (Saxon) settlements dating from the Middle Ages, with the German inhabitants being, until a few decades ago, the dominant population. The German ethnicity in Transylvania enjoys a large cultural capital (see Stroe 2011).

and, more generally, how transformations in consumer culture enable the establishment of a market for artisan preserves.

The presentation leaflet of the Presidium of Saxon Village Preserves portrays Greta, one of the Presidium jar producers, with an apron inscribed with the Slow Food logo (a red-and-white snail) in the courtyard of her house at sunset, filling a series of small, hexagon-shaped jars with freshly prepared jam, poured with a ladle out of a red domestic pot. The text reads:

> "[the jam] is prepared using fruit cultivated in the garden or picked from the nearby forests. The most special jams are rhubarb, forest fruit (rosehip, wild strawberries, blackberries, mirabelles), as well as apple and cinnamon, prepared out of the local variety [of fruit] called 'skin apples' […] Housewives prepare this extraordinary variety of fruit preserves for their domestic, family consumption, diversifying recipes every month in order to harness everything the domestic orchard offers. The recipes are very simple, based on fruit, sugar and – in some cases – on natural pectin, made of unripe apples. The jams are cooked on a slow fire, but not for a long time, in order to preserve the taste and perfume of fresh fruit."

I have chosen to present a longer piece of text, as it includes several of the sources of value claimed by the preserve-makers in my research: the fruits are cultivated by the producers themselves, or foraged from the spontaneous flora. The use of local, ancient fruit varieties (such as skin apple and rhubarb) is marked as relevant, as is the synchronicity of the natural rhythms and the preparation work. The hint to the domestic consumption as one of the destinations of production stands as a warranty of quality. The use of natural pectin, instead of the typical aspirin and synthetic preservatives used by modern makers of domestic preserves, places the producers in a horizon of ancestral knowledge. A restrained simplicity (only two ingredients) acquires sophistication, through the minimal intervention on the quality of the raw fruit, through a brief preparation procedure. More importantly, the text suggests that the very domestic production for self-consumption is transposed, unaltered, to the commercial, market production.

The producers have a range of products that include several jam varieties, syrups, some types of *zacusca*, and various pickles and sauces, but they have each cultivated one or two flagship products, for which they are best known. The latter are typically novelty products, drawing value from a vegetal repertoire outside the typical range of jam fruit that one might expect to find in stores, with a large proportion based on wild fruit: cornelian cherry, elder fruit, bitter cherries, rosehip, rhubarb, sea buckthorn, or rose petals.

The dominant feature of the preserve production surveyed is that, even though they are all registered producers, with official forms, the market value of their artisan production seems to lie in the ability of their "brand" to embody domestic intimacy and programmatic non-seriality. The systematic non-standardized character of production can be summed up in the words of Andra, one of the younger producers: "No batch is exactly like the others because it is artisan production." In what follows, I will outline a discussion about the sources of value of my informants' preserves.

The Symbolic Repertoire of Meaning in the Artisan Market

The producers I have done ethnographic work with entertain a logic of "proper" scale, where being a *small* producer allows them to retain control over the results. The pride of being small scale is infused with a discourse of morality. Commenting on the 2011 outbreak of the *E. coli* epidemics in Europe, traced back to a large-scale organic crop of sprouted foods in Germany,[38] Tudora, one of the producers, the co-owner of a small family farm and production unit, offers her opinion: the outbreak must have been caused by the farmer losing the sense of proportion and extending his crop far beyond his control. The small scale is also closer to the self-provisioning model from which they have emerged as producers. The business is adamantly kept in the family and within the limits of the household. The principle recalled is "we work as much as we can achieve with our hands." Autonomy of production is infused with a moral dimension of just, sustainable, and controllable size of production, where scale is also placed in direct connection with quality. The common sense professed by the producers sanctions any potential surpassing the boundaries of handmade, outside of which, they believe, lies industrial production and a morally corrupt territory.

The production is unpredictable, with an inconstant production flux, variations in the quantity, quality, and range of products prepared from one season to the other. The unpredictability is often an effect of one of the product's sources of added value, the self-provisioning of ingredients, which depends on seasonality, success of domestic garden crops, trustworthy suppliers, and fluctuations of the informal foraging activity:

> "You have just two weeks every year to preserve wild strawberries or cornelian cherries. If you don't manage, then you've lost your chance until next year" (Andra, producer).

An additional factor is the producers' reluctance to project themselves in entrepreneurial roles:

> "I cannot make as much jam as I could sell, but I keep selling until I am left with however much I need for my family and for my tourists. [...] You cannot really plan ahead; sometimes, when a fruit is in season, I may be busy with other things and I just cannot make the jam" (Greta, producer).

Pressures to standardize their serendipitous production sometimes come from offers by large distributors (supermarket chains). Some of the offers received by the producers go so far as to condition the distribution "deal" by the provision of the jars under the supermarket's private brand (with no credentials for the producers' authorship). No such offer has so far been accepted, with producers reluctant because of fears that such engagements would force them to expand their production capacity

[38] A food safety scandal in the summer of 2011 associated an *E. coli* epidemics to batches of organic cucumbers produced on a farm in Spain. The suspicions were later proved erroneous.

and alter the quality of their jars.[39] A stoic stance is present in the discourse that embraces the rhythm and pace of nature, even if it hinders productivity.

The seven producers function legally and have to obey food safety regulations, such as using stainless steel kitchen appliances, but they keep the prerogative to introduce variation to the production: recipes are not fixed and they might be adapted according to inspiration or spontaneous sensorial evaluation of fruit and vegetable properties (a sweeter batch of fruit might necessitate less sugar). Recipes and ideas are transmitted within a social or family network, from mothers, aunts, neighbors, and other older women, but also greatly inspired by consumer feedback.

Performing Domesticity and Simplicity: Fighting Standardization with Quality Signs

Even if some producers hold or have held occasional certifications (for organic or traditional jar preserves), there is a recurring discourse of rejecting formal credentials. In order to compensate, transparency and direct, unmediated contact is crucial for certifying the products' authenticity and wholesomeness, as well as for gaining consumers' trust. This is why they encourage farm-door sales and direct sales through farmers' markets and festivals, which create an opportunity to attach a human face to the products and bring it closer in character to an informal transaction (farm sales in particular).[40] Among the producers, there is a critical discourse towards conventional certifications (as an ecological or a traditional product), which hints to an envisaged pool of consumers that they target as stable customers: those whose consumer competence allows them to be more reflexive and receptive to more discreet and less formalized sources of value. The reception of these products is conditioned by the possession of specific cultural competences, associated to cultural capital, to decode the product meanings.

A valuable tool for quality certification is the invocation of self-consumption. The "homemade" food category has rich marketing value and, during direct sales, producers insist on the double destination of their jar production: what is being sold is also destined to be consumed at home by the producers and their family.

Quaint imperfections constitute another important attribute that consumers look for while attempting to authenticate artisan jar production. Suspicions are raised when the jars look too "perfect," and Andra, the younger among my artisan infor-

---

[39] During my participation at an agriculture and food fair in Bucharest, Dumitru, one of the producers who, by his own account, can produce a maximum of 5000 jars of preserves per year, was shocked by a contract proposal made by a Japanese investor, who asked him how many train wagons of rose petal *dulceață* he could supply.

[40] As reported by the sales assistant of the souvenir shop in one of the tourist sites selling the products of the surveyed producers, the jars labeled as Jams from Rozi (*Gemuri de la Rozi*) sell first, because "it says who made them," even if the same type of jam is available from several producers.

mants, whose appearance does not conform at all to that of a stereotypical rural woman devoted to domestic activities, often has trouble in convincing customers of markets and food festivals that she is the real author of the jars and also that the preserves really are handmade:

> "the cleaner-looking the jar is, the more they suspect you are not a small producer [...] they say 'oh, it cannot be homemade, it looks too beautiful, it is even labeled and all.'"

Domesticity as an authenticating strategy is performed by various bodily and discursive strategies of producers, and also incorporated in brand names, logos, labels, and packaging (cloth attached to the lids, rope to tie the jars) and by the appearance of the product itself: chunky bits are considered more rustic and more coherent with the homemade repertoire of possibilities. There is, however, a thin line between the quaint imperfections and quality signs, and customers look for a non-standardized sensorial reality. For example, they might tilt the jar to check whether the jam is reasonably thick, or "tied together." Color offers an additional repertoire of quality signs, as the jam should ideally not be too grim, but not too bright either, lest it might raise suspicions of usage of synthetic gelatin to make the color "hold."

The use of sugar is a thorny issue for the production of jam and *dulceață*: concerned, middle-class consumers are anxious about their sugar intake[41] and producers feel pressured to diminish or minimize the added sugar quantity or use rhetorical techniques to divert their customers' attention from the sugar content. As many younger female customers walk by the festival stands, asking for sugarless preserves and for products with a less sweet taste, producers explain to them, again and again, that sugar is necessary, as it acts as a preservative for the fruit, or change the topic to emphasize other attributes that make the products clean and pure:

"We unfortunately have to compromise on sugar, as we could not identify a sugar replacement in jams. But at least we do not add anything extra, no additives," producer Dumitru stresses in an over-the-stand dialog with a customer. The choice for the local, conventional sugar instead of imported organic version places another value-embedded choice for the producers between purity (chemical-free agriculture) and locality.

Producers act and speak of ingredient thriftiness as if obeying a conscientious Occam's razor, with no added water, a minimal amount of sugar, and no aspirin or other artificial preservatives. Cultural competence is shared among consumers and producers and the producers have learned to "clean" their recipes of potentially tainted ingredients:

> "we have decided to stop using any preservatives [...] and no sort of gelatin. Only sugar and fruit. I took it up as a trial one year, to see how the jam would last and it turns out that it worked. [...] But being very cautious probably helped as well" (Greta, producer).

Using foraged ingredients (mushrooms, berries, and other wild fruit) is of particular value for my informants: the wild origins (associated with untainted nature) confer the products an aura of purity and place them outside suspicions of chemical or

[41] A public service communication broadcast regularly by televisions during ad breaks warns against the excessive consumption of salt, sugar, and fats.

symbolic pollution. The same principle of thriftiness applies—for some of the producers—to the range of products that they include in their offer: three to four is seen as the balanced number.

Ethics and Labor as Sources of Value

Painstaking, labor-intensive preparation activities enhance the product value. Small fruits and wild fruits are singled out as the most laborious: picking the stones out of bitter cherries, for example, or turning rosehip into a smooth paste, or picking the soft and small sea buckthorn fruit from the thorny stems of the tree. Andra brings up an additional limitation of the small-scale production, owing to the available labor that the producer family and occasional day workers can provide:

> "Everything that is forest fruit is hard to process. Bitter cherries, you go crazy until you take out all the stones; elder fruit, with its tiny-tiny fruit … you have to remove every piece individually if you care about quality. […] Cornelian cherries are just as difficult, plus you waste a lot of it, you can only use the pulp. […] When you make everything by hand, the quantities are really limited" (Andra, producer).

The various producers have devised various solutions, which rely either on coopting extra manual labor force during fruit high season or on devising special techniques to enhance production quality:

> "I would gather the rosehips and spread them on the ground at the end of October, for about a week, so that the hoarfrost fell on them in the mornings. It makes them softer and easier to boil. Oh, and sweeter, you know … These things … we've learned them from the old Germans, you know …" (Emilia, producer).

Greta, the producer featured on the Slow Food leaflet, offers her own version of "smaller is better":

> "I only boil one kilogram of fruit at once. This decreases the cooking time and allows the color and taste to keep better. From a business point of view, of course a bigger batch is better, but the quality will be poorer then."

The market for artisan-jarred preserves was positioned as a more meaningful and more trustworthy alternative to the industrial, mass production. The mutual influences circulated between the industry and the artisan producers, with the former adopting a discourse of domesticity and familiarity and the latter imitating business branding strategies.

To the standardization of mass production, artisans oppose a different set of values, as illustrated by the producers who were the focus of my ethnographic fieldwork. Sustainable size and production volume, labor-intensive techniques, domesticity, control of ingredients, inherited knowledge, lack of market savvy, and mercantilism are values that the observed consumers attach to the artisan production during my fieldwork.

The values are meaningful to consumers based, to a significant extent, on the analogy between artisan and domestic production. The shared meanings, reading of quality signs, interactional cues in face-to-face interaction, etc. empower the consumers to elude standardized, formal/conventional certifications of food safety, taste, and quality when acquiring trust into the artisan production.

Giving New Meaning to Domestic Self-Provisioning: Jars and Productive Leisure Among the Middle Class

Most of my consumer informants have recorded a shift from their former attachments and behavior regarding domestic preserves over the past few years. The findings indicate that the meaning of homemade preserves has shifted from the association with the drudgery, hardship, and shortage of their socialist experience to a practice associated more with creativity, leisure, and materialization of consumer competence. The continuation of domestic jarring attests to a conservative attachment to a certain domestic role, associated with caring for the loved ones. However, this meaning of preserve-making coexists with the sublimated, reinterpreted version of preserve-making as productive leisure (De Solier 2013).

In what follows, I will describe my informants' reflections and practices revolving around domestic preserves.

Divorced and with no grandchildren, currently in her early 60s, Cornelia sometimes uses jarring as a means to bond with her friends. For several weeks or weekends during summer, she is invited to various friends' countryside houses, where they make preserves outdoors together. Over the past years, she became a very active Internet user and a keen traveler abroad. The Internet and cooking media rubbed off on her cooking habits and she became keen to experiment in the kitchen. Her latest culinary discovery is rhubarb jam with ginger. She got the rhubarb jam idea from her daughter and she added ginger drawing inspiration from an Internet recipe. She associates having a full pantry of homemade preserves with emotional comfort. As she lives alone, she has reduced the quantities of preserves that she makes, but not the variety:

> "I like to have a bit of every kind. I made jars of many kinds of fruit, because they are tempting, they're beautiful and it's nice to have them."

She carefully labels the jars, and writes the year and the type of jam. She is extra-cautious to protect the content by putting foil under the lid. She has a set of printed, illustrated labels, she received as a gift, which she uses for certain batches, to create "market-style" preserves, a way to play the artisan producer. Sometimes, by naming their products (sometimes in a nondescriptive way), the domestic makers borrow the aesthetics and rudimentary branding of their jars from the artisans.

Eugenia lives with her husband and their adult son. Most of her cooking and jarring are designed around the eating preferences of her son, a very picky eater, inclined towards fast food. Also in her early 60s, her food supply relies significantly on the countryside home of her elderly parents. She is an enthusiastic cook and spends a lot of time online. She describes cooking as a hobby and a refuge: "cooking is my fight with monotony." She makes a lot more preserves than her family is willing to eat, but is not willing to readjust her preserve plan according to the consumption needs: she is happy to share surplus jars among her friends, relatives, or younger neighbors. Every year she makes a separate batch of preserves to send to her daughter in Bucharest, with jars made by recipes adapted to her daughter's taste preferences.

Quite often, the preserve-making decisions take into account the children's preferences and open up channels of creative interaction and reciprocal learning with the adult children: no vinegar pickles, no dill, no oily *zacusca*, less sweet jam, and spicier sauce. Several ingredients or recipes are introduced as the result of knowledge exchanges with the adult children: chutneys, chili jam, orange jam, plum jam with nuts and cinnamon, etc. Circulating preserves via food parcels, as an exchange of knowledge and material objects, is a prized way for my informants to bond with their adult children. Andreea, a copywriter in her 30s, considers herself very lucky from a food point of view, due to her mother's holiday cottage where the mother has grown a hobby garden from which she provides Andreea with all her vegetable supply and sends her homemade preserves for the winter.

Holidays abroad, television cooking shows, the brochures and catalogs supplied by the supermarkets, the abundance of food festivals, and farmers' markets have all contributed to the stimulation of the creative potential of cooking and preserve-making for my informants. Innovations and experimenting with new ingredients are often the result of a negotiation of taste and food values such as cosmopolitanism, sustainability, traceability, nutrition, and health, between them and the adult children, who encourage their parents to send food parcels.

A serendipitously acquired batch of good-quality fruit is often a trigger for a jam-making project. Fruit procured from someone's countryside garden or fruit or mushrooms picked during a hike are valuable raw materials that often spur an unplanned preserve-making campaign for my informants. My informants particularly appreciate the occasional open-air preserve-making experience, both for the experience itself and for the perceived improved quality of the resulting product. Roasting vegetables in open air is believed to give them a smoky flavor, and cooking in a cauldron, on an open fire, in large batches, is likewise believed to enhance the taste of *zacusca*. Cooking outdoors, foraging for wild ingredients, and picking someone's countryside garden or orchard are all preserve-related activities which enhance the authenticity of the experience.

A key choice for my informants, informed by health concerns, seems to be drawn between using sugar or aspirin and boiling the jars as a means to properly preserve produce. They all rationalize a "lesser evil," which usually now tilts towards the chemical-free options. As Cornelia reflects,

"With sour-cherries there is another way: to add a lot of sugar and aspirin, and then you don't need to boil them. But I don't want to add any preservatives and especially not sugar. I would need to add one kilo [of sugar] to each kilo [of fruit] and I do not want to use this much sugar and especially aspirin." Cornelia recalls laughingly of her aspirin-adding days: "I would add aspirin a bit everywhere. Aspirin or preservative. A little bag of powder. Now I do not want to use it anymore.

I even used to add it to the tomato juice. I don't even know why. You only need to sterilize them well and they will keep for as long as 2-3 years."

The attitudes towards sugar are ambivalent: the quality and quali-signs of the end product are in direct correspondence with the sugar quantity; the more the sugar content, the more dense ("*legat*") the jam. The watery aspect is a minus. However, too much boiling, which makes up for the lower sugar content, affects the color, giving the jam an opaque, dark hue.

The awareness of chemicals is acutely present in the discourse of my informants and it represents a key focus of their attainment of consumer competence. Clean sourcing, as a result, is among their main concerns. Cornelia admits that the store-bought preserves that she tried have a satisfactory taste, but she attributes the good taste on the abundance of the dreaded preservatives and "E"s that likely create flavor. The reluctance to use chemicals in jams is defended in relation to the exasperation that the fresh fruit and vegetables are already too chemical filled. Eugenia has her trustworthy sources of fruit and vegetables; when she cannot procure them from her parents' countryside, she buys from specific sellers at the farmers' market: "I have my peasants. And I have my green tomato lady." She claims to be able to sniff the pesticides from the vegetables, so she always smells the produce and relies upon her sense of smell to make the decision what to buy or to prepare.

The use of chemicals in domestic preserves is often described under a discourse of repented taste. Eugenia confesses that she has recently tried using Gelfix again (a powdered preservative especially popular in the 1990s) and that she decided to give away the batch of jam, as the perceived unnatural consistency and structure of the jam did not allow her to enjoy it. The attachment to making preserves at home is placed into the larger context of eating anxieties by Eugenia: "I know it's like a drop in the ocean, but at least it's something that doesn't add to all the other dubious stuff we eat."

The various secrets of jarring seem trivial but key to successful kitchen do-it-yourself. The interviewed women describe these skills passionately. Cornelia balances the sugar quantity according to the perceived water content of the fruit: she teaches me that fruit picked after the rain is more watery and the sugar quantity needs to be increased. She controls the consistency of the jams in real time, by pouring a drop onto a cold plate. The droplet needs to hold and not liquefy on the plate. Eugenia makes everything by the eye and is keen to specify that she can even bake cakes by approximating the needed ingredient quantities. Continuous evaluation and adjustment are named among the skills that my informants rely on for successful jarring.

Eugenia makes her own ketchup, often outdoors, for the extra smoky flavor. She proudly recalls a moment when she served her son and his visiting friends a homemade meal that reproduced a fast-food meal, with crispy chicken, ketchup, and pickled cucumbers, all homemade, that her son assumed would be a failure; it turned out to be incredibly popular among his friends. Her most recent preserve success was a quince jam, made serendipitously, with the batch of small fruit received as a gift from a neighbor's unpruned tree: inspired by a food blog, she added cinnamon to the mix. Upon my latest visit, Cornelia enthusiastically made me taste her homemade limoncello. The sweet liquor that I was tasting, lighter in color and slightly less thick compared to what I was accustomed with from store-bought versions, was made by comparing several Internet recipes which turned up on a Google search and the taste was adjusted according to the limoncello that she had tasted during two trips to Italy and to Greece:

> "I took it as a challenge; I thought buying it from Greece was too expensive, I looked on the internet and I figured it was very easy to make at home. Long live the internet! It was indeed very easy!".

Marcela, inspired by trips to IKEA, has found inspiration in the Scandinavian menu of the IKEA restaurant and has started to use—against the disapproval of her family—some of her homemade blueberry jam as a sauce for steak during domestic dinners.

My middle-class informants displayed many instances of treating jarring as productive leisure. Often, the informants—in their 50s and 60s—resume the practice at the pressure of their adult children's quest for their own self-authentication, through the consumption of safe, quality, authentic foods. The middle-class young adults perceive their parents' preserves as a source of food embodying these qualities (e.g., a facilitator for an identity performance of origins, family heritage, and access to rare, archaic, or exotic food resources, such as heirloom or regional varieties).

Following the argument of Isabelle de Solier I argue that the domestic production of preserves practiced by my informants is a form of productive leisure (De Solier 2013). De Solier starts her argument with the observation that cooking, as a social practice of production, has been historically "internally differentiated into forms of paid and unpaid labor along gender lines" (2013: 130), where domestic cooking, as opposed to professional cooking, is a form of feminized unpaid domestic labor. Her research on the emerging figure of the foodie supports the idea that home cooking is also experienced as a form of "domestic leisure." She quotes Luce Giard stating that activities of food preparation can be "a significant site of self-making" (De Solier 2013: 130). She finds that the technological changes and the affordability of convenience foods allowed the middle-class aspiring foodies that she had surveyed to experience cooking as a form of leisure. She refers to education, moral approach, and intentionality that mobilize creativity in cooking as the differentiating features of productive leisure:

> "the effort and commitment, the constant acquisition and deployment of knowledge and skill, and the emulation of the attitudes, values and practices of professional chefs that distinguishes their home cooking as the serious and productive leisure of amateurs" (2013: 132).

The moral dimension of producing food in the home lies in the belief that everything should be prepared from scratch. As de Solier states,

> "such material production held a higher moral value in their self-making because of anxieties over consumerism and the worth placed in productive pursuit" (2013: 137).

The creative character of domestic cooking shares features with craft activities, as Colin Campbell (2005), quoted in de Solier, suggests the term "craft consumption" to refer to what he believes is a hybrid practice.

The domestic postsocialist producers featured in my research seem to participate in a practice shared by a global category of postindustrial societies. The manual character of jarring is—under the terminology of de Solier—a type of "manual leisure" that the middle classes pursue to counterbalance the absence of manual labor associated with their work:

> "Where manual labor is working class, manual leisure is middle class" (2013: 142).

Jarring is a form of manual production—informed nonetheless by intellectually acquired knowledge—that the middle classes embrace as an experience in a postindustrial context.

As I have previously illustrated, several dimensions of the evolution of postsocialist preserve-making suggest a shift of the practice towards the side of productive leisure: enhancing the aesthetic, creative, and experiential side of jarring, as opposed to productivity, efficiency, and planning; the privilege of spur-of-the-moment preserving decisions; the reflection on taste and health implications; and the cultivation of values such as small scale, purity, innovation, etc. Domestic jarring acquires a new set of meanings and becomes the field for the exercise of newly acquired cultural competences among middle-class women past middle age in my research.

Conclusions

Throughout this chapter, I have positioned the preserve jar as a metaphor for broader transformations in the Romanian consumer culture. I have argued and illustrated how the consumption of artisan preserves, domestic production, as well as a rose-tinted retrospective appreciation for socialist-era preserves are all facets of the struggle against standardization professed by middle-class consumers in postsocialist Romania. I have examined the transformations in the culture of consumption of preserves of Romanian middle-class consumers emerging from postsocialist Romania as a shift in meaning, from the culture of shortage, to the repositioning as a form of consumption associated with authenticity and used for self-actualization.

My goal was to shed light on the practices and meanings attached to preserves under various spheres: domestic self-provisioning, the artisan market, and the mass market. I have examined the postsocialist symbolic "career" of socialist-era foods, I have illustrated how attributes and values sought in the consumption of artisan jars create a market of "quality products," and I have examined the revival of domestic jarring among middle-class women and its repositioning as productive leisure.

I have described the culture of shortage associated with late Romanian socialism and preserves as one of its material expressions that embody pragmatic, food-hoarding strategies. I have mapped the transition to capitalism, with the associated consumer strategies of domestication of foreign foods and of allowing capitalist modernity into domestic kitchens and cuisines.

Standardization and modernization, associated with globalization and Europeanization, is experienced as a loss of taste and as a source of anxiety connected to the lack of traceability, accountability, and "origin" of contemporary convenience foods. A counter-reaction emerges among concerned middle-class consumers seeking to regain control over what they ingest, increasingly turning to shorter food chains and more local production as a strategy to mitigate uncertainty. Such consumers oppose the "symbolic bulimia," associated with postsocialist consumerism, with a symbolic cleansing of the diet, which includes a revaluation of artisan, manual labor and products, purity, simplicity, and sustainability. Paradoxically, the socialist food industry becomes one of the unlikely objects of appreciation and nostalgia through a process of selective memory, where past products, including preserves, are invested with a memory of pre-modern trustworthiness.

The practice of homemade jars has itself shifted from the association with drudgery, hardship, and shortage of the socialist experience to a practice associated more with creativity, leisure, and materialization of consumer competence. A meaning of preserve self-provisioning as productive leisure emerges, which includes the aesthetic, creative, and experiential side of jarring (as opposed to productivity, efficiency, and planning); the privilege of spontaneous decision; and the cultivation of "artisan" values. The reframing of preserves materializes the middle-class consumers' aspiration to the construction of an authentic self and is projected unto a horizon of morality.

Acknowledgments This chapter was written as part of the project "Material projects of class distinction: An analysis of middle classness in post-socialist Romania from a material culture perspective," funded by the Romanian Executive Agency for Higher Education, Research, Development and Innovation Funding Programme "Human Resources," Project Type: Research Projects for Young Independent Teams (TE 2014), PN-II-RU-TE-2014-4-2650.

References

Anghel, Remus. 2004. Economia informală în comunism şi postcomunism: mere şi ţuică într-un sat din România [Informal Economy in Communism and Postcommunism: Apples and Brandy in a Village in Romania]. In *Economia informală în România: Pieţe, practici sociale şi transformări ale statului după 1989* [Informal Economy in Romania: Markets, Social Practices and Transformations of the State after 1989], ed. Liviu Chelcea and Oana Mateescu, 263–287. Bucharest: Paideia.

———. 2013. *Romanians in Western Europe: Migration, Status Dilemmas, and Transnational Connections*. Lexington, MA: Lexington Books.

Arndt, Stephan, and Wolfgang Becker. 2003. *Good Bye Lenin! [motion picture]*. Germany: X-Filme Creative Pool.

Arnould, Eric, and Linda L. Price. 2000. Authenticating Acts and Authoritative Performances: Questing for Self and Community. In *The Why of Consumption: Contemporary Perspectives on Consumer Motives, Goals, and Desires*, ed. Eric Arnould et al., 140–163. London: Routledge.

Baudrillard, Jean. 1998. *The Consumer Society*. London: Sage.

Berdahl, Daphne. 1999a. '(N)Ostalgie' for the Present: Memory, Longing, and East German Things. *Ethnos* 64 (2): 192–211.

———. 1999b. *Where the World Ended: Re-Unification and Identity in the German Borderland*. Berkeley, CA: University of California Press.

———. 2005. The Spirit of Capitalism and the Boundaries of Citizenship in Post-Wall Germany. *Comparative Studies in Society and History* 47 (2): 235–251.

Caldwell, Melissa. 2002. The Taste of Nationalism: Food politics in Postsocialist Moscow. *Ethnos* 67 (3): 295–319.

———. 2004. Domesticating the French fry: McDonald's and Consumerism in Moscow. *Journal of Consumer Culture* 4 (1): 5–26.

———. 2007. Feeding the Body and Nourishing the Soul: Natural Foods in Postsocialist Russia. *Food Culture and Society* 10 (1): 43–71.

———. 2011. *Dacha Idylls: Living Organically in Russia's Countryside*. Berkeley: University of California Press.

Campbell, Colin. 2005. The Craft Consumer: Culture, Craft and Consumption in a Postmodern Society. *Journal of Consumer Culture* 5 (1): 23–42.

Chelcea, Liviu. 2002. The Culture of Shortage During State-Socialism: Consumption Practices in a Romanian Village in the 1980s. *Cultural Studies* 16 (1): 16–43.

———. 2006. Marginal Groups in Central Places: Gentrification, Property Rights and Post-Socialist Primitive Accumulation (Bucharest, Romania). In *Social Changes and Social Sustainability in Historical Urban Centres: The Case of Central Europe*, ed. Gyorgy Enyedi and Zoltan Kovács, 127–146. Pecs: Centre for Regional Studies of Hungarian Academy of Sciences.

Chivu, Marius. 2016, November 17–23. "Statul mult timp în bucătărie e marca celor născuţi în comunism"—interviu cu scenaristul Alex Baciu ["Spending Time in the Kitchen is the Brand of Those Born under Communism"—Interview with Screenplay Writer Alex Baciu]. *Dilema veche*. Retrieved from http://dilemaveche.ro/sectiune/tema-saptamanii/articol/statul-mult-timp-in-bucatarie-e-marca-celor-nascuti-in-comunism. Accessed 20 Aug 2017.

Colquhoun, Anna. 2008, May 22. To Romania in a Spoon [Blog post]. *Culinary Anthropologist*. Retrieved from http://www.culinaryanthropologist.org/to-romania-in-a-spoon/#more-117. Accessed 30 Aug 2017.

Creed, Gerald. 1998. *Domesticating Revolution: from Socialist Reform to Ambivalent Transition in a Bulgarian Village*. University Park, PA: Pennsylvania State University Press.

De Solier, Isabelle. 2013. *Food and the Self: Consumption, Production and Material Culture*. London: Bloomsbury.

Diminescu, Dana. 2009. Exerciţiul dificil al liberei circulaţii: o introducere în istoria migraţiei recente a românilor [The Difficult Exercise of Free Movement: an Introduction to the History of Recent Migration of Romanians]. In *Sociologia migraţiei. Teorii şi studii de caz româneşti* [Sociology of Migration: Theories and Romanian Case Studies], ed. Remus Anghel and Istvan Horvath, 45–63. Bucharest: Polirom.

Dumitrescu, Florin. 2015. *Traditii la superoferta—Intre socoteala din agentie si cea de la raft* [Traditions on Offer: Between Agency Strategies and the Shelf]. Bucharest: Cartier.

Dunn, Elizabeth Cullen. 2009. Afterword. Turnips and Mangos: Power and the Edible State in Eastern Europe. In Food and Everyday Life in the Post-Socialist World, ed. Melissa Caldwell, 206–222. Bloomington: Indiana University Press.

Fehérváry, Katherine. 2002. American Kitchens, Luxury Bathrooms, and the Search for a 'Normal' Life in Postsocialist Hungary. *Ethnos* 67 (3): 369–400.

———. 2009. Goods and States: The Political Logic of State-Socialist Material Culture. *Comparative Studies in Society and History* 51 (2): 426–459.

Fischler, Claude. 1980. Food Habits, Social Change and the Nature/Culture Dilemma. *Social Science Information* 19 (6): 937–953.

Gille, Zsuzsa. 2009. The Tale of the Toxic Paprika: the Hungarian taste of Euro-globalization. In *Food and Everyday Life in the Postsocialist World*, ed. Melissa Caldwell, 57–77. Bloomington, IN: Indiana University Press.

Harkness, Nicholas. 2015. The Pragmatics of Qualia in Practice. *Annual Review of Anthropology* 44 (1): 573–589.

Hochshild, Arlie. 1989. *The Second Shift: Working Parents and the Revolution at Home*. New York: Viking.

Horváth, Istvan, and Remus Anghel. 2009. Migration and its Consequences for Romania. *Südosteuropa* 57 (4): 386–403.

Iancu, Bogdan. 2011. The Golden Age of Termopane. The Social Life of Post-Socialist Windows. *Martor* 16: 19–34.

———. 2014, June. *Certifying 'real food' through the incorporation of 'home': The rise of 'traditional products' and the re-imagination of grandma*. Paper presented at the Perugia Food Studies Conference, Umbra Institute, Perugia.

Jackson, Peter. 2010. Food Stories: Consumption in an Age of Anxiety. *Cultural Geographies* 17 (2): 147–165.

———. 2015. *Anxious Appetites: Food and Consumer Culture*. London: Bloomsbury Publishing.

Jung, Yuson. 2009. From Canned Food to Canny Consumers: Cultural Competence in the Age of Mechanical Production. In *Food and Everyday Life in the Postsocialist World*, ed. Melissa Caldwell, 29–56. Bloomington, IN: Indiana University Press.

Kideckel, David. 1993. *The Solitude of Collectivism: Romanian Villagers to the Revolution and Beyond*. Ithaca, NY: Cornell University Press.

———. 2008. *Getting by in Postsocialist Romania: Labor, the Body, & Working-Class Culture*. Bloomington, IN: Indiana University Press.

Klumbyte, Neringa. 2009. The Geopolitics of Taste: The 'Euro' and 'Soviet' Sausage Industries in Lithuania. In *Food and Everyday Life in the Postsocialist World*, ed. Melissa Caldwell, 130–153. Bloomington, IN: Indiana University Press.

Konstantinov, Yulian, and Andrei Simić. 2001. Bulgaria: The Quest for Security. *Anthropology of East Europe Review* 19 (2): 21–34.

Kopytoff, Igor. 1986. The Cultural Biography of Things: Commoditization as Process. In *The Social Life of things: Commodities in Cultural Perspective*, ed. Arjun Appadurai, 64–91. Cambridge: Cambridge University Press.

Lampland, Martha. 1995. *The Object of Labor: Commodification in Socialist Hungary*. Chicago, IL: University of Chicago Press.

Lankauskas, Gediminas. 2002. On 'Modern' Christians, Consumption, and the Value of National Identity in Post-Soviet Lithuania. *Ethnos* 67 (3): 320–344.

Ledeneva, Alena. 1998. *Russia's Economy of Favours: Blat, Networking and Informal Exchange*. Cambridge: Cambridge University Press.

Manning, Paul, and Ann Uplisashvili. 2007. "Our Beer": Ethnographic Brands in Postsocialist Georgia. *American Anthropologist* 109 (4): 626–641.

Mars, Gerald, and Yochanan Altman. 1987. Alternative Mechanism of Distribution in a Soviet Economy. In *Constructive Drinking: Perspectives on Drink from Anthropology*, ed. Mary Douglas, 270–279. Cambridge: Cambridge University Press.

Mateescu, Oana. 2005. Furt, vânzare sau dar: Bucuriile privatizării într-un sat din Oltenia [Theft, Sale or Gift: the Joys of Privatisation in a Village of Oltenia]. In *Economie informala in Romania* [The Informal Economy in Romania], ed. Liviu Chelcea and Oana Mateescu, 83–112. Bucharest: Paideia.

Meneley, Anne. 2008. Oleo-Signs and Quali-Signs: The Qualities of Olive Oil. *Ethnos* 73 (3): 303–326.

Merkel, Ina. 1994. From a Socialist Society of Labor into a Consumer Society? The Transformation of East German Identities and Systems. In *Envisioning Eastern Europe: Postcommunist Cultural Studies*, ed. Michael Kennedy, 55–65. Ann Arbor, MI: University of Michigan Press.

———. 1998. Consumer Culture in the GDR, or How the Struggle for Antimodernity was Lost on the Battleground of Consumer Culture. In *Getting and Spending: European and American Consumer Societies in the Twentieth Century*, ed. Susan Strasser, Charles McGovern, and Matthias Judt, 281–299. Cambridge: Cambridge University Press.

Micu, Cornel. 2012. *From Peasants to Farmers? Agrarian Reforms and Modernisation in Twentieth Century Romania: A Case Study: Bordei Verde Commune in Braila County*. New York: Peter Lang.

Mihailescu, Vintila. 2000. La maisnie diffuse, du communisme au capitalisme: questions et hypothèses [The Diffuse Household, from Communism to Capitalism: Questions and Hypotheses]. *Balkanologie. Revue d'études pluridisciplinaires* 4 (2): 73–90.

———. 2014. Sateni. A Diffuse Household in a Post-Peasant Society. *Acta Universitatis Sapientiae, Social Analysis* 4 (1/2): 31–43.

Mihăilescu, Vintila, and Bogdan Iancu. 2009. "Produsele de calitate" şi patrimonializarea gustului în România ["Quality Products" and the Patrimonialisation of Taste in Romania]. *Sociologie Românească* 7 (3): 37–49.

Mincyte, Diana. 2009. Self-Made Women: Informal Dairy Markets in Europeanizing Lithuania. In *Food and Everyday Life in the Postsocialist World*, ed. Melissa Caldwell, 78–100. Bloomington, IN: Indiana University Press.

Ministerul Agriculturii. 1960. *Sfaturi gospodaresti* [Household Advice]. Bucharest: Editura Agrosilvica.

Miroiu, Mihaela. 2004. *Drumul catre autonomie. Teorii politice feministe* [The Road to Autonomy. Feminist Political Theories]. Bucharest: Polirom.

Moisio, Risto, Eric Arnould, and Linda L. Price. 2004. Between Mothers and Markets: Constructing Family Identity Through Homemade Food. *Journal of Consumer Culture* 4 (3): 361–384.

Otzen, Hans, and Barbara Otzen. 2012. *DDR Kochbuch*. Koln: Komet Verlag.

———. 2014. *DDR Backbuch*. Koln: Komet Verlag.

Patico, Jennifer, and Melissa Caldwell. 2002. Consumers Exiting Socialism: Ethnographic Perspectives on Daily Life in Post-Communist Europe. *Ethnos* 67 (3): 285–294.

Pârvulescu, Ioana. 2012. *Intelectuali la cratiţă: amintiri culinare şi 50 de reţete* [Intellectuals in the Kitchen: Culinary Memories and 50 Recipes]. Bucharest: Humanitas.

Poenaru, Florin. 2008. On the Socialist Balcony: State, Citizens and Ideology in a Romanian Neighborhood. Saarbrücken: VDM Publishing.

Pratt, Jeffrey. 2008. Food values: The Local and the Authentic. In *Hidden Hands in the Market: Ethnographies of Fair Trade, Ethical Consumption, and Corporate Social Responsibility*, ed. Geert De Neve et al., 53–70. Bingley: Emerald Group Publishing.

Rausing, Sigrid. 2002. Reconstructing the 'Normal'. In *Markets & Moralities: Ethnographies of Postsocialism*, ed. Ruth Mandel and Caroline Humphrey, 127–142. New York: Berg.

Rozin, Paul. 1976. "The selection of foods by rats, humans and other animals", in: J. S. Rosenblatt; R. A. Hinde; E. Shaw; C. Beer (eds.). Advances in the study of behavior. 6, 21–76.

Ries, Nancy. 2009. Potato Ontology: Surviving Postsocialism in Russia. *Cultural Anthropology* 24 (2): 181–212.

Sampson, Steven. 1984. *National Integration Through Socialist Planning: an Anthropological Study of a Romanian New Town*. New York: Columbia University Press.

Smollett, Eleanor Wenkart. 1989. The Economy of Jars: Kindred Relationships in Bulgaria—an Exploration. *Ethnologia Europaea* 19 (2): 125–140.

Stroe, Monica. 2011. Ethnopolitical Entrepreneurship and the Political Role of "Saxonness without Saxons" in Sibiu. *Sociologie Romaneasca* 9 (2): 86–95.

———. 2016. *Gustul locului: productia de peisaje culturale agro-alimentare in sudul Transilvaniei* [The Taste of Place: the Production of Agro-Food Landscapes in Southern Transylvania]. Bucharest: Tritonic.

Syutkin, Olga, and Pavel Syutkin. 2015. *CCCP Cook Book: True Stories of Soviet Cuisine*. London: Fuel Publishing.

Teisanu, Ecaterina. 1954. *Conserve de legume şi fructe* [Fruit and Vegetable Preserves]. Bucharest: Comitetul femeilor democrate din RPR.

———. 1969. *Îmi reuşesc toate conservele de legume* [Successful Vegetable Preserves]. Bucharest: Ceres.

Verdery, Katherine. 1996. *What Was Socialism, and What Comes Next*. Princeton, NJ: Princeton University Press.

Von Bremzen, Anya. 2013. *Mastering the Art of Soviet Cooking: A Memoir of Food and Longing*. New York: Crown.

Watson, James L., ed. 2006. *Golden Arches East: McDonald's in East Asia*. Palo Alto, CA: Stanford University Press.
Wilk, Richard. 2006. *Home Cooking in the Global Village: Caribbean Food from Buccaneers to Ecotourists*. New York: Berg.
Yan, Yunxiang. 2000. Of Hamburger and Social Space: Consuming McDonald's in Beijing. In *The Consumer Revolution in Urban China*, ed. Deborah Davis, 201–225. Berkeley, CA: University of California Press.
Zerilli, Filippo. 2004. Jucand (cu) mita. Imagini etnografice ale coruptiei in Romania [Playing (with) Bribery. Ethnographic Images of Corruption in Romania]. In *Cercetarea antropologica in Romania. Perspective istorice si etnografice* [Anthropological Research in Romania. Historical and Ethnographic Perspectives], ed. Cristina Papa, Giovanni Pizza, and Filippo Zerilli, 269–300. Cluj-Napoca: Clusium.

The Pleasures of Being Global: Cultural Consumption of Pizza and Sushi in a Bulgarian City

Iskra Velinova

Introduction

The debate of what turn globalization takes is still at hand. Jan Pieterse summarizes the way different politics on multiculturalism define possible paradigms as (1) a gloomy *cultural differentialism* (closure and apartheid), (2) westernalized *cultural convergence* (the politics of assimilation with the dominant group as the center of gravity, westernalization or Americanization at large) (Ritzer 1993), or (3) a brighter, yet blurred idea of *cultural mixing* (integration without giving up cultural identities, and cohabitation yielding new cross-cultural patterns). The third concept implies open-ended outcome processes as much as of easternalization as of westernalization, as well as of many interstitial influences (Pieterse 2004: 57). While the complete economic and political sequels to those theoretical approaches are yet to be seen, the contemporary consumer culture seems to transcend those distinctions and to display all those aspects as different *scapes*, in Appadurai's terminology (Appadurai 1996). Western practices and modes of production dominate technological consumerism and its derivatives (Ritzer 1993). Cultural differentialism reigns in the sphere of religions and ideologies. Food culture, on the other hand, gradually transforms into a global *melánge*. Transportation of foods and food practices from one place to faraway destinations is already commonplace. Food consumption becomes a terrain of brave experiments of large groups of people eating the food traditionally eaten by foreign peoples. The appearance of *fusion cuisine* mixes up food preparation methods, recipes, cooking, and presentation through creative integration of different cultures. These are world-shaping phenomena.

These processes do not take place without impediments though. I do not entirely share the fear that global food homogenizes modern life and dissolves the subtleties of diverse local tastes (Caldwell 2004: 5–26; Mintz 2006: 7). Setting aside the fact

I. Velinova (✉)
Independent Scholar, Sofia, Bulgaria

E. Krasteva-Blagoeva (ed.), *Approaching Consumer Culture*, International Series on Consumer Science, https://doi.org/10.1007/978-3-030-00226-8_8

that we never eat the food of the unfamiliar other (Heldke 2005: 386), which I discuss further, even though we may consciously search for similar gest, we cannot help but transform the foreign into a kind of "our own." I argue that global food consumption puts people from different cultures in a situation of making similar social choices while trying to transform the foreign into something familiar. The specific ways of transformation depend on how existing food habits, economic options, and cultural traditions intersect with personal experiences and life encounters. Within this framework, people shape their own global (or glocal) identity. "Tastes both remind us of who we are and point out to us who we are not" (Heldke 2005: 386). Different principles of *domestication* work here and they are one of the ways through which we may trace the dynamics of modern culture.

My research explores the principles of transformation of foreign into domestic through the incorporation of two world popular foods in a Bulgarian city's culture, pizza and sushi. It envisages the mechanisms of the construction of domestic and foreign in the food habits and practices of contemporary city inhabitants.[1]

A useful methodological device to explain the stable elements and the change factors of food systems can be the analogy with language systems. The parallel between food connections and linguistic structures was suggested by Mary Douglas (Douglas 1983: 80). Roland Barthes has addressed the signifying and communicative nature of food coining the term "grammar of food" and using "structure" of food system in the sense that it has in linguistics (See Barthes 2008: 22–26). Later the same analogy has successfully been used by Massimo Montanari, who more closely connects the levels of language and categories of linguistics with food structure. The *grammar of food* informs the food system as a dynamic structure, pointing out its cultural and communicative values and potentialities (Montanari 2006: 93–113). The lexicon on which this language is based is the available animal and vegetable products very much like the kind of morphemes (the basic units of meaning). This lexicon "redefines itself in the changing context of environmental,

[1] This chapter is based on my investigation carried out in 2013 and a follow-up in 2015–2017. The ethnographic research on food consumption practices of urbanites took place in Sofia, the capital city of Bulgaria. The ethnographic data was collected after I conducted two unstructured group interviews with ten college and university students, aged 17–24; interviews with specialized respondents: two chefs of Japanese food restaurants and one chef of a pizza restaurant in Sofia—one interview with each of them. Especially illuminating was the interview with a big supermarket manager on the demand and supply of seafood as well as the structure of purchases of fish and other sea products of the restaurants. Also, I had a number of informal interviews with seven young professionals, aged 28–39. Two of them turned out to be my key informants. Four middle-aged Sofians provided my reference points when I had to outline the changes in local food tastes and food preferences.

Particularly useful were the customers' reviews and comments in the websites of pizzarias and Japanese restaurants. Those clients gave me interesting information on how they position themselves on the map of the global food consumption and what symbolic meaning they ascribe to the acts of visiting ethnic restaurants.

For the Japanese food part of the text I rely on my experience as a long-term participant observer having spent a month in Japan every year for the last 17 years. There I have had the chance to interview people on their food preferences and practices; observe Japanese home cooking, frequent restaurants, and sushi bars; and cook Japanese food myself.

economic, social and cultural circumstances." Morphology includes the ways in which products are developed and adapted to the different demands of consumption (Montanari 2006: 99, 100). Then the syntax in the sphere of gastronomy is "the meal that coordinates the dishes according to criteria determining sequence, combination, and reciprocal reltionships" (Montanari 2006: 101). Semantics and pragmatics of the food "text" are the meanings, situations, and contexts which the meal as a social and cultural device produces or is influenced by, when people choose the ingredients, preparation methods, and ways of consumption.

Linguistic analogies may be helpful in explanation of whether and how foods from one part of the world and from one culinary system can or cannot be transplanted into the food system of another. It can give us some clues of how certain foods are indigenized or become global.[2]

I will apply the mentioned linguistic analogy as a methodological device to analyze how *pizza* and *sushi* have been introduced into the Bulgarian postsocialist city culinary landscape.

Pizza is the dish which is intimately domesticated. It is transformed and turned largely into a local food. Local tradition finds closeness to its own taste. This dish has been hybridized and has become an indiscernible element of the contemporary Bulgarian eating out practices. I explain the blending through the nonconflicting interaction of economic and cultural factors while pizza is being spread as an ordinary street food and restaurant dish on the urban culinary scene.

Just the opposite, sushi restaurants and Japanese foods can be defined as markers of cultural non-belonging and "exotic strangeness." Interactions between the main factors do not enhance the process of domesticating this food. Japanese food, and more particularly sushi and sashimi, indicates economic, taste, and cultural barriers, showing the markers of what "we are not." This does not entail a suggestion that sushi restaurants in the cities, mainly in the capital Sofia, are not visited. On the contrary, a good number of citizens opt for spending their leisure time in those places. The motivation, though, is to be more profoundly explored. I argue that the enjoyment of eating Japanese food lies more in the realm of abstract symbolic consumption rather than in gustatory pleasures.

Before the talk about how global foods enter the culinary practices of contemporary people, I must briefly discuss the venues in urban landscapes where those two meet—restaurants.

---

[2] In her illuminating essay on the indigenization of Philippine food, Doreen Fernandez elegantly uses the main categories standing behind the linguistic terms in food analysis—names, ingredients, cooking process, flavoring, and social position—to show how elements from different culinary cultures interact, are Philippinized, and blend into a unique native cuisine (see Fernandez 1988).

City Restaurants

As researchers show, the idea of the restaurant has evolved from the humble village cook shops—places of feeding lower class people and travelers' inns in medieval times. Through the seventeenth to nineteenth centuries coffeehouses and teahouses appeared in big cities like Venice, London, Paris, and Rome, but foremost Middle Eastern Damascus, Cairo, and Istanbul. First two coffeehouses opened in Istanbul in 1554 (Markman 2004; Finkelsein 2004). They inspired the emergence of modern restaurants combining the basic function of those early forms—to be places that satisfy the biological need of nourishment and the social need of people to communicate (Ashley et al. 2004: Ch. 9).

When part of the Ottoman Empire,[3] Bulgaria developed the coffeehouse and tavern culture as early as the town life emerged. The Ottoman type of coffeehouses and taverns opened wherever Muslim communities lived on the vast territory of the empire. They became favorite places for men to spend their leisure time (Karababa and Ger 2011). First Turkish coffeehouses opened in Bulgarian towns as early as the end of the sixteenth and beginning of the seventeenth centuries to be followed by Armenian, Jewish, and Bulgarian taverns and coffee shops in the next decades and centuries (Kraev 2005: 46).[4] In the eighteenth and especially the nineteenth centuries there were coffeehouses (*kafeneta*) in almost every town. They would sometimes combine grocery shop, sweet shop, barbershop, coffee shop, and/or lunch place in one (Kraev 2005: 41, 42, 47). Nearby these there were taverns where the focus was on the alcoholic drinks and *meze* snacks. Men adopted the ubiquitous practice of spending hours in those places discussing worldly matters, politics, or just gossiping. The kafenetata became centers for social interaction (Kraev 2005).[5]

After Bulgaria achieved independence in 1878, a capitalist city culture quickly developed and set new recreational places. Influences from the West mixed up with the older Eastern traditions: a curious coexistence of old Middle East types of coffeehouses side by side with new Viennese-style sweet shops, for example. There followed some 60 years of capitalist development before the communist regime came to power. It is important to note that the years of capitalism were insufficient

[3] Bulgaria lost its independence at the end of the fourteenth century as the kingdom fell under the domination of Ottoman Empire and remained its province until the second half of the nineteenth century.

[4] The ethnic and religious separation of recreational places followed the pattern of the Metropolis. For a long period of time Istanbul set the norm of keeping the coffeehouses exclusively as Muslim venues, while taverns and other recreational places had different ethnic clientele, mainly Christians and Jews (Karababa and Ger 2011; Markman 2004). Later the provinces, such as Greece and Bulgaria, developed their own, more or less autonomous, town culture by opening coffeehouses run by and serving people of other ethnic groups and religious denominations (Kraev 2005: 46, 47). Gradually these boundaries were blurred and the clientele mixed while class distinctions dominated. There were coffeehouses and taverns for the rich notables and cheaper places for the town poor (Kraev 2005: 27).

[5] These places were visited almost exclusively by men. The only women who would visit such places at that time were belly dancers of low reputation.

to distinguish the well-known qualitative class distinctions in food consumption and therefore formulate the idea of *national haute cuisine* (Bourdieu 1984). Wherever new city-style culture appeared, it tried to catch up with the Western mode of life. On the other hand, the national bourgeoisie, consisting mainly of *nouveau-riches*, kept close at hand the old kitchen traditions and never abandoned the centuries-old consumption practices. The country remained in the periphery of the subtleties of the culinary explorations of the *Belle Époque* up until the 20s of the twentieth century. It stayed there for the next half of the century as it remained in the communist zone after World War II. Cooking and food consumption were predominantly at home, while going out was mainly to meet friends for coffee or drinks, or for family dining on certain occasions.

As I have discussed elsewhere, consumption culture during socialism developed in a paradoxical nexus of quick modernizing industrialization and standardization within the scarce economy and permanent crises. During socialism, a type of quasi-consumption culture was formed, deprived of the quintessence of consumption—freedom of choice (Velinova 2004). During socialism the epitomic public spaces for eating were not the restaurants, where professional chefs could experiment and transform food into art. The necessary excess resources and political motivation to produce such food specialists (Ashkenazi and Jacob 2000: 32) lacked for many years after communist party took power. Mass public eating spaces were school and workers' canteens offering affordable staples. Restaurants, of course, did exist, some of them (especially in the mid-1970s) showing features of luxury and particular chic in furniture and service. They were very few in number though. Long queues of people waited for a table. It was a matter of sheer luck to find a place to dine at such places. Standardized menus reduced the choice of the customers to just a couple of options. This—among other circumstances—explains the fact that the concept of *culinary taste*, rather than being enriched and refined due to new consumption practices as in the West, has shrunk to the simple "homemade" as a model of "good food."

It is noteworthy, though, that the culture of going out with family and friends has never declined. On the contrary, in this then-economically backward country, communism turned out to be a significant modernizing economic and cultural project. Urban transformations open up spaces and places for social life. Not necessarily high end, some *unpretentious eateries—mainly for grilled food (kebapchiinitsa)* or small Viennese-type *cafés and coffeehouses (often called sweet shops)*—satisfied the demand for emotional pleasure and continuous entertainment (Finkelstein 2014). There, over a glass of an inexpensive alcoholic drink and a plate of grilled meat and salad, or a cup of coffee, people would spend long hours enjoying each other's company. The centuries-old Balkan habit of having a good time at a table outside the home had been retained.

Pizza

History

Pizza is so popular in the world that it may be stated it belongs to no particular cuisine. Historically it can be defined as a paramount Indo-European archetype. Its origin can be traced in the lands of all peoples living around the Mediterranean who grew wheat. The easiest way to prepare food is to make dough, flatten it, put some toppings or just herbs on it, and cook it inside an oven or in a pan. Lebanese, Turks, Jews, Greeks, Arabs, and the peoples of India all have similar dishes, prepared out of the same basic ingredients (La Secla 2007: 35, 81). The spices which people put in are different and thus the taste differs. But pizza as we know it is definitely Italian, known first as Neapolitan invention (La Secla 2007: 40). An important circumstance is the fact that after pizza was transported across the Atlantic Ocean together with the Italian immigrants, it was successfully *creolized* in America. Then it traveled back to the continent and migrated in different recipe versions to other places. The substantial American amendments to the original simpler Italian ingredients are richer toppings such as ground beef, different types of sausages, chicken, fruit (as is the famous Hawaiian pizza with pineapple and ham on it), and sauces. Side by side with the notable American recipe augmentations, this dish undergoes considerable changes wherever it is transported.

Foods, together with their ingredients, flavors, culinary techniques, and food habits and rituals, form structured compositions of acceptances and rejections. Those compositions define food only partly for nutrition and very largely for ceremonial and social purposes (Douglas 1983; Bourdieu 1984; Slater 1997; Featherstone 2007; Finkelstein 2014; etc.).

The Culinary Grammar of Pizza

Morphology of the Dish of Pizza

Basic ingredients are dough (in its Italian version, leavened dough), with or without any topping, seasoned with a dash of olive oil, salt (or cheese), and some herbs. The thickness of pizza varies depending on local customs (Parasecoli 2004: 43–44). Toppings can be very diverse—they can be vegetables (tomatoes, eggplants, mushrooms, zucchini, onion, etc.), meats (bacon, sausage, salami, ground beef, prosciutto, etc.), fish and seafood (mussels, shrimps, salmon, anchovies, or other kinds of fish, etc.), or cheeses (the most prominent Italian cheeses are mozzarella, Parmigiano Reggiano, gorgonzola, Grana Padano, ricotta, etc.). Practically almost anything can be put on as topping in different assemblages, with some very particular exceptions in Italy—no rice, potatoes, or cabbage, and no sweet elements. "Hawaiian pizza is unheard of, and the very idea of putting sweet ingredients on pizza sounds whimsical" (Parasecoli 2004: 43, 44). Contemporary Italian (and most of European) cuisine tends to differentiate tastes: sweet, salty, bitter, sour, and spicy, reserving for each of these an autonomous space, either in a specific food or in the sequence of the meal (Montanari 2006: 62). This is related to the specific *taste filters*, which make a cuisine admit or not certain foreign food ingredients.

For my research it is important to mention specifically two types of pizza—calzone and *pizza bianca*. *Calzone* is an oven-cooked pizza folded in half and filled with ingredients, which in Naples (its place of origin) are ricotta cheese, diced mozzarella, diced salami or *prosciutto*, and egg for spread over it for a good crust and color (Parasecoli 2004: 43, 44). Calzones can be associated with many similar dishes in other geographical places. *Chebureki* (*or chibureki*) are traditional for the Caucasian and Turkic peoples. They are also popular as a snack and street food throughout Central Asia, Russia, and Ukraine. Fried or baked empanadas are popular all over Latin America and Spain. Samosas are prepared in the local cuisines of the Southeast Asia, Southwest Asia, Central Asia, the Arabian Peninsula, and north and South Africa. *Pizza bianca*, "white pizza," is the plainest type of pizza, simply made of flour, water, yeast, salt, and olive oil. Sometimes it is sprinkled with coarse salt and a bit of rosemary or thyme. It can be fairly thin, or thick but fluffy. Some cheese can be sprinkled too, according to taste. A version of it is *focaccia,* with olives and/or herbs added. *Pizza bianca* can be easily associated with plain flatbreads outside Italy.

Considering the morphology of pizza, it somehow has the status of a prototypal food, and this puts it in a privileged starting position to easily become one of the global foods. Yet there are much more factors at play, when we explain how such foods become domesticated and diffused within different communities' own eating habits. Such factors may be culinary traditions (themselves being formed through historical, cultural, and economic developments of people living in a place), political or even ideological circumstances (as is usually the case in the formation of national cuisines) (Mintz 1996: 96–97). "The foodstuff transported from one culture to another, has been rethought and repositioned in a sequence and structure different from that of its place of origin" (Montanari 2006: 88).

Put in another way, food syntax and semantics are decisive if, when, and how translocal food is implanted in a culinary culture. All factors together form the unique phenomenon of taste.

Culinary Syntax and Semantics of Pizza

How does pizza communicate with other foods and drinks in Italian food culture? How does it function in the culinary discourse?

Pizza first appeared in the late seventeenth and the early eighteenth centuries as a street food for poor city dwellers in Naples (La Secla 2007: 40–43). Since the very beginning, it has been consumed alone, as a separate dish or snack. It contains the elements and the taste of bread, and the complementary dish in one. It is elastic but tender, not very oily, easy to be eaten with hands as a snack, and can be cut in smaller pieces, each having the same taste. This makes it potentially shareable. It admits different condiments according to individual taste preferences—sauces, olives, and herbs. Salads and pickles may be the usual garnish (La Secla 2007: 36). The almost infinite varieties of toppings allow pizza to be consumed with the most diverse drinks—water and soft drinks, as well as all types of beer. It can be consumed with red and white wine. This last fact is essential. The consumption of pizza with wine rearranges its syntax from street food into being potentially apt to be served as a part of more refined culinary chain.[6]

Offered as street food, pizza functions as a late morning snack or light lunch. It is sold sliced in places similar to fast-food counters (Parasecoli 2004: 29, 151). In such shape and function it is very popular in Europe and America, and of course is adapted to the local taste (consuming sliced pizza is a bit rare in countries like Japan). Pizza can be served *a la carte* in restaurants too. When served by waiters at a table in a restaurant, pizza changes the discourse and functions as a main dish. The usual menu comprises a pizza, some *antipasti*, like marinated vegetables, cheese, salami, etc., and a dessert. Served with a glass of wine, pizza makes the perfect dinner. Since pizza contains flour (a grain derivative) and toppings (meats or vegetables) it successfully can play a central role in the structure of an Italian meal (Montanari 2006:101–103).

The semantics of a given food may connect the elements of the cuisine and community ideology in one cultural ensemble. Pizza undergoes a series of symbolic transformations since the time of Italian *Risorgimento*, the nineteenth-century unification movement. As an ideological, literary, and political movement, Risorgimento incorporated the culinary practices into an ideological ensemble to arouse the national consciousness. Pizza (together with pasta) became the gustatory equivalent of the self-consciousness of an Italian. Pizza *margherita*, named in honor of Queen Margherita of Savoy, as it bears the colors of the national flag—red tomato sauce, white mozzarella, and green basil—became a signature dish and a pivot of national cuisine. It was not a surprise when in 2010 *Pizza Napoletana*, the other name of pizza margherita, received TSG (Traditional Status Guaranteed), which acknowledged its specific character, raw materials, and production method as traditional.[7]

Of course, this last aspect of Italian pizza semantics remains within the realms of Italian cultural history only. When its inherent culinary meaning is addressed, pizza is discussed as an element of the "Mediterranean diet," which has a positive connotation in and outside Italy as the eating of healthy foods. It uses olive oil,

---

[6] All these circumstances are rather dubious. On the one hand they seem to support its transformation into one of those ubiquitous adaptable foods whose worldwide popularity is unanimously acknowledged. On the other hand though, peoples of East Asia and Japan, for example, may find it difficult to accept it as their own since abundance of thick sauces and herbs as condiments is not popular there, consumption of cheese is rather an exception, and touching food with hands during a meal traditionally is considered vulgar. These peoples would consume pizza as an occasional *foreign* food.

[7] See inta.org/INTABulletin.

vegetables, fresh tomatoes, and "the holy herb" basil.[8] This fame of Italian pizza facilitates its transition to the global food.

Domesticating Pizza in Bulgarian City Culture

Bulgarian Cuisine and Its Traditions

Sidney Mintz has argued that it is questionable to speak of national cuisine at all. The foods of a country do not, by themselves, compose a cuisine.

> "Cuisines, when seen from the perspectives of people who care about the *foods*, are never the foods of a country, but the foods of a place" (Mintz 1996: 96).

Places are defined geographically. This means that cuisines are regional and are not strictly contoured by national borders. "Cuisine" in a practical sense, as ingredients, methods, and recipes which people use on a regular basis to produce their daily or festive food, is always local. National cuisine, on the other hand, is an ideological totalizing product of nation-states, and is an attempt to link people's feelings about food in one particular culture (Mintz 1996). Regional cuisines of Balkans and other Mediterranean regions are very close, if basic dietary ingredients and calorie intake are taken into account (Bradatan 2003: 43–47). No doubt, geographically close regions usually have similar climate conditions. Peoples inhabiting such areas interact politically and culturally, and by trade or war. These circumstances can unite big areas in similar or comparable culinary traditions. Contrary to those early unifying tendencies, there are "localizing" processes through which different peoples choose certain basic ingredients to produce their, more or less, unique dietary systems. Some intrinsic social and cultural principles lead them in the food selection, which they call their "own cuisine." National culinary diet is formed when, out of a given pool of comestibles, a community picks up specific ingredients and cooking techniques and combines them in a unique ensemble of dishes and tastes according to its own economic, cultural, and/or religious regulations and discoverabilities. Put in another way, within one vast regional food area, there are national selections which make the fine particular community adjustments. Whereas those adjustments frame the concept of what people consider as their "own," they can trace the paths of the dietary cultural exchange. Only from such a perspective we can make sense of modern culinary globalization and domestication.

[8] Basil is widespread over Asia, lands around Mediterranean, north and central Africa, and Central and South America. For centuries it has accumulated the lore of being a remedial plant. In the Greco-Roman tradition it was considered as a "holy herb" and was used for preparation of aromatic oils and baths. In Eastern Orthodox tradition basil is familiar as an element of the religious rituals. Priests sometimes use it to sprinkle "holy water" in their blessing performances and sensing (Marinov 2003: 20). It is more often used in the burial rituals (Vakarelski 2008: 106, 282). Bulgarians (and people in other neighbor Eastern Orthodox countries) would sometimes place a sprig of dry basil over an icon at homes or in churches.

Although geographically and historically Bulgaria belongs to the Greco-Roman region, this development was interrupted in the fourteenth century as the kingdom became part of the Ottoman Empire. The cuisine was shaped within the vast Ottoman culinary culture. Being a part of the Empire for about five centuries, the country developed its economy and household as a peripheral agricultural land, which formed a predominantly lower class profile of the cuisine. The country was under the cultural influence of the Middle East for many centuries, and was not able to create its distinct national daily life characteristics. The daily routine of all Balkan peoples under the Ottoman domination was very similar. National elites, howsoever meagre, emulated the lifestyle of the Turkish or Greek wealthier classes. Haute cuisine, which in most emerging European nation states in the eighteenth and more visibly nineteenth centuries formed a specific patriotic symbolic pivot (Mintz 1996), did not develop specific characteristics. Because of its low social status and poor households, Bulgarians under the Ottoman domination identified as their national food only the restricted segment of nutritional resources available to them. The exclusion of the lower classes from the pleasurable culinary extravagances of the rich Ottoman aristocracy, in fact economic and symbolic exclusion, brought together the Medieval food of the poor Turks, Greeks, and Bulgarians with the kitchens of poor peoples inhabiting southern part of Western Europe—Italy, France, and Spain (Montanari 1994: 88–89). The features of the staples of southern European lands were very similar—grains and bread, legumes, naturally found nuts and local wild fruits, milk, simple cheeses, eggs, and limited variety of greens. Meat had a status symbol and a sign of luxury, and was kept for special occasions, annual festivities, and religious celebrations (see Montanari 1994:73).

For the need of my investigations it is important to mention the common tradition to use wheat products (mainly bread and dough derivatives), cheeses, vegetables, and spices. Meat eating is not of great importance since the use of meat products in pizza, especially in Europe, is limited.

For many centuries bread and its derivatives have been the key food in the nutritional code of the Bulgarians. Bread and dough products have been on the table daily and on festive days. The Lord's Prayer's words—*daily bread* —has quite a literal meaning when it defines what has been eaten for centuries. The special place of leavened bread lies within the basis of Bulgarian food tradition. "Bread and salt feed the world" (*hliabut i solta sveta hraniat*) is an old local saying.

A usual morning breakfast in Bulgaria is a slice of bread with sweet or salty topping—butter, jam, honey, cheese, *lyutenitsa* (roasted red peppers and tomato chutney), French toast, pancakes, or *buhti*, and *mekitsi* (batter fried in deep oil). Lunch and dinner are always served with bread. Very often, a light supper would include some *milinki* (buns with white brine cheese filling), or *banitsa*, the favorite Bulgarian pastry, made of phyllo dough, eggs, and brine cheese as filling, baked in the oven.[9] This last pastry can have varieties of fillings—spinach, leeks, sorrel, cabbage, mushrooms, pumpkin or (rarely, indeed only in one or two regions) potatoes, or even rice. *Banitsa* with ground meat is also prepared, and is almost indistinguishable from the

[9] Same or similar dishes exist in all Balkan countries.

Turkish *bürek*. Local people think that only homemade *banitsa* is worth trying, which may be referred to the already mentioned popular belief that homemade food (and wine) is tastier.[10] *Banitsa*, as well as most of the other dough products are usually served with the local staple—plain yogurt.[11] Industrial production has been recently adapted to this mass taste. Frozen *banitsa* (like frozen pizza) can be found in the supermarkets. Nowadays all the abovementioned dough products can be prepared and served at privately owned snack bars and luncheon booths.

As a southern European country, Bulgarian people consume a wide variety of vegetables. Onions, garlic, leeks, tomatoes, peppers, eggplants, zucchinis, cabbage, and potatoes are commonly used in cooking. If we ask anybody about the vegetables, which are blended in most of local dishes and salads, they would answer—tomatoes, peppers, cucumbers, onions, garlic, beans, leeks, and zucchinis.

Cheese has been present on Bulgarian tables since ancient times. Compared to other European cheeses, though, there are fewer varieties. The differences in the cheeses come from the kind of milk used for production—sheep, cow, or goat—and not the technologies used to prepare it. For many years there were only two types of cheese—white cheese (brine cheese, which in taste is close to feta) and simple yellow cheese, *kashkaval*. Kashkaval cheese is popular in all Balkan countries. Cheese is the usual topping on or filling in a lot of dough products. Local taste gladly embraces leavened dough pastries with vegetables and cheese toppings or fillings. This is a favorable precondition for accepting the taste of pizza.

Given same ingredients, the technologies and spices make all the difference in a culinary culture. This is how specific "culinary belts (zones)" within one bigger region, such as a continent for example, are formed. Bulgaria's spice taste favors local fresh and dry herbs such as parsley, dill, spearmint (*Mentha spicata*), paprika, summer savory (*Satureja hortensis*), and oregano (the last used rarely, indeed). Black pepper and bay (laurel) are also very common. According to local lore, "no meal should be cooked without spices"(*jadene bez podpravki ne se gotvi*), and "almost all meals should be well seasoned" (*bilki slagat v pochti vsiaka mandja*) (Markova 2011: 195).

---

[10] My respondents gave the following answers to the question about their taste preferences on homemade versus store or food booth-produced banitsas: out of 21 interviewed individuals 3 students answered that they had never tried homemade banitsa since their mothers did not cook and they did not have grandmothers to be treated with this product made at home. Two students answered that they could distinguish the difference in taste but had no specific preference. Sixteen answers were definitely more positive on the taste of the homemade pastry, but people admitted that they ate more often banitsa bought at the luncheon shops out of sheer lack of time to cook it at home.

[11] Here and below I refer to *banitsa* to make rough comparisons with pizza for two reasons: first, there are some similarities in ingredients and preparation of the two dishes, and secondly a great number of informants when interviewed have stated that they like pizza *because it somehow tastes similar to banitsa* (14 out of 21 answers). In this text I refrain from the discussion on taste as sensory experience and subjective preferences. I am trying to focus on objective economic circumstances and cultural conditions which enable pizza's quick and successful introduction to Bulgarian culinary culture after the fall of communism in the early 1990s.

How Has Pizza Been Domesticated

Pizza has been incorporated very successfully in the postcommunist culinary practices. Similar food ingredients, manner of consumption, and even, if we mind certain specificities, similar semantics of the culinary discourse make it close to the local taste and preferences. Pizza in Bulgaria has been almost fully domesticated in contemporary urban food industries. Now it is one of the most popular restaurant and snack foods, present in almost all eateries. It has a unique crossover status, being present at breakfast takeaway stands, middle-range restaurants, some higher category restaurants, and, of course, Italian ethnic pizzerias.

As already mentioned, the basic factors for identification of a given food as one's own (close) or foreign (remote, exotic, unusual, etc.) are mainly four:

1. Same or similar ingredients
2. Available culinary practices
3. Close culinary syntax: ways in which different foods are connected with the other elements of the culinary code of a given community
4. Close or familiar semantics: same or similar social meaning people give to some foods (as for example, Easter bread in Christian countries: recipes are similar but not identical, while cultural use of it is same)

I suggest that if all those four similarity aspects are present certain food could be successfully localized and transformed into communities' *own*.

Although pizza was served in some city restaurants before the fall of communism, it was not widely spread. The dish was known under the name "pita" (Bulgarian word for *flatbread*), and the recipe vaguely resembled the Italian original.[12] After the changes of 1989, when communist regime descended, new pizzerias emerged within a year, while the existing restaurants quickly acquired the recipes and began serving pizzas. Nowadays pizza restaurants are everywhere in the big or smaller cities, in bigger villages as well, sometimes more than one on a street.[13] Pieces of pizza are also sold at snack food stalls, altogether with traditional Bulgarian snacks. Bulgarians eat pizza very often, the adolescents and working people more frequently than the senior citizens.[14]

Pizza has successfully passed through the local taste filters and has been almost fully appropriated by the local culinary culture. There are specific causes of such cultural exchange.

---

[12] The recipes of such pitas were obviously "smuggled" by some ingenious chefs who had the chance to travel abroad. The name conceals the Italian origin of the dish.

[13] According to the National Statistical Institute as of 31.12.2016 the population of Bulgaria was 7,101,859; the capital Sofia had 1,323,637. A big city of the country is roughly considered a community of more than 100,000 people. There are eight such cities. Middle-size town population is between 40,500 and 100,000 citizens. There are 22 middle-size towns in the country (see http://www.nsi.bg/en/).

[14] My middle-aged informants have reported of consuming pizza once or twice a month, more often when eating out. Even though they like it, they consider some dietary restrictions, such as higher caloric values.

First, there is the close familiarity with the ingredients.

As has already been pointed out, bread and leavened dough products are staples in this part of Europe. Local basic bread is made of the same ingredients as pizza.

The *olfactory codes* of the spices are also very close. The herbs and spices which are used in pizza and other Italian meals are, in fact, used in a lot of traditional Bulgarian dishes, such as parsley, black pepper, garlic, bay (laurel), dill, cumin, cinnamon, and nutmeg (in fact, the last three rarely used in both kitchens). An interesting symmetry exists between oregano, which is used in Italian meals, and the ubiquitous Bulgarian spice, summer savory. They are very close in odor and flavor. Wherever oregano is used, summer savory successfully can substitute it. Summer savory can be used in the same way as *sage* is used in Italian cuisine. The local counterpart of mint is peppermint. Paprika is put in a lot of Bulgarian meals (indeed not so often in Italian). A local spice *sharena sol*, made as a mix of salt, ground fenugreek seeds, paprika, summer savory, and black pepper, is usually present on traditional Bulgarian table (not very often in modern city restaurants), and it may be used as a seasoning of a flatbread *hlebche*, which is similar to pizza bianca.[15]

Basil is by all means the most popular Italian herb, used in pizzas, soups, and many pasta dishes. Basil as well as thyme are not traditionally known as cooking herbs in Bulgaria, but are familiar in old healing recipes. Once basil has been introduced through the rapid Italian cuisine recipe dissemination, it has spread very quickly as a much-loved local spice as well. Basil perfectly matches the favorite vegetables, common to both cuisines.

Both food dietary systems moderately use spices. In the two kitchens the ingredients, especially vegetables, can be distinctly tasted. In the local versions of pizza the original ingredients are freely substituted with regional elements. No substantial difference in taste and appearance can be recognized. Local taste preferences exclude almost same ingredients, notably pineapple. Hawaiian pizza is among the least popular dishes in the local restaurants too.[16] A lot of the original recipes are not strictly followed. Some new versions appear, having new names, given by imaginative chefs.

Secondly, pizza culinary techniques are completely accessible.

Traditionally bread and dough products have been prepared by hand, as it is almost everywhere in the world. When *banitsa* or other local pastries are made, the dough is rolled out by hand or by rolling pin, the same way as pizzas. The difference is that *banitsa* requires much thinner dough, as thin as a "sheet of paper." The filling is put on top of it, and then the thin dough sheets are rolled in long tubes which are coiled one after another on a big tray. In pizza preparation it remains as topping, but in calzones it is folded making the taste similar to that of banitsa. Except for

[15] See below.

[16] One of my informants, Villie aged 28, once told me: "Most probably I am among the very few people here who like sweet and salty mixed taste. When I order pizza hawaii in a restaurant, there is always somebody in the company who asks me: 'Why do you choose this? You want to experiment, or what?'"

banitsas, almost all other local snacks are made of leavened dough, with or without topping or filling.[17]

There is a curious similarity in an outwardly aesthetic aspect of the preparation of the two dishes. The good *pizzaiolo* (professional pizza maker) is the restaurant's celebrity. "The mounds of dough, the smack of his palms and thumbs as he flattens one, flying arms as he forms a disk, his light touch as his fingers and eyes control the quantity of the ingredients, the fistful of flour he throws on the peel, and his warrior's thrust as he brings the shiny white round of dough to rest near the mouth of the oven, knowing that its first contact with heat is the most important one. No one is more respected than the pizzaiolo as he waits, seeming to do nothing, as the transformation takes place inside the oven …" (La Secla 2007: 39–40). Same words can describe the skills of the banitsa maker when the dough sheets are handmade (including the "flying arms" as much thinner and much bigger discs of dough sheets are tossed in the air). The difference though is that traditionally the *banitsa* makers are women, and the dish was originally homemade; thus the performance used to be for the family audience.[18] While pizza emerged as street food, *banitsa* in Bulgaria first appeared as homemade pastry. Later, as the town culture developed baker's shops and banitsa vendors could be seen in the local neighborhoods.

The baking of pizza, as well as the baking of bread and *banitsa*, is identical—traditionally in brickwork or electrical oven (Markova 2011: 148). The cooking technique of pizza making is completely familiar and very easily adaptable.

Thirdly, we may compare the culinary syntax of the two dishes. A correspondent culinary syntax exists if the ways in which food connections within the culinary code of a given community are the same as or similar to food links within the cuisine of another community. The systems of culinary syntax shouldn't be ignored. There might be identical or suchlike ingredients and technology of production, i.e., cuisine morphology, but some prohibitions (not necessarily religious) and allowances, which, together with the social meaning of food, make a different cultural system with different culinary rules. Even though cuisine hybridization is now

[17] As a comparison, laminated dough, used in croissants and other puff pastries, which are very popular in other parts of the continent, was not traditionally used. The layered texture of the pastries is achieved by folding phyllo dough many times.

[18] Banitsa or a similar product is a very old food on the Balkans. Its origins could be traced back to the Byzantine times or even before, but the techniques of its preparation, as we know them today, are mastered during the Ottoman domination. Local cuisines have their own versions with a variety of fillings. It has emerged as a home food in the villages. As town life developed banitsa and pastry bakeries were opened at many places, sometimes catering for neighboring places. (One of my respondents, 84-year-old lady from the town of Tryavna, remembered that in her childhood the products, especially banitsa, of the local bakery were transported early in the mornings to the neighboring towns of Gorna Oriahoviza and Tirnovo, sent by the existing back then railway). Food industrialization in the twentieth century brought about factory-produced banitsas and snacks, which middle-aged citizens remember as untasty, sticky, oily, and never fresh. These days, as many privately owned snack kiosks have been opened and fresh *banitsa* snacks are sold there, in the early mornings one can see the skillful hands of young women or men "rolling on" first breakfast *banitsas* and can sense the flavorful smell of the golden brown crunchy crust.

almost a matter of fashion, such fine distinctions exist and make blendings compatible or not.

In the realm of culinary syntax—ways in which foods are considered compatible or not with other foods—the differences in the two culinary cultures are clearly discernible.

Bulgarian *banitsa* dough is unleavened. The filling of the most popular *banitsa* consists of whisked eggs, yogurt, and white brine cheese. These are unthinkable pizza toppings. Other very popular *banitsa* or pastry fillings are rarely or never found as pizza toppings—cabbage, leeks, spinach (docks, nettles, and sorrels), possible rice, or potatoes.[19] Pumpkin, walnuts, currants, milk and sugar, apples, or sometimes cherries are possible banitsa fillings transforming it into a dessert. Italians would not recognize such tastes as familiar. Proportions of dough to fillings in the local products and Italian pizza are different, too. Usually Italian pizzas are richer in toppings than Bulgarian *banitsa* or other pastries. The Italian dish uses more varieties of cheese while the Bulgarian one uses predominantly white brine cheese or local *kashkaval*, similar in taste to Italian *caciocavallo*.

Syntactical structure of culinary discourse may also include the combinations and sequence of dishes as well as side dishes and beverages. In this aspect, distinctions between the two culinary products are also highly distinguishable. *Banitsas* these days can be both homemade and street food. As homemade product it is normally eaten as a breakfast or a snack, a side dish, or a light supper. The fillings define the place banitsa takes in the culinary syntax. When "heavier," such as meat, potatoes, onions and mushrooms, and leeks, the dish can be consumed even as a main course. If the filling is sweet it is served as a dessert. Banitsa is incorporated in the festive meals, traditionally on two occasions—Christmas and New Year's Eve. Therefore, only occasionally and at home it can be put up as main food in the course of meals. Outside the home, however, *banitsa* and other pastries are consumed as snack foods in street kiosks.[20] Pizza, on the other hand, is not meant to be home food. It can be a street food snack; it could be a "carryout," fast-food lunch on the spot. But it may be served as a restaurant dinner as well. Logically, following the syntax, the beverages consumed with the two foods are different. Bulgarian pastry is accompanied by nonalcoholic drinks, while pizza can go with beer and wine as well. Thus we may conclude that, despite similar ingredients and identical culinary techniques, the culinary syntax shows local specificities in the two meals, placing one of them as foreign.

---

[19] Rice is an ineligible pizza topping, but in the East Asian countries pizza base can be made of cooked rice, as an attempt of culinary creolization. Obviously local peoples' palates are trained in such combinations.

[20] Up until a few years ago banitsas were consumed as luncheon by office workers, builders, shop assistants, etc., in the big cities. We can explain this with the fact that back then there were very few inexpensive eateries preparing fresh hot dishes and soups. Such places have appeared within the last 10 years. Nowadays working people most often would opt for such heartier foods or slices of pizza with their salami, bacon, or other meat and cheese toppings: obviously perceived as closer to a filling meal.

We may add more on the subtle gustatory distinctions which define food as *own* or *foreign* if we discuss the culinary semantics of food. Pizza domestication follows the logic of constant oscillation between these two categories. Certainly, it has been creolized. This brings us to the argument that people do not eat the food of the totally "unfamiliar Other." Even when the eaters consider the dishes as undeniable foods,[21] if the constituents or flavors do not communicate in any way with their previous sensory experiences or other types of knowledge on the food, they would try or consume the exotic foreign as a culinary adventure, as an educational experiment, or simply as an occasional event. Foreign dishes can become food on a daily basis, if some *meaningful links* between local culinary culture and the foreign other exist. This would suggest that people usually are ardent culinary patriots. This fact may pose some questions, such as to what extent can food globalization expand, the answer to which goes beyond the scope of this text.[22] Culinary transactions described here may throw some light on the choices which different cultures make when allowing pervasion of certain globalizing (food) trends.

There are fine *semantic* distinctions which attribute pizza to the foreign culinary area, despite the above-outlined correspondences. *Pizza Napoletana* with anchovies—a *par excellence* Italian pizza—is almost completely absent from Bulgarian pizzerias. Also, pizza with seafood toppings is not accepted on the local table for reasons which I will discuss further down. Fish is not consumed as a snack (and not very often as a main dish, indeed). Thus pizza with anchovies or any *fruits de mer* could be automatically excluded from the snack stalls and kiosks. Yet snacks constitute a large segment of the pizza food market. Economic and cultural logic forms a filter through which such types of pizza dishes cannot easily pass through in the local food habits. On the contrary, if a pizza recipe is too close to the local taste, it is not recognized as a pizza at all. Such is the case of *pizza bianca*. In the local eateries one can find identical product, which is not served under the name of pizza. It is offered as seasoned flatbread, *hlebche*. Usual toppings are garlic, cheese, onions, summer savory, pepper, rosemary, or the already mentioned *sharena sol*. Under such names the hlebche substitutes plain bread. As plain bread it is not consumed as an only dish but can be a supplement to soups, main dishes, salads, or grilled meat. In the ethnic Italian restaurants, *pizza bianca* is rarely ordered. Customers would not take food which they could order everywhere else as bread. In those restaurants they would expect to experience authentic Italian food, *pizza napoletana* included.

What is the point, then, at which both eating practices come nearest? I would argue that it is the *social meaning* of pizza consumption that approximates to local eating habits.

---

[21] I borrow the term "unfamiliar Other" from the already mentioned article of Prof. E. Heldke, and I echo Prof. Heldke's remark of refrain from the discussion of how different cultures define edibles and inedibles.

[22] Drastic changes in peoples' diet may happen only in cases of unforeseen food shortage: notorious is the case of the reluctant introduction of potatoes in the eighteenth-century Europe. History teaches us that even in cases of famine, the survival strategies follow the general rule to "adhere as closely as possible to the basic individual culture and to the familiar, already known "language." First potato flour was tried as a substitute for wheat in bread making (Montanari 2006).

When we talk about food *semantics,* we also mean the social contexts in which people consume foods and the local cultures the foods support or enhance. In Bulgaria, pizza eating is outside home. Thus we may assess its value within the context of existing or emerging (predominantly urban) mass consumption practices.

Pizza in Bulgarian Restaurants

The changes after the fall of communism fostered a proliferation of new eateries. Pizza restaurants appear to be those places where new mass consumer culture was formed. Free of the restrictions of scarcity economy, yet not reaching the splendor of the luxury eating venues of the West, those restaurants have become the most suitable *loci* of social contact. Pizza consumption is a meaningful device for the formation of new leisure practices.

At restaurants people meet friends, dine with their families, and spend their leisure time. Pizza restaurants have acquired the functions of the coffeehouses of the time of the Ottoman Empire. As in the past, people enjoy the friendly atmosphere there. Sounds are always familiar: loud conversations, hearty laughter, and pleasant clinking of food dishes and cutlery. Pizza restaurants are fostering the city culture of eating out. These restaurants are usually unpretentious.[23]

In Bulgarian pizza restaurants, people usually order twice—first, pizza and side dish (salad or pickles), and second, coffee and a dessert. Beer, wine, or fizzy drinks are the usual drink choices. The traditional Balkan cold yogurt beverage, *ayran*, also goes very well with pizzas.[24]

Pizza consumption disrupts not only classical bourgeois food order of the West[25] (see Bourdieu 1984: 196) but also the modest traditional Bulgarian full meal order of dishes. The latter would start with salads (or pickles according to the season) and hard liquors (most popular is a locally produced grape or plum brandy, *rakia*), then soup, followed by a main dish—usually meat and a cooked vegetable side dish (or a casserole), bread, wine or beer, and a dessert and coffee. Compressing the length of course servings (pizza being a kind of all-in-one) it somehow eases the management of time spent on eating. Pizza eating diverts the attention from the food protocol to the investment in time spent in pleasure and togetherness. Duration doesn't

---

[23] Exceptions are special Italian restaurants, where the owners, the chefs, and the ingredients used are Italian. There Italian ethnic food is consumed, and the dishes are more expensive.

[24] *Ayran* is not consumed with seafood, though. This drink is popular in wide regions: Balkans, Turkey, Armenia, and beyond the Middle East—Kazakhstan, Kyrgyzstan, and the north Caucasus. It is made of diluted yogurt with salt. It is served chilled and often as an accompaniment to almost all Bulgarian snacks and foods—grilled meats, stews, etc. Since it is nonalcoholic and non-carbonated drink, parents who are health concerned would often order ayran with the food to their children. "When we dine out I'd order plain ayran to the kids rather than sweetened with God knows what soda. They like it" (Ina, 36, mother of a boy, 12, and a girl, 7). Adults, who do not drink alcohol, and do not like heavily sweetened sodas, would opt for ayran too.

[25] On the classical bourgeois meal order see Bourdieu 1984: p196.

matter. Served as a restaurant food it is no longer a fast-food street snack. Pizza consumption compactness obliterates the formality of a classical menu and turns eating out into a spontaneous immersion into the pleasures of communication. Thus pizza eating becomes a social event that democratically "levels up" up social distinctions and enhances the conviviality of community life. Very often consumers would describe pizza as fun.[26] A pizza party can be a favorite teenage leisure time, a friends' Saturday-night eating-out gathering, or part of firms' team-building agenda.

Local consumers are fond of the liberty of manners when pizza is consumed. It can be eaten as a classical dish with knife and fork. But just like bread or banitsa it can be served as one unbroken (round) whole and then cut into pieces to be shared. The sense of shared food adds some coziness of taking part in a communal feast, like on a family table. On the other hand, the opportunity to be consumed in a public space enhances the pleasure of being within the group solidarity of new urban culture. Pizza consumption epitomizes the functional core dialectics of the very institution of restaurant—the desire for privacy and anonymity while in a crowd (Finkelstein 2014:181). If I may go a little further, such experience can be comprehended within the conception of aestheticization of everyday life (Featherstone 2007: 64–81). The playfulness between the triviality of feeding (the compact intake of nutritional substances) and the much higher experience of emotional transactions within companionship does have some aesthetic dimension. It is the objectification of feelings on the social stage of city life experienced as an intimate exploit. Conversation is an end in itself (Finkelstein 2014:181). A young couple, Nelly and Deian, put it as this:

> "We prefer to meet people outside, in a restaurant, because there we can focus on our friends and the conversation, leaving the service to the personnel. If we meet them at home we have to pay attention to the food serving, dishes, food sequence, etc. It is very difficult in a bigger company. Moreover, now people are more fastidious: one is a vegetarian, another – a vegan, third – allergic to some foods. You cannot make dinner suitable for all. Going out to a pizza restaurant gives opportunity to everyone to choose … Anybody can order whatever they want."

Last but not least, alongside pizzas, these restaurants offer a rich variety of traditional restaurant foods—grilled meats, French fries with cheese, locally cooked meals, fried or grilled vegetables, salads, and side dishes. Served almost everywhere in the city eating places, pizza is comprehended as part of the local cuisine, which it very often is.[27]

[26] All my young respondents described pizza eating as fun, and thus preferable food for their gatherings.

[27] Now pizza is not served only in the restaurants that are specialized exclusively in Bulgarian traditional food, ethnic restaurants, such as Indian, or Japanese, and the highest priced top-category places. Eateries that people visit on more or less regular basis usually offer locally prepared pizzas.

Summarizing the influence of pizza's appearance in the Bulgarian culinary landscape it can be pointed out that this process has produced a couple of new culinary practices:

Firstly, Italian original recipes have been emulated by substituting imported foreign ingredients with cheaper local ones. This process might seem to be "downgrading" the original recipes and might not be hailed by the taste purists. But it can also be assessed as a way of spreading the culture, while the economic restrictions on imported ingredients are still to be considered. Some 27 years ago, before 1990s, the very word "pizza" did not exist in the language. Now people are aware of this food and can enjoy it.

Secondly, the practice of pizza making has inspired chefs to creatively use home-produced ingredients to make new kinds of pizzas, experimenting with, for example, peppers, onion, eggplants, local sausages, spinach, and white brine cheese. By enriching the variety of pizzas with local components, the domestic kitchen develops and opens up to culinary experiments.

Thirdly, Bulgarian recipes, influenced by this culinary novelty, have appeared, such as leavened dough snacks with olives and cheese, sausages, or meats as fillings or toppings. Another new product is banitsa with fillings, inspired by pizza toppings (for example, banitsa with chicken and olives, bacon and cheese, or even *banitsa-pizza*).[28]

Fourth, pizza, this "stateless world citizen" (La Secla 2007: 87), is here to stay as an enjoyable global dish. It is among those products that strive for worldliness without being dismissive to local culture (Finkelstein 2014: 86), which makes it among the most agreeable culinary novelties of the last century.

Last, but by no means least, the proliferation of city restaurants, mainly as pizza eateries, has expanded new social experiences of leisure consumption.

Japanese Food as a Symbol of Unfamiliar Otherness

When we speak of Japanese food, it is a truism to mention its exceptional exoticism. Yet the very notion of exotic food in the globalizing world is anachronistic. Bizarre foods are discussed not only in professional literature (Harris 1985) but also in popular publications, TV shows, tourist brochures, culinary blogs, etc. The businesses of culinary tourism are engaged in the transportation and accommodation of people who travel to far distant places just to taste the "exotic" foods there. Modern shipping and preservation food technologies allow supermarkets all over the world to easily provide products thousands of kilometers away from their source. As people become better informed about foreign cuisines, and as they can taste more of the

[28] The Internet culinary site *gotvach.bg* has more than 1500 recipes for *banitsas* with varieties of fillings. There one can find *banitsa a la lasagna*, as well as *banitsa-pizza* with frankfurters, cheese, olives, and gherkins—obviously an attempt to "hybridize" the dish.

products grown in remote lands, they change their ideas of extraordinariness. The world becomes a culinary "village."

While it has become easier to access foreign foods and information about them, it is much less easy to understand the cultural codes of a foreign cuisine, even harder to assimilate them and to transform them into a local taste. Taste is a cognitive activity, involving memory, experience, emotions (Heldke 2005: 388), and social interactions. "Exotic foreign" now is not the unfamiliar, but the food which cannot be domesticated, not creolized, and which, when tasted, immediately displays differences to the local food practices.[29] Within such framework of reference, Japanese cuisine takes a special position. Being the regional food of a distant people, it has a syntax and semantics which are almost unrecognizable to the foreigner. Yet, today it is a global culinary product.

Transformation of Japanese Food into Global

The economic, social, and cultural grounds and circumstances of transformation of Japanese food—mainly sushi—into global food have been widely discussed. Authors have mentioned challenges and barriers which Japanese cuisine had to face on its way to the fame and triumph it has today in culinary cultures of modern Western societies (Bestor 2000, 2004; Issenberg 2007). For the purposes of my research, it is worth noting the main circumstances which supported the transformation of Japanese foods into global delicacies. They might help us examine and envisage how Bulgarian consumers would accept Japanese food and food culture.

The United States is the country that plays the role of a globalizing agent. Japanese restaurants and sushi bars opened in the 1930s in New York and California, but the food gained real popularity in the 1970s and 1980s. At approximately the same time Japanese cuisine spread to big West European cities. Now it is an indispensable part of the urban culinary stage of affluent societies. Political, economic, and cultural factors contribute to this process.

Theodore Bestor mentions that in 1929, the *Ladies' Home Journal* introduced Japanese cooking to North American women but "discreetly skirted the subject of raw fish" (Bestor 2000: 56). In the 1930s the first Japanese restaurants served cooked foods (grilled, broiled, or crumbled)—*sukiyaki, teriyaki, or tempura.* Those restaurants carefully avoided raw seafood, unacceptable to the American taste at that time (Mariani 1991: 80).

---

[29] It is necessary to make a distinction between *fusion cuisine* and *creolized food*, which I use as a near synonym of "domesticated." *Fusion kitchen* is an intentional combination of ingredients or elements of dishes belonging to different cuisines. It is a *conscious* culinary experiment, a *cognitive process* of focusing on, selecting, intellectually working on ingredient blending, and visually representing new foods so as to create a kind of nouvelle cuisine—a chef's artifact. Domestication or *creolization* is a grassroots, more or less a spontaneous, manipulation of an original dish so as to transform them into local, familiar, edible products.

After World War II, together with the returning military personnel and especially after Japan took a course to politically ally with the United States, the interest in Japanese life grew, yet Japanese cuisine stayed away from American tables for the next decade. The traditional local taste could not accept raw seafood with its specific flavors. Additionally, there were not many available dexterous hands of Japanese sushi chefs to display the aesthetic aspects of this cuisine. The food remained locally confined within the small ethnic communities of Japanese immigrants in the so-called Little Tokyo areas of some American cities, mostly on the West Coast.

As Japan quickly recovered after the war and economically boomed in the 1970s, a considerable number of Japanese professionals and managers came to live and work in the United States. Some Japanese food restaurants were open to satisfy their consumers' needs. Unlike other ethnic foods though, Japanese cuisine, especially as a restaurant serves, has never been cheap and has always been rated as haute cuisine (Issenberg 2007: 92). This fact, together with the use of raw seafood and nearly uncooked meat in some dishes, is a unique challenge for its acceptance and transformation into popular food in the United States and elsewhere (Bestor 2000; Issenberg 2007). As Theodore Bestor puts it "sushi isn't an easy concept to sell to the uninitiated" (Bestor 2000: 56). More factors were needed to the process of popularization of the food.

Since mid-1970s Japan has already been an important world economic player. Japan's much higher living standard has raised fish and seafood demands, more particularly bluefin tuna, which is the best loved traditional Japanese delicacy. Many countries on both sides of the Atlantic develop their fisheries under the guidance of Japanese professionals and keep Japan as their exclusive trade partner (Bestor 2000, 2004; Issenberg 2007). Japan's economic influence on fish industries and trade draws attention towards the cuisine. Japanese food preparation has become a matter of exceptional interest in the luxury restaurants in the West. This interest is boosted by the expanding consumption needs of the well-off generations and the appearance of *the nouvelle cuisine* in the 1980s.

In the 1980s the States and Great Britain celebrated the emergence of *foodies*—a gourmet culture of young, financially well-set people who spent their free time visiting fashionable restaurants and experimenting with alternative healthy foods. They were the first group of people who promulgated the *nouvelle cuisine* and sushi eating. Nouvelle cuisine itself, which was created by the French chefs at that time, inscribed Japanese food principles in their own cooking postulates, such as minimalist aesthetics, small portions, high-quality fresh ingredients, and very short time of cooking with almost no oil. The tendency to preserve original colors and texture transformed the plate into a work of art. Healthy food principles required the use of fish and vegetables rather than meat and potatoes. As the *nouvelle cuisine* became the norm for the gourmet restaurants in the West, Japanese food found its way as the epitome of the exquisite aesthetic way of eating, which was and is an aspect of the overall aestheticization of the lives of the middle class (Featherstone 2007: 64–81).

Starting out as an elegant culinary experiment of the young cosmopolitan middle classes in the 1970s and 1980s, Japanese food, especially sushi and sashimi, made its triumphant march towards the plates of not only high-end but also middle-category eateries, supermarkets, as well as local food stores in the West, Hong Kong, and other east Asian countries. This last process is enhanced by the next *millennial generation* preferences, growing up entirely into the digital era. Many of those young people, "falling under the spell" of Japanese manga and anime culture, and "cool Japan" lifestyle borrowed from Tokyo Shibuia and Harajuku regions, have embraced enjoying Japanese foods altogether with the aforementioned symbolic cultural messages. Japanese sushi culture has become a part of Japan's soft power and cultural propaganda policy of the last 20 years or so (Reynolds 2014; Nye 2004; McGray 2009).

Features of Japanese Food: Sushi and Sashimi

Basic Ingredients and Preparation (Culinary Morphology)

Japanese food specifics have been widely discussed in the professional cultural, anthropological, and culinary literature (Ashkenazi and Jacob 2000; Ashkenazi and Jacob 2003; Bestor 2004; Cwiertka 2006; Goulding 2015; Hosking 1996; Issenberg 2007; Rath and Assmann 2010; Ishige 2011, etc.). For the purposes of my research, I need to mention those of its distinctive features, which face and interact with Bulgarian eating principles to produce or not a domesticated version of a cuisine.

In terms of ingredients and preparation it is very hard to think of a dish simpler than *sashimi*. Thinly sliced pieces of raw fish are dipped into a mix of soy sauce and wasabi. The dish could be served over a canapé of shredded radish, not necessarily consumed but considered as adding freshness to the dish. As for sushi, there are many varieties, but the basic ingredients are a ball of cooked vinegared rice and pieces of fish or vegetables, usually compressed into one or several shapes (Ashkenazi and Jacob 2003: 183). Raw or cooked fish or other seafood (octopus, cuttlefish, urchin, shrimp, roe, scallops, etc.) is the usual sushi topping. Nori (dried pressed seaweed) is often used to wrap sushi pieces (*norimaki* or *temaki* sushi). Sushi can be prepared with a lot of vegetarian toppings or other fillings—cucumber, *umeboshi* (Japanese pickled plum), *natto* (fermented soya beans), *tamago yaki* (a slightly sweet, moist square-shaped egg omelette), etc. Japanese restaurants serve a very wide range of sushi. In fact sushi and sashimi can be made of almost any kind of fish.[30] Japanese people consider *toro sushi* (prepared with the fat belly part of tuna fish) particularly tasty. It is the most expensive part of the fish. *Maguro sushi* (a sliced piece of raw tuna over a rice ball) is the usual first choice of people in Japan.

[30] Perhaps the only fish which is not used as food is carp, as it has some symbolic cultural value. Starting at the end of the nineteenth century, carps (*koi*) have been selected in different colors and looked after as decorative fish in koi ponds.

These distinctive taste preferences make Japan the number one consumer of bluefin tuna fish in the world.[31]

Sashimi and sushi are by far the most favorite dishes for Japanese people (Ishige 2011: 164). Preparation of sushi in sushi bars and restaurants in Japan is a true performance. The chef at the counter has the uneasy task of feeding people while showing his mastery. Sushi chefs are always male individuals.[32] Highly praised by the customers of sushi restaurants are the restaurants' attempts to create an intimate homelike atmosphere, albeit it may be rather fake one. In traditional sushi restaurants, the sushi chef is positioned very close to the clients—either in the center of the bar with a belt counter-rotating around him on which he puts small plates with ready pieces (*kaiten-zushi*), or standing behind a counter in front of customers' tables (*sushi-ya*). This is reflected in the price: in cheaper sushi places the customer does not see the full preparation, only the end result (Ashkenazi and Jacob 2000: 207). In both types of restaurants the client may order sushi of their own choice if it is not on display at the moment. The order is served within minutes. From this perspective, sushi may be put in the group of fast foods.

As it has already been mentioned, sushi and sashimi can be served at very expensive sushi places as well. There are high-category restaurants where sushi is prepared individually and especially for particular clients. A little conversation between the chef and the customer can precede the food preparation. Talking to the customer the chef gets oriented as how to satisfy the most intimate palate desires of the person that very day. Then the sushi morsels are prepared and served in a strict order out of absolutely fresh products and according to chef's creative imagination. Sometimes it is *omakase*, the chef's choice. An ordering of flavor, texture, and color of the pieces is strictly followed. As a complement to the highest confidence between the customer and the chef, and in accordance with the oldest top-end traditions of serving, sushi balls are served by the hand of the master into the hand of the client and then put in the mouth. As Ashkenazi and Jacob put it:

> "The message is clear: shape and form, perfect action, are what define not only good service and thus good food, but perhaps Japanese perceptions of selfhood and appropriateness as well" (Ashkenazi and Jacob 2000: 207).

The refinement of the Japanese way of food preparation is best demonstrated through the cleaning, cutting, and beautiful arrangement of sushi pieces or sashimi plates according to their shape, color, and flavor. Transformation from raw ingredients into culinary specialties follows these three main steps. Some very fine seasoning can be added. The proverbial lore states: "Not cooking is the ideal way of cooking" (Ishige 2011: 238). The principles of the restraint of many culinary techniques and the emphasis on natural flavors are leading in preparation of most Japanese dishes, sushi and sashimi included. To appreciate the mild taste of Japanese

---

[31] www.reportlinker.com/report.

[32] Theodore Bestor reports the popular Tsukiji seafood market folklore that women's hands are warmer than men's and hence adversely affect the flavor of raw seafood (Bestor 2004: 83–84, 126–127).

food one needs highly sensitive taste buds. It takes time and years of tasting. Thus every consumer becomes a connoisseur.

Speaking about sushi preparation, the mastery of cooking rice should be noted. Many years chefs learn how to choose the best rice brand suitable for the specific kind of sushi and how to carefully cook and flavor it. Ideal serving temperature, molding, and precise decorating of the plate is what makes *a shokunin* (master). "Sushi is eighty percent rice" (Goulding 2015: 11, 12).

Culinary Syntax and Semantics: Table Manners

Although sushi very often is consumed at home, nowadays it is mostly enjoyed as *public* food (Ashkenazi and Jacob 2000: 201). In Japan going out for sushi could be a special event, but very often it is just a quick lunch or refreshment on the way home. Of course, takeouts are common. Carryouts can be catered for different festive celebrations as well. In such cases sushi shops arrange the pieces in beautiful lacquered trays ready to be served on the table. Takeouts position sushi as potentially capable of becoming popular in the new global eating practices. Indeed, it has gradually been transformed into mass urban restaurant food, takeaway dish, element of food-ordering system, or a humble lunch box, prepared in advance at the supermarkets. In Japan it is usually accompanied by hot or cold green tea, or beer. Japanese traditional taste regards sushi as incompatible with wine, perhaps because of the slightly sour taste of the dish.[33]

The order in which sushi is consumed is unimportant: the ambience, setting, and quality are (Ashkenazi and Jacob 2000: 206). Seasonality and fishery products matter a lot. Contemporary catches of new fish and seafood from world oceans, as well as fish farming, overcome a lot of seasonal constraints on seafood consumption of the past times. Although there is not a particular season of eating sushi, local folklore defines sushi as a summer dish, probably because of the cool residual freshness in the mouth after consuming it.

Semantics of sushi and sashimi consumption is rather different from the consumption of public Western food, as pizza, for example. Sushi is not a food to share. Families and collegial and friendly dining parties go out for sushi, but eating it is a matter of individual choice. *Kaiten zushi bars* (conveyor-belt sushi bars) usually physically do not allow sitting around a table. Those bars are supposed to be highly efficient, but they are, to a certain extent, impersonal consumption places, attracting fast (and often lonely) eaters (Bestor 2006: 115–127). Even when offered in usual sushi restaurants, sushi offerings are of a great variety, but served in a limited number of pieces. It is inconvenient to share.[34] There is a centuries-old tradition for food

[33] Whereas in the Western countries and in Bulgaria sushi can be (usually) served with white wine, wine is not easily connected with any of the traditional Japanese dishes. The country has not been a wine producer for centuries. In recent years wine consumption has been widely popularized; however it is considered to have the best taste when consumed with Western food, *youshoku*.

[34] An amusing aspect of Japanese home "etiquette" is, before ordering a takeout tray of sushi, to ask

to be served as individual settings on trays with or without legs in front of each diner. This custom has framed serving in individual portions (Hosking 1996: 193). One's chopsticks come into contact only with one's personal serving of food. Even when the meal requires taking from a large one-pot dish (as in *nabemono*[35]) within same family, touching common food with the personal chopsticks is considered a breach of etiquette. Instead, special serving chopsticks are provided to transfer pieces into one's own bowl or plate (Ishige 2011: 193; Hosking 1996: 193). This practice creates a sense of privacy and enhances the sanitary rules. Chopsticks are not shared even by family members. In public places single-use chopsticks are provided. Thus sushi and, to a large extent, Japanese food do not invite people to enjoy the too-close commonality of sharing. This somehow brings a different structural pattern of togetherness when families or other diners go out for lunch or dinner.

In addition, there is a different order of the dishes served in Japanese cuisine as compared to dish order in Europe. It takes time for a non-familiar eater to become accustomed to consume sashimi in the first half of the meal, while the bowl of rice to be eaten at the second half, and a bowl of miso soup served often as a finish to the main meal before the light desserts, usually fruit (Ashkenazi and Jacob 2003; Hosking 1996). Sushi is considered a meal in which a staple and another food are put together as a single dish (Ishige 2011: 168). So it is well served as a separate light lunch or dinner, accompanied or not by a bowl of miso soup.

Sushi and sashimi are favorite Japanese foods. Through their ingredients, way of preparation, taste, color, eating places, and ways of consumption they constitute the underlying fundament of Japanese food culture. These foods school every Japanese how to value *washoku* (national cuisine). The two dishes teach people knowledge of how to read the social signs of national culture. They play a role in the national pedagogy and are an aspect of self-identification—part of the spirit of Japanese-ness.

Japanese Food in Bulgarian Urban Culture

In a warm September afternoon in 2015 I and a friend of mine sat for an early dinner at a restaurant in the center of the city. Having ordered two sets of sushi we anticipated spending some pleasant hours enjoying the food and talk. As the order was served, we focused on the neatly arranged plates with a set of six pieces of hosomaki tuna and a pair of glittering salmon nigiri for me and the same number of hosomaki salmon and a duo of pale pink shrimps for her. After struggling with the chopsticks for a couple of minutes, transforming the nicely wrapped pieces of

family members (or even guests if they are close friends) what kind of sushi pieces they would like and what number of pieces to order for each person.

[35] Nabemono is a hot-pot dish, prepared on a portable electric or gas cooker on the dining table. The ingredients could be meat slices, seafood, vegetables, tofu, noodles, or some greens in a broth. The diners pick up morsels from the pot and place them in small individual bowls to eat from them.

hosomaki sushi into a loose aggregation of rice and nori shreds soaked in enormous quantity of soy sauce, my friend Nia, 64, said: "Sorry but I'd rather order some normal food and a glass of wine."

This episode is not only an example of the sentiments of a lot of middle-aged Bulgarians towards the new fashionable foreign food. It also illustrates the cultural challenges, which Japanese food has brought with it after its appearance in the local culinary landscape.

The Bulgarian consumer has been acquainted with Japanese food very recently. In fact Asian food was first introduced through Chinese restaurants and booths which proliferated in the 1990s after the fall of communism[36] (Jung 2012: 579–598). In 2007 visiting such restaurants went out of fashion although they did not disappear. According to a popular site for eateries, in 2017 there were about 30 places serving Chinese food in the capital.[37] Big department stores have their usual Chinese food places among other fast-food eateries, but are not the most frequented. It seems that Chinese food, although remaining part of the urban culinary setting, has not become some particular fad. Consumption of Chinese food has now become to a "normalcy" of an average level, and by no means are these restaurants favorite places to spend leisure time.[38]

Another "exotic foreign," Japanese restaurants started emerging after 2007 in Bulgaria's big cities, most of them in the capital. In 2017 there were about 20 sushi restaurants in Sofia.[39] Their number is growing. A good number of restaurants serving the usual Western type of foods also offer sushi. Home delivery of sushi is orderable online. Several firms sell Japanese food products online. They transport their products in the capital and to the big cities. An interesting development of supermarket franchising has been noticed in the recent years. A couple of years ago almost all big supermarkets (especially those which had fish counters) started selling sushi. It seemed reasonably priced and convenient, and suggested potentially good purchases. But within a year or two this trade was nearly gone. This paradox is in the core issues explaining how Japanese food has been introduced and perceived in local consumer practices. I will address this later. More broadly put here, the contradictions in consumption of Japanese food illustrate the well-argued thesis that food is not just a way to satisfy bodily needs but to a greater extent it is a social construction. When facing the "exotic otherness," a very complex set of circumstances, economic and cultural interactions play a crucial role in formation of the food of a nation, or simply a fashionable trend in a cuisine.

---

[36] On the way Chinese food was introduced in postcommunist Bulgarian cities and the causes of the decline of its consumption; see the illuminating article of Yuson Jung.

[37] https://www.foodpanda.bg (2017.04.08).

[38] On the process of "normalization" of food consumption in postsocialist Bulgaria, see the above-mentioned article of Yuson Jung. My main point here is that the Bulgarian public have not had a long history of consuming ethnic foods, let alone East Asian. Apart from the already mentioned Chinese restaurants, there are a couple of Indian restaurants, one Thai restaurant, and one Korean in the capital. Against this backdrop the boom of Japanese restaurants and the interest in Japanese food are worth being studied.

[39] https://www.foodpanda.bg (2017.04.04).

The question to be answered is this: Can cultural food traditions in Bulgaria absorb Japanese culinary products and techniques? Can Japanese food be comfortably accommodated and become an indiscernible part of the culinary landscape as it is in many Western countries? Are local practices ready to domesticate it as is the case with pizza? What self-identification do Bulgarian consumers find in this new food consumption?

I will argue that to most of those questions the answer is negative, or it will remain such for a considerable time ahead. This does not concern the growing number of sushi bars and restaurants, and the increasing number of people visiting those places. I believe that Japanese cuisine will stay as a special, exotic food for a long time—on the borderline between domestic and foreign, a particular way of tasting and enjoying the different.

Fish and Seafood in Bulgarian Cuisine

If we look back historically at food habits of Bulgarians, fish has never been considered among the regular edibles. Fish (as well as mollusks, cuttlefish, frogs, snails, snakes, etc.) has been thought of as liminal, i.e., marking the boundary between edibles and nonedibles. Fish has been regularly eaten only in the regions along the Black Sea coast and the Danube River (Markova 2011: 187). The Black Sea and the Danube River[40] did not provide a rich variety of fish. Until the first half of the twentieth century there were no good refrigerating techniques and fast means of transportation, and thus import was insignificant. Historically fish and seafood did not have big economic and practical importance. Vast regions of the country consumed fish once or twice a year, mostly on special occasions, such as eating of carp on St. Nickolas's Day, celebrated as religious holiday on December 6th. For a long period of time fish was regarded as a wild food and potentially dangerous (Markova 2011: 224).[41] Bulgarians traditionally consumed domesticated food.

During communism, food consumption patterns did not change much, as the variety and quantity of fish consumption were not considered of essential importance.[42] Popular beliefs retained some distrust in nourishing and safety qualities of fish and seafood.

Local preparation techniques can be defined as opposite to what Japanese cooking is. Traditionally fish is cooked for a long time.

---

[40] In the past these water basins were the only two which could provide some subsistence fishing for poor families living along the seacoast and the bank of the river. After communism came to power in the mid-40s, within the process of industrializationa fishing fleet was built to provide raw material for the fish canning industry and trade.

[41] Since ancient times there was widespread prejudice that fish, game catches, and whatever grew in the forests (mushrooms for example) belonged to the wild, murky, and eventually contaminated worlds. Therefore those things should be kept away from the table (Markova 2011).

[42] Fishing industries satisfied the low local demands, but Bulgarian fishing fleet operated in the World Oceans trading its fish catch.

> "[I]n some regions it is noted that high-temperature cooking is vital for transforming fish flesh into human food. In northwestern Bulgaria it is believed that 'a person dies of raw fish' and that is why carp should never be eaten boiled, only roasted … Even more, in many regions of the country fish is considered dangerous, even after cooked" (Markova 2011: 223).

There are some "practical" prohibitions of consuming fish together with certain foods, especially fermented foods; for example, fish and yogurt cannot be eaten together, nor should fish be cooked in wine. The liminal semantics of fish defines it as incidental food, and it is not unconditionally put on the table (Markova 2011: 224).

However humorous those beliefs may be now, they have put some limitations on the consumption of fish and seafood in traditional Bulgarian cuisine. Of course, contemporary taste has substantially evolved and such accounts of the preparation of fish and seafood are anachronistic. Nowadays this market is considerably richer and such normalization works in favor of appearance of a new generation of consumers who more readily consume such foods. Yet the range of seafood products is neither very rich on the shop counters nor on the plate. Shrimps and mussels are available but are not widely liked. Much rarer is the consumption of octopuses, crabs, and oysters, rarely prepared at home.[43]

It is also important to mention the economic logic of the low fish consumption. Since there is local poor variety catch,[44] traders rely on import. A number of Bulgarian fish farms usually provide several freshwater fish kinds, such as trout, carp, bighead carp, and catfish. Marine black mussels also come from local private farms. Black Sea catch consists predominantly of mackerel, belted bonito, and horse mackerel. Most of the fish and seafood supplies are imported from the EU countries; therefore those goods hold international prices, which are rather high for the average consumer.[45] Thus, despite the positive tendencies, market potentialities do not stimulate and educate fish and seafood consumption taste.

Given such economic and cultural circumstances, the question at hand is:

Who Visits Japanese Restaurants and Why?

Historically food used to be a marker of class, wealth, and power. These features have never faded away. Yet in contemporary affluent and economically stable societies, such distinctions are rather blurred. Age and gender, cultural capital and education, and personal social position are more clearly displayed through food

[43] As has already been mentioned, fish is traditionally long cooked. To a much greater extent it refers to other seafood products.

[44] For local catch and seafood production, see http://iara.government.bg/?page_id=16173.

[45] As an example, in 2017 a kilo of salmon is sold at a price of about 30 Bulgarian levs, equal to 15 euro (1€ = 1.957 BGN). This is still considered a costly food product. National Statistical Institute data show that the average Bulgarian salary in December 2017 was 1123 levs (about 574 €) (http://www.nsi.bg/sites/default/files/files/pressreleases/EmplsSalary2017q4_LFZ0SQE.pdf).

consumption. I argue that foreign food consumption in Bulgarian cities is primarily a marker of distinction through knowledge and, to a certain extent, experience.

No doubt, visitors of city restaurants who would opt for Japanese or any other "exotic" foods[46] belong to the well-off part of society, very often young professionals, people who have traveled or lived abroad, usually in the West, and rarely in Japan. Often they have had some previous experience with Japanese food, mostly in the United States, Canada, or western European countries. There is not any recognizable distinctive group of gourmet consumers who would regularly eat in the Japanese restaurants just because they have the habit of doing so. On the other hand, there are young people who choose to visit different restaurants serving such food in order to try it. Some visit sushi restaurants to taste something different. Eating this food is still a culinary experiment. Here are some comments:

> "I have visited almost all restaurants serving sushi in Sofia, but this one I like most! If I am not mistaken, in the autumn of 2007 the assortment was enriched and the prices were raised. Yet there are many kinds of sushi, which are not offered in Bulgaria."[47]

> "It's my first experiment in ramen eating. The feeling after the restaurants was very pleasant. A sense of satisfaction and inside warmth."[48]

If we apply the culinary grammar analogy to view the possible compatibility of Japanese food with the Bulgarian food culture we may notice the striking contrast between the two. It seems nothing of the Japanese culinary morphology and syntax matches the local food. As already described, the ingredients used in Japanese cuisine do not have analogs in the local kitchen. Preparation techniques are not similar. The culinary traditions of the country are very far from those in Japan. Roughly speaking, Bulgarian cooking starts with cutting the raw products, while Japanese techniques (especially in sashimi preparation) end up with fine cutting and presentation of raw fish. Bulgaria, being a closed communist country, remained untouched by the first wave of globalization of Japanese food in the 1970s–1980s, so local people did not have the chance to taste it. Eating with chopsticks was and still is difficult for a lot of customers, especially middle aged and older. Japanese cuisine is transported in gastronomic models which suggest its ceremonial and social purposes, prompted by the exactness of preparation, the high aestheticism of serving, and the different dish order. Then, why is Japanese food becoming more and more attractive to (especially) young Bulgarians?

---

[46] For "exotic foods," see footnote 38 on the number of Asian restaurants in Bulgaria. Perhaps it is worth mentioning that food, served in Greek, Turkish, Lebanese, Syrian, and Moroccan restaurants, is not perceived exotic as Japanese, Indian, Thai, or Korean foods are. I presume this can be explained with the fact that Middle East cuisines have culinary grammar, similar to Bulgarian kitchen.

[47] (http://sofiacompass.com/) Here and further down I keep the sentence structure and punctuation of the comments as they appear in the restaurant sites.

[48] Umamido site.

I presume we may use the analogy with another linguistic term to better elucidate the process of introduction of this foreign food, *pragmatics*.[49] In other words, the answer to the aforementioned question lies in the way in which the new food consumption practices produce meaningful cultural contexts. Such contexts may suggest new consumer identities. Consuming Japanese food can be best explained as an emotional journey to an imaginary exotic world, creating or examining some expertise and, above all, enjoying the pleasure of eating world foods. All of these constitute cultural practice and therefore have symbolic meaning. I will discuss these three aspects.

Japanese food is consumed in two types of restaurants. First, those specialized in serving only Japanese dishes are called Japanese restaurants. They usually have Japanese names and a touch of Japanese furnishing. The second type is restaurants serving sushi, sashimi, and a limited number of Japanese side dishes and condiments, as well as other Western foods (advertised as European cuisine), and Bulgarian dishes. The first type restaurants are more expensive and are usually visited only on special occasions. How do people view and evaluate their experiences in these restaurants?

When going out for Japanese food people are usually prepared for tasting raw fish. As already noted, there is no complete ignorance on foreign food. Japanese restaurants are supposed to and they usually serve fresh raw fish. They have fresh supply from neighboring sea countries (mostly salmon, shrimps, sea bass, cuttlefish, or tuna from Greece or Turkey, but also from other, mainly EU countries). After 2012 these restaurants have expanded their menus and people can find a good range of Japanese dishes there.[50] Apart from the fish and seafood, a lot of ingredients are imported from Japan now (for example, panko bread crumbs, miso paste, frozen edamame, soy sauce). Some popular dishes are produced and served, such as tempura, teriyaki, yakitori, and soba. Thus people can taste the main Japanese dishes, found in Japanese restaurants in the other countries. There are certain limitations, though—chefs are not Japanese, rice is usually not Japanese, and the variety of fish and seafood is not that large (for example, bluefin tuna is usually not available). These circumstances, which would compromise Japanese food in high-profile restaurants abroad, do not seem to bother much the local consumers.[51] Knowing the limitations, people who visit such restaurants are not so much interested in the high gourmet aspects of eating authentic food from Japan. They would rather enjoy the

[49] As my idea is not to follow literally the linguistic analysis, my suggestions are only approximations. In this case I follow the meaning of pragmatics as "the study of the use of natural language in communication; more generally, the study of the relations between languages and their users" (https://www.britannica.com).

[50] Some economic investments and development of production, sales, and distribution of seafood products (including frozen and packed import from Japan) enhanced the expansion of the restaurant business about that time. A good example is AlexFish Company, providing a wide range of fish and Japanese food products to the restaurants (https://alexfish.bg).

[51] High-end restaurants in the world cities, such as New York, London, and Tokyo, have incessant flow of fresh products and ingredients from all world fish markets. Such good examples are high-quality Nobu restaurants (Shoko Imai 2010).

"exotic" ambience of the places. The restaurants create a fake atmosphere of "real" Japanese restaurants—tatami, bamboo, fans, hanging scrolls on the walls, and sometimes Japanese-style dressed personnel. The furniture and atmosphere trigger the imagination to create an experience of the "authentic foreign." Usual informant commentaries can be summarized as: "Expensive but it was worth being there. The atmosphere and the serving were wonderful." The restaurants are evaluated as *loci of authenticity* without having to travel abroad. Melissa Caldwell has described such culinary tourism in the city of Moscow as a creation of a virtual reality. In the same way as in Moscow, the popularity of Japanese food reflects the changing borders of people's navigable worlds. "Japan now represents the boundary between the familiar and the exotic" (Caldwell 2006: 108) A complex ambivalent mental image of *authenticity without the authentic* is created. Consumers are aware of such ambiguity and seem agreeable to the interplay of reproduction. Imagination would amend the vision in accordance with what their previous experience was and what they expect. This may be defined as *a quasi-aesthetic* experience—literal consumption is enhanced by the imaginary expectation. Japanese restaurants are those special places, where people dwell in for a short period of time. They are there in order to sense an exotic foreign culture through the active work of their memory, imagination, and knowledge. They are there as if they were in Japan but not leaving the comfortable and familiar locality. This is a "constructed authenticity," structured within the Bulgarian cultural expectations, and taste and food boundaries. "It is a *local* response to foreign trends" (Caldwell 2006: 99; emphasis mine).

Firstly, if we analyze the menus of the restaurants we notice that sushi and sashimi are made almost exclusively with two or three kinds of seafood and fish—salmon, tuna, shrimps, bass, and rarely eel. Except the eel, these are the most popular fish and seafood imports in the country (bass could be local catch), and they can be found in any fish shop.[52] Franchising companies offer almost the same prepackaged sushi, advertising them as customers' favorites: *nigiri salmon, nigiri eel, hosomaki* salmon, *hosomaki* smoked salmon, *nigiri* tuna, *hosomaki* cucumber, sushi Philadelphia, sushi avocado, sushi with smoked salmon and mango, etc.[53] Chefs report that people usually avoid consuming octopus, scallops, and roe, even if they are on the menu.[54] A lot of customers choose cooked food, California rolls, or vegetable sushi. In other words, people consume those sushi or sashimi dishes with which their palate is more or less familiar. Thus, taste seems to be following rather conventional preferences.[55] On the other hand, customers who have lived abroad readily opt for the unusual dishes. Expertise matters.

[52] https://edosushi.bg/menu/#toggle-id-9 (retrieved 12.04.2017).

[53] kayo.bg.

[54] When interviewed the chef of one of the Japanese food restaurants admitted that the rarest clients' choices are octopus sushi and scallops. Some restaurant menus present a considerable variety of Japanese dishes. See for example http://www.miyabi.bg/.

[55] Similar observations were made by Yuson Jung in her study on Chinese food consumption in Bulgaria in the late 1990s through 2007. "More successful Chinese restaurants in Sofia compromised 'authenticity' by preparing food in more Bulgarian styles" (Jung 2012: 587). Although sushi

Secondly, people are particularly sensitive to the quality of service. They associate politeness and hospitality with their knowledge of Japan, not always gained through personal experience. Critical commentaries suggest an expectation of Japanese service.

> "… The atmosphere in terms of the interior is good but the service is mediocre - the waitresses need to learn how to interact better with the customers. The menu needs expanding."

> "Overall quite disappointing. We were welcomed by a girl in everyday casual clothes who turned out to be the waitress. The interior was supposed to look contemporary but to me it had no soul and wasn't connected with Japan at all. We felt like in a fast food place - the furniture wasn't comfortable, the Chinese spoon was plastic, the chopsticks were of lowest quality … Much ado about nothing …"[56]

On the positive side comments are associated with an imagined picture of Japanese good service as being part of the authentic Japanese culture. One of my informants, a middle-aged lady, who had never been in Japan, humorously, but approvingly commented:

> "The waiter was so nice. He even bowed as he took the order, although he was a Bulgarian."

An indirect confirmation that customers visit such restaurants to enjoy an imagined authentic atmosphere is the fact that the only *kaiten-zushi* in Bulgaria is among the least visited. Situated on the third floor of a big department store in the middle of a food court offering other kitchen foods, it is hardly visited at all. The conveyor-belt sushi restaurants are among the favorite sushi bars in Japan for their reasonable prices and fast service. They may be called "authentic" as they "have become *sine qua non* of the contemporary urban commercial landscape" (Bestor 2006: 115). Usually there are queues of visitors in front of them in Japan. Yet the Bulgarian consumer logic does not recognize this restaurant as Japanese, perhaps because it lacks the imagined exotic Japanese-ness. Furthermore, conveyor-belt sushi restaurants offering plates of sushi moving around the sushi chef do not correspond to whatsoever Bulgarian food conviviality structure. Local table culture would require a party of diners to sit facing each other, eventually to share food and raise glasses to toast. Very often such groups are more than two people. Somehow this kaiten-zushi restaurant looks odd arranging diners in a line.[57] Visiting Japanese restaurants is viewed as a special occasion and it needs supposedly "cozier" atmosphere.

Japanese restaurants are also visited to examine some expertise, gained abroad, or to learn more about such food. Comments about the food in the restaurant sites usually come from customers who have lived in the West or in Japan. In most of the

---

and sashimi cannot be prepared in "Bulgarian style" the preferences follow familiar ingredient tastes.

[56] UmamidoSofia site.

[57] Such line arrangement is unfamiliar in any Bulgarian restaurant tradition. Lines of chairs can be seen in snack shops though suggesting the quick manner of eating.

cases, people compare their experience in the local restaurants to what they have tasted in the West.

> "I tried sushi in America and I'm not excited. In Canada it was better as was in Austria … I recommend this sushi bar, you'll get addicted …"

> "Too much rice and too little filling … I have tried sushi in America and Europe." (http://sofiacompass.com/).

> "I recommend the Japanese Miso soup … It is tasty and served in bigger bowls, and not as it is served in Europe and the States."[58]

Authenticity is examined through the experience, not so much the taste, of food. On the other hand, there are people (not many though) who have lived in Japan or have good knowledge on Japanese culture and lifestyle. They set a rather different aspect of identity. I often dine with two of my friends who have an avid interest in Japanese food and culture. One of them is a specialist in Japanese language and a translator who often travels to Japan. The other is a state expert and has a good conduct of Japanese. She has also visited Japan. When we dine together they never take westernalized sushi dishes but keep to the "pure" taste of raw fish. The usual remark they make is: "Sushi is not the same as in Japan but it is always good to remember the taste." Obviously the deeper knowledge on the authentic dishes places the locally produced Japanese food as a surrogate which triggers the memories of the distant culture. In this aspect food is notable as a sensory and as a social experience.

We come to the third aspect of Japanese food consumption popularity. Enjoying the pleasure of being on a par with the global consumption of exquisite food is an overarching experience, taste authenticity remaining secondary. In her research conducted in 1997 through 2007 Yuson Jung explored how Chinese food in Bulgaria had become emblematic of Western lifestyle. She suggested that the experience of socialist consumers with American films associated Chinese food with the Western lifestyle. In the postsocialist context of that time the consumption of Chinese food was perceived as Western experience (Jung 2012:583, 590). Ten years later consumers can assess the Japanese food on the basis of their own experience and knowledge acquired mainly in the West, but also in Japan. The authenticity of consumption is by all means a way of accumulating cultural capital. This authentic consumption also suggests a dynamic rearrangement of Bulgarian "position in the global political and economic hierarchy" (Jung 2012: 581). One of my Bulgarian informants, Ani, a university student in Amsterdam, once told me:

> "I live and study in Amsterdam. From time to time I pay visit to my friends who live in London or they come to see me in Amsterdam. We always have Japanese food when we meet: it's something as a tradition. It's very pleasing that when we come back on vacation we can have sushi together. It is nice that sushi here, in Sofia, is of good quality and cheaper than in Amsterdam and London. We love being at home, but enjoying things we like abroad."[59]

---

[58] http://www.capital.bg/.

[59] In 2017 the price of a portion of two pieces of nigiri tuna (80 g) in middle-range sushi bar in Sofia

The comments are closer to approbation of cultural adherence and openness to the global consumer condition.

The above circumstances explain the paradox of growing number of sushi and sashimi restaurants at the backdrop of the disappearance of sushi counters in the supermarkets. Japanese food is consumed as a global cultural product despite the fact that its taste is unusual or unfamiliar to Bulgarian consumer's palate. Going out for a sushi at a restaurant is a social event rather than a nutritional practice. There is next to no interest in buying prepackaged sushi or sashimi from the local supermarket or sushi shops just to eat it at home, as is the common practice in the countries accustomed to such food. Some sushi restaurants cater for sushi at homes. This type of consumption does not go beyond the common pattern, though. Sushi parties at home are occasional and usually organized by people who have been trained in sushi eating abroad. Not surprisingly, as restaurant chefs report, customers' favorites are Americanized versions of sushi, with Philadelphia cheese, avocado, mango fruit, strawberries, salmon (very often smoked), tuna fish, and shrimps.[60] All of these taste preferences highlight the aforementioned argument that consumers eat those modifications of foreign (Japanese) food which are closer or somehow familiar to the local flavors. The Japanese traditional palate would rather choose the pure taste of raw fish, seafood, rice, nori, and wasabi.[61]

Interesting restaurants are the eateries of the mixed type. At dinnertime those places are the most populated, sometimes overcrowded. There families and friends, colleagues, or just acquaintances meet over favorite dishes. Such dishes could be traditional Balkan appetizers, local grilled meats and salads, European food, pizza, pasta, grilled fish, grilled meats and vegetables, cocktails, and desserts. Such restaurants have sushi bars as well. Pizza and sushi, together with traditional choices, appear to be among the most suitable venues for spending pleasurable time these days. They are becoming the most desired places for eating out. There people find the best opportunities to choose whatever they are craving at the moment. As food preferences are becoming more diverse, everybody can find something to their liking on the menus. The freedom to either share common dishes, such as pizza, or have their own individual platter of sushi best corresponds to modern fastidious consumer subjectivities and the local idea of commonality. This is, as J. Finkelstein puts it, emotional capitalism in action: an emotional repertoire regularly played out through our consumer practices, including the pleasure we find in popular pastimes, such as eating out (Finkelstein 2014: 184).

After 2007 a new dynamics in the habits of eating out can be noticed.[62] Knowledge on Japanese food has expanded (including learning from blogs and Internet recipes).

---

is 4.50 levs (about 2.5 €).

[60] haikusushi.bg.

[61] Japanese people would enjoy also natto and tamago-yaki sushi, which are considered odd tasting outside the country.

[62] In 2007 Bulgaria became a member of European Union. Since then a lot of economic opportunities for new businesses and trade have developed. Many young people travel to study in the Western countries. Japan has a stable policy of promoting its culture and lifestyle in Bulgaria by organizing

Many people try and come to like this food. A new twist in taste formation appears—the palate follows the new consumption practice. More informants share that they enjoy Japanese food. The fact that the taste for sushi develops does not mean that culinary grammar of the dish operates unconditionally in the local cultural context. If we summarize the way Bulgarian food culture has accepted the food we can say that it is becoming fashionable in the city culture, but it still bears the aura of a culinary adventure, and its taste, appearance, and inherent culinary discourse cannot hold their own. It still remains the *foreign Other*, which has come to be a token of globalization.

Whether Japanese food will be recontextualized and creolized remains to be seen. A group of constant consumers have to become visible as having part on the culinary stage, perhaps a newly emerging middle class. It is not enough to visit Japanese restaurants just to experiment and to educate yourself. Such social and cultural capital has to be transformed into an intimate mechanism of experience of local and global as unified self-identification and lifestyle.

Contemporary cosmopolite inhabits many parallel cultural worlds. The two global foods, discussed in this text and their consumption, step in differently in the cultural spaces of everyday life. They enhance different social processes by which social subjects comprehend their own worlds.

By analogy with other contemporary cultural processes, two tendencies in the food culture developments can be distinctively visible now: (1) *culinary universalism*, set forth through globalizing food industries, but also (2) *culinary differentialism*—people like their traditional food and defend their local taste and ways of production. *Goût de terroir* is gradually acquiring broader meaning of protecting culturally and politically (and in some cases legally) the locally based foods and consumption practices. This culinary differentialism would always contest the "invasion" of foreign foods. In between these two opposite tendencies, the real life of food culture unfolds. Urban people every day make their better informed choice of eating—fluctuating between the familiar taste of traditional local dishes and sometimes the less confident yet very exciting experience of eating the foods of the foreigners. Such acts of tasting are the delightful ways of learning through the senses and better understanding what lies beyond one's cultural boundaries. As such experiences become more frequent and more diverse, the consumers feel the pleasures of being part of the global communities of those who know and accept the differences—the real connoisseurs. New Bulgarian cities gradually become part of those global communities.

---

annual "Days of Japanese Culture" and providing scholarships for education there. These circumstances could be considered as factors enhancing the interest in Japanese food as well.

References

Appadurai, Arjun. 1996. Modernity at Large: Cultural Dimensions of Globalization. In *Minneapolis*. London: University of Minnesota Press.

Ashkenazi, Michael, and Jeanne Jacob. 2000. *The Essence of Japanese Cuisine*. Richmond, Surrey: Curzon.

———. 2003. *Food Culture in Japan*. Westport, CT: Greenwood Press.

Ashley, Bob, Joanne Hollows, Steve Jones, and Ben Taylor. 2004. *Food and Cultural Studies*. London: Routledge.

Barthes, Roland. 2008. Toward a Psychosociology of Contemporary food Consumption. In *Food and Culture*, ed. Carole Counihan and Penny Van Esterik, 28–35. New York: Routledge.

Bestor, Theodore. 2000. *How Sushi Went Global*, Foreign Policy, November/December 54–63.

———. 2004. *Tsukiji. The Fish Market at the Center of the World*. Berkeley, LA: University of California Press.

———. 2006. Kaiten-Zushi and Konbini: Japanese Food Culture in the Age of Mechanical Reproduction. In *Fast Food/Slow Food. The Cultural Economy of Global Food Systems*, ed. Richard Wilk, 115–130. Lanham, MD: Altamira Press.

Bourdieu, Pierre. 1984 (2002 print). *Distinction. A Social Critique of the Judgement of Taste*. Trans. R. Nice. Cambridge, MA: Harvard University Press.

Bradatan, Christina. 2003. Cuisine and Cultural Identities in Balkans. *The Anthropology of East Europe Review: Central Europe, Eastern Europe and Eurasia* 21 (1): 43–47.

Caldwell, Melissa. 2004. Domesticating the French Fries: McDonald's and Consumerism in Moscow. *Journal of Consumer Culture* 4 (1): 5–26.

———. 2006. Tasting the Worlds of Yesterday and Today: Culinary Tourism and Nostalgia Foods in Post-Soviet Russia. In *Fast Food/Slow Food. The Cultural Economy of Global Food Systems*, ed. Richard Wilk, 97–112. Lanham, MD: Altamira Press.

Cwiertka, Katarzyna. 2006. *Modern Japanese Cuisine: Food, Power and National Identity*. London: Reaktion Books.

Douglas, Mary. 1983. Culture and Food. In *The Pleasures of Anthropology*, ed. Morris Freilich, 74–101. New York: New American Library.

Featherstone, Mike. 2007. *Consumer Culture and Postmodernism*. Singapore: Sage Publications.

Finkelstein, Joanne. 2014. Fashioning Appetite. Restaurants and the Making of Modern Identity. London, New York: I.B. Tauris.

Fernandez, Doreen G. 1988. Culture Ingested. Notes on the Indigenization of Philipine Food, *Philipine Studies* 36: 219–232. https://www.jstor.org/stable/42633085?seq=2#page_scan_tab_contents. Retrieved 16 Aug 2017.

Goulding, Matt. 2015. *Rice, Noodle, Fish: Deep Travels Through Japan's Food Culture*. New York: Harper Collins Publishers.

Harris, Marvin. 1985. Good to Eat. Riddles of Food and Culture. In *Prospect Heights*. Long Grove, IL: Waveland Press Inc.

Heldke, Lisa. 2005. But Is It Authentic? Culinary Travel and the Search for the "Genuine Article". In *The Taste Cultural Reader*, ed. Carolyn Korsmeyer, 385–394. Oxford: Berg.

Hosking, Richard. 1996. *Dictionary of Japanese Food: Ingredients and Culture*. Boston, MA: Tuttle Publishing.

Imai, Shoko. 2010. Nobu and After: Westernized Japanese Food and Globalization. In *Food and Social Identities in the Asia Pacific Region*, ed. James Farrer. Tokyo: Sophia University Institute of Comparative Culture. URL: http://icc.fla.sophia.ac.jp/global%20food%20papers/html/imai.html. Retrieved 06 Oct 2017.

Ishige, Naomichi. 2011. *The History and Culture of Japanese Food*. New York: Routledge.

Issenberg, Sasha. 2007. *The Sushi Economy. Globalization and the Making of a Global Delicacy*. New York: Gotham Books Ltd.

Jung, Yuson. 2012. Experiencing the "West" Through the "East" in the Margins of Europe. Chinese Food Consumption Practices in Postsocialist Bulgaria. *Food, Culture and Society* 15 (4): 579–598.

Karababa, Eminegül, and Güliz Ger. 2011. Early Modern Ottoman Coffeehouse Culture and the Formation of the Consumer Subject. *Journal of Consumer Research* 37 (5): 737–760.

Kraev, Georg. 2005. *Kafeneto kato diskurs* [Café as a Discourse]. Sofia: New Bulgarian University Press.

La Secla, Franco. 2007. *Pasta and Pizza*. Chicago, IL: Prickly Paradigm Press.

Mariani, John. 1991. *America Eats Out*. New York: William Morrow.

Marinov, Dimitar. 2003. *Izbrani proizvedina v 5 toma. Tom I, chast 2. Religiozni narodni obichai* [Selected Works in 5 volumes. Vol. I, part 2. Religious Folklore Customs]. Sofia: Iztok-Zapad.

Markman, Ellis. 2004. *The Coffee House: A Cultural History*. London: Weidenfeld & Nikolson.

Markova, Maria. 2011. *Hrana i hranene: mezhdu prirodata i kulturata* [Food and Nutrition: Between Nature and Culture]. Sofia: Prof. Marin Drinov.

McGray, Douglas. 2009. Japan's Gross Nationa Cool, in: *Foreign Policy*, November 11, 2009. http://foreignpolicy.com/2009/11/11/japans-gross-national-cool/. Retrieved 27 Aug 2017.

Mintz, Sidney. 1996. *Tasting Food, Tasting Freedom*. Boston, MA: Beacon Press.

———. 2006. Food at Moderate Speed. In *Fast Food/ Slow Food. The Cultural Economy of the Gobal food System*, ed. Richard Wilk, 3–11. Lanham, MD: Altamira Press.

Montanari, Massimo. 1994, 1996. *The Culture of Food*. Trans. by C. Ipsen. Oxford: Blackwell Publishers Ltd.

———. 2006. *Food is Culture*. Trans. by A. Sonnenfeld. New York: Columbia University Press.

Nye, Joseph S. 2004. *Soft Power: The Means to Succes in World Politics*. New York: NY Public Affairs.

Parasecoli, Fabio. 2004. Food Culture in Italy. In *Westport Connecticut*. London: Greenwood Press.

Pieterse, Jan Nederveen. 2004. *Globalization and Culture. Global Mélange*. Lanham, MD: Rowman & Littlefield Publisher, Inc.

Rath, Eric, and Stephanie Assmann. 2010. *Japanese Foodways, Past and Present*. Urbana, IL: University of Illinois Press.

Reynolds, Christian John. 2014. The Soft Power of Food: A Diplomacy of Hamburgers and Sushi? Food Studies: An Interdisciplinary Journal 1(2). https://www.researchgate.net/publication/261760629_The_Soft_Power_of_Food_A_Diplomacy_of_Hamburgers_and_Sushi. Retrieved 21 Aug 2017.

Ritzer, George. 1993. The McDonaldization of Society: An Investigation into the Changeing Character of Contemporary Life. Thousand Oaks, London and New Delhi: Pine Forge Press, Sage Publications.

Slater, Don. 1997. *Consumer Culture & Modernity*. Cambridge: Polity Press.

Vakarelski, Hristo. 2008. *Balgarski pogrebalni obichai* [Bulgarian Burial Rituals]. Sofia: Zahari Stoyanov.

Velinova, Iskra. 2004. *Za potrebnostite, potreblenieto i konsumaziata pri sozializma* [About Needs and Consumption during Socialism], In Antropologichni Izsledvania [Anthropological Researches], vol. V. Bulgarian: New Bulgarian University Press 71–81.

Websites

https://www.britannica.com/science/pragmatics. Retrieved 23 July 2017.

http://www.capital.bg/light/revju/restorant/2008/03/21/474286_vkusno_sushi_v_hamachi/. Retrieved 03 Nov 2013.

http://ec.europa.eu/agriculture/quality/schemes/index_en.htm.

https://edosushi.bg/menu/#toggle-id-9. Retrieved 12 Apr 2017.

https://www.foodpanda.bg/restaurants?user_search=&sort=&sort=&cuisines%5B%5D=78&page=1. Retrieved 04 Apr 2017.

https://www.foodpanda.bg/restaurants?user_search=&sort=&sort=&cuisines%5B%5D=64&page=1. Retrieved 08 Apr 2017.

http://haikusushi.bg/cat/. Retrieved 20 June 2017.

http://iara.government.bg/?page_id=16173.

http://www.inta.org/INTABulletin/Pages/EUROPEANUNIONPIZZANAPOLETANAObtainsTraditionalSpecialityGuaranteedStatus.aspx.

http://kayo.bg/produkt-kategoria/%d0%bc%d0%b5%d0%bd%d1%8e-%d0%b4%d0%be%d1%81%d1%82%d0%b0%d0%b2%d0%ba%d0%b0/. Retrieved 23 Mar 2017.

http://www.miyabi.bg/.

https://www.facebook.com/Miyabi.BG/. Retrieved 13 Apr 2017.

http://www.nsi.bg/en/content/6704/population-districts-municipalities-place-residence-and-sex. Retrieved 23 July 2017.

http://www.nsi.bg/sites/default/files/files/pressreleases/EmplsSalary2017q4_LFZ0SQE.pdf.

http://www.reportlinker.com/report/best/coverage/World/keywords/Tuna?utm_source=adwords1&utm_medium=sitelinks&utm_campaign=RLSA_Food&utm_adgroup=RLSA_Tuna&gclid=CPmYkZqig9MCFUqNGwodU20EXQ. Retrieved 01 Apr 2017.

http://sofiacompass.com/%D0%B5%D0%B2%D1%82%D0%B8%D0%BD-%D1%81%D1%83%D1%88%D0%B8-%D0%B1%D0%B0%D1%80-%D0%B2-%D1%81%D0%BE%D1%84%D0%B8%D1%8F. Retrieved 01 Apr 2001.

http://thetravelbite.com/recipes/red-cabbage-and-gorgonzola-pizza/. Retrieved 25 July 2013.

https://www.tripadvisor.com/Restaurant_Review-g294452-d808082-Reviews-or20-Hamachi-Sofia_Sofia_Region.html#REVIEWS.

https://www.facebook.com/UmamidoSofia/. Retrieved 10 Apr 2017, 12 Apr 2017, 21 June 2017.

http://winewitandwisdomswe.com/2017/03/13/pizza-napoletana-tsg-traditional-status-guaranteed/.

Consumption of the Past: Constructing Antiquity of an Archaeological Site in Bulgaria and Marketing the Ideological Narrative

Tsvete Lazova

Approaching the Production of Antiquity of an Archaeological Site: Its Role in the Politics of Consumption of Nationalized Past

This chapter is supposed to contribute to the amassed corpus of literature on the practice of archaeology and its role in the politics of producing archaeological sites, which shape the national identity represented as archaeological narrative. The text developed by a research project and realized in the Department of Anthropology at New Bulgarian University examines new consumer practices in post-socialist Bulgaria in anthropological perspective. The elaborated ideological and therefore problematic interpretations of archaeological record in the 1970s and 1980s and their marketing in the 1990s up to nowadays are discussed, asking a question: Does the academic scholarship in post-socialist Bulgaria draw a line between academic professional and ethical responsibilities and popular entertainment? Therefore the focus in this chapter is on how ancient periods are prioritized for construction of national identity and thus selected for promotion and consumption by the state with the implicit consent of the academy as well.

The "eye of anthropology," which gives priority to cultural phenomena, makes it possible to evaluate archaeological practice and the nature of its narratives and discourses as cultural product in the context of the imagined nation (Appadurai 1996).They are to be understood then within a cultural matrix and mainly as consumption of signs (Featherstone 2007: 82–87). The archaeological material traces from the past and the narratives and discourses produced about them provide the nation-building with signs that testify the prolonged and specified historical existence of a nation. The deep roots of a nation or its ancient-ness are supposed to

T. Lazova (✉)
New Bulgarian University, Sofia, Bulgaria
e-mail: tlazova@gmail.com

E. Krasteva-Blagoeva (ed.), *Approaching Consumer Culture*, International Series on Consumer Science, https://doi.org/10.1007/978-3-030-00226-8_9

be considered as cultural capital being a resource of construction of national identities and "economic capital" as well. This fact gives arguments to be considered that each national archaeological practice has its specific regional traditions, which takes into account the complexity of the phenomenon of nationalism. The reflexivity in many disciplines including archaeology reveals different faces of dependence on nation-state formation. Moreover, many recent publications studying the relationship of archaeology and nationalism are based on the postmodern critique of science, which takes the form of post-processual archaeology (Hodder and Hutson 2003; Trigger 2008). These new trends in archaeological research practices emphasize the social, cultural, and political contexts in which archaeology is conducted (Trigger 1984; Kohl and Fawcett 1995; Meskell 1998). International organizations, such as the World Archaeological Congress (WAC) created in 1986, and the European Association of Archaeology established in 1994, also highlight the political and ideological dimensions of the discipline. As it became a truism that archaeology has political dimensions there is something more to be added—many scholars explore the inherent political nature of archaeology and its impact on the practice of the discipline. Therefore they reopen a serious discussion of archaeology as political action. They situated the discussion of ethics in the political realm and ask the question that "never fully answers but … never quit asking, archaeology for whom?" (Hamilakis and Duke 2007: 10). This question leads to another issue—the growing phenomenon of marketing archaeological heritage which culminated in a session at the American Anthropology Association meetings in 2001. A scholarly research was produced drawing on examples from many areas of the world in order to examine the ways in which archaeology and heritage are becoming commodities in the marketplace (Rowan and Baram 2004). Recognizing this context as inevitable and having in mind the extreme commoditization of archaeology in the last 30 years or so a suggested satisfactory answer can be found in the disciplinary power of professionalization and its effect on the ethical debates in archeology (Hamilakis and Duke 2007: 21).

This chapter adds a place from Bulgaria that might contribute to the debate concerning the sociopolitical nature of archaeological thinking and practice in contemporary archaeology and the politics of its commoditization. The study of the processes of renewing the excavations on the site called Perperikon (located in Southeastern Bulgaria, in the Rhodope mountains) and embedding it in the collective archaeological imagination of everyday life is based on the reflexive nature of contemporary anthropology and archaeology. Theoretical reflections in anthropology turned problems of description into problems of representation (Marcus and Fischer 1986: 9). An important point becomes then that "all associations of place, people, and culture are social and historical creations to be explained, not given natural facts" (Gupta and Ferguson 2001: 4).

A very fruitful approach in the field of reflexive studies in archaeology is the "archaeological ethnography" which includes studying various kinds of documents concerning archaeological sites. This field of research focuses on the problem of how a site's archaeological data is acquired by examining the social, political, and ideological contexts in which it is produced. It is an approach that tends to be realized by the "thick description," meaning the use of a very wide range of documentation including various descriptions, publications, touristic guides, various media products, interviews with different participants in the archaeological excavations, exhibitions, Internet publications, etc. (Hamilakis and Anagnostopoulos 2009). This approach evaluates the process of developing the site: how the knowledge about it is created, becomes popular, and becomes integrated into the national values and identity, and how academics communicate with local experts to gain knowledge about the ancient past or how this knowledge is transmitted in the media. The approach of archaeological ethnography revealed the fact that the archaeological discipline in Bulgaria is still informed mostly by the culture-historical perspective practiced actively at the end of the nineteenth century and the beginnings of the twentieth century (Lazova 2016). It produces usually ethnic archaeology used in service of the national ideologies. The local elites seek to glorify the antiquity and authenticity of its ethnic cultures and to embed it in everyday life. In Bulgaria these processes were supported actively in the period after World War II by the Soviet theories of ethnogenesis which constructed "new" rhetoric after the 1940s when the Marxist methodology was explicitly introduced. The key question in academic scholarship became how to elaborate a glorious history so that to provide the nation with significant remote past. The ethnic archaeology of antiquity and the philological model of archaeology in particular were activated during the time of late socialism from the 1970s and 1980s as a resource of (re)legitimating the national identity. The studied archaeological site Perperikon manifests the most spectacular symbiosis of the cultural nationalism practiced by the communist ideology of this period and its uses after the 1990s in the tourism industry.

Archaeology as Historical Science in Bulgaria: The Context of Culture-Historical Approaches

In Bulgaria, as in most European countries, especially in southeastern Europe, archaeology is a historical science. Therefore trends within the disciplines of history and archaeology are one and the same. At the beginning of the 1990s, in the context of the changes in the countries of Eastern Europe, many expectations, and real opportunities, appeared for Bulgarian academics to offer a review and a reappraisal of archaeological practice and to discard the ideological burden imposed on it by the communist past. Some international scholarly periodicals offered rubrics devoted to the nature of the expected transition in Central and Eastern European scholarship. Very few academics took the opportunity to contribute to historiographical studies in order to reveal the contexts and their conventions of writing history. In her subtle analysis of Bulgarian historiography, M. Todorova presents the character of the Bulgarian historical scholarship as shaped by the traditions within the historical discipline. Bulgarian historiography was born in the age of nationalism and was developing in the context of nation-state formation as one of its most important pillars. It has evolved exclusively according to the percepts of its duty—to shape the national consciousness fulfilling its important social function. Thus the "national(ist) continuum" of the nineteenth and twentieth centuries was permanently revitalized by the vast range of intellectuals—protectors and promoters of the "national interests." Outlining the main aspects of the transformation after "the changes in November 10, 1989," Todorova goes deeper in her analysis. She recognizes that there was a large-scale theoretical isolation as a result of the political setting in which the Bulgarian historical discipline is nourished (Todorova 1992). This means that archaeology as an integral part of Bulgarian historical scholarship has existed and developed in the same setting as an active ideological and political factor.

A special section of "Antiquity"—the academic journal dedicated to the subject of archaeology—was devoted to Central European archaeology in transition. There appeared a brief review on Bulgarian archaeology focusing on the dominant role of the state in controlling archaeological practice. It stated that this guardianship was weakened immediately after the changes in November 10, 1989, because state funding has been reduced (Velkov 1993). The article failed to notice, however, that the communist state lavishly financed a number of programs asserted to be national which activated the studies of the ancient past. These critical glances designed for foreign scholarship are far from profound analyses concerning the archaeological practice in Bulgaria. The discipline itself being an integral part of ancient history does not even make an effort to inform itself about the new trends in the development of archaeology outside Bulgaria. The only serious anxiety after the fall of communism remained the financing of archaeological excavations rather than the ways of overcoming its methodological insufficiency. Yet, the subsequent reappraisals in historical discipline marked a shift toward applying new approaches to the study of history supported by scholars in philosophy, literary criticism, and linguistics. They produced a number of valuable studies by Bulgarian scholars on Bulgarian history entangled with the history of the Balkans (Daskalov and Vezenkov 2015). However, the new critical approaches here applied were (and still are) insufficiently publicized and institutionalized in order to popularize alternatives to the nation-centric model in Bulgarian historical research.

The reflexive perspective of analysis in archaeology shows clearly that critical trends in the Bulgarian archaeology are found in the works of foreign archaeologists. Still, they provide a basis for including Bulgaria in the debates concerning the ideological and political character of archaeological practice in Eastern Europe. Yet, the foreign archaeologists open up the way to analyze the Bulgarian case in the context of the relationship between archaeology and ideology in southeast Europe and in the Eastern Mediterranean—notwithstanding the absence of Bulgarian archaeologists (Kaiser 1995; Bailey 1998). The ideological nature of the search of continuities emerged in a number of studies which compare the processes of tracing and representing antiquity as ethnic constituent of the present nations on the Balkans (Danforth 1984; Kotsakis 1998).

Territorializing the Nation by Means of Ancient and Medieval Ruins: A Longue Durée Perspective

The presented case study tries to turn away from the commonsense idea that locality is simply given. It focuses on ideological and political processes of place making that shape national identities and its appearance to be natural (Gupta and Ferguson 2001: 6). This case study resulted from the critical study which places the research of the archaeological site of Perperikon within a larger political and historical context. It revealed the conditions which produced interpretative frame that places the archaeological research in a context that feeds the so-called culture-historical heritage in Bulgaria today (Lazova 2016: 72–95). Culture-historical approach produces always an imagined relationship between artifacts and people (Trigger 2008: 211–313). It has already been observed that Bulgarian archaeology remains deeply historical using culture-historical perspectives. Its goal was to extend history back into more remote past combining written Greco-Roman sources with archaeological materiality. This philological model of archaeology tends to explain origins and changes of the archaeological cultures mainly by means of diffusion and migration. Culture-historical approaches nourish the cultural nationalism which is progressively banalized through the increasing multiplication of "the national" narratives and discourses by archaeological finds saturated with enduring symbols of national identity.

Today, nationalism is analyzed in numerous studies and is put in many different categories grouped by different qualifiers—diachronic, geographic/territorial, typological (civic, democratic, popular, populist), etc. Recently it has been argued that it would be useful to introduce a needed sensitivity to different intensities of nationalism across time and space, as well as within the same space (Todorova 2015: 681–699). It is in accordance with the suggestion that the significance of archaeology for national projects has varied greatly in duration and intensity. Social and political changes stimulate interest in a nation's past (Trigger 2008: 249–250). A general model on the Balkans practiced with different dynamics in different countries is to derive a sense of ethnic continuity and identity from their combined prehistoric, classical, and medieval archaeological legacy. The local elites in the Balkan countries sought to celebrate the authenticity of their ethnic cultures stressing more on ethnicity than on the ideas of universal human rights (Trigger 1995: 269). Thus the problem of boundaries emerges and concerns a territory in antiquity occupied by multiple modern nation-states, including Bulgaria, Greece, Turkey, Romania, Serbia, Macedonia, Moldova, Ukraine, etc. The political agendas of the twentieth century impacted so greatly modern scholarship that the political fragmentation on the Balkans has been inscribed in the ancient landscape (Bouzek and Graningen 2015: 12). Therefore different national narratives developed in continuous historiographical battles with one another (Marinov 2015: 3). In this case some authors rightly insist that cultural nationalism still exists, the aim of which is the construction of distinctive collective identities rooted deeply in history. Although these identities may be mythical, they played a part in political nationalism and thus in the making of modern societies (Hutchinson 1994). In the contemporary setting of neoliberal consumer culture, culture-historical archaeology still produces archaeological narratives shaping national identity and also actively marketing it. Thus the market and the consumers are mobilized in the production of the collective "us" or "our homeland." Cultural tourism and its institutions including academic fields and popular media support its management. Therefore the category of cultural nationalism might be considered still useful in Bulgarian (Balkan) context.

The archaeological site Perperikon is a place most actively represented in the last 20 years as "national resource." This case study is analyzed with the purpose of presenting the mechanisms of embedding academically produced knowledge of antiquity in the surface of contemporary life. The "resurrection" of Perperikon with the added value of antiquity has to create a narrative flagging a prestigious ancientness of the nation. The archaeological narrative will reproduce it as natural environment of today. In this case banal nationalism operates with popular ancient imagery, which makes the nation unforgettable taking it for granted.

This location was established as a bishop's residence from the fourteenth century by Konstantin Jirecek, a Czech scholar who came to Bulgaria in 1879. His work, *History of the Bulgarians* (1876) published in Czech, German, Russian, and Bulgarian, became considered as a "people's book." During his earliest tours in Bulgaria K. Jirecek began the process of territorializing the land by means of ancient and medieval artifacts. His activities in Bulgaria after the creation of the independent Bulgarian state (de facto 1878 *de jure* in 1908) marked the beginnings of the historical scholarship in Bulgaria. K. Jirecek introduced the culture-historical orthodoxy, including archaeology, whose developments in Europe were accompanied by the growing ethnic nationalism called upon the shaping of the national histories. The growing interest in the concept of archaeological culture gained speed and later was fully realized by Gustaf Kossinna in Germany.[1] Kossinna as the leading icon of Nazi ethnic and racial prehistory casts a long shadow over modern German and Balkan archaeology. His work was based on a well-established interest in defining archaeological cultures and equating them with specific peoples. This form of interpretation began in the early 1860s and became increasingly common in central, eastern, and northern countries where it was frequently associated with increasing nationalism. After the 1930s his approach gained an unprecedented Nazi support. Thus Kossinna and his German followers became part of a much wider pattern of racist and ethnocentric views. They contaminated the work of archeologists and their interpretations including the Bulgarian archaeology.

In Bulgaria this early academic impetus to produce knowledge about the past was launched at first by academic figures coming from "outside" after the end of the nineteenth century (Lazova 2016: 144–150). They greatly contributed to the processes which later made the Bulgarians and their antiquity visible to foreign

[1] Gustaf Kossinna (1858–1931) is a linguist and researcher of Indo-European culture, and professor of German archaeology. He developed the theory that a regionally determined ethnicity can be defined by the material culture excavated from a site (culture-historical archaeology).

scholars. In spite of the fact that the main focus was medieval history Jirecek initiated the processes of territorializing and establishing continuity between ancient and medieval times which was typical for the culture-historical approach. He associated artifacts of various sorts with written texts produced in a Greco-Roman cultural context. His actions, in romantic-patriotic view, are considered by Bulgarian scholars to be as ones of the "fathers" or "founders" of Bulgarian historical science and archaeology, respectively. The East European archaeologists felt that it was their mission to stimulate a sense of national identity for the Poles, the Czechs, the Hungarians, and the Bulgarians who had lived in multinational empires. K. Jirecek also dictated the structures of the main scholarly institutions, i.e., libraries and museums, which were supposed to create the new national policies in the production of knowledge about the past. These institutions were designed to manage the interaction of this information with various public groups. Since then the public dissemination of the values of Bulgaria's archaeological finds has become more and more intensive and different audience are affected in different ways by the knowledge of the remote past.

The interwar period was the period of active realization of Bulgarian *Altertumswissenschaft*, "the science of antiquity" (Lazova 2016: 150–185). It was shaped by a great number of Bulgarian scholars who studied mainly in Germany. Coming back to Bulgaria, they developed the field of classical studies. The main figure in the field of archaeological scholarship was Bogdan Filov (1883–1945);[2] he organized fully the archaeological discipline and its institutionalization in Bulgaria and created departments for its main research fields among which was Thracian antiquity. He took the lead of the Sofia University department of archaeology and its programs, and was influential both at home and internationally. His research activity and wide-ranging expertise were not only visible abroad but foreign scholars were eager to follow archaeological investigations in this region interpreted by Filov. He devoted much effort to establish foundations in order to finance properly the archaeological practice in Bulgaria (Lazova 2016: 159–171).

The loss of territories after World War I incited the Bulgarian-Greek debate about ancient Thracian heritage. Developing within a larger ideological background, the question of Thracian "ancestry" was treated with academic caution by the Bulgarian archaeological discipline during the interwar period. Yet, Perperikon remained interpreted as a medieval episcopal residence from the fourteenth century following Jirecek's identification. The time between World War I and World War II is considered however to be unsuccessful in the national integration. Therefore a number of Bulgarian intellectuals turned to the task of uncovering Bulgarian *Volksgeist*, "the national spirit." Influenced by the Western studies of antiquity, many of them became obsessed with searching the origins of the Bulgarian nation by means of "resurrection" of antiquity. The lack of a strong international patron or movement comparable to philhellenism for the Greeks or the "Latin" kinship of the

[2] Bogdan Filov (1883–1945) is a famous Bulgarian archaeologist, art historian, and politician. He was the Prime Minister (1940–1943) of Nazi allied Bulgaria. Sentenced to death he was executed on the 2nd of February 1945.

Romanians stimulated and activated the intensive search for heroic figures. In the second half of the nineteenth and the beginnings of the twentieth century some Western archaeologists and classical philologists claimed that the Cult of Dionysus usually associated with Orpheus was of Thracian origin. They associated them with the belief of immortality and presented it as "salient trait" of the Thracian "national religion" (Marinov 2015: 17–18). Thus the archetypal figures of Orpheus and Dionysus are ancestral even if mythical figures began to occupy a central position. This trend became visible in some ethno-philosophical writings searching for the Bulgarian "national character" and "essence." These writings gave the Bulgarians an important Thracian ancestry making them "the focus of the world history" (Marinov 2015: 86–87; Lazova 2016: 150–159). These ideas would attain exclusive significance and would become the mainstream in the theories of Bulgarian Thracological School from the 1970s, onward.

About the end of the 1940s, and mainly in the 1950s, the strong modernization impulse of the communist national(ist)-ideological project intensified the production of knowledge about the ancient past. It is archaeology that gained a crucial role for representing the material "truths" necessary to forge a valuable past for the nation. A specific characteristic of historical research in Bulgaria was marked by the Soviet theory of ethnogenesis (Lazova 2016: 110–124). The "national(ist) continuum" institutionalized by the Bulgarian *Altertumswissenschaft* in the interwar period is remarkably reinforced by the "new" rhetoric nourished by the Soviet theory of ethnogenesis under the dictate of historical materialism. Methodologically, it reanimated the symbiosis of the romantic ideas and the positivistic approaches of the nineteenth century, typical for the culture-historical approaches. Still more, ethnic archaeology was strongly inspired by the G. Kossinna concept of the archaeological culture and widely popularized by Go rdon Childe.[3] It attached an ethnic group to objective, relatively durable, and fixed criteria, such as language, territory, dress, and other cultural traditions (Gellner 1980; Shnirelman 1995: 120–128; Kohl 1998: 230–233). Thus, in parallel with the virulent critique of the "bourgeois" science of antiquity, the "new" communist rhetoric was supposed to overcome the "bourgeois culture," the "Bulgarian fascism and chauvinism" which would help to develop "new scientific programs." This "new line" in Bulgarian historical scholarship supported the officially sanctioned Soviet conception of *ethnos* characterized as primordialist or essentialist (Kohl 1998: 231). Introducing this concept, Bulgarian academic development in the field of history and archaeology remained isolated from the contemporary debates and new methodological insights produced in Western scholarship. It contrasted sharply with the more situational and relational concepts of ethnic identity developed by most Western anthropologists (Eriksen 2010: 1–22). All methodological devices in Bulgaria were supposed to be coordinated with the Soviet archaeology as "the true science." Guided by the quest

[3]Gordon Childe (1892–1957) is an influential Australian archaeologist and philologist who was the proponent of the culture-historical approach to archaeology. He adopted the concept of "culture" from G. Kossinna and was influenced by Marxist ideas on societal development. His works are still influential in Bulgaria.

for origins, the function of antiquity remained unchanged—to supply the nation with a prestigious remote past. In the 1960s the Thracians were canonized as one of the three components of the Bulgarian nation together with the Slavs and Proto-Bulgarians (Iliev 1998; Marinov 2015). Stigmatizing prewar nationalism, communist modernization project implicitly used its discourse but with new rhetoric of the specific Thracian "spirituality." Still more, the uniqueness of the Thracian culture has been embedded in the national imagination on a much greater scale through a series of national research programs; the ideological institutions of Bulgarian Academy of Science and the centralized sponsorship of the state fully realized them.

In the 1970s and 1980s many schools in the social sciences attacked the incapacity of culture-historical approaches in archaeology with the goal of explaining the artifacts properly outside their nationalist interpretations. New paradigms try to provide explanations for social processes lying behind the descriptive accounts of culture-historical approaches. Thus the archaeological practices in many universities began to follow the mainstream of sociocultural anthropology. The "innocence" of the archaeological discipline had been questioned and it began its shift towards ambitious theoretical innovations including reflexive research instruments. The ultimate academic challenge became to comprehend the economic and political factors that shaped these intellectual movements. A number of intellectual and broader social and political processes increased criticism of the objective and value-free nature of processual archaeology. They resulted in a fundamental change in the disciplinary culture of archaeology (Hamilakis and Duke 2007: 18–19). The reflexivity of the discipline revealed the processes of production of knowledge and the limits of the archaeological interpretation (Hodder and Hutson 2003). Therefore today archaeology of ethnicity is considered to be an impossible undertaking for the constructivist perspectives on ethnicity and national identity (Kohl 1998: 223–246). On the contrary, it is still very easy for the cultural nationalists to equate archaeological cultures with ethnic groups living there in the past. Many academic traditions influenced by Kossinna refuse to discuss their discipline's past. Although seminal collections of analytical papers on the history of German archaeology appeared and are considered to be a milestone in the study of German archaeology the old concept of G. Kossinna continues to work undisturbed by critical analyses (Härke 2002): many archaeologically outlined regions still correspond to certain peoples in all periods of time ("Bulgarian lands in antiquity"). The pursuits of ancient pasts remain unchangeable as the principle of the unswerving culture-historical approaches of the communist modernization projects including Bulgaria.

The theoretical unrests mentioned above do not affect the Bulgarian culture-historical archaeology as well. Instead, the "new" rhetoric of the modernizing communist project was activated by strong national programs sponsored by the state. It was framed in the "anniversary activities" especially the most spectacular of them—the 1300th anniversary of the establishment of the Bulgarian state. Thus at the beginnings of the 1970s, a powerful ideological imagery activated the study of antiquity. Bulgarian culture was considered to be an amalgamation of past-present-future built on the ground of the "national(ist) continuum." The knowledge about the Thracian *ethnos*, activated in the 1950s through the Soviet theory of ethnogenesis later in the 1970s, becomes crucial in the production of knowledge about the remote past. Still the nation has to be an ethnically homogeneous entity with common and inherited values of history, language, religion, and territory. It becomes legitimate through its origin from ancient communities, whose "revivals" are permanent care of the intellectual elite (Hutchinson 1994).

The modernizing communist project established an academic rhetoric based on two main trends. The first is directed toward cultivating "a true patriotism" of the socialist citizen. The second called for turning excavated archaeological sites into tourist attractions. This is also the time when tours of the "Thracian art from the Bulgarian lands" started to be exposed in a great number of museums around the world. This period might be defined as a time of intensive production of archaeological knowledge and encouraging its consumption. This so-called culture-historical heritage is marketed on the basis of the "unique spirituality" of the Thracian culture, a culture that is considered to be the legitimate heritage of the Bulgarians.

As was mentioned above, the ancient Thracians were canonized in the 1960s as one of the three components of the Bulgarian nation together with the Slavs and the Proto-Bulgarians. Therefore, the study of the Thracians has been institutionalized and most of the archaeological material has been reinterpreted according to the fabricated theories of the Bulgarian Thracological School—active mostly after the 1970s. The 1970s and the 1980s might be qualified as a period of flowering of culture-historical archaeology in Bulgaria, which has been associated with the Thracological School. Bulgarian Thracology was based on the so-called complex studies of the Thracians including studies in history, archaeology, linguistics, and ethnology. In this context, the specialized Institute of Thracology and the Department of Thracian archaeology within the Institute of Archaeology and Museum began their joint academic work. Thus, the philological pattern of archaeology typical for culture-historical method was fully established. Most of the scholars still easily relate archaeological evidence with the texts of Greek and Roman authors. Thracian antiquity was beginning to achieve high social status in public sphere. Bulgarian archaeology has been equated with the so-called Thracian archaeology. The process of ideological institutionalization also includes the organization of international congress activities centered around "The Thracian Gold" exhibitions.

The theories of the Bulgarian Thracological School were constructed, in fact, on the basis of the eclectic methodology shaped by a number of influences. The fundamental concepts were based mostly on the heritage of the Western European classical studies and history of religions from the nineteenth century and the first half of the twentieth century. As "the cradle of the orgiastic cult of Bacchus," Thrace was associated with the most influential theory—"the belief in immortality" as a "salient trait" of the Thracian "national religion." This claim had an enormous impact on the European classical scholars. Hence "Thracian" origin of the Pythian prophecies in Delphi (Greece) was proclaimed. These claims gave further grounds to identify the homeland of the ecstatic Cult of Dionysus with the Pangaean

Mountains in Southeast Macedonia (Marinov 2015: 17–18). It has to be added the Soviet concept of "Indo-European Studies," and the old-fashioned and anachronistic theories of evolutionist survivalism. After the 1950s these concepts were activated by the Soviet theory of ethnogenesis, helping to solidify the uniqueness of the Thracian culture. Thus the eclecticism of these out-of-date theories produced the so-called ideological doctrine of "Thracian Orphism"—an intellectual forgery of the Thracian "uniqueness." Following the interwar imagery of Bulgaria as a highly "spiritual culture" situated at a space of cultural crossroads, this theory is considered to represent the "ideology" of the "royal" and "aristocratic" Thracian elite. It became central in the construction of the "grand narrative," wherein antiquity occupies a privileged position in the national past. It was established by dubious explanations of ancient texts, which became the main focus of the interpretation of archaeological material. A number of national programs produced ideological constructions of ancient Thracian "spirituality" as an archetypal construction of contemporary Bulgarian culture (Marinov 2015: 94–95).

The symbiosis between these highly problematic identifications realized by the national programs from the 1980s and 1990s, sponsored by the state, and then marketed as culture-historical "authentic" heritage, supplied the touristic market with new products. They were proclaimed by the media and the newly liberated book market to mass publicity. The representations make visible the undisturbed "national(ist) continuum" between the late socialist and the postcommunist period following the main trends of interpretation before World War II. Thus, a number of archaeological "resurrections" were imbedded in social phenomena, which continue to constitute popular worldviews and mental orientations.

Production of Archaeological Narrative of the Site of Perperikon: The Archaeologist-As-Hero

As already mentioned the most spectacular "resurrection" of an archaeological site was that of Perperikon in Southeastern Bulgaria in the Rhodope mountains. The name of Perperikon was created out of several names similar in their articulation. Now Perperikon has been associated with Thracian antiquity because of the prestige attributed to it by the professional thracologists from the 1970s. The "resurrection" of Perperikon was realized by attributing the figures of Orpheus and Dionysus to the ruins known until then as a medieval site. These images, being central for the Bulgarian Thracological School, shaped the archaeological narrative, associating it with the early age of the site. Thus the theories of the Thracological School became the key to understanding the archaeological material considered up to now to belong to the Byzantine period. It had been presented as an ancient place with an acropolis, ancient sanctuary, a shrine, and a tomb. The fabricated narrative entered the public space through various media sources, publishing centers, guides, advertising materials, film representations, museum expositions, and many popular brochures.

Thracian antiquity, canonized in the ideological construction of the national identity, then turned into a marketable product for the tourism industry.

The ancient past of the site was inserted into the archaeological narrative by the leading archaeologist who is named and later self-proclaimed "Bulgarian Indiana Jones."[4] The figure of the archaeologist-as-hero was never explicitly discussed in Bulgarian archaeology, although the narrative became omnipresent. Very often this kind of narratives hinders professional archaeological publications. Such figures, in the role of activist/mouthpiece of the past, are omnipresent in the media and the Internet. The archaeologist-hero exploring the site of Perperikon shaped and heralded the centrality of this archaeological site for the last 20 years as "the top archaeological discovery in Bulgaria" notwithstanding the abundance of important archaeological sites in Bulgaria. After the active media campaigns—TV productions and newspaper publications—the archaeological work at Perperikon has been supported by state sponsorship. The state now tolerated only those archaeological sites whose participation in the tourist industry was unquestionable because of their ascribed national character. Today antiquity is needed not only as prestigious demonstration of national identity, but also as an asset in the touristic industry. Therefore, the site known before only as a medieval place now receives an additional narrative as a result of its forged life in antiquity. In the quest for continuity, a basic narrative has to be established in order to legitimize our remote past.

The "Bulgarian Indiana Jones" who comes from academic circles is obsessed by the theories of the so-called Thracian Orphism. It was fabricated in the 1980s as an aristocratic Thracian doctrine or "ideology" dating back to the 2nd millennium BCE, transmitted orally between those who were initiated in it preceding the Greek Orphism by centuries (Marinov 2015: 102–107). The institutional and emotional power of this theory in academic context becomes overgrown with formulations derived from its basic concepts; they had to be accommodated to material artifacts and thus the Thracian past would be "read" properly. This academically sanctioned doctrine forged by ideological academic institutions paved the way of producing a number of coherent narratives and thus marketing many archaeological sites as commodities. Thus power structures being internal to the archaeological discipline in Bulgaria influenced its nature. All kinds of archaeological narratives bear one and the same ideological messages designed for testifying the ancient-ness of the nation and for profit as well. A number of archaeological narratives are produced in a campaign called *The Wonders of Bulgaria* and realized by media competing enterprises.

The archaeological narrative needs its moderator. Therefore the main figure in constructing the narration is an archaeologist-as-hero who manifests abilities to launch important ideological interpretations by coupling the archaeological data from the site with the imagery of Orpheus and Dionysus. It represents a well-known narrative pattern discussed already as "an effective literary form to legitimize

---

[4] Nikolai Ovcharov (1957–) is a Bulgarian archeologist and thracologist, Associate Professor at the Archaeological Institute with Museum, Bulgarian Academy of Sciences. He is famous for his work on Perperikon and its tourist representations.

sudden changes or revelations in our understanding of the past" (Silberman 1995: 252). Thus the "Orphic" interpretation colors the general public's understanding of the archaeological data and gains currency among various publics. It was targeted for popular consumption mainly through the media, where these ancient figures were loudly pronounced as "ours." This ideological activism established a new setting for social communication. A popular discourse was born accusing the Greeks of taking away these figures from "us," the Bulgarians. As there is no academic debate on these issues in Bulgaria, it seems likely such a thesis to be generated in quasi-academic centers of power, which ensured financial support. This kind of interpretations easily took form of archaeological narrative as they are coined by the archaeologist-as-hero, who focuses on the continuum of historical development with beginnings, middles, and ends (Silberman 1995: 250). These archaeological narratives are used to legitimize modern territorial claims coupled with a kind of cultural uniqueness and thus they are transformed from mere historical description into a political essay (Silberman 1995: 253).

The dramatic "resurrection" of many sites transferred in the remote past is associated with Bulgarian culture revealing its "true" ancestors. These "revivals" accomplished by an archaeologist-as-hero actually produce cultural capital and thus turn into a resource for cultural nationalism. In the period after 2000, Perperikon occupied this central position with media assistance and the liberated possibilities of publishing popular literature. The market now requires an archaeological narrative focused on the national continuum restoring the primordial character of the nation and establishing its "otherness" as compared with the Greek-ness. Visibility is achieved by the figure of the archaeologist-hero who always unearths "unbelievable" artifacts, presenting them immediately to the media and its publics as something "unique." The uncovered secrets very soon become a matter of immediate common knowledge, mainly seen in the Internet. The newly uncovered places or artifacts are always named by the hero-archaeologist as he is the only one familiar with their ancient-ness. The archaeological narrative enriches periodically because of "new sensational discoveries." Sponsored by the Bulgarian Ministry of Finance, the results of the excavations are briefly reported in the professional publications of *Archaeological discoveries and excavations*. They are presented, however, in the medieval section reporting that cult activities from antiquity are registered from the Late Eneolithic period to the time of Late Bronze Age. The archaeological reports use the rhetoric suitable to advertise these "monumental" and "gorgeous" discoveries. This kind of rhetoric is quite atypical for archaeological publications, which focus on describing the artifacts found in situ (Lazova 2015).

In 2004 a brochure was produced—it announces that "a Dionysus sanctuary" was unearthed. It was compared with the Greek site Delphi, receiving the name of "The Northern Delphi." The name associates the old notion of already mentioned Western classical scholars who suggested that the Pythian prophesies in Delphi were of "Thracian origin." Mapping this association it tends to the success of the marketed ancient-ness of the place.

Very soon it was fabricated that this monumental rock complex was the residence (court) of the Thracian kings, including the sanctuary of Dionysus. It suits well the culture-historical approach to the Thracian culture phenomena whose main purpose is to outline the distinctive features of the Thracian "spiritual culture" in the context of its royal-ness. Later the rock complex was proclaimed as a "rock city" associated with a stone construction, famous for its identifying with the grave of Orpheus (considered to be located near the village of Tatoul). The ornamentation of these places with Greek imagery is a clear sign of forging a narrative by producing the desired antique roots of the site and respectively of the nation. It closely follows the interpretation fabricated by the Bulgarian Thracological School associating many artifacts with the Orphic doctrine. This school has already produced various scholarly discourses on the "otherness" of Thracian antiquity in the context of a well-defined Hellenic past. The statements of the archaeologist-as-hero produced a "memory place" which is accepted by the local population as a place of their "own" past. The "resurrection" of Perperikon is a result of the abilities of nation-state to politicize culture-historical methodology. It names freely the material traces identifying an archaeological site known before as medieval fortress with images from the Greek mythical past. The constructed archaeological narrative enters the media and becomes embedded in popular perceptions. A recent sociological research devoted to historical places considered to be formative for the Bulgarian national identity is indicative. Perperikon is one of the three stable markers which produces an ethnically homogeneous population because of sharing one and the same remote past (Lazova 2016: 259–260).

Scant are the announcements about this site in professional periodicals publishing the archaeological excavations. It does enter, however, into a number of luxurious editions entitled *Perperikon*. The rhetoric is ornamented with language typical of a tourist brochure, with texts describing a "mysterious civilization" with a "grandiose" ancient palace. It also finds its way as resounding news in the media. Alongside Bulgarian TV news, radios, and newspapers—CNN, RTL, and Euro News also reported the "sensational" discoveries. "The imposing excavations" are supposed to reveal 7000 years of history beginning in prehistory and ending in the Middle Ages. This long history of Perperikon is considered to be comparable only with that of Constantinople. This is emphasized as the reason why tourists are increasing in number and the state continues its sponsorship. We never understood however what do the tourists want to see and where do they come from.

As was already mentioned, the archaeologist-as-hero announces his discoveries almost every week in newspapers and in TV programs. His activist position forced a campaign *The Wonders of Bulgaria* which started in 2010. It takes the model of *The Seven Wonders of the Ancient World*, which is the first known list of the most remarkable creations of the classical world. It is known that this list was renewed by several companies in 1994 and in 2007 in order to find candidates for the present wonders of the world. The Bulgarian "wonders" are *sui generis* referendum not only to define the most important archaeological site but also to stimulate state sponsorship. The "scholarly" criteria are committed to the popular knowledge of different publics. This campaign aims at preserving and making popular the Bulgarian symbols of remote past but also at creating touristic site not only for the Bulgarians but also for foreign tourists. At the height of the campaign the managing editor of the newspaper proclaimed that "the historical heritage became again a national politics." The choice of the most important site is committed to the *vox populi*. Therefore, several booklets were published containing the "miracles" of the place. One of them discusses the predictions associated with Perperikon, some of which are of ancient origin associating them with the Greek Pythia. The other brochure is devoted to Orpheus as the oracle of the nearby site of Tatoul—widely considered to be his grave. The archaeologist-as-hero revitalizes earlier suggestions based on ancient Greek allusions that this is prehistoric cult place used later as sanctuary of Orpheus.

This line in the archaeological narrative corresponds to the propensity for occultism and esoterism typical for the cultural messianism of the communist regime from the 1980s (Marinov 2015: 95). The archaeologist-as-hero brings to light similar revelations communicated in some media who were anticipating the interests of future tourists. This embedded Perperikon in the esoteric discourse already institutionalized in the communist nationalistic discourses. Perperikon is related with mysterious solar gods and fire rituals. It is also associated with a mysteriously died-out script. The prophecies and oracular activity were a natural continuation of the interest in secret stories. A lot of narratives are devoted to fabulously rich treasures carried away from that place. Thus, the treasure hunter's folklore is also involved in the archaeologist's narrative expecting to gain the tourist attention. Thus, the tourist brochures are abundant with narratives about sensational discoveries, associated with the "civilization of the rock peoples."

These discoveries and their interpretation according to the theories of the Thracological School are absent from professional archaeological periodicals. The archaeologist-as-hero does not take part in any discussion provoked by his colleagues. He does not answer any questions concerning the invented narrative about the site of Perperikon. Many questions appeared not only on the Internet but also in the professional periodical "Archaeology." The hero-archaeologist also takes up the role of antiquity's spokesperson by visiting different TV studios. This kind of behavior is typical for an untouchable representative of power structures which are external to the discipline. This kind of archaeologists are welcome guests on many programs, including the culinary ones. The process of commoditization makes visible the process of transforming a dubiously constructed narrative about the Thracians through state-sponsored programs into popular knowledge—mainly through the Internet. In the postcommunist free market of "ancient heritage" the nationally approved interpretations of history gain much greater prestige. The cultural nationalism tolerated before exerts even greater influence on the professional standards of behavior and on the inner state of the discipline.

These "grand discoveries" which fuelled the "grand narratives" remain separate from the contemporary debates in archaeology. The interpretations serve the construction of the archaeological narrative considered by its author as suitable for the tourist market. They have however quite a short life, and after exhausting attractive plots for the national "grand narrative" the hero-archaeologist rushes off again in quest for the next great adventure.

The processes of commoditization of archaeological sites and artifacts raise questions on how ancient periods and sites are selected for consumption by the state, by the academy, and by individuals and in what ways archaeology and heritage are becoming commodities in the marketplace (Rowan and Baram 2004). This process is related to another set of questions concerning the ethical standards. The reflexive approaches reveal a number of archaeologies which form their research programs according to different viewpoints. The seminal work of Bruce Trigger (1984) outlining alternative archaeologies such as nationalist, colonialist, and imperialist might be completed with much greater number of archaeologies. The question is how to use disciplinary power of professionalization to provoke the ethical debates in archaeology. It is evident today that archeology develops highly technological devices of research whose results are difficult to be thrust in archaic epistemological paradigms. The archaeologists have to be able reflexively to outline the epistemological boundaries of their interpretations instead of announcing various phantasms as the only possible readings of the ancient past. The ideological interpretation is often hidden behind the scholarly categories of interdisciplinarity and objectivity. In order to prevent the nation to become a parody of itself, the idea to codify the basic ethical principles that archaeology should adhere is reasonable and has to become workable (Silberman 1995: 261; Hamilakis and Duke 2007: 21–22). Something more, the forged antiquity does not add much to its own value as many of the visitors might be aware of criticisms in the field of historical disciplines and their impact on the marketed heritage. As is well known today the essence of heritage is social activity embedded in a changing contemporary context. Therefore the nature of authenticity and the role of interpretation have to be constantly reexamined and redefined. This is the way to recognize the value of intangible traditions and social life they represent (Silberman 2006: 7). Thus the adoption of contemporary methods in professional academic archaeological practice contributing to its adequate interpretation is the device which might help to draw a line between ideology and epistemology.

References

Appadurai, Arjun. 1996. *Modernity at Large. Cultural Dimensions of Globalization*. Minneapolis, MN: University of the Minnesota Press.

Bailey, Douglass. 1998. Bulgarian Archaeology: Ideology, Sociopolitics and the Exotic. In *Archaeology under Fire. Nationalism, Politics and Heritage in the Eastern Mediterranean and Middle East*, ed. Lynn Meskell, 87–110. London: Routledge.

Bouzek, Jan, and Denver Graningen. 2015. Geography. In *A Companion to Ancient Thrace*, ed. Julia Valeva, Emil Nankov, and Denver Graninger, 12–20. Oxford: Wiley-Blackwell.

Danforth, Loring. 1984. The Ideological Context of the Search of Continuities in Greek Culture. *Journal of Modern Greek Studies* 2 (1): 53–85.

Daskalov, Roumen, and Alexander Vezenkov, eds. 2015. *Entangled Histories of the Balkans*, Shared Pasts, Disputed Legacies. Vol. 3. Leiden/Boston: Brill.

Eriksen, Thomas. 2010. *Ethnicity and Nationalism: Anthropological Perspectives*. London: Pluto Press.

Featherstone, Mike. 2007. *Consumer Culture and Postmodernism*. Los Angeles, CA: Sage Publications.

Gellner, Ernst, ed. 1980. *Soviet and Western Anthropology*. New York: Columbia University Press.

Gupta, Akil, and James Ferguson. 2001. Culture, Power, Place: Ethnography at the End of an Era. In *Culture, Power, Place. Exploration in Critical Anthropology*, 1–29. Durham: Duke University Press.

Hamilakis, Yannis, and Aris Anagnostopoulos. 2009. What is Archaeological Ethnography. *Public Archaeology: Archaeological Ethnographies* 8 (2–3): 65–87.

Hamilakis, Yannis, and Philip Duke. 2007. *Archaeology and Capitalism*. Walnut Greek, CA: Left Coast Press.

Härke, Heinrich, ed. 2002 [2000]. *Archaeology, Ideology and Society: The German Experience* (2nd revised ed.à Peter Lang). Frankfurt/Main: Wien.

Hodder, Ian, and Scott Hutson. 2003. *Reading the Past. Current Approaches to Interpretation in Archaeology*. Cambridge: Cambridge University Press.

Hutchinson, John. 1994. *Modern nationalism*. London: Fontana Press.

Iliev, Ilia. 1998. The Proper Use of Ancestors. *Ethnologia Balkanica* 2: 7–18.

Kaiser, Timothy. 1995. Archaeology and Ideology in Southeast Europe. In *Nationalism, Politics, and the Practice of Archaeology*, ed. Philip Kohl and Clare Fawcett, 99–119. Cambridge: Cambridge University Press.

Kohl, Philip. 1998. Nationalism and Archaeology: On the Construction of Nations and the Reconstruction of the Remote Past. *Annual Review of Anthropology* 27: 223–246.

Kohl, Philip, and Clare Fawcett, eds. 1995. *Nationalism, Politics, and the Practice of Archaeology*. Cambridge: Cambridge University Press.

Kotsakis, Kostas. 1998. The Past is Ours. Images of Greek Macedonia. In *Archaeology under Fire. Nationalism, Politics and Heritage in the Eastern Mediterranean and Middle East*, ed. Lynn Meskell. London: Routledge.

Lazova, Tsvete. 2015. Perperikon entre nature et histoire: les dimensiones multiples d'une site archeolgique et le peysage de identite Bulgare. In *Etudes Balkaniques: Paysage religious et memoriels en Europe du Sud-Est: visions anciennes, pratique et politiques recentes*, 221–247. Paris: Association Pierre Belon.

———. 2016. *Antichnost, Archeologia i Natsionalno Vaobrazjavane. Antropologichni perspektivi* [Antiquity, Archaeology and National Imagination. Anthropological Perspectives]. Sofia: New Bulgarian University Press.

Marcus, George, and Michael Fisher. 1986. Anthropology as Cultural Critique: An Experimental Moment in the Human Sciences, Chicago and London : The University of Chicago Press.

Marinov, Tchavdar. 2015. Ancient Thrace in the Modern Imagination: Ideological Aspects of the Construction of Thracian Studies in Southeast Europe (Romania, Greece, Bulgaria). In *Entangled Histories of the Balkans. Vol. 3. Shared Pasts Disputed Legacies*, Balkan Studies Library, ed. Roumen Daskalov and Alexander Vezenkov, vol. 16, 10–118. Leiden: Brill.

Meskell, Lynn. 1998. *Archaeology Under Fire: Nationalism, Politics and Heritage in the Eastern Mediterranean and Middle East*. London: Routledge.

Rowan, Yorke, and Uzi Baram, eds. 2004. *Marketing Heritage. Archaeology and the Consumption of the Past*. Walnut Creek, CA: Altamira Press.

Shnirelman, Victor. 1995. From Internationalism to Nationalism: Forgotten Pages of Soviet Archaeology in the 30s and 40s. In *Nationalism, Politics and the Practice of Archaeology*, ed. Philip Kohl and Clare Fawsett, 120–138. Cambridge: Cambridge University Press.

Silberman, Neil. 1995. Promised Lands and Chosen peoples: the Politics and Poetics of Archaeological Narrative. In *Nationalism, Politics and the Practice of Archaeology*, ed. Philip Kohl and Clare Fawcett, 249–262. Cambridge: Cambridge University Press.

Silberman, Neil. 2008. Chasing the Unicorn? The quest for "essence" in digital heritage – In: Yehuda E. Kalai, Thomas Kvan & Janice Affleck (eds). New Heritage. New Media and Cultural Heritage. London and New York: Routledge, 81–91.

Todorova, Maria. 1992. Historiography of the Countries of Eastern Europe: Bulgaria. *American Historical Review* 4: 1105–1117.

———. 2015. Is There Weak Nationalism and Is It a Useful Category. *Nation and Nationalism* 21 (4): 681–699.

Trigger, Bruce. 1984. Alternative Archaeologies: Nationalist, Colonialist, Imperialist, *Man* 19 (3): 355–370. New Series.

———. 1995. Romanticism, Nationalism, and Archaeology. In *Nationalism, Politics and the Practice of Archaeology*, ed. Philip Kohl and Clare Fawcett, 263–279. Cambridge: Cambridge University Press.

———. 2008. *A History of Archaeological Thought*. Cambridge: Cambridge University Press.

Velkov, Velizar. 1993. Archaeology in Bulgaria. *Antiquity* 67 (254): 125–129.

Modernization and the Department Store in Early-Twentieth-Century Japan: Modern Girl and New Consumer Culture Lifestyles

Tomoko Tamari

Introduction

This chapter focuses on the way in which the department store became a key site for the constitution of Japanese modernity in early-twentieth-century Japan. The department store not only provided new goods along with pragmatic ideas of how to use and how to evaluate them, but also sought to promote images and advice on how to integrate the "new" into existing lifestyles and value systems. These pragmatic exercises carried particularly significant meanings for expanding new middle class and increasing urban working women to construct their new femininities. The department stores were also a new urban consumer space. They provided spectacular theatrical space utilizing atmospheric lighting and well-organized combination of colors, calculatedly set out commodities, provoked a dream-like theatricality to create visual and sensory pleasures, which evoked a new type of aesthetic sensibility. Urban middle class, particularly female modern consumers, who were often identified as new women who sought to be modern as opposed to be traditional, enjoyed and embodied new consumer experiences.

The Japanese department store also fitted closely with the state's governmental policy, "reform of everyday life," which educates people to be modern citizen and emphasized rationalization and efficiency in many elements of lifestyles. In this sense, the department store played a key role as a political institution to implement the government policies into new lifestyles they provided.

Hence in the Japanese case, the emergence of modern consumer culture can be understood as one of the consequences, coupled with both a reflection of the desire to be modern with new lifestyles which department store provided and the government-led reform of everyday life policy which department store helped to implement as part of the Japanese modernization process.

T. Tamari (✉)
Goldsmiths, University of London, London, UK
e-mail: t.tamari@gold.ac.uk

E. Krasteva-Blagoeva (ed.), *Approaching Consumer Culture*, International Series on Consumer Science, https://doi.org/10.1007/978-3-030-00226-8_10

In these processes, women were responsible for organizing a range of new lifestyle practices and acted as domestic engineers. Therefore, housewives were particularly targeted as a major consumer for the department store. The department store was also one of the key sources for the new woman who sought fashionable and stylish urban lifestyles, which in many ways resembled Western styles.

In order to better understand the complex dynamic between the burgeoning consumer culture, new lifestyles, new woman, and new urban spaces, the aim of this chapter is to explore how a particular important department store, Mitsukoshi, contributed to the formation of modern lifestyle and provided a significant women's public sphere in early-twentieth-century Japan. It would be useful to address the following questions as our point of departure: In what ways did department stores actually play an important role to translate, and deliver modern lifestyles and new values to people? To address this question, we will discuss the birth of the department store in general and the historical background to Japan's first department store, Mitsukoshi, in particular, especially focusing on its role as a forerunner, providing a new style of merchandising. The focus will also be on architectural and interior design as a new urban cultural form in order to consider how such carefully designed spaces could evoke new sensitivities, the sensory pleasure of consumer experiences.

The Department Store and New Consumer Experience

The Birth of the Department Store

The first department stores in the West developed and became the vanguard of retail merchandising in the second half of the nineteenth century. The new type of retailing space was one of the responses to urban development, industrialization, new pattern of distribution, production, and consumption. They also provided a new form of women's public spheres. The definition of a department store did not emerge until 1890 in the West, but it briefly refers to two different types. One was a general shop in town which supplied commodities for the local market, and the other was an urban shop which dealt with specific commodities with a narrow range of goods. As urbanization transformed towns into cities, the general shop eventually became a large-scale retailer, the forerunner of the department store (Benson 1986: 13).

Japanese department stores also have their forerunners which came from different historical trajectories to their Western counterparts. It is often argued that the original inspiration of Japanese department store as a new type of retailing space could be linked to Japan's experience of international exhibitions.

Department stores globally developed over the same period as the rise of international exhibitions—especially the London International Exhibitions in 1851. The 19th international exhibitions were crucial in developing a global stage that displayed the Western nations' hierarchy via a classification system that displayed the power differences between nations. Japan soon learnt the cultural potential and political power of exhibition and started to participate in future exhibitions, such as Paris in 1869, Vienna in 1873, Philadelphia Centennial Exhibitions in 1876, and the World's Columbian Expositions in Chicago in 1893. Japan also started to organize domestic exhibitions, such as *Kokunai Kangyo Hakurankai* (Domestic Marketing Promotion of Industry Exhibition) held in Ueno Park, Tokyo, in 1878.

The exhibition displayed various goods and handicraft from all over Japan and gained massive public interest. After the exhibition, a good number of remainder goods were often sold off at the site, which was called Kankoba. The first Kankoba opened in 1878 and many others followed throughout Japan. They were not just places where goods were more attractively displayed and customers invited to walk around and inspect them, but they were also entertainment places with many of the similar functions found in the department store. They usually had a coffee house and confectionary parlor and sometimes hairdressing salon, photographic studio, and ornamental garden with teahouse. Although their buildings were effectively much smaller than department store, they seemed to draw on many of the architectural features of department store, with brick construction and flat roofs with towers. The term *Kankoba* in Japanese means "a seeing place." This emphasized that all the goods were designed to be displayed in front of the eyes of their customers. This new type of consumer place, consequently, captured retailers' and merchants' interest. Hence, it could be argued that *Kankoba* could be seen as a forerunner of the Japanese department store (Hatsuda 1993).

Department Stores as New Urban Spectacular Spaces

While *Kankoba* as "a seeing place" often offered a limited space, the early department stores were usually more spectacular large buildings in cities.

The large scale of building which was a distinctive feature of department stores can be traced back to the history of the Western department stores. Interestingly we can find that the burgeoning department stores have similarities with nineteenth-century European architecture characterized by application of new technologies at that time.

It is generally accepted that the first true large-scale realization of glass and cast-iron architecture was, as Wolfgang Schivelbusch (1986) pointed out, the Crystal Palace, which was built for the Great Exhibition in London 1851. This was

> "a hothouse that has drawn inwards everything that was once on the outside" (Sloterdijk 2014: 12).

This extensive space with its huge glass areas was well lit and created new spatial experiences for the nineteenth-century Victorians.

In the following decades, in the wake of Crystal Palace, the style was adopted in the grand buildings of the Universal Expositions, which were held in many cities in Europe and the United States. This occurred at the same time as department stores developed. Department stores were among the first to follow the use of the new glass and cast-iron technology to make possible relatively huge, bright, and airy consumption places (Williams 1982). They often had a multistory top-lit atrium which enabled display on a massive scale in the store building. They also incorporated show windows with large plate glass at the street level. All these aestheticized retailing space were devoted to attracting customers to visit and spend the day inside the store. It evoked an unprecedented spectacular imagining in urban space. Hence, department stores in the nineteenth-century Europe have been variously described using terminologies such as "cathedrals of consumption" (Crossick and Jaumain 1999) and "panoramatic" space (Schivelbusch 1977). This terminology, which emerged contemporaneously with the birth of the stores, shows the multi-faced character of the department stores as a new cultural form.

The First Japanese Department Store, Mitsukoshi

We can see some similarities in the historical development of the Japanese department store. Japan's first department store, Mitsukoshi Gofukuten,[1] completed a new headquarters "flagship" building in Nihonbashi, Tokyo, in 1914.

The building was applied Renaissance style with the use of white brick and the format of the building comprised of an underground floor and five stories with a total area of 13,210 square meters. This magnificent spectacular premise was well equipped with modern technological facilities: elevators, escalators, and sprinkler system for extinguishing fires. There were also an elegant Western-style dining room and an elaborately outfitted common room for both staff and customers. The building expanded to contain a second basement floor and seventh story with a total area of 51,000 square meters by 1935.

Mitsukoshi applied a variety of designs decorate its interior to enhance the theatrical effect. The most impressive aspect was the central staircase and the huge glass ceiling which let in a lot of light along with the huge scale of the interior space, which helped creating an overwhelming atmosphere. The high-celling main hall had a huge stained-glass roof which reminds us of the Crystal Palace International Exhibition in London in 1851. The interior design also recalls that of the world's first department store, Bon Marché in Paris.

Mitsukoshi from an early point started to recognize the power of theatricality and paid attention to the details of interior design to create a spectacular space. Reflecting to this new merchandizing, Hayashi Kohei, Mitsukoshi's first chief interior designer

[1] It is generally accepted that Mitsukoshi was established as the first Japanese department store in the 1900s. "*Gofukuten*" in Japanese means draper store. (Mitsukoshi Gofukuten started using the official name "Mitsukoshi" in 1928.) Mitsukoshi was originally a draper's store, "Echigoya," founded by Mitsui Takatoshi in 1673. He opened drapery shops in Kyoto, Osaka, and Edo (Tokyo) to expand his business, which included not only a drapery shop, but also banking activities in 1683. This business provided strong financial background for Echigoya (later became Mitsui Gofukuten) to eventually become part of the Mitsui group ("*Zaibatsu*").

who allegedly became the first professional interior designer in Japan, was sent to the United States in 1904 to study window displays and then got a job in the first-class interior design shop, Maples in London, for a year.

Thanks to the advent of new technologies in the West, many retailers, such as department stores, could use large glass panel for window displays. By using atmospheric lighting, along with the well-organized combination of colors, and the carefully calculated theatrical display of commodities, a new range of visual and sensory pleasures could be stimulated.

Window Display, Architecture, and Sensory Pleasure

In the window displays, each commodity was carefully located in relation to each other and the objects were initiated into various scenarios drawing on everyday narratives.[2] Windows superficially displayed aspects of the everyday landscape along with new consumer commodities; the displays conveyed not just separated or fragmented images from everyday practices, but rather provided a wider continuity with everyday narratives through dramaturgy.[3] Hayashi was quick to learn and implement the power of theatricality and explore its effect on the consumers' sensory apparatus and feelings by manipulating the designed material environment and sense of aesthetics. He was fully aware of the importance of the "total coordination" of retail spaces in order to enhance both dreaming imaginaries and potential realities of luxury experiences (see Tamari 2016a: 90).

Here the emphasis is on the total coordination of a range of consumer spaces, such as distinctively designed architecture, interior detail, product design, and carefully organized display. All these create multi-sensorial stimulation. This aspect of spatial design has been discussed by Juhani Pallasmma, when he argues that architecture evokes a multitude of sensory experiences (Pallasmaa 2012: 75).[4] He is critical of ocular-centric visions of the world and emphasizes the importance of the tactile sense to understand our being-in-the-world. He also underlines the link between art and architecture stating that

> "(T)he spaces and places enticed by a work of art are real in the full sense of the experience" (Pallasmaa 2012: 74).

---

[2] There would seem to be some overlap with the concept of "the frame" in cinema theory referred to by Deleuze. "All framing determines an out-of-field," he explains (Deleuze 1986, 2017: 19). He remarks that the out of field "refers to what is neither seen nor understood, but it is nevertheless perfectly present" and "the frame teaches us that the image is not just given to be seen" (Deleuze 1986, 2017: 16), rather it can encompass all the potential component or the whole world in some way.

[3] Mitsukoshi sometimes used mannequins in the window display to enhance its narratives and theatricality (Mitsukoshi 1919 Vol. 9 issue 8).

[4] In his explanation of the bodily sensation and architecture, he argues that there might be a dialectic unconscious communication though bodily sensation between the architect and the person who encounter the work (Pallasmaa 2013: 71; Tamari 2016b).

This can be illustrated by the way the carefully designed consumer space can be understood as a site for arousing somatic multi-sensory experiences that lure consumers into the pleasure of luxury with the sense of aesthetics. The range of sensory experiences could activate the consumer's imagination and stimulate the desire to pursue fantasies and emotional experiences.

Accordingly, the new Mitsukoshi department store changed not only the way of selling, but also provided the new form of retail space, through grandiose architecture with theatrical forms of lighting and display. The goal was to create "spectacular space, a site not just for the provision of commodities, but for a new unban public space along with sensory and aesthetic experience." Hence for the customers, the new department store could aptly be referred to as a "dream world" (Bowlby 1985; Williams 1982), the place of phantasmagoria where desires could play (Williams 1982; Kawashima 1996). The place was also

> "a temple in which goods were worshipped as fetishes" (Featherstone 1991: 73).

Flâneur and Symbolic Consumption

Aestheticized consumer space and visual merchandizing can be traced back to the eighteenth century and become fully established in the large department stores in the mid-nineteenth century (Parker 2003). Such new type of merchandizing was famously expounded in relation to symbolic consumption by Baudrillard (1981, 1996, 1998). He contended that commodities were not consumed because of their use value, but because of their sign value. Modern consumers were attracted by the symbolic attributes of an object. To transfer the semiotic features and images of goods into the judgment of value of goods, forms of promotion and advertisement became significant. In this process, "cultural specialists" or "cultural intermediaries" (Bourdieu 1984; Featherstone 1991) often played a significant role. They could be seen as producers of symbolic goods and services in cultural industries (e.g., marketing, advertising, and mass media). It was indeed that visual merchandizing was one of the most effective components. Hence, department stores became ideal sites for cultural specialists and intermediaries who applied advertising with carefully considered sales slogans and designed visual promotion in order to manipulate the signs that could be attached to the commodities.

In Simmel's account of the modern life, he explicates the metropolitan personality who is an inhabitant in abundance of the signs in the metropolis. He states that

> "The psychological basis of the metropolitan type of individuality consists in the *intensification of nervous stimulation* which results from the swift and uninterrupted change of outer and inner stimuli" (Simmel 1950: 409–10 cited in Wolff 1985: 38. Italics in original).

Williams introduced Tarde's claim about "social man" who is an inhabitant in the metropolis:

> "(his) attention to the new environment is so potent and concentrated that 'these stupefied and feverish beings invincibly submit to the magic *charm* of their new surroundings; they believe everything they see' (Italic in original). --- In less extreme form this trancelike state is chronic among city-dwellers. The abundance of models to imitate renders their minds at once overexcited and numb"[5] (Williams 1982: 348, Italic emphasis added).

Tarde tried to understand city dwellers who were also modern consumers.[6]

The city dweller could also be seen as a *flâneur*, a central figure made famous in the writing of Benjamin on Baudelaire about the nineteenth-century Paris. The *flâneur* was the stroller who enjoyed observing and being observed, someone who loved to be free, to be in the urban crowd, and

> "celebrated artificiality, randomness and superficiality of the fantastic *mélange* of fictions and strange values" (Chmabers 1986; Calefato 1988 cited in Featherstone 1991: 24).

They were a type of modern metropolitan-character consumers who utilized a mobile gaze to enjoy the constantly changing flow of commodities, images and new sensations in the city, including the site of hallucinogenic dream worlds, the department stores.

The idea of the *flâneur* often focused on man's urban lifestyle and was criticized by a feminist Janet Wolff in a paper titled "The Invisible *flâneuse*" (Wolff 1985). She claimed that absence of women's lives in modernity and pointed out "the non-existent role of a *flâneuse*" in the cities (Wolff 1985: 41). For Wolff, women were less paid attention to articulate their urban lives and marginalized by theorists of modernity, since it was believed that women were caretakers for families, confined to the domestic sphere of the home, and had little chance to appear in public. It is also because

> "the literature of modernity ignores the private sphere and to that extent is silent on the subject of women's primary domain" (Wolff 1985: 44).

As we will see, however, the reality was more complex in modernity. Women became more visible in the city as working women and were also active and visible in public space (such as the department store) as a consumer as well as a

[5] Tarde wrote, "The movement and the noise of the streets, the store window, the frenetic and impulsive agitation of their existence, affect them like hypnotic spells. Now urban life, is it not social life concentrated and taken to an extreme? --- Society is imitation and imitation is a type of hypnotism" (Tarde 1900: 91, 95 cited in Williams: 348).

[6] Tarde's intention was to reveal modern consumer's mobile vision and sensory experience in expositions, automobile shows, movies, and perhaps department stores in the city. Williams explains Tarde's approach:

> "When he is faced with such spectacles, in the consumer's mind are mixed emotional hyperactivity and paralysis, envy and scorn, conscious choice and semiconscious obedience initiative and submission, desire and repulsion. The analogy with hypnosis emphasizes these ambiguities" (Williams 1982 349).

Hence, Tarde concluded that social man, the city dweller, is "a veritable somnambulist" (Williams 1982: 350).

salesperson. Nava pointed out that women in modernity were often depicted as the prostitute or actress-entertainer and with these featured as the major female figures in the urban landscape, and ordinary women were ignored. In fact, the middle-class women who engaged with

"the proliferation of philanthropic schemes in order to cope with the perceived crisis of the city - with threat of social disorder, disease destitution and inadequate housing Middle-class women as bearers of particular kind of knowledge, were involved on a huge scale in the process of disseminating information about morality, domestic economy, hygiene and child care to women of the working class." (Nava 1997:5) They were increasingly seen as unaccompanied women highly visible in the urban landscapes (- e.g. galleries, libraries, restaurants, tearooms and department store (see more details Nava 1997: 5).

Department Store and Women's Public Sphere

It could be argued that those who enjoyed most such new consumer spaces and experiences were the new middle-class women. They were the *flâneuse*'. At the same time, it was true that such designed and planned consumer spaces and new experimental innovations tended to be carefully calculated and accommodated to ensure that women consumers in particular could enjoy new aesthetic experiences.

The theatrical setting of the department store also offered a performing platform, "front-stage" area (Goffman 1971), which was not just for spectators or an audience, but for those who could enjoy performing ideal persona with new commodities. The front-stage areas also offered spaces where women could enjoy "looking" as well as "being looked at."

Department stores also provided "back-stage" areas in the changing rooms and powder rooms where women could try on novel commodities and enjoy an experience with new sensations. Furthermore, women also obtained a good deal of information and advice to help enhance their presentation skills. Through all these practices, women gained a complete package of resources for new identity construction through purchasing the commodities, which were needed to "get into role," and participate in the front-stage drama.[7]

Berger observed women and commented on their consciousness of their presence. He remarks:

> One might simplify this by saying: men act and women appear. Men look at women. Women watch themselves being looked at. This determines not only most relations between men and women, but also the relation of women to themselves. The surveyor of woman in herself is male: the surveyed female. Thus, she turns herself into an object—and most particularly an object of vision: a sight (Berger 1972: 47).

[7]Yet, at the same time, the department store offered women the capacity to engage in relatively independent action outside the control of men. On the other hand, it reinforced the traditional stereotype of femininity with the emphasis on dressing-up and making-up skills.

Hence department stores offered themselves as new aestheticized and sensory spaces which allowed women not just "looking" at others, but to be looked at, as both subject and object. The department store thus provided women with a new urban space to enjoy novel forms of consumer activities and to explore in relative freedom and safety in a range of urban sites outside domestic space. Here we can see the emergence of a woman's public sphere (Tamari 2006: 107 onward).

Woman as a Domestic Engineer

The department stores were not just a woman's public sphere, but also a political institute for the government. The period referred as "Greater Taisho" (Garon 1998), from 1900 to 1930, in Japan was the era in which "kindaiseikatsu" (modern lifestyle) suggesting a new or reformed way of life and "bunkaseikatsu" (cultural/cultured living) suggesting a more stylish, rational, and efficient way of life were developed. The term, cultural/cultured living (bunkaseikatsu), would seem to have become prominent in the 1919 Lifestyle Improvement Exhibition (Seikatsu Kaizen Ten) organized by the Ministry of Education, Science and Culture. In the wake of the conference, the ministry established the Alliance for Lifestyle Improvement (Seikatsu Kaizen Domeikai) in 1920, which sought to encourage improvement in all areas of everyday life in domestic space. The reform of everyday life basically encouraged thrift, saving and recycling.

This involved a redefinition of family life in the domestic spaces. Women were the arbiters of these new lifestyles. They needed to learn how to organize and order new things in ways which were deemed economic and rational.

As the department stores were always sensitive not only to women, but also to the government policies, they were affected by the governmental-led reform of everyday life movement. It can be argued that while on the surface there would seem to be a clash between the rationalizing austerity message of the reform of everyday life and the hedonistic consumer culture, in reality they fitted together well (Garon 1997, 1998). In fact, the reform of everyday life movement helped to generate a consumer culture with its emphasis upon changing fashions, styles, aesthetics and "new lifestyles." Consumer culture always sought to instill a calculating hedonism in consumers, who could plan and check, as well as succumb to the power of images and impulses.

Women as domestic engineers had to learn the new classification systems, the placement of objects, and the ordering things in domestic sphere. A constant introduction of new objects, styles, and ideas required continuous update classification systems. The department stores not only provided a tremendous range of new products and large amounts of information of new styles with new meanings and values, but also offered practical advice on the techniques and technologies of everyday life. As women became drawn into the world of consumption, they were increasingly asked to acquire the capacity to switch contexts between calculation and hedonism, rationality and emotion, and new public spaces of consumption and domestic domain of the home, as they grappled with the new lifestyles.

Working Woman as a New Type of Woman

The tendency for women to become a major marketing target could also be related to the increasing number of working women in the city. There are several reasons for the expansion of working women. Firstly, in the postwar reconstruction phase after the Russo-Japanese War (1904–1905) and during the First World War (1914–1918), there was a growth of women's job opportunities. However, the picture is more complicated, as the First World War boom led to rapid inflation and increases in wages with more favorable terms of trade for Japan, but after the war there was a sustained period of deflation and recession in the 1920s (Yamamura 1974: 302).

The first three decades of the twentieth century caught the Japanese economy in a number of cycles whose effects are difficult to evaluate. Yamamura captures the tensions and difficulty of reading the Taisho (1912–1926) and early Showa (1926–1989) economy:

> "The difficulties in evaluating the Taisho period and the early Showa years become obvious when we attempt to summarize significant events of these years. The effects of the First World War boom, with the strong impetus it provided for the industrialization of Japan, must be considered against the prolonged recession of the 1920s. The continued development of the heavy metal, chemical and other industries which made Japan an industrial power must be evaluated against the Rice Riots, stagnant real wages, a hard-pressed agricultural sector, the weak Factory Act, and other 'costs' to the Japanese people. The increased power of the *zaibatsu* banks and the emergence of a dual structure were an integral part of the Taisho economy (Yamamura 1974: 325)."

Chizuko Ueno, a leading Japanese feminist, argues that war causes a massive rise in both production and consumption (Ueno 1990: 184). Given this social-economic situation, women were seen as a ready source of cheap labor. This meant that it was possible for capitalists to employ large number of women at low wage levels.[8] A similar condition occurred after the major Tokyo earthquake of 1923, which took place in an economic recession, with the reconstruction boom generating a wave of prosperity. The same assumptions can be used here as that used to explain the "war boom."[9]

The idea to become a working woman was acclaimed by some intellectuals, who wanted to encourage women to become economically independent. For example, a socialist critic Hajime Akaba (1875–1912) was critical of women's economic reliance on men in the *Tokyo Shakai* newspaper, 5th June 1908 (Hayashi and Nishida 1961: 262).

In the research on working women by Tokyo City[10] conducted in 1922, an earlier Tokyo Recruitment Centre report from 1919 is cited—which shows the number of

---

[8] Ueno (1990: 184) regards war as a necessary "dumping ground" for an expanding economy.

[9] Women normally worked in more menial work for lower pay, and their position was more that of unskilled or semiskilled workers. They were not able to work in mainstream business management, but had to be content with the role of assistant or typist. It was very rare that women could become a manager.

[10] The 1922 data was incorporated in the 1924 report. This is the most significant early data.

working women at 3,581,183 (Tokyo City Research 1924: 65; Murakami 1983: 55).[11] With the total number of women in Japan at 27,000,000, working women made up 13%. With the expansion of the service sector, many new types of women's jobs became popular in the 1920s, such as shop girls, bus conductresses, telephone operators, and cinema ushers, which meant that women had to learn the new presentational skills, which we now referred to as "emotional labor" (Hochschild 1987; Smith 1999: 115).[12]

These new occupations not only improved women's employment opportunities, but also provided ambivalent images of working women. On the one hand, their image was more active, competent, modern, and (to some extent) glamorous. For example, the women's magazine, *Fujin Kurabu* in 1926 introduced women's new jobs, such as shop girls (August) and typists (September) (Saito 2000: 46–47). On the other hand, there were negative images and feelings that working women had become a "moral panic." This negative view was derived from the traditional dominant ethical view, which saw working women as morally irresponsible, and they were often criticized (Kawashima 1996: 114–115; Saito 2000: 90). The self-perception of some of the working women was, however, clearly positive. One working woman remarked that she only went to work to support her family, and that before this she was negative and in a hopeless state. Once she started to work, her self-esteem increased rapidly (*Jogaku Sekai,* Women's World *1921*, cited in Konno 2000: 76). Some women, then, gained confidence and enjoyed the challenges and difficulties of work.

Hence, the increasing demand for cheap labor, especially in the service sector, along with the positive attitude of women who sought the chance for self-realization, led to the situation in which greater numbers of women workers began to flow into the city. They started to enjoy the "new image of working women" which has much in common with the image of the "new women."[13]

Although the increasing numbers of women's workers were noticeable, the Meiji and Taisho government did not conduct research (Murakami 1983: 54). Therefore, it is hard to find reasonable statistical data. In 1923, the Osaka local recruitment center (大阪地方職業紹介事務局) compiled data from 69 recruitment centers and made a report on wage levels. This data could well be the first reliable data on working women (Murakami 1983: 55). In his investigation of working women, Murakami focused on the Tokyo City Research Report of 1924, which is the most reliable data on the conditions of working women.

[11] Hereafter this and subsequent research by Tokyo City will be referred to as "Tokyo City Research." All the researches cited which was conducted over a number of years between 1922 and 1938 were surveys of women's employment. Confusingly, there were also a number of women's employment reports carried out by the Tokyo Prefecture (i.e., larger metropolitan area) which are also referred to by year. Information for further research on women's employment for both Tokyo City and Osaka City is referred to in the same way.

[12] According to the 1924 Tokyo City research report, the increase in numbers of working women resulted from the financial crisis of the middle classes, the effects of the women's emancipation movement, and the transformation of the economy producing new types of jobs (Tokyo City Research 1924: 63).

[13] The Modern Girl is often described as one of the key types of New Woman. There were, however, some differences between them in the case of Japan. New woman was usually well-educated intel-

Shop Girl as a Symbol of Modern

Here we need to consider the department store not only as a consumption site for women, but also as a place where women worked. They were shop girls. They tended to be identified as a type of new woman. The term, "shop garu" (shop girl), was arguably coined by Shuichi Kitazawa in 1925 (Yoshimi 1995: 34). In his essay in the magazine *Kaizo*, he discussed sales women in department stores. *Kaizo* was one of the popular magazines which regularly featured new thought, new trend, and general interest topics. He wrote that saleswomen in the shop were often referred to as "jyotenin" which became the popular modern women's job in the 1920s. Kitazawa also asserted that saleswomen should be called "shoppgaru" (shop girls), since they were becoming a new type of woman who acquired a new sensibility and attitude. They were more tuned into modern tastes.

Kitazawa went on to remark,

> The best way to describe these saleswomen now, is to use the English term, '*shop-garu*' (shop girls). This expression seems to best express the characteristics of today's saleswomen: 'modern' (cited in Yoshimi 1995: 34).

The use of the Western language term ("*shop garu*") suggested something sophisticated and modern. Although they wore Japanese traditional kimonos into the 1930s, the image of modern could be inscribed into an image of shop girls who were seen as glamorous modern working women. They worked in the key modernizing institution for everyday living, the department store, which was full of the latest goods from the West and their Japanese imitations. It was a professed practical educational institution overtly concerned with spreading to the public the new skills and virtues of consumer culture.

As discussed earlier, Mitsukoshi was a good example in the way it prompted the flow of Western goods and tastes into Japan, and established "Mitsukoshi taste" which often compromised and bridged Japanese and Western styles. In order to introduce these new hybrid commodities and consumer lifestyles, the saleswomen were then one of the key groups who operated and explained this process to customers. They were encouraged to develop knowledge of the new modern tastes and lifestyles and to be informative to customers. This was the difficult task of learning how to operate in the new world of consumption and mediate this world to department store customers and the wider public. It entailed a complex learning process in mastering the new rites of consumption and their translation and mediation for customers.[14] In this process, they became to be seen as fashion leaders and tastemakers

lectually and often engaged with women's social and cultural problem. Writers, such as Hiratsuka Raicho, Yosano Akiko and Ito Noe were some of the famous figures as New Women. Unlike the New Woman, the Modern Girl often rendered as a girl who is apolitical, emotional rather than rational, and a hedonistic consumer in urban life.

[14] But they were also taught to educate/guide customers in a subtle way, which did not threaten established notions of gender roles. In effect, they not only had to successfully mediate Japanese and the modern Western culture, but also had to learn to mediate between the neo-traditional "good wife, wise mother" doctrine and the exciting style of the new modern girl.

for the public. Consequently, the shop girls obtained a symbolic power far outweighing their number in employment and became seen as prototypes for the new modern way of life.

Modern Girls and New Femininity

Despite the increasing number of working women in the service sector, such as department stores, we had to wait to the advent of the new term, "modern girl" which refers to a girl who looked modern, in a magazine. In his letter from England to his sister, it was Shuichi Kitazawa who probably first used the term, "modern girl" (*modan garu*, The letter entitled "The modern girl and self-expression - a letter to my younger sister in Japan" was published by *Jyosei Kaizou* woman's reform) in 1923. He explained about new type of women who had appeared in the West. They had become conscious of their capacity to live out their own lives and sought the new virtue of self-expression by rebelling against traditions and conventions. Kitazawa presumably used the term "modern girls" to refer to "recent girls, girls of the present moment, or today's girls." The images and connotations of modern girls were closely associated with the term "modern."[15]

In the aftermath of 1923 Great Kanto earthquake, metropolitan Tokyo recovered rapidly not only through physical rebuilding of the city, but also via resilient psychological strength among the dystopian landscape. Increasing hope for the future along with the continual "shocks of the new" enhanced the sense of intense modern life. The emergence of modern girls became seen as a part of this urban mass cultural phenomenon. A journalist, writer, and anarchist Itaru Nii defined and fleshed out the image of modan garu (modern girl). He promoted modern girls who were intelligent and witty enough to practice what they want without ulterior motives, or any specific political reasons. He explained that their lifestyle lives up to their desires and their practices were based on the individual freedom.

Both Kitazawa and Nii shared had the common assumption that modern girls were liberated from conventional women's ideology and had strong principles of self-respect and individualism. They could be considered to be a new type of women that emerged as a modern cultural phenomenon.

Another person who actively circulated the term modern girl in the 1920s was the journalist Kiyoshi Kiyosawa (Ueda 1983: 112). Kiyosawa saw the emergence of new type of women and their appearance as a clear reflection of a changing society. He argued that these women who projected the changing society should be seen as "jidai no sentan" (newest, most novel, and most modern of the time). Hence,

[15] The term modern and its derivatives modernity, modernism, and modernization derive from the Latin, meaning "just now," "of today," to the new moment as seen as a departure from tradition and previous times (Buci-Glucksmann 1994; Habermas 1981, 1985; Hansen 1995; Miyoshi and Harootunian 1989; Harootunian 2000; see the latter especially for a discussion of the use of the term by intellectuals in Japan in the 1920s).

women who have the newest styles and values were found to be the most modern of the time. We could call them modern girls.

Hatsunosuke Hirabarashi also thought that emergence of the modern girl was seen as heralding the start of a new age. Yet he further developed his insights into the emergence of modern girls from the perspective of modernism.

He argued that the emergence of the modern girl was not just an example of a new "fashion" among young women, rather it could be seen as an engine to change social mores, popular culture, and tastes (Hirabayashi 1928, reprinted 1975a: 389). For him, women were central to modernity and had the capacity to change society and to generate a new culture.

Interestingly both Kiyosawa and Hirabayashi saw modern girls as reflections of the far-reaching social changes accompanying rapid modernization. Hirabayashi however went further and argued that modern girls should not be regarded as merely passive projections of social change, but were active "creators" of new culture and lifestyles (Hirabayashi 1928, reprinted 1975a).

New Women, the Modern Girl and Consumption

Although female educators, intellectuals, and writers (e.g., Akiko Yosano and Raicho Hitatsuka) also discussed the Modern Girl in both a celebratory and critical manner, the Modern Girl was generally described and analyzed by influential male intellectuals, journalists, and politicians. For them, the Modern Girl was a new phenomenon, evidence of a new type of women born in the new era—modernity. In this respect, it can be argued that the Modern Girl could be emerged through male intellectuals' gaze and their imaginations. Hence, on the one hand, no matter whether she existed or not, the modern girl was seen as a reflection of modernity. Yet, on the other hand, it should be noted that, in fact, the Modern Girls were widely witnessed around the world in the first half of the twentieth century. The Modern Girl was a global phenomenon in the 1920s and 1930s (The Modern Girl Around the World Research Group 2008: 2). She was discovered

> "[i]n cities from Beijing to Bombay, Tokyo to Berlin, Johannesburg to New York, the Modern Girl made her sometimes flashy, always fashionable appearance" (The Modern Girl Around the World Research Group 2008: 1).

In this respect, we can think that she was not just an image and reflection of modernity, but incresingly noticeable as a new type of woman who was characterized not only by their new fashionable style, but also by their spirited challenge of the conventional and normative gender image.

It is often discussed that they were consumers. This is because they had to internalize stereotypical narratives of the Modern Girl and embody certain styles and tastes through consumption. A set of the commodities for the modern girls, such as face cream, powders, perfumes, cigarettes, cloche hats, and lipstick, were globally advertised and purchased. All these were important elements and tools for women to become modern girls. In fact, the expanding business of advertising agencies in the 1920s played a key role in promoting representations of "the Modern Girl as an advertising icon" along with "global flow of Modern Girl commodities" such as cosmetics (The Modern Girl Around the World Research Group 2008: 20). Consuming Modern Girl commodities and learning their immaterial signs and values, women were able to become active agents who could define themselves as modern girls through "technologies of the self" (Foucault 1988) in consumer culture. Consequently the modern girl became globally visible. She was seen not only in mass media such as advertisements and magazines, but also increasingly appeared in the new urban spaces, such as dance halls, cafés, theatres, beaches, tennis courts, streets, offices, and department stores. Inhabiting such public space, becoming a gaze object was central to the nature of the modern girl. She also objectified herself to perform as a modern girl.

She performed surrounded by a plethora of consumer goods. The real struggle arose in choosing among the abundant materials with different signs and values. Here she had to discover how to fit together various goods, values, and signs in a new harmonious hierarchy. This was a process that entailed the invention of a new form of associating values and signs. Hence, she played the role of a cultural agent seeking to new sets of cultural values and signs. In this process, she not only internalized all the traits and philosophy of the modern girl, but rather she became the dynamic creator of a new type of woman in modern society. Hence, according to Hirabayashi, her possibility and ability to redefine or to subvert existing dominant narratives and values in society became a matter of modernity.

Conclusion: The Aestheticization of Everyday Life

Hence, modern girls were incorporated into the public imagination not only as exemplars of the new modern styles, but also as prominent tastemakers. They established their social images as new women in a distinctive era. This era can be characterized by the expansion of women's work opportunities and the growth of urban culture along with an increasing number of consumer sites such as the dance hall, café, cinema theatre and department stores. All these offered theatrical space ("front stage") where modern girls could enjoy performing new type of femininity. Modern girls as modern consumers need careful guidance and advice about how to deal with all the new consumer products and new type of sensibility. They also acquired more extensive knowledge of modern in order to integrate them into existing meanings, knowledge, and narratives of everyday life. In all these processes, the department store, like Mitsukoshi, as a women's public sphere, particularly played a crucial role as an important information source and guide for new urban lifestyles by developing a significant cultural crossroad between the new and the old, the West and Japan, and modernity and tradition. All this helped to create conditions in which the modern girl could flourish.

Mitsukoshi not only become an important cultural reference point for the modern consumers such as the modern girls, but it also played a part in the wider sociocultural role in Japan's twentieth-century modernizing process. Mitsukoshi was a site of cultural intermediation in the formation of "the aestheticization of everyday life" (Featherstone 1991: 65).

According to Featherstone,

> "the aestheticization of everyday life refers to the rapid flow of signs and images which saturate the fabric of everyday life in contemporary society" (Featherstone 1991: 67).[16]

The domination of signs and images over the use value and exchange value of commodities was conceptualized by Baudrillard, who coined the term "sign value." The commodities of advertising, billboard, show windows and various spectaculars in urban and consumer space, like the department stores, constantly produce dazzling dream images which can stimulate people's imagination. The dream world, the department store, therefore inevitably becomes inseparable from consumers' fantasies. "The consumer tries to realize fantasies through merchandise," Williams (1982: 108) remarked. Especially when the fantasy cannot be materialized in actual life, people buy commodities which are associated with their fantasies so as to pretentiously perform or to compromise with their unrealizable desires. This could be a self-deception, but it enables consumers to enjoy their daydream. Hence,

> "people don't buy things to have things, but they buy things to work for them. They buy hope" (Leach 1994: 298).

The commodity has now a "hope value" which could be associated to a potential future one might/might not realize.

In modernity, the more real world becomes unstable with ever-changing dominant ideas and values with saturated signs and information, the more people's psyches begin to tune to a possible positive brighter future, and at the same time to expect negative dark uncertainty. In this light, we can understand that the emergence of the modern girl was a pure reflection of modernity. On the one hand, she was a hope. She was a new woman who cultivated herself as an independent, confident, and self-determined personality. Therefore, she was a new cultural phenomenon which suggested a beginning of desirable future in a new phase of society. On the other hand, she was an uncertainty. She could be a vehicle of the moral panic and destabilize established cultural values. Therefore, she was an undesirable phenomenon which created a fear of the destruction of conventional society. Hence, we can see that the modern girl herself was a product of modernity. She was born in the middle of burgeoning urban consumer culture and nurtured by modern consumer institutions, such as the department stores. The modern girl as a daydreamer in the

---

[16] Featherstone characterized "the aestheticization of everyday life" by three aspects: the effacement of the boundary between art and everyday life; the project of turning life into a work of art; and the rapid flow of signs and images in everyday life which is, he remarks, central to the development of consumer culture (see Featherstone 1991, Chap. 5).

department store was also a central figure in modernity. Hence, she turned herself into a "sign" of modernity.

Hence it can be said that both development of department stores and emergence of modern girls were understood as part of social and cultural phenomenon of the incipient period of Japanese modernization. In other words, they can be seen as a projection of social consciousness in new urban consumer culture. What they have in common is that the nature of department store's identity has always been changing, being a multi-faced reflection of an ever-changing society. This can also be found in the formation of female gender identity. This means that modern girls can be found in any times and perhaps in any society and culture.

Mitsukoshi's corporate advertisement in 2013 still reinforces this assumption.

They ask themselves what the department store should or would be.

Their answer is that "the future department store, to be a real department store, should rigorously and continuously transform" and their main motto used in publicity is "keep pursuing, keep transforming." Indeed, the same could be said for women.

References

Baudrillard, Jean. 1981. *For a Critique of the Political Economy of the Sign*. St Louis, MO: Telos.

———. 1996. *The System of Objects*. London: Jerso.

———. 1998. *The Consumer Society: Myth and Structure*. London: Sage Publications.

Benson, Susan P. 1986. *Counter Culture, Saleswomen, Managers, and Customers in American Department Stores 1890-1940*. Urbana and Chicago: University of Illinois Press.

Berger, John. 1972. *Ways of seeing*. London: Penguin Books.

Bourdieu, Pierre. 1984. *Distinction. A Social Critique of the Judgement of Taste*. London: Routledge.

Bowlby, Rachel. 1985. *Just Looking*. London: Methuen.

Buci-Glucksmann, Christine. 1994. *Baroque Reason: the Aesthetics of Modernity*. London: Sage.

Crossick, Geoffrey, and Serge Jaumain. 1999. *Cathedrals of Consumption: The European Department Store*, 1850–1939. London: Ashgate Publishing Limited.

Deleuse, Gilles. 1986. *Cinema I, The Moving-Image*. Vol. 2017. London: Bloomsbury.

Featherstone, Mike. 1991. *Consumer Culture & Postmodernism*. London: Sage Publications.

Foucault, Michel. 1988. In *Technology of the Self: A Seminar with Michel Foucault*, ed. Luther Martin, Huck Gutman, Patrick Hutton, and P.H. Amherst. MA: University of Massachusetts Press.

Garon, Sheldon. 1997. Molding Japanese Minds: the State in Everyday Life. Princeton, N.J.: Princeton University Press.

Garon, Sheldon. 1998. Fashioning a Culture of Diligence and Thrift: Saving and Frugality Campaign in Japan 1900-1931. In *Japan's Competing Modernities: Issues in Contemporary Culture and Democracy 1900-1930s*, ed. Sharon A. Minichiello. Honolulu: University of Hawai'i Press.

Goffman, Erving. 1971. *The Presentation of Self in Everyday Life*. Harmondsworth: Penguin.

Habermas, Jurgen. 1981. Modernity versus Postmodernity. *New German Critique* 22: 2–14.

———. 1985. Modernity: an Incomplete Project. In *The Anti-Aesthetic: Essays on Postmodern Culture*, ed. Hal Foster, 3–16. Port Townsend: Bay Press.

Hansen, Mark. 1995. America, Paris, the Alps: Kracauer (and Benjamin) on Cinema and Modernity. In *Cinema and the Invention of Modern Life*, ed. Leo Charney and Vanessa R. Schwartz, 362–403. Berkeley: University of California Press.
Harootunian, Harry. 2000. *Overcome by Modernity*. Princeton: Princeton University Publisher.
Hatsuda, Toru. 1993. *The Birth of Department Store*. Tokyo: Sanseidou Shoten.
Hirabayashi, Hatsunosuke. 1928. *Women in the Era of Falling Authority – Social Factor of the Emergence of Modern Girls*. The collection of Hatsunosuke Hirabayashi's Literary Critic Essays, Second Volume (1975a), 383–389. Tokyo: Bunsendo Shoten.
———. 1975. *The collection of Hatsunosuke Hirabayashi's Literary Critic Essays, Third Volume*. Tokyo: Bunsendo Shoten.
Hochschild, Arlie. 1987. *The Managed Heart: the Commercialization of Human Feelings*. Berkeley: University of California Press.
Kawashima, Yasuyoshi. 1996. *The Beginning of Columns for Women and Family*. Tokyo: Seiabou.
Leach, William. 1994. *Land of Desire: Merchants, Power, and the Rise of a New American Culture*. New York: Vintage Book.
Minako, Konno. 2000. The Creation of Office Lady, Gender as Semiotic World. Tokyo: Keiso Shobo.
Mitsukoshi's House Magazine. 1919. Mitsukoshi. 9(8).
Miyoshi, Masao, and Harry Harootunian, eds. 1989. *Postmodernism and Japan*. Durham: Duke U.P.
Murakami, Nobuhiko. 1983. *Working Women in Taisho Period*. Tokyo: Domes Shuppan.
Nava, Mica. 1997. Modernity's Disavowal: Women, the City and the Department Store. In *Modern Times: Reflections on a Century of English Modernity*. ed. Mica Nava and Allan O'Shea, 38–77. London: Sage Publications. http://roar.uel.ac.uk/4252/1/Nava%20modernity%27s%20disavowal%20falk%20ed%20version.pdf. Accessed 8 Aug 2017.
Pallasmaa, Juhani. 2012. *The Eyes of The Skin: Architecture and the Senses*. London: Willey.
Parker, Ken W. 2003. Sing consumption in the 19th-century department store: An examination of visual merchandizing in the grand emporiums (1846-1900). Journal of Sociology 39 (4): 353-371
Saito, Minako. 2000. *An Essay of Modern Girl – Two Successful Career Paths for Young Woman*. Tokyo: Magazin Hause.
Schivelbusch, Wolfgang. 1977. *Geschichte der Eisenbahnreise, Sur Industrialisierung von Raum und Zeit im 19Jahrhundert*. Munich: Hanser Verlag.
———. 1986. *The Railway Journey: The Industrialization of Time and Space in the 19th Century*. New York: Berg Publishers Ltd.
Shigeru, Hayashi and Taketoshi, Nishida. 1961. Heimin Newspaper Editorial Collection. Tokyo: Iwanami Shoten.
Simmel, George. 1950. In *The Metropolis and Mental Life, in The Sociology of George Simmel*, ed. Kurt H. Wolff. New York: The Free Press.
Sloterdijk, Peter. 2014. In the World Interior of Capital. Trans by W. Hoban. London: Polity.
Smith, Pam. 1999. Introduction: Emotional Labour and the Politics of Emotions. *Sounding* 11 (Spring): 114–119.
Tamari, Tomoko. 2006. The Rise of the Department Store and the Aestheticization of Everyday Life in Early 20th Century Japan. *International Journal of Japanese Sociology* 15 (1): 99–118.
———. 2016a. The Department Store in Early 20th Century Japan: Luxury, Aestheticization and Modern Life. *Luxury, History, Culture, Consumption* 3 (1–2): 83–103.
———. 2016b. The Phenomenology of Architecture. *Body & Society* 23 (1): 91–95.
Tarde, Gabriel. 1900. *Les Lois de l'imitation, etude sociologique*. 3rd ed. Paris: Felix Alcan.
The Modern Girl Around the World Research Group. 2008. *The Modern Girl Around the World, Consumption, Modernity, and Globalization*. Durham and London: Duke University Press.
Tokyo City Research. 1924. Tokyo City Social Affair department, Archive Document in Tokyo Metropolitan Library.
Ueda, Yasuo. 1983. *Modernism in Women's magazines, special issue Japanese Modernism, L'esprit d'aujourd'hui (Today's Spirit)*, 112–113. Tokyo: Shibundo.

Ueno, Chizuko. 1990. *Patriarchy and Capitalism*. Tokyo: Iwanami Shoten.

Williams, Rosalind H. 1982. *Dream World: Mass Consumption in Late Nineteenth-Century France*. Oxford: University of California Press.

Wolff, Janet. 1985. The Invisible Flaneuse: Women and the Literature of Modernity. *Theory, Culture & Society* 2 (3): 37–46.

Yamamura, Kozo. 1974. The Japanese Economy 1911-1930: Concentration, Conflicts and Crises. In *Japan in Crisis: Essays in Taisho Democracy*, ed. B.S. Silberman and H.D. Harootunian. Princeton, N.J: Princeton University Press.

Yoshimi, Shunya. 1995. The World of Depart Girls (2), RIRI, Vol. 247. Tokyo: Ryutsu Sangyo Kenkyujyo.

A Cultural Reading of Conspicuous Consumption in China

Min Zhou

With its rapid economic development, China is now gradually entering into the era of consumer society, in which consumption, rather than production, has become the dominate mode of social life. Consumption is not only an act that speaks of the individual consumer's personal choices, but also a symptom of general social reality that reflects the society's mode of existence and operation. It is via consumption that people get access into society and obtain a certain social status. Also, via consumption and commodity signs people interact with each other. It is the symbolic value, not the use value or exchange value of goods, which has become central. Therefore, as Mike Featherstone argues,

> "consumption can no longer be seen as an innocent act, but as part of the chains interdependence and networks which bind people together across the world in terms of production, consumption and also the accumulation of risks" (Featherstone 2007: Xviii).

Consumption is therefore not merely an economic act but also a cultural one, deeply and closely intertwined with culture and politics. In this chapter I will analyze a special form of consumption, conspicuous consumption, and I will try to examine the cultural and historical logic of conspicuous consumption in China.

A General Review of Conspicuous Consumption

"Conspicuous consumption" as a concept was introduced in the nineteenth century by Thorstein Veblen (1857–1929) to describe behavioral characteristics of the new rich class who used their great wealth to ostensibly manifest their social status, either real or perceived. In the twentieth century, the term "conspicuous consumption" was more broadly attached to people who had obtained a type of financial

M. Zhou (✉)
Institute of Literary Studies, Shanghai International Studies University, Shanghai, China

E. Krasteva-Blagoeva (ed.), *Approaching Consumer Culture*, International Series on Consumer Science, https://doi.org/10.1007/978-3-030-00226-8_11

freedom that allowed them to engage in the consumption of goods and services. They were motivated by symbolic value embedded in commodities and services, rather than by their practical use value. Conspicuous consumption of luxury goods in China is generally believed to have developed in the wake of China's entrance into a consumer society in 1990s. In fact, however, consumption of luxurious objects had existed in China's history. Philosopher Yang Zhu was the first person in Chinese history to encourage luxury consumption based on his philosophy that life is short and, therefore, it is important to realize oneself and enhance one's self-esteem, even if it means the owning of material goods. If Yang Zhu encourages consumption for the sake of self-realization out of a hedonist view of life, in an earlier period—in the time of Guan Zhong (719 BC–645 BC)—luxury consumption was encouraged as a way to increase employment and to boost the development of economy. Guan Zhong wrote in the book of Guanzi that before boiling an egg on fire, painters should be hired to paint the egg and to cut the piece of wood so that opportunities of employment could be increased. Doesn't this sound familiar? In his The General Theory of Employment, Interest and Money Keynes gave the example of filling a used bottle with banknotes, burying it in an excavated mine shaft, filling up the hole with city garbage, and leaving the money to be excavated by private enterprise again. As a result, unemployment would be resolved and social wealth would be increased (Keynes 1936: 129). The only difference between Guan Zhong and Keynes is that the former's method was stated 2000 years earlier and is more aesthetically appealing. Another example happened in the northern Song dynasty (960–1127). After a flood in the city of Hangzhou, instead of following the common practice of endorsing frugality in times of scarcity, the governor Fan Zhongyan (989–1062) promoted luxurious consumption of food, travel, and basic infrastructure construction so as to increase employment, which was so successful that it made Hangzhou the only prosperous city among the flood-stricken areas. Until the Ming Dynasty (1368–1644), conspicuous consumption had been very popular. Lu Ji (1515–1552) believed that if consumption was encouraged, this would consequently make common people's lives easier and if frugality was encouraged, it would be more difficult for them to make a living.

At various times, luxury consumption had been considered a moral issue. Sumptuary laws had existed almost everywhere including Ancient Greece and Rome, China, Japan, the Islamic World, and England. Such laws regulated people's attitude toward luxury consumption. They concerned mainly the imperial privileged classes. For the nobility, consumption of luxurious items was an expression of taste and a symbol of privilege, and for the lower classes it was judged as wasteful and immoral behavior. Mike Featherstone acknowledges that the spreading of luxury consumption in modern society is a democratic movement, thanks to the influence of media as well as the increased purchase power of the middle class (Featherstone 2014: 89). The consumption of luxurious goods is made conspicuous largely because of the symbolic meaning embedded in them, as well as their connection with status, identity, taste, and so on. Unlike ordinary commodities, they don't simply function in a utilitarian manner to satisfy a particular need; instead, they manifest, speak of, and radiate the desires of the consumers. Longing of symbolic power of the luxury goods, consumers fall under their spell—this reflects the way they perceive the world (Featherstone 2014: 93). Through conspicuous consumption the inner desire of the consumer who believes he/she is the one in control of consumption is shown. But in fact, it is consumption that controls the consumer. Thus the position of goods is transformed—instead of being owned by the consumer they are "the owners." The relationship between the consumer and the luxury goods is a dialectical one, like that of Hegel's master and slave.

Conspicuous consumption is not a privilege of the rich only. According to Virginia Postrel conspicuous consumption comprises not only socioeconomic behaviors practiced by rich people, but also socioeconomic behaviors common to poor social classes and economic groups. Displays of wealth are used by such groups to psychologically combat the impression of poverty, usually because such men and women belong to a socioeconomic class perceived as poor by the society (Postrel 2008: 1). Stanley and Danko found that Americans with a net worth of more than one million dollars are likely to avoid conspicuous consumption and that millionaires tend to practice frugality—that is, prefer to buy used cars with cash rather than new cars with credit, in order to avoid material depreciation and paying interest for a loan to buy a new car (Stanley and William 1998: 32).

The Development of Conspicuous Consumption in China

Although there are ancient precedents of the consumption of luxury goods in China, the practice did not become a major economic and cultural phenomenon until the late twentieth century. Since the 1990s, with the constant increase in the number of people of high salaries, luxury brands began to enter the Chinese market and the consumption of luxury goods among Chinese began to explode. Although the consumption of luxury goods in China started comparatively late, it developed very quickly. In 2005, China was the world's third biggest consumer of luxury goods. Only 6 years later, by 2011, it had become the second biggest consumer of luxury goods (Yuan 2013: 33). Not only in big cities like Shanghai and Beijing, but also in middle-sized cities like Chengdu, Dalian, and Zhengzhou, shops of luxury brands have been opened in large numbers. In 2015, Chinese people spent $118.6 billion on luxury goods, which amounted to 46% of such goods consumed worldwide ("Fortune Research Institute") (2016). Apparently, China has now become a superpower of luxury consumption. Why does conspicuous consumption thrive in such a way in a developing country like China, while its economy as a whole still lags far behind other developed countries?

To answer this question, we should keep in mind that before entering into a consumer society China was an underdeveloped society where frugality used to be enthusiastically encouraged as a great virtue. This transformation from frugality to extravagance is intrinsic to the structural changes of Chinese society and its transition from a planned economy to a market economy. The rise of consumerism is, therefore, an inevitable outcome of China's social transformation, as well as a result of the nation's political strategy in which consumerism was encouraged so as to maintain the government legitimacy. In other words, China's transformation into a consumer society is not only an outcome of economic development; it is also due to the fact that old social structure could no longer sustain the fragile economic and political structure of the society. The reason why people choose to pursue either frugality or consumerism is because the nation has successfully reconstructed the structure of their desire. In the years between 1949 and 1979, frugality was encouraged as a national objective or goal due to the political and social conditions of that period, when the People's Republic of China had just been founded and there was a mass shortage of commodities. "Thrift," as is generally understood, is a kind of psychological mechanism or mode of desire that restrains individual's desire to consume. Instilled as a longtime resistance to consumption, thrift is built into the mindset of the subject as an instinct and a habit, even an objective. Under this psychological mechanism, the subject's desire is restricted to a basic survival level. When thrift was advocated as a national objective, desire for consumption of something other than what was necessary was often condemned and looked down upon, whereas thriftiness was respected as a virtue. Luxury consumption, as opposed to frugality, is deemed immoral, even reactionary. For a long time, any consumption beyond the satisfaction of basic needs was condemned socially and politically.

If frugality is a rational habit of consumption typical of a developing or a premodern economy, consumerism tends to be more prone to instinctive consumption and is evident more often in wealthy societies. Consumerism, according to Wang Ning, is the outcome of industrial society, especially its postindustrial variant (Wang 2010). It is a psychological mechanism and a desire format that suits the surplus economy. It follows the principles of hedonism, materialism, and expressionism. Consumerism is a type of psychology format that is forever chasing new desires and the satisfaction of such desires. The transition from an agricultural society into industrial one is followed by transition of subjects' desire format (Wang 2010: 19). In agricultural or traditional society, the mainstream psychology for consumption is thrift; in industrial (consumer) society the mainstream psychology format is consumerism. The transition from thrift to consumerism looks like a transformation of subject's desire pattern, but in its essence it is a result of structural transition from the society of production to consumer society. In a planned economy, the desire pattern of the consumer tends to be edited according to the macroeconomic situation while in the market economy the desire pattern is let loose according to the macroeconomic situation. In the mode of consumerism, what people desire usually surpasses their basic needs; the search for pleasure, status, and self-realization is emphasized. Desire becomes a type of constructive force that transcends the restriction of basic physical needs. It is shapeable, moveable, and increasable, similar to the "desiring production" of Deleuze who sees every social order as built around particular systems of desire. What made mass consumption possible, according to Daniel Bell, is technological revolution, the wide spread of the use of home appliances like washing machines, refrigerators, and vacuum machines, as well as production lines and a credit system (Bell 1976: 57). Technological revolution and mass production constitute the technological-economic foundation for consumerism while the credit system and the mortgage system work as its financial basis. On the other hand, consumerism is also a cultural mechanism creating desires of the consumers.

Social Changes that Make Conspicuous Consumption Possible in China

Both China and the West have experienced this transition toward consumer society and consumerism where people's desires for material goods are set free and encouraged. What is unique about consumerism in China is that, unlike the West, where this process took about a century to transpire, in China it took only about 30 years. The transition happened so quickly because of the ideological work that the national government put into abetting and encouraging it. With the transition from a planned economy to a market economy, the nation's attitude toward consumption transformed significantly. Without the change of the nation's political strategy, this change would not have happened so soon, if at all.

In the first years after the foundation of the People's Republic of China in 1949, in order to realize industrialization nationwide as soon as possible, so as to catch up with and surpass capitalist countries, the development of heavy industry was prioritized. Therefore, the major resources of the nation were used in the development of heavy industry. The emphasis then was on accumulation rather than consumption. To reduce the cost of industrialization, the salary of the workers had to be reduced. To realize this, the prices of basic life necessities had to be put under control. The government therefore had to monopolize the buying and selling of agricultural and sideline products so as to control their prices. The principle of low salary and a rationing system was thus applied in order to bring the basic consumption level under control. Within such a system, people led a life of extreme austerity. In a nation that lacked necessary resources, control of consumption itself was not enough; it also had to cultivate the laborers' motivation and their enthusiasm, which was actually the only advantage that China could draw on at the time, so they could put all their energy into national production. The Chinese Communist Party was good in connecting individual needs with the needs of the party and the nation. The objective of the individual was combined with the objectives of the nation so thoroughly that only the objectives of the nation remained. Through ideological and political propaganda at different levels, in a manner similar to what Foucault described as the "panopticon," individuals interiorized the national objective of frugality and made it their own personal belief. At the same time, methods like "criticism" and "self-criticism" were constantly used to condemn and diminish ideas like "individualism" or "hedonism." With such methods, the nation successfully made hedonism, consumerism, and individualism shameful notions as they were not in lines with the nation's collective needs. People who opposed such ideas were tagged as reactionary. They were seen as lusting after the life of the capitalists and were politically persecuted and socially excluded. Such mechanisms functioned as suppliers of meaning to instill ideas of collectivism, idealism, and asceticism.

In the time of the planned economy, people's consumption practices were thus instrumentalized and all desires that were not pertinent to the basic survival needs were viewed as contradictory to the great national objective. It was even considered a threat that was illegal and unjustifiable. Within this mechanism, thrift was made doubly significant. On the one hand, as a production of meaning mechanism, thriftiness was culturally legitimate. On the other hand, by combining the needs of the individual with the needs of the nation, the thrifty lifestyle was made materially more bearable. People were willing to live a life of austerity because they believed that by doing so they were making it possible for later generations to live a life of affluence and abundance. However, as the contradictions of the planned economy became more and more obvious—the lack of consumer goods and the decrease of people's living standards—the nation's promise of deferred consumption was manifested as vain and people's motivation was shaken. While their complaints of shortages kept increasing, people became less and less tolerant to frugality, which led to the decrease of their motivation. This lack of motivation further effected production of material goods and as a result a vicious circle came into being. Reform seemed the only way out of it. Since the traditional way to motivate people had lost its momentum, new ways had to be found. The Reform policy, which the nation began in late 1970s, propagated liberation of minds, which meant that the old ideological system based on frugality would face new challenges. In this historical and cultural context, the nation had to give up the old utopian ideology as the provider of meaning, while an ideological vacuum appeared as new guiding ideologies had not been formed yet. At the same time, due to Opening and Reform policy, as well as due to massive introduction of Western thoughts and ideas, old ideologies which kept China away from the rest of the world could no longer hold out. It became harder and harder to persuade the public that by practicing frugality, they were pursuing a sublime national objective. A vacuum of ultimate objectives appeared as the nation could no longer be the provider of overall meaning. This absence of national objectives led the nation to a state of uncertainty. It seemed that both the nation and the people had lost their sense of orientation.

It was under this political, historical, and cultural context that the famous "Shekou Storm" (2016) happened in 1988. Shekou used to be a small fishing village. In 1979, with the approval of the State Council, it was experimentally transformed into a special industrial area. In 10 years Shekou became a modern industrial port city and a focus of the whole nation as well. Everything that happened there attracted national attention. On January 13, 1988, a group of famous educators from Beijing visited Shekou. They traveled around China to deliver ideological lectures to the young people. Unlike any other places on their lecture tour, where young people accepted what they said wholeheartedly, in Shekou they were met with unprecedented questions and challenges. When one of the educators claimed that some people came to Shekou only to seek money and that the special zone should not welcome such gold-diggers, he was challenged. Someone of the audience said that there was nothing wrong with moneymaking if it was done in legal ways.

According to the young people, even though the gold-diggers came to Shekou for the sake of money, they also contributed to the development of the city. The educators then pointed out that there were some businessmen who donated what they earned to the nation and that such deeds should be encouraged. Some young people disagreed and said that those who donated did it not of their own will, but out of fear of the leftist belief that making money and being rich were wrong. For the young people, businessmen should proudly put the money they made into their own pockets as they contributed to the country when they accumulated wealth for themselves. One of the young people from Shekou sharply declared that there was no place for the educators' "old-fashioned" ideas in Shekou. He said that one should express one's love of the country in practical ways, not in vain, fake, and empty ways:

> "We express our love of China with our labor. We work for the country and should have the right to enjoy the fruit of our labor" ("Shekou Storm").

Triggered by this, very heated discussions arose regarding individualism, the meaning of life, the role of the market, and so on. The next day after the discussion, 14th of January 1988, one of the educators published a paper criticizing how polluted the minds of the young people in Shekou had become. On the 1st of February, Shekou Newsletter published an article criticizing the three educators' ideas as being out of date and rigid. Ten days later, Yangcheng Evening reported on this debate again. Soon discussions regarding this case expanded and on the 6th of August 1988 the most famous national paper, People's Daily, published a 7000-word essay about what had happened in Shekou and it opened a column for discussion. From August 8th until September 14th, People's Daily received 1531 readers' letters. Among them only 17.4% were on the side of the educators. Hundreds of local media got involved and it was commonly accepted that new ways were needed to implement ideology education and new standards should be established ("Shekou Storm").

Not many people would think of the "Shekou Storm" when talking about the consumer culture in China today. Yet it actually established the basic cultural soil for a consumer culture to flourish in China. The legitimacy of individualism, as well as people's right to enjoy the fruit of their labor advocated then, was very important for the emergence of luxury consumption in China because, as we have already seen, for many years consumption itself was something to be ashamed of in Chinese culture. In the context of the discussion around "Shekou Storm" young people's demand to express their will and their individualist spirit was combined with the psychological motivations of conspicuous consumption.

In retrospect, the development of the phenomenon of luxury consumption in China can be roughly divided into three periods. The first period from 1979 to 1997 coincides with the time when China entered the World Trade Organization. In the beginning of the Opening and Reform, few reports on consumption were published because the majority of Chinese people were still struggling for basic food and clothing at the level of survival. The first two famous foreign brands that entered China were Pierre Cardin and RADO, both in 1979. RADO's first TV advertisement ran for 1 min on the Shanghai TV Channel at 6 pm on the 15th of March 1979. In the same year, Pierre Cardin had its first fashion show in Beijing. Roughly speaking, this was a period when luxury consumption in China started increasing and slow cultivation of people's sense for and appreciation of luxury commodities began. Chinese people commenced learning about and enjoying luxury goods, which together with the new social zest for being rich had become a very conspicuous phenomenon nationwide. The second stage of luxury consumption can be roughly put between the time when China entered the WTO in 1997 and 2013, when the national anti-corruption campaign swept the country. In this period conspicuous consumption was completely rooted in China and it became an important social indicator of the fluidity of social classes. Unlike the first period when people mainly shopped for luxury goods inside China, with the deepening of the opening policy more and more Chinese began to travel and shop abroad. In 2010, more than 50% of the consumption of luxury goods was acquired outside China. Besides the fact that there are more choices in foreign shops, another very important reason is that because of the taxes China imposed on imported goods, the prices of luxury goods could vary drastically inside and outside of the country. During this period, China became the world's second biggest market for luxury goods. The third stage of luxury consumption began with a drastic drop in sales. It is commonly attributed to the anti-corruption movement in China since gift culture had played a large role in the rise of luxury consumption in China (buying luxury goods as gifts (for bribery) was not an uncommon practice before the anti-corruption campaign in the country).

Characteristics of Conspicuous Consumption in China

From the beginning of the development of luxury consumption in China, some prominent characteristics made it distinctive from the process in the West. First, in terms of the group of luxury consumers, unlike the West, where people between the age of 40 and 70 are the majority of consumers of luxurious goods, in China frequent shoppers of luxurious goods are people under the age of 40, chiefly businessmen, their teenage children, and popular stars. Many young people born in the 1980s are fans of luxury goods as well—the so-called Guan Erdai (second generation of the officials) and Fu Erdai (second generation of the rich, who are more aware of luxury brands). Second, the purpose of conspicuous consumption in China tends to be more irrational. Many people buy out of vanity, for the sake of "image," without considering the cultural and historical connotations or consequences of the product. Very often consumers' choice of luxury goods is solely based on price, because they buy in order to impress other people. Third, differently from the West where people buy luxury goods for themselves, Chinese using luxurious goods don't buy them and people who buy them don't use them. This unique phenomenon is due to the so-called gift culture by which luxury goods have been significantly instrumentalized as a means for bribery. That is why all the buyers care about is the price of goods. The object exists in this gift economy only to function as a bearer of price. What comes next is that most people choose to buy luxury goods outside

China because of high taxes of luxury goods. Lastly, most luxury goods consumed in the country are foreign brands; only few of them are local products. This is so because consumers tend to be more attracted by foreign products and because Chinese luxury goods have not been fully developed and just few products are comparable with the foreign ones.

In addition, in China there is a type of luxury consumption practiced by ordinary people for special cultural events. Luxury consumption in the context of cultural domain does not necessarily refer to expensive goods owned by the minority group of the rich, but it can also refer to some rituals and habits. People often resort to extraordinary acts of consumption to express or obtain what they really need in social life, which is closely connected with issues of power, desire, regulations, and emotions. To understand luxury consumption comprehensively, we need to look at it not only from economic point of view but also from cultural point of view. What makes luxury consumption a cultural event is the cause as well as the consequence of conspicuous consumption.

As mentioned above, the concept of conspicuous consumption of Veblen is used to describe acts of consumption for the purpose of showing off. Mason has a similar idea: the motivation of conspicuous consumption is to impress other people with the consumers' ability to pay for expensive commodities. For him, it is a form of consumption that is defined by its social effect rather than its economic or physical effects (Mason 1983: 16). Belk argues that conspicuous consumption is a type of purchasing behavior that consumer conducts in order others to feel about oneself in ways one wants them to (Belk 1988: 146). No matter how complicated the psychological motivation may be conspicuous consumption refers to public consumption of expensive and luxurious commodities and service (Belk et al. 1982: 14; O'Cass and Frost 2002: 71). The reason why consumers are willing to pay higher prices for goods is because they long for a kind of status that is associated with material wealth (Bagwell and Bernheim 1996: 152). Actually, according to Richins, very often people would judge whether someone is successful or not according to the material objects he/she owns (Richins 2004: 213). Conspicuous consumption has, therefore, become a significant means of expression in people's daily behavior. People would buy conspicuous products associable with their social status to imitate or to differentiate themselves from other consumers, which creates the bandwagon or snob effect (Leibenstein 1950: 190). However, apart from rich people, there are also people of low economic status engaged in conspicuous consumption (Banerjee and Duflo 2007:152; Charles et al. 2009: 436; Christen and Morgan 2005: 157). Compared with the rich, these people of low income tend to spend more on conspicuous consumption at the sacrifice of education, entertainment, and health insurance. What puzzles economists is why relatively poor people would demonstrate stronger desires for "unnecessary" conspicuous goods. Research shows that when consumers are of relatively low or unstable social status, they tend to be more willing to pay for specific things that will help compensate for their psychological losses (Gao et al. 2009: 32; Sivanathan and Pettit 2010: 567). When subjects are under self-threat, they demonstrate a desire to pay for things that are associated with higher social status and when the self-threat is restored such desires lessen.

Moreover, individuals of lower self-esteem show a higher tendency toward luxury consumption. Obviously, people hope to compensate their inferior status, lack of power, and low self-esteem with luxury consumption (Banerjee and Duflo 2007: 153; Charles et al. 2009: 437).

For Chinese consumers, another factor is worth paying attention to—the influence of traditional Chinese culture. Research shows that traditional Confucian values are most closely connected to luxurious, conspicuous, and signifying purchasing activities (Zhang 2006: 109; Yuan et al. 2009: 81). The three Confucian cultural values that affect Chinese consumption of luxury commodities are consistency between behavior and status, family reputation, and other people's influence (Zhang 2006: 27). Among them "consistency between behavior and status" is the most influential one: the more a consumer cares about the consistency between behavior and status, the stronger his/her interest in conspicuous consumption is (Yuan 2013: 63). According to Zhang Mengxia, the idea of "consistency between behavior and status" teaches people to consider whether a certain behavior is in consistence with the respective social status (Zhang 2006: 25). Traditional Confucian culture emphasizes the relationship between individuals as well as the relationship between individual and community. People are taught to acknowledge one's social status as well as one's difference from others because this maintains stability and harmony in society.

In regard to consumer activities, the idea of "consistency between behavior and status" teaches people to consume according to their social status. Individuals with lower social status should buy things that match their position and spend their money in a rational way, while those of a higher social stand should buy more expensive products to demonstrate their identity and status in society. This way harmony between individuals and community can be sustained. Under the influence of the idea of consistency between behavior and status, those who believe they are of a higher social status tend to actively demonstrate themselves through conspicuous consumption so that their appearance matches what is defined by their identity and status. A "conspicuous" way of behavior as a way to demonstrate one's social status for both sexes is also reflected in the ancient Chinese traditions. Noble classes wore long nails as a demonstration of their social status, meaning they didn't have to be engaged in manual labor. And according to the symbolic self-completion theory, many activities that the individuals are engaged in, for example, purchase of commodities, are performed in a way to support the definition of the self so as to express the individual's identity (Wicklund and Gollwitzer 1981, p. 93). Accordingly, the more a person believes his/her behavior should match his/her social status, the more active he/she will be in purchasing so that he/she can strengthen his/her self-definition. Consumers can show their status with the act of consumption of certain things (Belk et al. 1982: 12), especially with the consumption of luxury and rare products (Han et al. 2010: 17).

Another important element in Confucian cultural values is the "consciousness of the face" (Pan et al. 2009: 82; Zhang et al. 2010: 17). "Face" refers to the individual's positive self-image gained through his/her interaction with other people. Specifically, the face means the social, open, and fluid self that is connected with other people's behavior and attitude. It also means a desire to sustain or improve one's image, to avoid losing one's face in social interactions, especially with important people (Bao et al. 2003: 749). As social beings, we all have experiences related with our "face." People strive to sustain or improve their face; when their face is under threat or attack, they always try to keep or protect it. In a culture which emphasizes on the spirit of collectivism, this is even more so. In China, what needs to be protected is not only one's own face, but also the face of those important to oneself. One's face is always also that of one's family. The face is, therefore, very important for Chinese people. The more a person pays attention to ones' "face," the stronger is one's desire to buy expensive things (Yuan 2013: 19). This sense of face will connect consumption with social relationships and affect many other facets in social life, from one's own physical needs to the need of self-realization (Belk 1988: 15). Studies show that because of the emphasis on "face," consumers in south-east China pay more attention to commodities that will attract public visibility (Wong and Ahuvia 1998: 431).

These factors influenced by Confucian values demonstrate that for Chinese consumers, the major motivation for conspicuous consumption is out of the "signaling motive," not the "compensating motive" shown in the behavior of Western consumers. For them, luxury consumption to a large extent leads to the growth and expansion of the self. Therefore, luxury consumption is practiced for the purpose of demonstrating individual's social status as well as a sense of privilege.

Conclusion

Conspicuous consumption in China, as we have seen, has a long history and is of particular importance in understanding today's China because it functions as a signifier—or rather a chain of signifiers—that reveals characteristics about society the same way as symptoms uncover diseases of a body. As a mechanism of distinction, cultural politics of conspicuous consumption in China distinguishes itself from the Western mode because it is more deeply interwoven with state power that either gives rise to it or tears it apart according to its own agenda, as is seen above how social changes led to the development of luxury consumption in China. On the other hand, conspicuous consumption is but one form of consumption in China; it is not even the dominate mode, because in general there still exists a big gap of difference between the rich and the poor in China. There are still many places in China which are not developed enough to even speak of conspicuous consumption. Unlike consumers of luxury goods who subject themselves to the signifying system of commodity signs, a large number of Chinese consumers in the poor areas still crave for the use value of commodities as such.

References

Bagwell, Laurie Simon, and Douglas B. Bernheim. 1996. Veblen Effects in a Theory of Conspicuous Consumption. *The American Economic Review* 86 (3): 349–373.

Banerjee, Abhijit, and Esther Duflo. 2007. The economic Lives of the Poor. *Journal of Economic Perspectives* 21 (1): 141–167.

Bao, Yeqing, Kevin Zheng Zhou, and Chenting Su. 2003. Face Consciousness and Risk Aversion: Do They Affect Consumer's Decision-making? *Psychology and Marketing* 20 (8): 733–755.

Belk, Russell W. 1988. Possessions and the Extended Self. *Journal of Consumer Research* 15 (2): 139–168.

Belk, Russel W., Kenneth D. Bahn, and Robert N. Mayer. 1982. Developmental Recognition of Consumption Symbolism. *Journal of Consumer Research* 9 (1): 4–17.

Bell, Daniel. 1976. *The Cultural Contradictions of Capitalism*. New York: Basic Books.

Charles, Kerwin Kofi, Erik Hurst, and Nikolai Roussanov. 2009. Conspicuous Consumption and Race. *The Quarterly Journal of Economics* 124 (2): 425–467.

Christen, Markus, and Ruskin Morgan. 2005. Keeping Up with the Joneses: Analyzing the Effect of Income Inequality on Consumer Borrowing. *Quantitative Marketing and Economics* 3 (2): 145–173.

Featherstone, Mike. 2007. *Consumer Culture and Postmodernism*. 2nd ed. London: Sage.

———. 2014. Luxury Dynamics. In *New Agenda of Cultural Studies: Property, Aesthetics and Globalization*, ed. Yu Jianhua and Jin Huimin, 86–104. Shanghai: Shanghai Foreign Language Education Press.

Fortune Research Institute. *Report on Conspicuous Consumption in China in 2015: Down from the Altar*. Tengxun Fashion. 8 Jan. 2016. http://www.199it.com/archives/414572.html

Gao, Leilei, Chrisitan Wheeler, and Shiv Baba. 2009. The "Shaken Self ": Product Choices as a Means of Restoring Self-View Confidence. *Journal of Consumer Research* 36 (1): 29–38.

Han, Young Jee, Joseph C. Nunes, and Xavier Drèze. 2010. Signaling Status with Luxury Goods: The Role of Brand Prominence. *Journal of Marketing* 74 (4): 15–30.

Keynes, John Maynard. 1936. *The General Theory of Employment, Interest and Money*. London: Macmillan.

Leibenstein, Harvey. 1950. Bandwagon, Snob, and Vablen Effects in the Theory of Consumer Demand. *Quarterly Journal of Economics* 64 (2): 183–207.

Mason, Roger. 1983. The Economic Theory of Conspicuous Consumption. *International Journal of Social Economics* 10 (3): 3–17.

O'Cass, Aron, and Hmily Frost. 2002. Status Brands: Examining the Effects on Non-Product-Related Brand Associations on Status and Conspicuous Consumption. *Journal of Product and Brand Management* 11 (2): 67–86.

Pan, Yu, Gao Li, and Wang Fanghua. 2009. Behavior Research on Chinese Consumers: A Confucian Perspective. *Chinese Industry and Economy* 9: 80–84.

Postrel, Virginia. 2008. Inconspicuous Consumption: A New Theory of the New Leisure Class. *The Atlantic* 302 (1): 148–150–151.

Richins, Marshal L. 2004. The Material Values Scale: Measurement Properties and Development of a Short Form. *Journal of Consumer Research* 31 (1): 209–219.

Shekou Storm. *Baidu Encyclopedia*. 12 Jan 2016. https://baike.baidu.com/item/%E8%9B%87%E5%8F%A3%E9%A3%8E%E6%B3%A2/3881915?fr=aladdin.

Sivanathan, Niro, and Nathan C. Pettit. 2010. Protecting the self through Consumption: Status Goods as Affirmational Commodities. *Journal of Experimental Social Psychology* 46 (3): 564–570.

Stanley, Thomas, and D. Danko William. 1998. *The Millionaire Next Door*. New York: Simon and Schuster.

Wang, Ning. 2010. The Cultural Logic from Thriftism to Consumerism. *The Journal of Lanzhou University* 3: 11–23.

Wicklund, Robert A., and Peter M. Gollwitzer. 1981. Symbolic Self-completion, Attempted Influence, and Self-depression. *Basic and Applied Social Psychology* 2 (2): 89–114.
Wong, Nancy Y., and Aaron C. Ahuvia. 1998. Personal Taste and Family Face: Luxury Consumption in Confucian and Western Societies. *Psychology and Marketing* 15: 423–441.
Yuan, Shaofeng. 2013. *Conspicuous Consumption of Chinese: Antecedents and Consequences*. Beijing: Chinese Economic Publishing House.
Yuan, Shaofeng, Yan Gao, and Youxin Zheng. 2009. Consciousness of Face, Status Differentiation and Conspicuous Consumption: Theoretical Modes and Practice Tests. *Forum on Finance and Economics* 5: 81–86.
Zhang, Mengxia. 2006. Definition and the Value Study of Luxury Consumption. *Economy Management* 12: 23–29.
Zhang, Xin-an, Jie Li, and Yuan Ma. 2010. Chinese Consciousness of Face and Status and Consumption Behavior. *Journal of Management Science* 6 (4): 14–28.

Middle Stratum Consumption Patterns as a "Key" for Understanding Japanese Society

Maya Keliyan

Introduction: Japan Seen Through Its Consumption

From the very start of my study of Japanese society, which began in 1994, I was impressed by the leading position held by modern Japan in the world with respect to consumption and lifestyle. Observation of Japanese consumption society shows very clearly the importance of consumption in today's global world, and the need for using the concept of "consumption patterns." Japanese society is a rewarding object for the study of these patterns: due to the exceptionally great significance of social group status in Japan, consumption patterns there are distinctly and quite visibly status oriented (Keliyan 1999: 117). Status is something that can be plainly observed there, and it leaves its distinct mark on individuals and groups as present in all spheres of public life. In Japan, due to the great variety of consumer opportunities, it is much easier to distinguish the differences in consumption patterns of separate social groups, categories, and strata. The country is known for all sort of extravagance, of bizarre whims, in consumption. Until 2008 Japan is a leader in avant-garde consumption and a country became "the first mass luxury market." The Japanese were "the most avid buyers of luxury products in the world" (Haghirian 2011: 108). But which are the social groups and categories that embody these trends? Who are the adherents of specific fashionable tendencies, movements, and phenomena, for which Japan has become proverbial[1]? During 1990s the Japanese middle class "was the most interested in purchasing luxury goods" (Haghirian 2011: 113).

Japan has a developed postmodern society, and is a leader in modern-style consumption. Its consumption patterns are exemplary for postmodern lifestyle in an

[1] For instance, whether *all* Japanese women use women's designer handbags Louis Vuitton, and which social groups consume such highly prestigious brands.

M. Keliyan (✉)
Institute for the Study of Societies and Knowledge, Bulgarian Academy of Sciences, Sofia, Bulgaria

E. Krasteva-Blagoeva (ed.), *Approaching Consumer Culture*, International Series on Consumer Science, https://doi.org/10.1007/978-3-030-00226-8_12

age of growing globalization (Keliyan 2008: 22–27). Ever since its opening to the world in 1868, Japan has looked to the West as a model to be emulated in all respects. Today, concerning the sphere of consumption, the Japanese have succeeded in surpassing their teachers in some respects. The case of Japan can now suggest the trends in consumption models that may be expected to come about in other societies. Japanese influence and leadership in the area of postmodern consumption culture and lifestyle have even become not only a source of economic recovery and strengthening but also one of the sources of its contemporary *soft power*. It is no coincidence that to foster industries the Ministry of Economy, Trade, and Industry created the concept of "Cool Japan." The most important aspects of this policy are expansion strategies for overseas promotion of famous Japanese products, consumption and lifestyle practices, values, and attitudes (Cool Japan Initiative 2014).

The rapid development, expansion, and stabilization of the middle strata in Japan after World War II, especially the new middle strata, was a factor that contributed to the country' economic success. These are the active and innovative postmodern consumers, and a model for studying the role of the middle strata as an important social-structural formation in modern consumption.

Consumption Patterns and Middle Strata in Contemporary Societies

After World War II, global changes took place, as a result of which status differences between people and groups became increasingly defined according to their consumption patterns and lifestyle. Changes in labor and production during 1960s in developed societies led to the "age of high mass consumption" (Rostow 1960). As indicated by Featherstone, in "modern capitalist consumer societies" consumption has become a significant source of status differentiation for all social groups (Featherstone 1990). The self-assessment and self-identification of the representatives of separate social strata depends to a great degree on the quantity and quality of consumption, on their lifestyle.

The phenomenon of sign value has become an essential constituent of the commodity and consumption which leads to "active manipulation of signs," so that both sign and goods turn into a product, which is a "commodity sign" (Baudrillard 1970). In postmodern societies job position, market situation, and opportunities for acquiring commodities, on the one hand, and consumption patterns and different lifestyles, on the other hand, are considered to lie at the basis of the distinction between class division and stratification division. Class differences might grow stronger owing to variations in the lifestyle and in "tastes" in the sense in which Bourdieu (1984) used the term.

Consumption plays a leading and decisive role in today's global world: by their very nature, developed societies are consumer societies. After a certain level of material and economic prosperity is attained, and with the transition from modern to postmodern, societies enter a new historical era, in which new dependencies prevail: among these, consumption plays a significant role for "economic freedom," for growth, and for our understanding of the nature of the society. In social stratification self-identification term people consider themselves in terms of consumption, rather than of their relation to production (Featherstone 1995). That is why the new importance attached to the factor of consumption is linked to the birth of postmodern society. Since consumption did not play this structure-determining role before the emergence of this new type of society, it should be stressed that it now has a new social significance that it did not, and could not, previously have.

The recent trends in stratification theory show that consumption has a key place in the analysis of social structuring processes, while the introduction and use of the concept of consumption patterns permit making a more comprehensive characterization of social group status in today's postmodern societies. This is the reason for choosing a stratification approach to the topic. We assume that in postmodern societies consumption patterns are among important indicators of the social status one occupies, both objectively and subjectively (Keliyan 2008: 45–49). These patterns determine not only the stratification position of the various social groups and strata, but their subjective self-identification as well.

The consumption patterns are *significant structure-determining* characteristics of social subjects; to a great degree they define their status position in society, their belonging to a specific social group, category, or stratum. In defining the concept of "consumption patterns" we assume that they are a *key indicator of social group status.* Hence it is the concept that characterizes *consumption in its stratification aspect*, i.e., not in general and in itself, but as a *mark of status*. While the concept of "consumption" expresses the act itself, that of "consumption patterns" characterizes the way, forms in which the various social group formations effectuate consumption.

Among the leading structure-determining characteristics of postmodern society are its large *middle strata*, firmly present in society, which are emblematic and especially important for modern consumption. Without their active, innovative role as consumers, no consumer society would be possible. Moreover, the birth and development of this society are linked to the growth and stabilization of the middle strata.

In the text use is made of a specific *methodological approach* to the surveyed phenomenon. *Consumption* is not viewed in opposition to production or as an alternative to relations of production, but is taken as *the point of departure for stratification analysis.* The author bases her discussion on the neo-Weberian tradition in the field of theories of classes and of social stratification, elaborated by Goldthorpe (1982), Savage et al. (1992), Butler and Savage (1995), and Tilkidjiev (2002). According to the proponents of this view, the middle class is defined on the basis of an aggregate of criteria. They include not only ownership of the means of production, income, and assets, but also the type of employment, work situation, profession, occupation, education, prestige, power resources, cultural status, lifestyle, consumption patterns, value system, political views and behavior, etc. The middle class holds an intermediate place in the stratification ladder, in the so-called stratification middle. Due to the *heterogeneous nature* of this class, it would be more appropriate to speak, not of a single middle class, but of middle classes in *plural*, or more precisely of *middle strata*.

Since the middle class in Japan is not a homogenous social group, within it we distinguish old and new middle class, and upper-middle, middle-middle, and lower-middle class. The *old middle class* encompasses all the strata whose existence as social groups is derived from the pre-industrial and pre-modern society. These are predominantly the small artisans, traders, farmers, and people exercising independent professions, such as doctors, dentists, and lawyers. By *new middle class* we mean all the social strata that have been created in modern times. These are people connected with large social organizations, institutions, etc., and include managers, specialists, professionals, experts, technicians, civil servants, etc.

In postmodern society, consumption becomes the foundation for "the construction of a lifestyle"; "consumption patterns of the middle class are perceived as the norm" and "standardized ideal" that all others strive to achieve (Bell and Hollows 2006: 3). Commodities are no longer produced for anonymous and undifferentiated masses of consumers but are aimed at *concrete social strata,* the most important of which are the *middle strata.*

Postmodernization of Japanese Consumption Patterns and Lifestyle

By the late 1920s, thanks to the growing urbanization, "consumption began to expand rapidly" in Japan's largest cities, "giving birth to a true mass consumer society," which "existed primarily for city dwellers and particularly for the urban middle class" (Miura 2014: 4–7). Immediately after World War II, Japanese consumption was characterized by poverty, shortage of commodities, a growing black market, and smuggling. Since the mid-1950s the country began to restore its economy; the emblematic commodities of consumption at that time were the washing machine, refrigerator, and television; by the mid-1960s these items were indeed found in every home. When Japan achieved the level of second strongest economy in the world in the late 1960s, shopping had come to be considered something *patriotic.* All this radically changed the nature of Japanese consumer society, which underwent a "transition from quantitative to qualitative consumption" (Skov and Moeran 1995: 28). It became important and at last possible for middle stratum consumers to display their grown living standard by the use of prestigious brands of commodities and services. At that time there began a development and gradual growth of *conspicuous consumption,* which attained a mass scale and characterized Japanese consumer society throughout the 1980s.

In the 1970s Japan was a leader in the development of the so-called fifth-generation computer systems and robotization. By the mid-1980s the country had achieved its goal and turned into an information society. Typically, Japan emphasizes foremost the social values of the media, communications, and information technologies, and their use not only in the sphere of production but also in leisure, recreation, and consumption. Since then high technologies have found a permanent place in Japanese consumption patterns, especially those of the *new middle strata*. They have become a characteristic feature of the Japanese consumer society and lifestyle in general. Japan has practically realized its postwar ideal, and is a real example of the postindustrial society described by Daniel Bell (1974/1973). Japan has become a society oriented mostly to information and services, and its industry is based on the development of science and technology, particularly modern technologies. Japanese products symbolize high quality, and the country has a well-established image as the land of high technologies.

> In 1985, in the city of Tsukuba, Ibaraki prefecture, north of Tokyo, the International Science Technology Exposition - Expo '85 was held. It popularized Japanese achievements and confirmed the status of the country as a world power in the field of science and technology (Creighton 1998: 220-221). Advocated among the public and the media was the idea that information is of paramount importance for achieving and leading a "meaningful life"; especially receptive to this message were the new middle strata. Knowledge-related professions have enhanced their influence, and this has changed the stratification structure of society and the place of the new middle class in that structure.

According to Imada Japan passed from the stage of "consumer society" in the 1960s and 1970s to that of a *yutakana shakai* or "affluent society" in the 1980s (Imada 1998). He uses this term to characterize the changes taking place in postmodern Japanese society. Due to these changes, the *status* differences between people and groups were now defined not only and not mostly by the material dimensions of their social situation but increasingly by their consumption patterns and lifestyle.

In the 1960s and 1970s, the growth and stabilization of the middle class became the goal of the ruling elites, and also the model of material success at the individual and social levels. Japan was regarded as "general middle-class society"—*sōchūryū shakai* (Chiavacci 2008: 6). The increasing number of white-collar workers in the Japanese economy at that time was a factor leading to the development of mass society and mass consumption, which in turn promoted the myth that Japan was a society in which "wealth and income were distributed fairly" (Chiavacci and Hommarich 2017: 4). The political party platforms at that time were elaborated in this direction. These changes led to the emergence of another myth, according to which the country was turning, during the 1970s, from a middle-class society into a "new middle-mass society" (Murakami 1984). The new middle mass is understood to be a mass middle stratum, homogenous in respect to lifestyle, consumption patterns, and value system. This massification was due to the increased proportion of the new middle class of professionals, experts, and managers.

Starting from the 1980s, Japan turned from a "society of the middle mass" into a "divided middle mass" society (Imada 1998). The "divided middle mass" has consumption patterns and lifestyle that do not directly result from its achieved status, i.e., from the profession, income, and education of its members, unlike the "middle mass society." "Divided middle mass" consists of differing social strata whose lifestyle is centered on the values of a good family, satisfaction derived from personal life and leisure, display of personal qualities, ample social contacts, possibilities for exercising leadership, and self-expression in informal relations. The concept of "divided middle mass" is used to characterize the middle class in postmodern societies like the Japanese one, in which values are reoriented from the achievement of material status to greater spiritual self-expression.

Other authors define that in the 1980s and early 1990s Japanese society entered a period of "post-scarcity" (Bookchin 1971: 10). The greater part of the population had by then no problems satisfying its basic needs, and could even afford to consume luxury goods (Tamura 2007). The contrast between the deprivations of the postwar years and the subsequent plenty was quite sharp and this change took place within a single generation. At that time the new stratifying role of consumption in Japanese society became increasingly distinct—by then society had achieved the material-economic freedom for such consumption.

There were indisputable differences between the status positions of the different social strata in Japan during this period. The question is not whether differences existed or whether they grew or decreased—the important point is that in a postmodern Japanese society, consumption patterns and lifestyle, together with economic situation, are significant, in fact key factors defining the status positions of the separate socio-professional groups. The views of various authors quoted above confirm this important finding: consumption patterns of separate groups and strata are increasingly differentiated and this testifies to the status differences between these groups. Research interest is focused primarily on what is happening in the *middle strata:* inner differences engendered by the specific consumption patterns of the separate socio-professional groups are analyzed. The processes occurring in these consumption patterns have shaped the main trends in the social stratification of postwar Japan and show the significance of the middle strata as bearers of the most important, symptomatic, and emblematic changes in society.

Since the mid-1980s Japanese postmodern consumer society entered a stage in which the stress shifted from conformism of the "consumer masses" to an individualism influenced by Western values. Consumer groups, in their striving to express most fully that they are "different," have become increasingly segmented (Schutte and Ciarlante 1998: 103; Creighton 1998: 219). Consumer culture in this period was dominated by the values of individualism and self-expression, which sought adequate projection in the lifestyle. The educated *new middle strata* of the so-called "new middle mass"—*shin chūkan taishu* (Murakami 1984; Imada 1998)—are the suitable target group of consumers with the necessary income but also with the cultural potential to adopt the ideas of "diversified" consumption patterns and lifestyle.

In reality, after World War II the share of the middle class, especially that of the new middle strata, did increase, but Japan was never a "middle-class society," a "general middle-class society" much less a "new middle-mass society" (Keliyan 2012: 95–101). Starting from the mid-1960s, lifestyle, consumption patterns, and cultural patterns certainly did become factors of growing importance for stratification, but this does not mean that economic criteria had lost their impact. Past inequalities have intensified since the 1980s, not only in the direction of growing differences in values, leisure, and cultural status. Under the impact of the "bubble economy," the prices of real estate and land grew several times higher, thus engendering considerable inequalities between those who had these resources and those who did not (Hashimoto 2003). The "new rich" and "new poor" emerged: the former have the resources for leading an affluent and even lavish lifestyle, which the latter cannot afford even when they are employed and with an income above the poverty line. In studying the financial resources and capacity for savings of the households, Ozawa states that society is entering an "era of neo-stratified consumption," connected with the "birth of the divided masses" (Ozawa 1985). Similar conclusions are presented by Yamazaki, who writes about "the emergence of fragile individualism" of "masses divided with regard to consumption and lifestyle" (Yamazaki 1984); Fujioka nostalgically entitled his article about these trends "Goodbye, masses" (Fujioka 1984).

In the late 1990s the Japanese postmodern consumer society underwent changes in values: the preference shifted to simple and functional products, in which the most important aspect was utility, not design and brand. These values have been shared especially by the *new middle strata*, who express the ideas of globalism, pragmatism, and "new refinement of taste." These processes are stimulated by economic recession, which makes the cheaper stores not only increasingly popular, but even "in vogue" among certain social groups of consumers.

As a result of the social, economic, and structural transformations in the country and worldwide, important changes can be observed in the consumption patterns and lifestyle of various social strata in Japan. In the media appeared indicative expressions such as *kachigumi* (the group of the successful) and *makegumi* (the group of losers). The growing income inequality in Japanese society made it be defined through key phrases, such as *kibou kakusa shakai*—"the hope disparity society" (introduced by Yamada 2004), and *karyu shakai*—"lower-class society" (expression first used by Miura 2005). These terms are a sign of the increasingly perceptible social and economic changes that are depriving Japanese society of its past aura of a homogenous middle class, and ending the myth about Japan as a "middle-class society."

The issue of growing economic inequality is being raised with increased emphasis in Japan, together with the notion of the "working poor" among the low-educated social strata and part-time employees (Tachibanaki 1998, 2005, 2006). It is regarding these problems that the discussion among the academic community and the general public first began: the ongoing structural processes and their disturbing social consequences. Public debate is going on about the "new forms of social exclusion" (Chiavacci and Hommarich 2017: 3), creating a completely new self-image of Japan as a "gap society" (*kakusa shakai*). Using empirical evidence about household income inequality, measured by Gini coefficient for the period of several decades, starting from 1980s, Shirahase concludes that trends of growing income inequality are evident during that period and "Japan was not a country of such equality as people imagine" (Shirahase 2014: 23). The rapid aging of population is a serious socioeconomic problem—in combination with the unwillingness of young people to have families of their own, and the decreasing number of children born, it predicts insecure future.

Middle Classes: Stratified Consumption and Leisure

Lifestyle and the prestige connected to it are among the important criteria by which contemporary Japanese sociology distinguishes *the middle strata* from other stratification groups (Keliyan 1999: 68–85, 97–103). In Japanese we can recognize three major notions pertained to the concept of middle class: "middle economic class"—*chūsan kaikyū,* "middle prestigious class"—*chūryū kaikyū,* and "middle strata"—*chūkan kaisō* (Odaka 1966: 543; Kosaka 1994: 95–97). "Middle economic class" is used to denominate the middle class which some conceptions define as "bourgeoisie," or as a middle class defined on the basis of owned means of production and economic power. "Middle strata" is used as a concept characterizing the middle class as regards their intermediate position in the stratified social space. After 1970s, the sociological concept, equivalent to the understanding of a middle class in Western sociology, is "middle prestigious class," or in Japanese *chūryū kaikyū,* situated between the upper and lower classes (Kosaka 1994: 103–104). Since the 1970s in Japan the term *class—kaikyū—*means precisely *"middle class,"* whereas before the country became a postmodern society the term referred primarily to "working class" due to the latter's importance for industrial development at that time.

The growing economic well-being after the World War II caused the gradual expanding of the middle class in Japan. According to SSM[2] surveys the Japanese middle class share, defined on the base of objective criteria, grew from 30% in 1955 to over 50% in 1985 (Seiyama 1993: 26); it remained relatively stable during the following decades. The share of those who self-identify with the middle class in Japan in 1964, according to the data from PMO (Prime Minister Office) survey, reached 90% (Kosaka 1994: 9). These data differ from those of the SSM survey, according to which 70–75% of the population self-associate with the middle class during the same period, mainly because of differences in the classification categories and schemes used.

The data on people identifying themselves as middle class show that those who have placed themselves in this category, i.e., the so-called subjective middle class are far more than those who fall into the "objective" one; this is a phenomenon that can be observed in all societies (Kelley and Evans 1995: 157–158; Tilkidjiev 2002). The explanations for this can be found in the impact of the following factors: the growing share of nonmanual labor professions in postmodern Japanese society; the symbolic significance of the middle strata for the modern lifestyle; the prestige of the middle class; and the changes that have taken place since the mid-1960s in

[2] Social Stratification and Mobility National Surveys (SSM) are held every 10 years since 1955 and are representative for the Japanese population.

living standard, consumption patterns, and lifestyles of large groups in Japanese society (Kosaka 1994; Imada 1998; Ishida 1993).

There is a certain difference between those who believe they belong to the "middle prestigious class" and the "middle economic class." The majority of those who identify themselves as belonging to the middle class do so from the viewpoint of prestige, consumption patterns, and lifestyle, as well as of their position as a middle stratum in the stratification environment, but not according to their economic resources (Keliyan 1999: 97–103).

The economic prosperity after World War II and the fact that within two generations Japan turned from a poor country into a rich society provide the foundations of the myth of "a middle-class society," zealously maintained by political parties and the media.

In Japan during 1960s and 1970s there was a state policy of purposeful and methodical support for the development of the new middle strata. They enjoyed high social prestige and received income corresponding to it. In the mid-1950s Japan was an "old middle-class society" (Hashimoto 2003: 18).[3] The numerical size of this old class sharply declined in the following 40 years, while the *new middle class* nearly doubled in size in the same time. The latter's most rapid growth as a proportion of the population was in the period between the mid-1950s and the mid-1960s. In the following decade its growth slowed down slightly, but in the mid-1990s it again started to speed up considerably. In the mid-1990s the share of the *new middle strata* grew to nearly one-fourth of the occupied population (24%) and has remained at this proportion ever since. One-third of these people work for large companies, one-fourth for state institutions, and about 40% for small and middle firms (Hashimoto 2003: 61). According to Hashimoto the *new middle class*[4] is a little more numerous than the *old middle class*[5] (22% of all occupied), but its relative share is two and a half times bigger than that of the *capitalist class*[6] (9%). The *working class*,[7] with its relative share of 45%, is nearly equal in size to the new and old middle classes put together.

The representatives of the *new middle class* are the youngest: their average age is nearly 42 years, which is 10 years younger than the average age of the old middle class. The members of the latter class, together with those of the capitalist class, are the oldest by average age. The new middle class has the highest proportion of men and the share of women in it—about one-fifth—is the lowest, compared with other

---

[3] The quoted author has used the findings of an SSM survey conducted in 1995, and regroups some of the data to fit his neo-Marxist class schema of four classes: capitalist class, new middle class, old middle class, and working class.

[4] It includes professionals, administrators, specialists, officials, and office workers.

[5] In this class Hashimoto includes leaders and directors of enterprises with a staff of less than five persons, as well as entrepreneurs, self-employed, and family members working for the latter.

[6] Falling under this category are leaders and directors of enterprises with a staff of five persons or more, as well as entrepreneurs, self-employed, and family members working for the latter.

[7] Hashimoto assigns to this class all employed excluding professionals, administrators, and officials.

classes. More than half of the working class are women (56%), and the proportion of women among the old middle class is about 10% points lower than this (47%). One-third of the members of the capitalist class are women. Women are most widely present in lower status positions, and their proportion is lower in leadership positions within firms. They are present in stable proportions in family businesses, where their role is often that of unpaid workers.

The highest percentage of married persons is that in the capitalist and old middle class: 90% of the former and 88% of the latter have a family. More than 80% of men and only two-thirds of women in the new middle class are married. The average age of these women is 39, which indicates that a high share of them have preferred their professional career to making a family. According to the data, the new middle class is the most highly educated: more than half its members (52%) are university graduates.

The living standard of the members of the new middle class is above the average for the country: their income level is the second highest after that of the capitalist class. The old middle class is in third position, the difference between second and third being negligible. The representatives of the new middle class have a considerable autonomy in their work, possess authority in their firm, and take part in decision-making, especially as regards distribution of work tasks. They have much better possibilities for growth in their professional career. Their social contacts are usually with professionals, administrators, and managers, which means with people of their own class or of the capitalist class (Hashimoto 2003: 110).

Nearly two-thirds of the new middle class are satisfied with their life, by which indicator they are in the second highest position, coming after the capitalist class. Half of the satisfied have specified they are "more or less satisfied," and one-seventh have indicated "satisfied."

Over one-third of the members of the new middle class self-identify as upper or upper-middle class, and 41% as "middle class," which once again puts it in second place after the capitalist class. Two-thirds of the new middle class are not supporters of any political party: in this it is similar to the working class and differs from the capitalist and old middle class. Nearly half of the people belonging to the latter two classes are not sympathizers of any party but approximately 40% of them are supporters of the Liberal Democratic Party (the share of supporters of this party among capitalists is slightly higher than among old middle class).

The composition of the *old middle class* at the end of the twentieth century was different from that in the middle of the century. Farmers were the main component then but now they are a minority; instead, self-employed traders and industrialists make up two-thirds of it. It has the best gender balance, but it has the highest average age: nearly one-third of its members are over 60 years old.

The old middle class also proves to be the least educated, and more than one-third of its members (36%) have completed only the obligatory educational level,[8] which is the highest share of this level of education among all classes. The average

[8] In Japan the obligatory education is 9 school years, which comprise the full three levels of basic education.

level of household income is equal to that of the new middle class, but their individual income levels are much lower, which shows that the household revenues come from the active participation of family members in the business. Since they are self-employed, they have a high degree of work autonomy and can decide how to organize their work. Most of the people they socialize with belong to their own class or to the new middle and working class. They maintain very good contacts with local administrators, with high-ranking officials from the trade associations, and with politicians, contacts that are necessary and useful for their business.

According to the data, by its degree of satisfaction with life, the old middle class is in third highest position, after the capitalist and new middle class (but the difference between it and the new middle is slight).

By status and class self-identification, the members of the old middle are in a slightly lower position than those of the new middle, but here too the difference between the two groups is small. The old middle class has a much larger percentage of supporters of the Liberal Democratic Party—more than one-third of the members of this class, which is twice more than the share of the party's supporters in the new middle class. Slightly over half of its members do not support any political party, which is nearly 15% less than the non-supporters among the new middle.

The working class has a low level of education (next to last, with only the old middle class below it) and the lowest income level. The average household income for this class amounts to two-thirds that of the households in the new and old middle classes. Among workers is registered the lowest degree of satisfaction with life. They self-identify as part of the lower and lower-middle class, but more than one-fifth of them define themselves as belonging to the middle class. Workers have the lowest degree of autonomy in work, and they are least able to determine the rate of work and the organization at their job. They show the lowest degree of political activeness: three-fifths of them indicate that they are not supporters of any political party, and one-fourth feels that "politics is too complicated for me to understand" (Hashimoto 2003: 93).

What has been said so far allows us to generalize that in Japanese postmodern society the proportion, social role, and importance of the *new middle class* are growing; it is the class with the fastest and steadiest growth in the last few decades. The relatively young age of its members, its high educational level and income level, the ample social contacts of its members, its high degree of satisfaction with life, and its class and status self-identification have made it the bearer of the latest trends in consumption and lifestyle. Unlike the new middle, the old middle class is more conservative, as its members are older, less educated, more connected with other household members in the framework of the family business. The tendencies in the postwar stratification structure of Japanese society have determined the stratification in the consumption patterns of the various classes, as well as the growing internal class differences within the middle class itself.

The new middle class is in third position as regards the average amount of its possession of consumer durables, house ownership, and financial assets, and by this criterion seems nearer to the working class than to the old middle and capitalist classes. The situation of this class is similar as regards the rate of house ownership;

nearly two-thirds of its members, which is almost as much as in the working class, live in a home of their own. The data show that this class has the highest share of members—nearly one-tenth, who live in company-owned dwellings. This fact is indicative of the advantages provided by the status of "people belonging to the organization." The *new* middle class is in second place, below the capitalist, with regard to consumer durable ownership.

This trend is especially clear with respect to the rate of ownership of a computer and piano, a criterion by which the new middle follows consumption patterns very similar to those of the capitalist class and quite different from those of the old middle and working class (the latter two prove to have approximately equal percentages of owners of these two items). Because of its higher educational level, the *new middle class* invests in objects related to high technology and culture. The percentage of people possessing a computer and piano is indicative of what this class would prefer to invest its money in, and of its interests and occupations in leisure—these are connected with *high culture.* This class is in second place with respect to the level of the individual salary but in third place with regard to house ownership. Its members can rely on "the organization they belong to" so they do not feel they must buy property as an eventual source of income should the need for this arise. The *new middle class* prefers to spend money on consumer durables and leisure activities, due to its higher educational level and more developed esthetical taste.

According to the criteria "rates of consumer durables ownership, house ownership and financial assets" the *old middle class* is in second place, following the capitalist class. By the indicator "rate of house ownership" it is even in first place, ahead of the capitalist class. Most of its members are self-employed and they want to be able to rely on this property in case of need. By investing in a home, real estate, and movable property and savings, they are providing for their family members actively engaged in the family business. By the rate of consumer durable ownership, the old middle class is in third place, following the capitalist and new middle class, but is in second place after the capitalist class by the criterion sport club membership and ownership of art objects and antiques.

The capitalist class is oriented above all to objects and property of high value and prestige. It has the highest percentage of owners of a home plus a country house. In Japan the possession of a country house is something rare, for three reasons: the high price of dwellings; the high tax rates on buildings, which grow in geometric progression for every following dwelling owned; and the small amount of leisure time to go to a country house even in case of having such. The people belonging to the capitalist class and possessing a country house are four times as many as those in the new and old middle class. Also, the capitalists possessing a drawing room set (an expensive possession and a mark of high social status, as it requires a large dwelling and Western-style furniture) are a higher percentage by one-fifth than those in the old and new middle class. Members of sport clubs among the capitalist class are three and a half times greater as a percentage than those in the new middle and 2.8 times greater than those in the old middle class. A similar proportion is evident for the indicator "ownership of art objects and antiques"—these owners are

2.4 times more among the capitalist class than in the new middle, and 1.6 times more than in the old middle class.

The working class has a similar level with regard to house ownership as the new middle class, but has the lowest level of consumer durable ownership.

The leisure patterns of the four classes differ considerably from one another. Of all four classes, the most active one during leisure time is the new middle class. This shows it has a lifestyle in which leisure holds a special place. The highest relative shares of people performing activities such as reading sports newspapers, women's weekly magazines, fiction, and history books and of karaoke users are in the new middle—80% for each of these activities (Hashimoto 2003: 105–107). Members of the new middle class are the most frequent visitors of art exhibitions and museums—about 70% of all members. The same proportion of it takes part in costly recreation activities such as golf, skiing, and tennis, while 40% go to concerts of classical music. It has the same percentages for these two indicators as the *capitalist class,* even though the latter has higher income. This confirms that the new middle have a leading place in activities requiring high esthetical taste and education.

Professionals and managers, though they, respectively, amount to 7% and almost 12% of respondents, represent more than one-fifth of the group with the highest level of "information literacy" (Hashimoto 2003: 208). The latter dimension has a strong influence on the consumption patterns and lifestyle of the various social strata in Japan, and modifies them to a considerable extent. The groups differentiated on the basis of information literacy represent separate consumer groups with specific lifestyles. The social differences between groups distinguished by their various skills in using the information media are closely linked to differences based on the use of traditional media. As may be expected, the groups with the highest level of "information literacy" are also the most active users of Internet: nearly 90% of them are regular users. Two-thirds of them read literary fiction and specialized literature in their spare time, nearly 80% read magazines and comics, and more than half go to the theatre and movies. By comparison, in the group with the lowest level of "information literacy" only 3% use the Internet, 12% read fiction and specialized literature, one-third read comics and magazines, and one-fourth go to cinema and the theatre.

Unlike the new middle class, the members of the old middle class are not very active in their leisure time. Their leisure patterns are the most passive; that is, with regard to the listed activities they are least active of all classes, even less than the working class. Unlike the new middle class, they do not belong to an institution to which they must be loyal and on which they can rely. This limits their leisure time and orients them above all to so-called social activities—they are the most active class next to the capitalist one in this respect. Forty percent of the old middle class and nearly half the capitalist class take part in various social activities.[9] For the old middle these activities are helpful for creating and maintaining valuable connections with members of local government, with politicians, with members of trade and

[9]Including activities in the local community, in various neighborhood clubs, in volunteer organizations, etc.

industrial associations, with business partners, etc. The leisure time of the old middle is not as distinctly separate from their working time as that of the new middle class.

Despite differences in leisure patterns between the different classes, there are evident similarities in their preference for two activities: reading sports newspapers and women's magazines, and karaoke. People attending classical music concerts account for the smallest share in all classes. The explanation for this may be that this activity requires specific taste, knowledge, and feeling of the music; also, tickets for such concerts are expensive. Still, about 15% of the old middle class and even 20% of the working class go to classical music concerts. This fact confirms how important high culture is for the Japanese and the impact of school education in taste formation.

The working class is the most active in playing *pachinko* (pinball machines): more than half its members do this in their free time. Next in order regarding this activity are members of the capitalist class and the new middle class, with about 45% each, while old middle class has less than 40% of its members who share in this recreation.

Conclusion: Middle Stratum Consumption Patterns of the Late Twentieth and Early Twenty-First Century

Prevalent in Japanese society are egalitarian values; this is a communitarian society with a developed group culture, which makes it very sensitive to the growing inequalities in income, education level, consumption, and lifestyle. The distinction that Ferdinand Tönnies (1887/2011) made between "community" (*Gemeinschaft*) and "society" (*Geselschaft*) as two different types of sociality was at the core of the *romantic notion* of the Japanese society as based on mutuality, cooperation, and mutual aid among its members. This is one of the views that contributed to the widespread, even mythical, representation regarding Japanese society and its unique difference from Western civilization, regarding the specific feeling of community and community spirit that make up the essential quality of being Japanese. The creation and spread of such highly ideological and mythologized representations are certainly connected to some real characteristics of Japanese society. This society has a developed community culture, which has been preserved over the centuries and continues to perform an important role and function even now, in postmodern society. In Japan there are certainly strong social bonds between individuals within the framework of the group to which they belong, between the communities and society at large. Japan is a communitarian society (Etzioni 1998), in which social responsibility and duty towards the group and the community are of paramount importance, despite the intense current of individualism that comes through Western influence. In fact, this trend is a result of not only foreign influence but also the impact upon society and its structures of modernization, industrialization, urbanization, mass culture, post-modernization, and social transformations all of these provoke.

During the period of high economic growth until the early 1990s Japan was portrayed as an egalitarian and predominantly middle-class society (Sugimoto 2010: 37) which was one of the main reasons for the widespread distribution of egalitarian values. It was suggested that basic inequalities were not those between social classes but between corporate groups (Nakane 1970/1992); some authors were arguing that classes no longer existed in Japan (Murakami 1984).

The middle class, both old and new, was protected on the labor market up until the late 1990s. The new middle strata benefited by the system of lifelong employment and the salaries of people in this group were set according to length of service and age. The old middle strata were protected through the existing regulations on the activity of large corporations, rules that alleviated the competition pressure on the self-employed and small entrepreneurs. However, at the end of the 1990s there was a reevaluation of the existing economic order. Since the second half of the 1990s Japanese society, as part of the increasingly global world economy, has been undergoing recessions and crises, followed by periods of recovery (Keliyan 2010: 35–42). The first crisis of this kind was in 1997, and the earliest signs of recovery were seen in 1999. The second crisis came in 2008; the economy began to revive slowly from it in the middle of 2009, but the disasters of March 11, 2011 led to a new crisis.

Two contrary trends are emerging in the consumption patterns of the various social strata. On the one hand there is a distinct group of upper strata demonstrating their affluent consumption. On the other hand there is an increasing share of people who must restrict their consumption because of their lower income. These two contrary trends in social stratification have determined the "boom" of stores and shopping centers meeting the different needs of these social groups: there are expensive stores offering luxury items and services, and there are shops offering cheap,[10] second-hand, and recycled commodities. The demographic trends of population aging, low birth rate, and growing share of unmarried young and middle-aged people are having an impact on producers and on various categories of consumer and lifestyle centers. In this context, the representatives of the new middle strata have a stable, though relatively slowly rising, income. The various kinds of stores and centers for consumption and recreation are offering increasingly varied products in order to meet the needs and demands of the consumers belonging to these different strata.

---

[10] These are stores where goods are priced at 100 yen (around 0.80 Euro); they are found near all the central stations of the public transport in Japanese cities and offer a great variety of goods, ranging from stationery to household appliances.

References

Baudrillard, Jean. 1970. *La sociètè de consommation*. Paris: Gallimard.

Bell, Daniel. 1973/1974. *The Coming of Post-Industrial Society: A Venture in Social Forecasting*. London: Heinemann.

Bell, David, and Joanne Hollows, eds. 2006. *Historicizing Lifestyle: mediating Taste, Consumption and Identity From the 1900s to 1970s*. Aldershot: Ashgate Publishing.

Bookchin, Murray. 1971. *Post-Scarcity Anarchism*. Berkeley, CA: Pamparts Press.

Bourdieu, Pierre. 1984. *Distinction: A Social Critique of the Judgment of Taste*. London: Routledge and Kegan Paul.

Butler, Tom, and Mike Savage, eds. 1995. *Social Change and the Middle Classes*. London: UCL.

Chiavacci, David. 2008. From Class Struggle to General-Middle Class Society to Divided Society: societal Models of Inequality in Postwar Japan. *Social Science Japan Journal* 11 (1): 5–27.

Chiavacci, David, and Carola Hommarich, eds. 2017. *Social Inequality in Post-Growth Japan: Transformation During Economic and Demographic Stagnation*. New York: Routledge.

Cool Japan initiative. 2014. *Ministry of Economy, Trade and Industry*. http://www.meti.go.jp/policy/mono_info_service/mono/creative/file/1406CoolJapanInitiative.pdf. Accessed 11 Aug 2017.

Creighton, Millie R. 1998. Something More: Japanese Department Stores' Marketing of 'A Meaningful Human Life'. In *Asian Department Stores*, ed. Kerrie L. MacPherson, 207–230. Richmond Surrey: Curzon Press.

Etzioni, Amitai. 1998. *The Essential Communitarian Reader*. New York: Roman & Littlefield.

Featherstone, Mike. 1990. Perspective on Consumer Culture. *Sociology* 24: 5–22.

———. 1995. *Undoing Culture: Globalization, Postmodernism, and Identity*. London: Sage.

Fujioka, Wakao. 1984. *Sayonara, taishu* [Goodbye, Masses]. Tokyo: PHP.

Goldthorpe, John H. 1982. On the Service Class, its Formation and Future. In *Social Class and the Division of Labor*, ed. Anthony Giddens and Gavin Mackenzie, 162–185. Cambridge: Cambridge University Press.

Haghirian, Parissa. 2011. Indulging in Luxury? Japan's New Rich' Consumers. In *Japanese Consumer Dynamics*, ed. Parissa Haghirian, 108–121. New York: Palgrave.

Hashimoto, Kenji. 2003. *Class Structure in Contemporary Japan*. Melbourne: Trans Pacific Press.

Imada, Takatoshi. 1998. *Divided Middle Mass and Quality-of-Life Politics: Middle Class in Post-Material Society*, 1995. Tokyo: SSM Project.

Ishida, Hiroshi. 1993. *Social Mobility in Contemporary Japan*. London: Macmillan.

Keliyan, Maya. 1999. *Yaponiya i Balgariya: modernizatsiyata, srednite sloeve i selskite obshtnosti* [Japan and Bulgaria: Modernization, Middle Strata and Rural Communities]. Sofia: Publishing House M-8-M.

———. 2008. *Yaponiya i Balgariya: razsloenite modeli na potreblenie* [Japan and Bulgaria: Stratified Consumption Patterns]. Sofia: Publishing House "Valentin Trajanov".

———. 2010. *Stil na jivot na lokalnata obshtnost: savremenna Yaponiya* [Local Community Lifestyle: Contemporary Japan]. Varna: Publishing House "Alex Print".

———. 2012. *Consumption Patterns and Middle Strata: Bulgaria and Japan*. PECOB (Portal on Central Eastern and Balkan Europe), Bologna: University of Bologna Press. file:///C:/Users/user/Downloads/Pecob_Volume_Keliyan.pdf. Accessed 11 Aug 2017.

Kelley, Jonathan, and M.D.R. Evans. 1995. Class and Class Conflict in Six Western Democracies. *American Sociological Review* 60 (April): 157–178.

Kosaka, Kenji, ed. 1994. *Social Stratification in Contemporary Japan*. London: Kegan Paul International.

Miura, Atsushi. 2005. *Karyushakai: aratana kaisoushudan no shutsugen* [Low Class Society: The Emergence of New Social Strata]. Tokyo: Kobunsha Shinsho.

———. 2014. *The Rise of Sharing: Fourth Stage Consumer Society in Japan*. Tokyo: LTCB International Library Trust/International House of Japan.

Murakami, Yasusuke. 1984. *Shin chukan taishu no jidai* [The Era of New Middle Mass]. Tokyo: Chuokoron-sha.

Nakane, Chie. 1970/1992. *Japanese Society*. Tokyo: Charles E. Tuttle.

Odaka, Kunio. 1966. The Middle Classes in Japan. In *Class, Status, and Power: Social Stratification in Comparative Perspective*, ed. Reinhard Bendix and Seimour Martin Lipset, 2nd ed., 541–551. New York: The Free Press.

Ozawa, Masako. 1985. *Shin kaisou-shouhi no jidai* [The Era of Neo-stratified Consumption]. Tokyo: Nihon Keizai Shinbunsha.

Rostow, Walt Whitman. 1960. *The Stages of Economic Growth, a Non-Communist Manifesto*. Cambridge: Cambridge University Press.

Savage, Mike, James Barlow, Peter Dickens, and Tom Fielding. 1992. *Property, Bureaucracy and Culture*. London: Routledge.

Schutte, Hellmut, and Deanna Ciarlante. 1998. *Consumer Behavior in Asia*. New York: New York University Press.

Seiyama, Kazuo. 1993. Is the Japanese Mobility Pattern Consistent? *International Journal of Japanese Sociology* 2: 17–35.

Shirahase, Sawako. 2014. *Social Inequality in Japan*. New York: Routledge.

Skov, Lise, and Brian Moeran. 1995. Introduction: Hiding in the Light: From Oshin to Yoshimoto Banana. In *Women, Media and Consumption in Japan*, ed. Lise Skov and Brian Moeran, 1–75. Richmond Surrey: Curzon Press.

Sugimoto, Yoshio. 2010. *An Introduction to Japanese Society*. Cambridge: Cambridge University Press.

Tachibanaki, Toshiaki. 1998. *Nihon no keizai kakusa* [Economic Inequality in Japan]. Tokyo: Iwanami Shoten.

———. 2005. *Confronting Income Inequality in Japan: a Comparative Analysis of Causes, Consequences, and Reform*. Cambridge: MIT Press.

———. 2006. Inequality and Poverty in Japan. *The Japanese Economic Review* 57 (1): 1–27.

Tamura, Yuichi. 2007. School Dress Codes in Post-Scarcity Japan: Ccontradiction and Changes. *Youth and Society* 38 (4): 463–489.

Tilkidjiev, Nikolay. 2002. *Sredna klasa i sotsialna stratifikatsiya* [Middle Class and Social Stratification]. Sofia: LIK Publishing House.

Tönnies, Ferdinand. 1887/2011. *Community and Society (Gemeinschalf und Gessellschaft)*. Mineola, NY: Dovel Publications.

Yamada, Masuhiro. 2004. *Kibou kakusa shakai: "makezoku"no zetsubokan ga nihon o hikihasu* [Society of Big Social Differences: the Disparity of "Losers" is Tearing Japan]. Tokyo: Chikumashobo.

Yamazaki, Masakazu. 1984. *Yawarakai kojinshugi no tanjou* [The Birth of Fragile Individualism). Tokyo: Chuokoronsha.

Index

E. Krasteva-Blagoeva (ed.), *Approaching Consumer Culture*, International Series on Consumer Science, https://doi.org/10.1007/978-3-030-00226-8

T

The manufacturer's authorised representative in the EU is Springer Nature Customer Service Centre GmbH, Europaplatz 3, 69115 Heidelberg, Germany. If you have any concerns regarding our products, please contact ProductSafety@springernature.com

Printed and bound by CPI Group (UK) Ltd, Croydon, CR0 4YY
22/09/2026
02221061-0014